ID0786593

HISTORICAL DICTIONARIES OF RELIGIONS, PHILOSOPHIES, AND MOVEMENTS
Jon Woronoff, Series Editor

1. *Buddhism,* by Charles S. Prebish, 1993
2. *Mormonism,* by Davis Bitton, 1994. *Out of print. See No. 32.*
3. *Ecumenical Christianity,* by Ans Joachim van der Bent, 1994
4. *Terrorism,* by Sean Anderson and Stephen Sloan, 1995. *Out of print. See No. 41.*
5. *Sikhism,* by W. H. McLeod, 1995
6. *Feminism,* by Janet K. Boles and Diane Long Hoeveler, 1995. *Out of print. See No. 52.*
7. *Olympic Movement,* by Ian Buchanan and Bill Mallon, 1995. *Out of print. See No. 39.*
8. *Methodism,* by Charles Yrigoyen Jr. and Susan E. Warrick, 1996
9. *Orthodox Church,* by Michael Prokurat, Alexander Golitzin, and Michael D. Peterson, 1996
10. *Organized Labor,* by James C. Docherty, 1996. *Out of print. See No. 50.*
11. *Civil Rights Movement,* by Ralph E. Luker, 1997
12. *Catholicism,* by William J. Collinge, 1997
13. *Hinduism,* by Bruce M. Sullivan, 1997
14. *North American Environmentalism,* by Edward R. Wells and Alan M. Schwartz, 1997
15. *Welfare State,* by Bent Greve, 1998
16. *Socialism,* by James C. Docherty, 1997
17. *Bahá'í Faith,* by Hugh C. Adamson and Philip Hainsworth, 1998
18. *Taoism,* by Julian F. Pas in cooperation with Man Kam Leung, 1998
19. *Judaism,* by Norman Solomon, 1998
20. *Green Movement,* by Elim Papadakis, 1998
21. *Nietzscheanism,* by Carol Diethe, 1999
22. *Gay Liberation Movement,* by Ronald J. Hunt, 1999
23. *Islamic Fundamentalist Movements in the Arab World, Iran, and Turkey,* by Ahmad S. Moussalli, 1999
24. *Reformed Churches,* by Robert Benedetto, Darrell L. Guder, and Donald K. McKim, 1999
25. *Baptists,* by William H. Brackney, 1999

Historical Dictionary of Utopianism

James M. Morris
Andrea L. Kross

Historical Dictionaries of Religions,
Philosophies, and Movements, No. 51

The Scarecrow Press, Inc.
Lanham, Maryland • Toronto • Oxford
2004

Contents

SCARECROW PRESS, INC.

Published in the United States of America
by Scarecrow Press, Inc.
A wholly owned subsidary of The Rowman & Littlefield Publishing Group, Inc.
4501 Forbes Boulevard, Suite 200
Lanham, Maryland 20706
www.scarecrowpress.com

PO Box 317
Oxford
OX2 9RU, UK

British Library Cataloguing in Publication Information Available

Library of Congress Cataloging-in-Publication Data

Morris, James M. (James Matthew), 1935–
  Historical dictionary of utopianism / James M. Morris, Andrea L. Kross.
      p. cm.—(Historical dictionaries of religions, philosophies, and movements ;
  no. 51)
  Includes bibliographical references.
  ISBN 0-8108-4912-7 (hardcover : alk. paper)
  1. Utopias—History—Dictionaries. I. Kross, Andrea L. II. Title. III. Series.
HX806 .M626 2004
335'.02'03—dc22
                                                                    2003023551

Editor's Foreword

Utopianism has been with us since the beginnings of recorded history, and for all we know even earlier, with the first precursors appearing among the ancient Israelites and the Greeks. Most of this has been in the Western world, but not only there as it spread and has emerged in other parts of the globe. Indeed, given the tendency of some persons and societies to seek perfection and given the dissatisfaction of infinitely more with their imperfect lives, it can be assumed that many more utopias will be formulated in the future. Unfortunately, almost all of the utopian projects turned out to be far less attractive in practice than in theory, leading to a generalized concern that utopianism can be futile and impractical, so "utopianism" is not always a positive expression. It can even turn into something far worse in the sense of a dystopia. But although utopian writings can age and become obsolete, and although utopian communities may fail to achieve their goals or simply be dissolved, their assumptions regarding human and societal perfectibility have not necessarily faded away or been rejected. Quite to the contrary, they have often been incorporated in our present state structure and society and are so familiar that they are no longer even regarded as "utopian."

Given the significant role of utopianism in human society, it is about time that this series produced a *Historical Dictionary of Utopianism,* which fills an important gap. This book covers the ground very broadly, running from the early theoreticians and thinkers over many centuries, including those who proposed republican, democratic, and authoritarian innovations; those who sought equality of classes, races, and genders; those who insisted on hierarchy under some supreme leader (or god); and those with more practical economic, social, or ethical plans. Also included in this volume are the concrete realizations of utopian thought and the various communities and organizations, both the successful ones and the failures. Knowledge of these is essential in determining historically what works and what does not. They are described along with utopian (and dystopian) writings in the dictionary section. The introduction offers a necessary overall view, and the chronology makes the progression of utopian projects and writings easier to trace. Thanks to the bibliography, it is possible to read further on aspects of particular interest to the reader.

This volume, which ties in with all three themes of the series—religions, philosophies, and movements—was written by James M. Morris and Andrea L. Kross. This is not their first historical dictionary, Dr. Morris having already produced one on the U.S. Navy, so it expresses their wide interests and a fascination with what actually is a very captivating topic, so much so that Dr. Morris is presently completing a manuscript on the United States as a utopia, a valid project given the extent to which utopian writings have appeared and utopian communities and other experiments have been attempted in the United States, along with the ardor with which many Americans regularly propose it as a world model. He has been a professor at several universities, most recently Christopher Newport University, teaching history with a specialization in military and naval history.

Jon Woronoff
Series Editor

Preface

Utopianism continues to exist, if not thrive, in the modern world, whether in the more popular and widespread form of individualism attained through governmentalism or in isolated cult millennial groups. From this fact follows the need or obligation for persons of curiosity and intelligence to explore this subject to better understand the strands of thought that have become part of the makeup of the Western mind and are even now emerging in the mindsets of the non-Western and developing countries of the world. For this reason, we have carefully prepared this *Historical Dictionary of Utopianism* for the interested student of historical developments and the underlying assumptions upon which they are based, the key to understanding any society, nation, or period of history of the past and in the present and future. Appended to its entries is an extensive bibliography on the subject divided according to logical subsets of utopian inquiry. This is presented in the hope that our efforts in this volume will lead to greater interest in and appreciation of utopian thought as it has influenced the world through the centuries down to our own.

Our special thanks go out to the staff of the Captain John Smith Library of Christopher Newport University and in particular to Mrs. Amy Boykin, Ms. Susan Barber, and Mrs. Leslie Condra, without whose help this task could not have been completed. Needless to say, any errors that appear in this volume are our own.

James M. Morris
Andrea L. Kross

Chronology

ca. 395 B.C.   Aristophanes' *Ecclesiazusae* (Women in Parliament) composed

360 B.C.   Plato's *The Republic* and *The Laws* published

350 B.C.   Aristotle's *Politics* published

Early 5th c.   Augustine's *City of God* written

431   Council of Ephesus rejects literal interpretation of The Apocalypse

Late 12th c.   Joachim of Fiore's *Concordance of the Old and New Testaments* published

1325   First of Yorkshire Communities established in England

1478   Birth of Thomas More (d. 1535)

1516   Thomas More's *Utopia* first published in Latin

1522   Anton Doni's *I Mondi* (The Worlds) published

1534–1536   Reign of John of Leyden over Anabaptists in Munster

1552   Family of Love, first Familist community in England, established

1567   François Rabelais' *Gargantua and Pantagruel,* including description of Abbey of Theleme, published

1619   Johann Andreae's *Reipublicae Christianopolitanal Descriptio* (Description of a Christian Republic) published

1621   Robert Burton's *The Anatomy of Melancholy* published

1623   Tommaso Campanella's utopian *City of the Sun* published

1626	Francis Bacon's utopian *New Atlantis* published
1641	Utopian *Macaria* published
1656	James Harrington's utopian *The Commonwealth of Oceana* published
1683	Bohemia Manor, first Labbadist colony in America, established
1736	Birth of Mother Ann Lee (d. 1784), founder of Shakers
1755	Morelly's utopian *Nature's Code* published
1757	Birth of George Rapp (d. 1847), founder of Harmony Society
1762	Jean-Jacques Rousseau's *The Social Contract* published; Sarah Scott's feminist utopian *A Description of Millennium Hall* published
1771	Louis Mercier's utopian *L'An 2440* published
1772	Birth of Charles Fourier (d. 1837), utopian socialist
1774	Claude-Nicolas Ledoux's Royal Salt Works begun
1776	Mount Lebanon (or New Lebanon), first gathered Shaker community, established
1785	Daniel Moore's utopian *An Account of Count D'Artois and His Friend's Passage to the Moon* published
1788	Birth of Etienne Cabet (d. 1856), founder of Icarian movement
1790	Gracchus Bebeuf's *Manifesto of the People* published
1795	Birth of Frances Wright (d. 1852), founder of Nashoba; birth of Barbara Heynemann (d. 1883), second leader of the Amana Society
1800	New Lanark established in Scotland by Robert Owen
1804	Harmony Society established by George Rapp
1809	Birth of Albert Brisbane (d. 1890), popularizer of Charles Fourier's ideas in the United States

1811	Birth of John Humphrey Noyes (d. 1886), founder of the Oneida Community
1814	George Rapp and Harmonists move to Harmony in Indiana
1820	Birth of Helena Blavatsky (d. 1891), founder of Theosophy
1822	St. Ann, first Canadian utopian community, established in Nova Scotia
1824	George Rapp and Harmonists move to Economy in Pennsylvania
1825	Robert Owen's New Harmony established in Indiana
1825	Comte de Saint-Simon's *Nouveau Christianisme* published
1826	Mary Wollstonecraft Shelley's dystopian *The Last Man* published; Frances Wright's Nashoba established in Tennessee
1829	Frances Wright's Nashoba abandoned; Wilberforce, first of six black utopias in the United States and Canada, established
1830	Joseph Smith's *The Book of Mormon* published
1831	Ralahine community in Ireland established
1833	John Adolphus Etzler's utopian *The Paradise within Reach of All Men* published
1839	Etienne Cabet's utopian *Voyage en Icarie* published
1840?	Queenwood community in England established
1841	Brook Farm, first Fourierist colony, established
1843	Ebenezer, first Amana community, established; North American Phalanx established
1845	Sylvester Judd's utopian *Margaret, a Tale of Real, Blight and Bloom* published
1846–1847	Mormons, led by Brigham Young, trek to Utah

1848	Karl Marx's *The Communist Manifesto* published; Icaria, first Icarian community, established in Texas; Oneida Community established
1851	James J. Strang's Beaver Island colony, or Kingdom of St. James, established
1852	Waipu in New Zealand established
1853	Herrnhut Commune, first Australian community, established
1862	Herbert Spencer's *First Principles* published
1863	Nicholas Chernyshevsky's utopian *What Is to Be Done?* written in prison
1867	Death of Christian Metz (b. ?), first spiritual head of the Amana Society
1870	Annie Cridge Denton's feminist utopian *Man's Rights* published
1874	Bon Homme, first Hutterite colony, established in South Dakota
1875	Theosophical Society founded
1877	Friendship Community, last Fourierist colony, ended
1879	Henry George's *Progress and Poverty* published
1881	Am Olam founded in Russia by Jews; Oneida Community transformed into joint-stock company, Oneida Community, Ltd.
1885	Emile Zola's utopian *Germinal* published
1887	Anna Bowman Dodd's dystopian *Republic of the Future* published
1888	Edward Bellamy's utopian *Looking Backward: 2000–1887* published
1889	Mary E. Bradley Lane's feminist utopian *Mizora: A Prophecy* published

1890   Ignatius Donnelly's utopian *Caesar's Column* published; Arthur Dudley Vinton's dystopian *Looking Further Backward* published

1891   William Morris's utopian *News from Nowhere* published; Chauncey Thomas's utopian *The Crystal Button* published

1893   Bournville, near Birmingham, England, established; Charles Nismonger's dystopian *The Isle of Feminine* published; Alice I. Jones and Ella Merchant's utopian *Unveiling a Parallel* published

1894   William Dean Howells's utopian *A Traveler from Altruria* published; Cosme Colony in Paraguay established

1895   William Bishop's feminist utopian *The Garden of Eden, U.S.A.* published; New Icarian Community, last Icarian community, ended

1897   Charles W. Caryl's utopian *New Era* published

1898   Garden City movement promulgated by Ebenezer Howard; three Salvation Army colonies established

1902   Theodor Herzl's utopian *Altneuland* published

1903   John Macmillan Brown's satirical utopian *Limanora* published

1905   H. G. Wells's utopian *A Modern Utopia* published; Harmony Society ended

1907   Jack London's dystopian/utopian *The Iron Heel* published

1909   E. M. Forster's dystopian "The Machine Stops" published

1915   Charlotte Perkins Gilman's feminist utopian *Herland* published

1916   Charlotte Perkins Gilman's feminist utopian *Our Land* published

1918	Most Hutterite colonies migrate to Canada during World War I
1921	Yevgeny Zamyatin's dystopian *We* published
1930	Nation of Islam established by Wallace D. Ford
1932	Aldous Huxley's dystopian *Brave New World* published; Amana Society reorganized as joint-stock company
1933	James Hilton's utopian *Lost Horizon* published
1935	K'ang Yu-Wei's utopian *The Great Equality* published in China
1937	Ayn Rand's dystopian *Anthem* published
1938	Teilhard de Chardin's *Phenomenon of Man* first published in French
1940	Arthur Koestler's dystopian *Darkness at Noon* published
1945	George Orwell's dystopian *Animal Farm* published
1948	B. F. Skinner's utopian *Walden Two* published
1949	George Orwell's dystopian *Nineteen Eighty-Four* published
1952	Kurt Vonnegut's dystopian *Player Piano* published
1953	Evelyn Waugh's dystopian short story "Love among the Ruins" published; Ray Bradbury's dystopian *Fahrenheit 451* published
1954	William Golding's dystopian *Lord of the Flies* published
1955	Herbert Marcuse's *Eros and Civilization* published
1968	Arthur C. Clarke's dystopian *2001: A Space Odyssey* published
1970	Charles Reich's utopian *The Greening of America* published; Hal Lindsey's *The Late Great Planet Earth* published

1974	Suzy McKee Charnas's feminist utopian *Walk to the End of the World* published; Ursula Le Guin's feminist utopian *The Dispossessed* published
1975	Joanna Russ's feminist utopian *The Female Man* published
1976	Marge Piercy's feminist utopian *Woman on the Edge of Time* published; Zoe Fairbairns's feminist utopian *Benefits* published
1977	Jonestown in Guyana established
1978	Jonestown in Guyana ends in mass suicides; Suzy McKee Charnas's feminist utopian *Motherlines* published
1984	Suzette Elgin's feminist utopian *Native Tongue* published
1985	Margaret Atwood's dystopian *The Handmaid's Tale* published
1986	Joan Slonczewski's feminist utopian *A Door into Ocean* published
1987	Ursula Le Guin's *Always Coming Home* published
1988	David Koresh assumes leadership of Branch Davidians at Mt. Carmel near Waco, Texas
1993	Siege of Branch Davidians at Mt. Carmel ends in fire
1997	Heaven's Gate millennial cult ends in mass suicides
2004	Sabbathday Lake, last Shaker community, remains in existence in Maine

Introduction

The words "utopia" and "utopian" have come into common usage in the West, referring in almost all cases to an idea or scheme far beyond the range of possibility, though perhaps intriguing in theory. The use of these words in common parlance can be credited to the fact that "utopia" and "utopian" have assumed such an ambiguity in meaning in modern times that they can be used without precision to denigrate any idea the user finds implausible if not ridiculous. Accordingly, any plan for economic abundance for all, a world without war, a world in which all persons of all nations and all races respect the rights and humanity of all others, and so on, can be and usually is dismissed as utopian, as the idle musings of incurably romantic and unrealistic dreamers or "do-gooders" whose common sense has somehow gone astray.

Yet, whatever the possibility of creating a perfect, or at least notably more perfect, society, nation, or world in actuality—and history suggests strongly that it is not possible given the nature of human beings and the failure of virtually all utopian projects—the dream has always lived on in the hearts and minds of at least a few individuals, sometimes waxing, sometimes waning, but always present from ancient times to the present. Because it is one of the components that make up the mental imaginings of humanity to the present day, and because many utopian demands or proposals have actually been achieved, at least in the West, such as the equality of classes and the sexes, generalized democracy, improved health and education, and other gains, utopianism in theory and in fact deserves attention and careful scrutiny from those who would seek to understand why the people of the world, and especially of the West, day after day not only dream of utopia but also live under the influence of utopian assumptions buried deep—and unrecognized—in the thoughts, judgments, and aspirations that direct their daily lives.

UTOPIANISM DEFINED

Although most people are at least dimly aware that the word "utopia" is derived from the title of a book of the same name written by Sir Thomas More, few are aware of More's intention in setting his thoughts in print in the early 16th century. Indeed, by titling the book *Utopia* (a play on two Greek words, *ou topos*, meaning no place, and *eu topos*, meaning an ideal place) More was in fact manipulating words to make a crucial point about his times. This was exactly the lord chancellor's intention: to describe not a society that could and should be created but, rather, to point out to the English ruling classes the faults of their own nation. *Utopia* was, as has been said by Robert Nisbet, the late distinguished professor of humanities at Columbia University, a kind of hair shirt for the nobility of England. Nevertheless, whatever More's intention by his artful play upon words, the title stuck and not only added to the utopian literature in existence but also gave impetus to other works of this type and to the dream of a perfected society and world as the West emerged from the Renaissance into modern times.

Thus utopianism took on new life, sometimes Christian, sometimes secular, in principle and practice. It came to fruition in the 19th and 20th centuries, most often in the form of communities based on communal living but also in the expectations of the general public. The dream of these modern utopianists was to replace contemporary harmful institutions with those in which peace, prosperity, and justice would reign without alteration, the formula for success having been discovered and applied once and for all.

Yet, despite the continuing thread of utopian literature and attempts at establishing a utopian way of life, these dreams and schemes have not been without their critics, who point out the pitfalls and even the dangers of attempting to build utopian societies. Just as utopianism has often appeared in Western life, so too has its antiutopian counterpart, dystopianism. Surfacing now and again in literature, in philosophical and theological writings, and in precautionary novels, from Augustine's *City of God* in ancient times down to the well-known dystopian 20th-century novels of Aldous Huxley and George Orwell, *Brave New World* and *Nineteen Eighty-Four,* respectively, dystopian authors have been persistent critics of utopian thought and the danger of the stultification of humanity inherent within it.

Given the vagueness of the concept of utopianism—currently being applied to everything from a world without war and poverty to an educational system where *every* student will be trained to be a knowledgeable and productive citizen (education being the key to success in all utopian societies) and to the short-lived communes of the 1960s and 1970s dedicated to finding Nirvana in sex and drugs—a definition is in order in preparing this historical dictionary. Accordingly, we have adopted the following guidelines in selecting entries for this dictionary:

1. The subject or entry included, whether a philosophical, instructional, or implementational idea or a person involved with utopianism, must refer to, describe, or outline a perfect or near perfect group-based human condition that is without basic conflict and is attainable by a nation, a society, a subgroup of that society, or the world. This group-based proposed state must be in time and be of this world, as opposed to otherworldly, thus eliminating religious communities or orders of professed members who seek perfection primarily in the afterlife; or,

2. The idealized subject must in the mind of its author be an improved state that not only could be but also should be implemented, by definition excluding pipe dreams or idle musings of solitary and dysfunctional thinkers; or,

3. The subject must include the assumption of malleability of persons because inherent within utopianism is the idea that by means of rational and/or moral education, a fundamental and total change in a society's laws, customs, and mores, an improved state, society, or societal subgrouping can and should be brought into being, whether through gradual or dramatic change or by fixed and inherent stages of development; or,

4. The subject, presented as a concrete plan, a new model (whether based on religion, reason, or science) to be followed in time (whether in the form of a work of literature or of credible philosophical, political, or economic reflection), must represent a superior alternative to the present to those who would give credence to it. Thus politically, whether ruled by an oligarchy made up of a natural aristocracy, a theocracy, a republic, or a democracy, it must promise total peace and fundamental justice for all persons within it. Socially it must promise a perfected family structure based on

kinship and brotherhood or sisterhood with class and sexual distinctions usually eliminated to assure a community of equals in all respects. Economically it must promise equality, cooperative effort toward a common and understood goal, and at least equity (if not equality) in income or reward; or,

5. The subject must be dystopian in nature, that is, a criticism of utopian ideas and schemes as unworkable in practice and contributing to, if not guaranteeing, the lessening or destruction of the humanity of its practitioners despite the loftiness of the goal or goals to be attained; or,

6. The subject must not represent mere escapism or the desire of a group with like interests (such as artists or voyeurs) to associate only with those of the same interests for their own enjoyment or edification. Nor must it represent mere reformism, that is, improving one or another factor in a nation's, a society's, or a societal subgrouping's existence; it must include both totality and perfectionism as basic components of its vision.

This historical dictionary, then, is an attempt to present to the interested reader the most vital information on the persons, plans, and attempts associated with utopianism that have been seen since ancient times. Although including all salient subjects that fall within the parameters listed above, we will present in over 600 semiencapsulated entries the necessary information or guidance to enable the reader to explore the Western mind's desire to improve the world and the lives of the people within it as utopianism has persisted over the centuries.

UTOPIANISM FROM ANCIENT TO EARLY MODERN TIMES

In ancient times, the people of Greece held tightly to the mythological Kingdom of Cronus, where in bygone days life was without worry or care; indeed, it was idyllic. But this dream took on a more concrete form in the speculations of the noted thinkers of ancient times: the poet-farmer Hesiod, who described a bucolic age of old in his *Works and Days*; the dramatist Aeschylus in his *Prometheus Bound*; and Socrates, Plato, and Aristotle. Each in his musings speculated as to how a more perfect state, that is, a Greek city-state, should be organized and governed. Especially influential were Plato's *The Republic* (more accurately translated as *The State*), in which civilization advanced in successive steps, and Aristotle's *Politics* and *Laws,* in which it was argued that humans advance by the use of reason. Each of these works had a powerful impact on political speculation and governance both at the time and for centuries thereafter. During the same centuries, the Jewish people and nation also cherished their own dream of triumph and perfection drawn from their sacred writings, especially the Genesis account of the fall of humankind and the promise of a New Eden of ascendancy and peace with the coming of the Messiah as promised by the prophets, including chapter 7 of The Book of Daniel.

In the early centuries after the death of Christ, the story of a perfected society to be realized in time continued to influence the gradually Christianizing early medieval world. Becoming especially popular and influential in these troubled times was the promise held out in St. John's Book of Revelation, or The Apocalypse, of a thousand years of peace when, after the great battle between good and evil, Satan and his minions would be held in chains for a millennium, leaving the world in peace for a thousand years and ending only with the Parousia (the Second Coming of Christ), the final destruction of Satan, and the end of time as the New Jerusalem descends from heaven. The literal acceptance of the prophecies contained in the Book of Revelation pretty much held sway during these early centuries until the advent of Augustine, bishop of Hippo, when his *City of God* came to dominate Christian thought in the fifth century. The Book of Revelation, St. Augustine argued, was to be read allegorically, not literally, as was demonstrated in his writings and reflected in the influence he held over theological studies for centuries thereafter. Still, the writings of Joachim of Fiore in the 12th century and the preaching of the Spiritual Franciscans during the same era enjoyed a small but critical following and kept the idea of a heaven on earth alive during the Middle Ages despite the Church officially frowning on the idea of perfection to be found in time on earth. And the Christian humanist Thomas More's *Utopia* and other utopian works kept the spirit of a perfected world alive during the Renaissance.

The age of the Reformation, despite the fact that it was basically a revolt against the medieval Church's blend of faith plus reason in favor of faith alone and *sola Scriptura* (the Scriptures alone) as the foundation stones of the Christian religion, witnessed the reemergence of utopian ideas in religious garb. The Bohemian Jan Hus had already reintroduced the concept before his execution for heresy, and with the successful attacks on Rome's domination over the religious precepts of human life there emerged numerous radical religious groups and persons who argued for and even attempted to set up perfect Christian societies on earth. These included the Taborites, the Anabaptists, Thomas Muntzer, John of Leyden at Münster, and even Martin Luther himself. All were determined that, with the guidance of God, perfect societies could be created on earth in time.

It can be argued that these religious utopians were also reacting to their more perilous living conditions as European society witnessed the first stirrings of the commercial revolution and saw the world shifting under their feet, but the fact remains that they turned in hope and solace to creating their own more perfect world even though clinging to their newfound faith in a better and more secure world meant, in many cases, death or ostracism in defense of their ideas. They remained a minority in their faith and hopes, but they helped to reinstate in the West the utopian dream of a life on earth free from hardship and united in faith under God's holy guidance.

Europe was not alone in finding itself confronted with enthusiastic utopianism defying law and custom if necessary. This idea also spread to the New World. Witness the Puritans' belief that they were on a holy mission from God to create a perfected society on the far Atlantic shores of North America. They were, in the words of John Winthrop, to build a "city on a hill" in their new home on their "errand into the wilderness." They were to be a light for the decaying European world as part of God's divine providence. This new and more perfect society would be a religious oligarchy led by the chosen of God; it would serve as a beacon for a troubled world and be emulated back home to the glory of God. This dream went unfulfilled, as it turned out, because their fellow Puritan dissenters back in England were willing to compromise with the Anglican Church and the Crown after the demise of the Commonwealth and Protectorate. It is also worthy of note that the dream of creating a more perfect society had previously immigrated to the Western Hemisphere during the 16th century with the work of the Spanish Franciscan Jeronimo de Mendieta in Mexico. Mendieta had envisioned the Spanish as the divinely commissioned power charged with establishing the New Jerusalem in the New World. And a fellow Spaniard and government official, Vasco de Quiroga, had envisioned a perfected society in Mexico based on communal villages.

Subsequently the European rationalists of the Enlightenment during the 17th and 18th centuries seized on the idea of perfectionism in order to provide it with a rational and scientific basis and move it toward a new vitalization freed of nonrational and nonscientific religious ties. This co-opting of utopian perfectionism by the rationalists helped to reinvigorate it in Western thought. But religious-based utopianism refused to die and remained vital to challenge the precepts of reason and scientism both then and in the centuries that followed.

For example, a Lutheran theologian by the name of Johann Valentin Andreae published *Christianopolis: An Ideal State of the 17th Century* in 1619. In it, he visualized his "Christian City" as a square town, 700 feet long and located on an island. It featured the College of Christianity with the study of the mysteries of God and of the world as the basis of all education. It was governed by a triumvirate made up of the "father of strength," the "father of help," and the "father of knowledge." The chief mark of the city was its stability because, dedicated as it was to unchanging Christian principles, it had no reason to change. Read literally or allegorically, Andreae's description of a utopian city stands as proof that perfected existence was at least a part of Western thought in the 17th century.

Of greater impact on that century was *The City of the Sun* by Tommaso Campanella, a Dominican priest who spent his years being alternately accepted and imprisoned by Church authorities until his death at the age of 71. First published in 1623 and widely read in its time, *The City of the Sun* describes in a dialogue format a perfected city two miles in diameter and seven miles in circumference located on an island named Taprobana. The city is governed by an oligarchy; marriage, sex, and procreation are controlled by the state; all citizens work only four hours per day and are well cared for during their entire lives; and private property is forbidden. The result is a place of tranquility on earth.

Oceana, the work of James Harrington in that same century, is a thinly disguised description of England and how it might be established by Oliver Cromwell. Property ownership in this mythical city is limited to ensure equality, all religions are tolerated (except Catholicism and Judaism), residence is divided into 50 tribes subdivided into 1,000 hundreds of persons and 10,000 parishes, and government is representative and features a separation of powers and rotation in office. Although *Oceana* can only be classified as literary utopianism, it was immensely popular at the time and, it is interesting to note, had a direct impact on the forming of the constitutions of various American states as well as the U.S. Constitution.

UTOPIANISM OF REASON AND SCIENCE

But this religion-based utopianism of the 17th century, reflective of an earlier utopian tradition, was being seriously challenged by the voices of reason and science. Prominent among rationalism's devotees and popularizers was Sir Francis Bacon, who can truly be said to have ushered in the age of scientific reasoning with his insistence on achieving truth only through inductive reasoning. And although Bacon wrote his own utopian work called *New Atlantis* (1624) about a perfected kingdom named Bensalem located on an island in the South Sea, his greatest contribution to utopian perfectionism lies not in this but in his insistence on human progress being based on reason utilizing the scientific method, as he spelled out in his *The Advancement of Learning* (1605) and his *Novum Organum* (1620). Bacon's impact on the Western mind was successfully supplemented by the works of Rene Descartes and Isaac Newton. Scientism also gained ground by the works of the German Gottfried Leibniz, at one time both a scientist and a utopian famous for his *Republica Christiana,* a work that visualized a perfected state that encompassed the entire world and in which scientific academies had replaced religious institutions.

These scientific writer-philosophers were complemented on a more pedestrian and popular level by the utopian Fifth Monarchists in England, who believed that the millennium had begun with the Reformation and that the reign of King Jesus was at hand, and by the egalitarian Levellers and Diggers. But more scientific and philosophical utopian perfectionism held its own with the work of the Cambridge Platonists led by Joseph Mede, who was Christian in outlook but rational in his approach to the truths of Christianity. Mede's ideas were reenforced by the writings of fellow Christian Platonists Thomas Burnet and Henry More. However much they differed in approach, whether philosophical or political, these rational millennial perfectionists, along with more pedestrian popularizers, kept the dream alive of necessary progress in the Western world. This dream would become increasingly secular as the 18th-century phase of the Enlightenment made its impact felt on modern values.

This Age of Reason witnessed the increasing influence of Blaise Pascal in the 17th century; of Claude Helvetius in the 18th century, who argued that power belongs rightly to the state and that human beings are rightly controlled by the state; of Denis Diderot, the major force behind the influential, rationalist *Encyclopédie*; and of Jean-Jacques Rousseau, who argued that individual moral freedom can be attained only by persons submitting their individual interests to the General Will of the community, even if they must "be forced to be free" to attain an idyllic state of nature, Rousseau's concept of utopia. These writers were joined by Claude-Henri de Saint-Simon, whose fevered mind envisioned utopias in the form of phalanxes or phalansteries presided over by the scientists, the natural outcome of the world evolving in three great stages, the last being the postmillennial present, the Age of Reason.

Other prophets of progress to perfection during this time were Immanuel Kant, known primarily for his idealism and his categorical imperative but who also argued for the creation of a better world as the end of history through reason and education; Anne Robert Turgot, who rewrote human history in the light of progress through a series of stages; the Marquis de Condorcet, who argued for the inevitable creation of a new man in 10 stages from the agricultural to the scientific, this new person being a superman with no need for God in his perfected state; and Auguste Comte, the founder of positivism and sociology, who offered to humankind a new god (the divinized human race following the Religion of Humanity) created through three successive stages by continued rational and scientific investigation and resulting in a positivist, totalitarian utopian state of perfection.

Clearly, by the end of the 18th century both in England and on the Continent, a faith in human salvation to perfectibility by means of knowledge was coming to dominate in important intellectual circles, with traditional religion being scuttled in favor of reason and science. When the writings of the Marquis de Sade, in which he pictured an aristocracy of libertines enjoying carnal pleasures with both abandon and purpose, and those of Restif de la Bretonne, the "Rousseau of the gutters," are added to the intellectual concepts of such men as Diderot,

Rousseau, Saint-Simon, Kant, Turgot, Condorcet, and Comte, it becomes obvious that although the 18th century cannot be labeled as fully utopian, the ground had been laid for the emergence of the belief that humankind was capable of achieving perfection in time, creating an "Age of Earthly Happiness," a utopia by means of reason and science. Thus modern utopianism is clearly the child of the Enlightenment, coming to dominance in the centuries that followed.

UTOPIA COMES TO THE UNITED STATES

Although the belief in progress to perfection, to utopia, may have been born out of European sources, it was hardly confined to that continent. Indeed, it was in the United States that utopianism bloomed brightest in the 19th century, building on the ideas carefully planted in the soil of the New World during colonial days. This can be seen, as noted, in the early New England settlements of the Puritans, who believed they had been sent on a holy mission, an errand into the wilderness, to create a perfect society freed from the faults of the Old World on the far shores of the New as active instruments of God moving toward the millennium. It can be found in the writing of the Connecticut clergyman Joseph Morgan, who described an otherworldly utopia on earth preceding the Last Judgment; and in Daniel Moore's story of two Frenchmen taken by balloon to a perfect moon world populated by Hebrew-speaking Lunarians. It can be seen in John Eliot's creation of 19 "praying towns" in 1651 to civilize and Christianize native Algonquians through four steps to perfection. It can be seen in the 17th- and 18th-century creations of the Valley of the Swans for Mennonites in Delaware, of Bohemia Manor in Maryland, and of the Society of the Woman in the Wilderness in Pennsylvania, in addition to the Ephrata Cloister and Moravian communities in Pennsylvania and in the southern colonies.

It can also be found in the preachings and writings of the Great Awakening of the 18th century, filled as they were with apocalyptic thoughts of bringing humans to perfection in the period of the Sixth Vial, the last before God's final judgment, and thus accepting an eschatological vision of perfection here on earth as part of God's final plan for humanity. And progress to perfection can be found in the American colonialists' assumptions during the English-French "Wars for Empire" of the late 17th through mid-18th centuries as they saw themselves on a holy mission by God to defeat the heretical French. This was religious millennialism being transformed into civil millennialism, the same concept that would dominate many colonists as they struggled to gain their independence from the Crown between 1763 and 1783. This quasi-religious millennialism would enjoy a resurgence among Unionists as they fought the Confederates between 1861 and 1865, Julia Ward Howe's "The Battle Hymn of the Republic" visualizing their apocalyptic holy march to a more perfect nation.

It comes as no surprise, then, to witness in the pre–Civil War decades of American history the establishment of dozens of utopian communities, some religious, some secular, their inhabitants convinced that a perfected society could be created in time in the United States, the worldwide symbol of progress for the world. Among these were the postmillennialist Shakers under Mother Ann Lee, followed by Joseph Meachem and Lucy Wright; the Harmony Society under George Rapp that at one time boasted of 10,000 followers; Robert Owen's ambitious but short-lived colony called New Harmony located on the Wabash River in Indiana; and the North American Phalanx, the intelligentsia's Brook Farm, and other phalanxes, these representing the dream children of Charles Fourier's imagination but brought to fruition in the United States through the influence of the editor and enthusiast Albert Brisbane. Perhaps most prominent was the Oneida Community in upstate New York, the creation of postmillennialist John Humphrey Noyes and the subject of contemporary and long-term enthusiasm, noted—and condemned by its neighbors—for its unique sexual practices.

Among the religious communities created in these decades was the Amana Society under the leadership of Barbara Heynemann (or Heinemann) and Christian Metz, the longest fully functioning society in American utopian history dating well back into the 18th century. First established in upstate New York as the Ebenezer Society, in the 1850s its followers moved to Iowa and established seven separatist villages that thrived in the years thereafter. Only 80 years later was the society reorganized as a joint-stock corporation; today the Amana villages remain popular tourist attractions.

A second prominent religious community developed during these years as the Church of Jesus Christ of Latter-Day Saints, or the Mormons, under the leadership first of Joseph Smith and later of Brigham

Young. Their story of hardship, persecution, and eventual survival is very well known, although few recognize it as utopian in its implications. Another at least quasi-religious utopian dream came from the mind of the Frenchman Etienne Cabet, who saw Christ as a communist and captured the public's imagination with his 1840 utopian novel *Voyage en Icarie* (Voyage to Icaria). Unfortunately for Cabet, his attempts to establish perfected communal societies, first in Fannin County, Texas, then in Illinois, failed even before his death in 1856, although some of his intellectual followers continued to establish colonies through the remainder of the 19th century.

Other utopian colonies were also established in the United States in the pre–Civil War years, especially in the 1820s, 1830s, and 1840s, sometimes called "The Golden Age of Utopian Communities," among them Bishop Hill in Illinois, the Separatists of Zoar and the Yellow Springs Community in Ohio, and Frances Wright's controversial free love and abolitionist colony of Nashoba in Tennessee. Yet to concentrate on these colonies during the Golden Age alone—only a small number of Americans took part in these utopian projects—would miss the persistence of civil millennialism widespread among the American people. For this was the era of Manifest Destiny, the religious-political belief that God had intended that the United States spread from ocean to ocean and in the process bring the benefits of a superior civilization and true Protestant Christianity to all inferior peoples in its environs in what has been termed "republican eschatology." And each success, as in driving the Native Americans from their lands and in defeating the Mexicans and seizing almost half of their land in the Treaty of Guadalupe Hidalgo in 1848 (that great swath of land from the Rio Grande to the Pacific shores of California) only convinced the American people even more that God was on their side in creating a more perfect, if not perfected, society. By the middle of the 19th century, then, not only was the United States seen as the testing ground for utopian-perfectionist communal projects by a determined minority of its people but also the nation's history was seen in its totality as the working of the hand of God in time as He willed the United States to be not only a "city on a hill" but also "the light of the world." Such hallowed beliefs would continue to flourish in the decades to follow, especially if not exclusively in the area of literature.

UTOPIANISM AND THE CHALLENGE OF CHANGE

The decades of the 19th century were times of great change in the United States as well as in the industrializing Western world as agricultural dominance gave way to industrialization and urbanization with all the attendant problems and dislocations these caused. And although in the long run these changes meant greater prosperity and a higher standard of living for those affected by them, in the short run they raised the question as to the essential fairness of a nation's economic, political, and social standards, especially on those who seemed to be most adversely affected by the emerging way of life. Accordingly, men and women began to search for answers to basic questions raised by the new and dominant way of life.

Some continued to see progress in modern life. Among these was the German idealist Johann Fichte, who wrote of the Five Ages of Humanity leading to the final stage, the millennial kingdom of the apocalypse and the reign of the Spirit, all to be accomplished through and embodied in the all-powerful nation state. In fundamental agreement with Fichte was Georg Hegel, who saw the absolute political state (the German state) as the embodiment of progress on earth. Of equal importance, Hegel became the apostle of necessary progress in the form of his famous dialectic between theses and antitheses leading inevitably to a perfected state, a utopian state, with all causes of conflict removed.

In contrast, Britain's William Godwin argued that progress would result not through subjugation to the state but, rather, when individuals would follow the dictates of reason and the greater good for themselves alone. Complete individualism and the removal of all sensual restrictions, especially the sexual, he asserted, along with cooperation and the abolition of marriage, would result in a state with no crime, no disease, no government, and no war, that is, a state of utopia. Godwin's successor as an apostle of individualism was John Stuart Mill, the 19th-century English philosopher and economist, as evidenced by his *On Liberty* (1859), an extended argument for individual freedom and social improvement. Mill was familiar with the writings of Auguste Comte and accepted his law of the three stages of humankind, individualism necessarily leading to progress providing that no barriers to individualism be erected by the state. Comte, too, was utopian, arguing that his positivist-scientific method alone would take the world out of its economic and spiritual crisis into spiritual reconstruction, his projected new world without blemish thanks to the priest-scientists of the "Religion of Humanity," the sociologists and anthropologists. Sharing the faith in progress and the spotlight of interest in fundamental change to cope with the evolving new world with Godwin, Mill, and Comte was Karl Marx, who, as a consummate utopian—much as he denied it—envisioned a scientifically inevitable march of the working class toward a socialism via Hegel's dialectic to a perfected state of equality and peace with the collapse of the individualizing capitalism stage of history.

These solutions were fueled and ironically complemented by what would appear to be their opposite, 19th-century romanticism with its emphasis on the nonrational or irrational, and on untapped human creativity. Yet, in the 19th century, the rational-scientific response and the romantic response with its conviction that humans progressed in time toward perfection became fused in a new enthusiasm for perfectionist utopianism, the possible blending into the rational and the rational into the possible and leading to new utopian solutions.

Darwinism with its struggle of the fittest was optimistically blended into the rational through the writings of the most prominent Social Darwinist of the age and conduit of European ideas to the United States, Herbert Spencer. Spencer argued that everything in the universe, whether physical, intellectual, or moral, was evolving upward by natural selection to a more perfect stage—indeed, to perfection—by the "law of evolution." His progressive-evolutionist ideas were reenforced by the writings of Frank Lester Ward and John Fiske, both of whom argued for social engineering to assure progressive evolutionism. Thus the mainstream of intellectualism in the 19th century absorbed increased rational scientism, romanticism, and necessary evolutionism as optimistic answers to the problems of society. Continued progress in the face of temporary difficulties and problems would thereby be assured to a nation and a Western world racked with pain in the face of fundamental wrenching changes in the lives of its citizens.

Yet there continued to be persons who were convinced that communal alternatives to the evolving individualist-rationalist-evolutionist society should be attempted. Between 1865 and 1900 over 100 communal, or utopian, communities came into existence in the United States, the most prominent being those of the Hutterites. All were rural; virtually all were short-lived. Some of the leaders of these colonies believed that cooperation was the key to a better life; others were charismatic perfectionists, political or social radicals, Christian socialists, or anarchists. All believed they could establish a better order of things through their ideas of planning and control, reason, and science, thereby unshackling humans from the debilities of the present. However, utopian ideas reemerged in a major way in the post–Civil War years in the United States not in these dozens of communities but through literary works reflective of the same ideas.

Between 1865 and 1917, "The Golden Age of Literary Utopias," at least 120 utopian literary works appeared in the United States, almost one third during the 1890s alone, all wedded to the idea of human progress toward some future stage of history. Chief among these were Henry George's *Progress and Poverty,* Edward Bellamy's *Looking Backward,* Ignatius Donnelly's *Caesar's Column,* William Dean Howells's *A Traveler from Altruria,* and Charlotte Perkins Gilman's *Herland.* And although not strictly utopian in outlook, Thorstein Veblen's *The Theory of the Leisure Class* added another voice raised in opposition to the status quo. All in one way or another pictured a new and better nation standing in sharp contrast to the United States as it existed in the late 19th and early 20th century. And from Europe came Theodor Hertzka's *Freiland* (Freeland), and from New Zealand came John Macmillan Brown's *Limanora, the Island of Progress.* In the United States, the call for reform in a utopian genre also came from the Theosophists under Helena Petrovna Blavatsky, who followed Buddhist and Brahmanic theories of life, pantheistic evolution, and reincarnation.

These utopian literary works were challenged, however, by other authors who saw in utopian schemes the very real possibility of oppression and dehumanization. Dystopian authors such as the early Jack London in his *The Iron Heel* (1908) and Anna Bowman Dodd in her *The Republic of the Future* warned against totalitarian governmentalism. And abroad, Mary Shelley had published her frightening dystopian novel *Frankenstein* back in 1818; now H. G. Wells was sounding his own warning against dehumanizing government in his *The Time Machine* and *The War of the Worlds.* But despite these warnings, as the United States and the Western world moved into the 20th century, necessary and inevitable progress, if not clear-cut utopianism, stood at the very heart of the West's picture of itself and its possibilities for the future. Aiding this movement toward a belief in inevitable progress was the shift among religious leaders from issuing warnings about the basic fallibility of humans inherent in the Judeo-Christian tradition to offering placations in modernist Social Gospelism, a form of religious positivism that took root and became prevalent in the Western world. The path was now becoming clear for secularizing utopianism in its quest to dominate the Western mind.

UTOPIANISM AND DYSTOPIANISM IN THE TWENTIETH CENTURY

The early 20th century was marked in the West by a sense of malaise arising to a great extent from the horrors of World War I. The confidence in progress inherent in 19th-century life appeared to be shattered by the war and by problems arising out of the emerging dominance of the new industrial elites and their political allies that more and more seemed to dominate the lives of individuals, leaving them at the mercy of forces beyond their control. In response to these forces, activist governments throughout the West assumed more power as the guarantors of justice and fairness for all. As a result, 19th-century individualism was folded into political activism in order to produce the perfected state in time. The goal of happiness and abundance for all had not changed; the means of attaining that goal had, that is, greater governmental activism in the lives of the citizenry.

This movement was aided by the influence of Friedrich Nietzsche with his assertions of the "death of God" and the creation of Superman as the end of infinite perfection resulting in a new heaven on earth; by the writings of Sigmund Freud with his emphasis on circumstance and its effects on the person; by the scientific positivism of John Dewey with its emphasis on individualism according to rules discovered pragmatically within society and imposed from without; by the influence of John B. Watson, the father of behaviorism; by the famous experiments of Ivan Petrovich Pavlov; and by the existentialist Martin Heidegger, whose teachings played a major role in moving modern humans from being to always becoming, since there are no transcendent truths or essences, and whose pupil, Jean-Paul Sartre, concluded that human beings are simply on their own in an absurd world. All suggested or openly preached that organisms, including humans, are shaped by external conditioning. If so, it followed that paternal governmental interventionism was the key to heightened individualism and happiness.

These ideas of individual autonomy via governmental interventionism—the individual must be forced to be free—leading to perfectionism, to utopias in time, came to dominate Western thought throughout the 20th century. In many tragic cases it took the form of governmental dictatorships, as in under Lenin, Stalin, Hitler, and Mao. In other cases it led to such tragedies as Jonestown and Waco at the end of the century. But whether in the form of "hard utopianism" by the "children of darkness" (evil persons) or in the form of "soft utopianism" propagated by the idyllic intellectuals of the West who consider themselves the "children of light" and seek to impose their gospel of personal autonomy for all through greater governmental intrusions on all, the end has never changed: a perfected or utopian state led by themselves, the politically powerful, the enlightened, the progressives, the modernists.

Aware of these tendencies during the 20th century, a number of thoughtful writers saw within these propensities a specter of the destruction of the very freedom and self-realization Western citizens were seeking. Through literature they attempted to warn the people of the world that the utopian path to freedom they embrace leads to its very opposite, the loss of that freedom. Thus early in the 20th century the Russian novelist Yevgeny Zamyatin, disillusioned by the Bolsheviks who had seized power in his native land only three years before, penned his novel *We,* where in the name of freedom the people live under rigid regimentation. His warnings were followed some years thereafter by Aldous Huxley, author of *Point Counter Point* (1928) and *Brave New World* (1932), the latter one of the most insightful dystopian novels ever written, a case study in effective preconditioning taken to its logical extreme in the name of "happiness" and a frightening and eerie preview of the West in the late 20th century.

Joining Huxley as one of the leading dystopians of the 20th century was George Orwell with his *Animal Farm* (1945) and *Nineteen Eighty-Four* (1949), the latter the story of Winston Smith and his final subjugation to the state, to Big Brother, in a world where transcendent Truth has vanished along with human freedom and dignity in the name of personal happiness. And although the popular enthusiasm for the antitotalitarian works of Huxley and Orwell has faded in the later decades of the 20th century as the continued popular Western belief in progress to utopia via governmentalism has grown, other writers have continued to issue their warnings to the West through their dystopian novels. One of these is Evelyn Waugh's short story "Love among the Ruins: A Romance of the Near Future" (1953), a picture of an England of the future. Another is *Player Piano: America in the Coming Age of Electronics* (1952), the first novel of Kurt Vonnegut, an extended commentary on lives being dominated by machines when not guided by rational and moral agencies; the novel argues that, people being fallible, there can be no utopia.

Yet, despite these grim warnings and others, belief in the possibility of achieving a utopia on earth has persisted in the 20th century and into the 21st. Some have argued that the root cause lies in the death of a belief in God and a paradise beyond the grave, this giving rise to a substitute to assure humans that their Promethean struggles on earth have a purpose after all. Others have argued that it lies in the belief that society, since it cannot be God-made, must be man-made, encouraging or demanding that humans be free to do with society whatever they wish. Therefore, people must create a good society without delay, this being realized through an elite seizing (or being given) power to create and maintain that good society by the best "scientific" means possible, including the "science" of government and the "science" of education.

A third explanation is that humans need optimism for the future in order to bear the burdens of today, the belief in a perfected society being the logical extension of this psychological craving for hope. They must be assured that T. S. Eliot, the leading 20th-century poet, was wrong when he concluded his "The Hollow Men" with the words: "This is the way the world ends/ Not with a bang but a whimper." To prevent either unthinkable denouement from occurring, to keep hope alive, these persons as necessary optimists agree that more and more external controls must be imposed to keep society moving in the "right" direction, and they agree that these restraints should be formulated by the government, the grand guarantor of everyone's well-being, and by the self-styled intelligentsia of academe and the media.

As a result, utopian fiction continues to be found in modern society. Early in the 20th century, H. G. Wells produced his *A Modern Utopia* (1905), wherein all are ensured a good life, even the Dull and the Base, under the benevolent rule of the *samurai,* a power elite of scientists and technicians. Wells's *Men like Gods* (1932) and *The Shape of Things to*

Come (1933) maintained the same optimistic, utopian theme. The same can be said for James Hilton's *Lost Horizon* (1933), Ralph Borsodi's *Flight from the City: The Story of a New Way to Family Security* (1933), and, at a later time, the behaviorist psychologist B. F. Skinner's *Walden Two* (1948) and *Beyond Freedom and Dignity* (1971). And the feminist movement since the 1970s has produced a resurgence of utopian novels in the United States. Building on the foundation of the writings of Charlotte Perkins Gilman early in the century, such feminist utopian novelists as Ursula Le Guin with her equivocal *The Dispossessed: An Ambiguous Utopia* (1974) and *Always Coming Home* (1985) have kept the utopian vision alive. Another major feminist utopian is Marge Piercy, author of the feminist utopian novel *Woman on the Edge of Time* (1976), in which men have been "maternalized" and all persons, women and men alike, have become "mothers."

When it is recalled that during the turbulent 1960s and 1970s utopian communities of various size and longevity became popular again—one estimate places the number of communal groups at more than 3,000 in the 1960s and early 1970s; another places the number at 100,000; whatever the number, almost all were small, urban, temporary, and undocumented— and that autonomous individualism to be attained by governmental activism (however contradictory in ends and means) continues to be accepted as the norm in the Western world and beyond, it becomes clear that utopianism remains a major current of Western thought and belief in the early 21st century.

UTOPIANISM PERSISTENT

Perfectibility to utopianism, now secularized, this-worldly, and committed to reason and science, continues its hold on the Western, and especially the American, mind. This is reflected in the political and educational worlds, where it has become a stock in trade for leaders to make promises that assume the malleability of the human person. This is also evident in the popularity, especially in academic circles, of New Ageism and postmodernism, blends of Eastern and Western mysticism that find their locus on the freedom of the individual to attain happiness and self-salvation by rejecting any imposed constraints of conformity, with deconstructionism coming to dominate the study of

Western literature. Unencumbered autonomy, aided historically by faith in democracy and equality, has come to be accepted as the essential ingredient of happiness and freedom. Personal freedom, now a quasi-religious ideal, has come to be the new utopia, but, contradictorily, it is to be gained by increased governmentalism, by politicians and bureaucrats, the new power elite—who bear a strong resemblance to Plato's Guardians.

Still, forms of more traditional group-based utopianism continue to find an audience in the West and especially in the United States. Witness the continued popularity of the feminist utopianism of Marge Piercy and Ursula Le Guin or the emergence of the Nation of Islam, laced through with millennialist ideas from its founder, Wallace D. Ford, through Elijah Muhammad and Malcolm X to Louis Farrakhan. Tragically, utopianism lay at the base of Jim Jones's leadership that resulted in the mass suicide of over 900 persons in Guyana in 1978 and in the case of the Branch Davidians under David Koresh, waiting out the reign of the Antichrist before Christ's victory at Armageddon near Waco, Texas, 73 of whom died in a fiery confrontation with law enforcement officials in 1993. A third tragic example of cult-millennialism occurred in 1997 in the mass suicide of 38 followers of Marshall Applewhite near San Diego, California, who expected their bodies to be whisked away by extraterrestrials as the earth was about to be recycled in an apocalyptic event ushering in the millennium. Clearly, utopianism—recognized as such or not—remains a vibrant strain in the Western world, and there are signs—sometimes hopeful, sometimes fearful—that it is spreading around the globe. Students of the history of the world, therefore, must be aware of its nature and effects as they seek to understand the world of the 21st century.

The Dictionary

– A –

AACAN. *See* ASSOCIATION OF ALL CLASSES OF ALL NATIONS.

ABBEY OF THELEME. The Abbey of Theleme was a fictitious religious house created by François Rabelais (ca. 1483–1553) as presented in his *Gargantua and Pantagruel*, published in 1567 after his death. Drawing on his monastic experience as a Franciscan and as a Benedictine, Rabelais in this derisive, satiric tale describes a religious order and abbey as envisioned by the Monk, who would rule over them. In the Monk's abbey there would be no clocks or bells to control activities, the women to be admitted would all be "faire, well featur'd, and of a sweet disposition," and the men would be "comely, personable and well conditioned." Members of each sex could leave at any time, and both could be wealthy, married, and at liberty to do what they wished (in obvious contrast to the ordinary monastic vows of poverty, chastity, and obedience). The rooms of the abbey would be rich in ornamentation, tapestries, statuary, and floor coverings and include galleries, baths, a theater, and a riding court, plus a swimming pool, tennis courts, riding stables, an orchard, and a falconry. The ladies would be elegantly dressed with their gowns corresponding to the seasons; the men would be dressed in matching luxury. In contrast to the religious houses Rabelais was satirizing, the Thelemites would live according to "their own free will and pleasure," the only rule for personal conduct in the abbey being "Do what thou wilt." The resulting liberty, according to Rabelais speaking through the Monk, would create men and women of virtue who were literate, could sing and play several musical instruments, and could speak five or six languages and who, being

1

freed from imposed subjection and constraint, would live in spontaneous cooperation in peace and virtue within the abbey. The description of the Abbey of Theleme as contained within *Gargantua and Pantagruel* was one of many satirical tales written by Rabelais that led to his condemnation by the Church but have enthralled readers since their publication in the 16th century.

ABRAM BROOKE'S EXPERIMENT. *See* MARBOROUGH ASSOCIATION.

ACCOUNT OF COUNT D'ARTOIS AND HIS FRIEND'S PASSAGE TO THE MOON, AN. This is the first known example in American utopian literature that tells the story of a flight to another planet upon which an imaginary more perfect society is discovered. Written by Daniel Moore (1764–1822) of Connecticut and published in 1785, it contains such **millennial** images as Eden and a **New Jerusalem**, and it reflects the utopian idea of a perfectible human society. It tells the story of two Frenchmen whose out-of-control balloon takes them to a lunar world populated by Hebrew-speaking humans who are perfectly religious, having never fallen from grace as humans did in the Garden of Eden, and, therefore, live in an idyllic setting free of want and abounding in harmony. The Lunarians they encounter assume that these humans represent a superior race and are enthused over their description of earth, another of God's worlds. Moore's point in *Passage to the Moon* is that humans can become like the Lunarians by means of Christ's sacrifice and God's grace. They can return to their lost innocence by an act of the will. They can, if they will, create a Christian utopia on earth.

ADAMITES. This 15th-century religious group was a radical faction of the **Taborites** in Bohemia. Holding that God dwelled within them as the Saints of the Last Days, they believed themselves to be superior to Christ. They also did away with the Bible, the Creed, and all book learning. Furthermore, they declared that the chaste were unworthy to enter the Kingdom. Accordingly, marriage was outlawed in favor of free sexuality, and the Adamites held naked ritual dances re-creating the state of innocence of Adam and Eve in the Garden of Eden. They also confiscated everything they wanted in the name of God. The Adamites were exterminated by armed Taborites in 1421.

ADONAI-SHOMO CORPORATION. In 1861 the Adonai-Shomo ("The Lord Is Here") Corporation was established as a Seventh-Day Adventist colony in Athol, Massachusetts, by Frederick T. Howland, a former Quaker. Howland was accompanied by 10 others, mostly women, who decided they should establish themselves as a commune. Their Athol commune was based at the home of Leonard Fuller; thus the members were often known as "Fullerites." By 1864 the community had 30 members, and that year they moved eight miles south to Petersham, where they took possession of 840 acres of farmland and lived in a common building. They observed their holy day on Saturday in keeping with the Seventh-Day Adventists. Howland believed in the coming **millennium** and taught his followers that they would have immortal life in the flesh. After Howland died from an accident, the community rallied behind a new leader, a man named Cook, who proclaimed that God had sent him to lead them. Soon afterward the members were horrified by the bizarre sexual practices that Cook tried to enforce, so they brought him before a grand jury. He was indicted and imprisoned. The membership fluctuated over the years, and they were consistently unable to keep their younger members. In 1896 the heirs to the property, those younger members who had left the group, sued the member who was then leading the colony, a man named Richards. The heirs claimed that Richards was using the property and proceeds for his own gain, a claim that was supported by the courts. The charter was broken, and the farm was forcibly sold off in 1897. However, the property only brought $4,390, just enough to pay off Richards's debts.

ADVANCEMENT OF LEARNING, THE. *See* BACON, FRANCIS.

AESCHYLUS (525–456 B.C.). Aeschylus, the Athenian poet and playwright, is famous for enforcing the Greek idea of progress through reform derived from **Hesiod**'s *Works and Days* in which the mythological god Prometheus was introduced to the ancient world. Prometheus, according to the cherished myth among the Greeks, braved the wrath of Zeus and thereby was punished for all eternity for bringing fire to humanity and thus moving civilization from poverty to plenty, from degeneration to universal justice through reform of the lives of persons and societies. This myth of Prometheus was most prominently kept alive in the fifth century B.C. in Aeschylus' *Prometheus Bound,* a reflection of a faith in progress as found in

Athenian life, and also by the works of **Plato** (ca. 427–347 B.C.) and others. Aeschylus' *Prometheus Bound,* then, was one of the building blocks of the Greek belief in progress, a conviction that continued as a vital part of Western thought in the centuries that followed.

AFRICAN AMERICAN UTOPIAS. *See* BLACK UTOPIAS.

ALABAMA COMMUNITY. *See* APPENDIX.

ALBERTSON, RALPH (1866–ca.1926). Albertson was born in Jamesport, New York. He became a Congregational minister in 1890 after attending Greenport Academy and Oberlin College and Theological Seminary. He served as a pastor in Ohio for the next five years but resigned in 1895 when many members of his Lagonda Congregational Church in Springfield went on strike against the nearby factories and Albertson's belief in Christian nonresistance did not allow him to support their actions. He left Springfield to join William C. Damon's **Willard Co-operative Colony** in Andrews, North Carolina. Damon's followers practiced the teachings of Jesus Christ in an attempt to re-create the Kingdom of Heaven on earth. The group, started in 1895, was a temperance colony named after the temperance leader Frances Willard. Through *The Kingdom,* published by the colony, Albertson made contact with George Howard Gibson. Albertson and Gibson forthwith established the **Christian Commonwealth Colony** in 1896. Under Albertson's leadership the colonists bought a Georgia cotton plantation; the colony was incorporated in 1899. Albertson had begun to edit *The Social Gospel* in 1897 and remained its editor until 1900.

The Christian Commonwealth Colony was very popular with over 300 people moving onto the land to live their lives according to the Sermon on the Mount, but the turnover rate was high. Everyone was welcome to join, all rewards were shared evenly, and none were required to pay or to work; unfortunately, this attracted many who took selfish advantage of this open policy. Though the colony boasted many industries plus agricultural endeavors, the members were unable to support themselves, and a typhoid epidemic took the lives of many. In 1900 the group disbanded, finally admitting that it was not financially able to continue the experiment. Albertson thereafter made his living in the publishing industry. In 1909 he and his second wife, Hazel, bought an old farmhouse in West Newburyport, Massachusetts, which became known as *The Farm*. They had many visitors, but, as before, Albertson allowed them to share his home with no demands on their time or money. Albertson's wandering eye led him to leave his wife to move to New York, where he continued to write. His wife continued to run The Farm on her own. Albertson died in obscurity, probably in 1926.

ALCOTT, AMOS BRONSON (1799–1888). Amos Bronson Alcott was born in Wolcott, Connecticut, on November 29, 1799. Although he did not have much in the way of a formal education, he became very interested in theories of educating young children. He worked as a peddler before establishing several schools in succession from 1823 to 1833 in Connecticut, Massachusetts, and Pennsylvania. In 1834 he began a school in Boston where instruction was built around the Socratic method. This school failed in 1839, however, when he enrolled a young black girl. This offended the parents of his other students, so they pulled their children out of Alcott's school. His subsequent schools failed after Alcott argued with his pupils' parents. With each setback, Alcott's family was rescued by a gift from his friend **Ralph Waldo Emerson** or by Alcott's wife begging from relatives or selling what she could. In 1842 Alcott made a trip to England to visit a boarding school in Ham Common, Surrey, named Alcott House, which was built upon his educational philosophies. Children aged three and older were awakened in the early hours of the morning to take cold baths; have a breakfast of cold water and beans, peas or lentils; and then begin a day of studies, music, and exercise. While at Alcott House he met **Charles Lane** (1800–1870), a fellow philosopher whose ideas on living a spiritual life were so in accord with Alcott's that Lane and his son accompanied Alcott back to the United States.

In June 1843 Alcott and Lane established a colony in Harvard known as Fruitlands. Life was harsh at Fruitlands, and though several people joined the two families in the small farmhouse during the next six months, most did not stay for long. The colonists subsisted on grains and fruit, wore loose linen breeches and tunic coats, took daily cold baths in the early morning hours, and tended the fields with spades. In living this way, the colonists shunned the slave industries that produced cotton and sugar and at the same time protected cows, sheep, pigs, chickens, oxen, and horses from exploitation. Following this regimen, the colony limped along, often facing starvation as the summer slipped away. By December the situation had become dire. Lane and Alcott had a falling out, and Abigail Alcott had come to the conclusion that her husband was going insane. When Lane and his son left Fruitlands to join a nearby **Shaker** village, Alcott's family refused to accompany them and Alcott fell into depression. When he recovered, they moved into rented rooms in a nearby village, where they were supported by Abigail's sewing abilities until they moved to Concord in 1843. There Alcott continued to teach and write, keeping his family in poverty until his daughter Louisa May's success as an author finally brought the family some money. In his later years until his death in 1888, Alcott loved to tell stories about his "little women."

ALFRED COMMUNITY. This long-lived **Shaker community** was located in the Town of Alfred in York County, Maine, and existed from 1793 to 1931. It was founded after a revival among the radical branch of the New Lights within the sect. Its maximum membership was 200 persons. In the early 1870s, the Shakers at Alfred considered moving to a milder climate and offered their entire property, which included 1,100 acres, for sale at $100,000. No buyer could be found. Some of the members still residing at Alfred joined the **Sabbathday Lake** Shakers in the same state.

ALLAIS, DENIS VAIRASSE d' (ca. 1630–ca. 1700). *See* SEVARAMBIANS.

ALLIANCE COLONY. The Alliance Colony, also known as the Vineland Colony, was established in 1882 in Salem County, New Jersey, with aid from the Alliance Israelite Universelle, a French organization dedicated to helping persecuted Jews. It continued in existence until 1908. This most successful of the Russian Jewish agricultural colonies, at least six in number in the Garden State, consisted of 1,150 acres of land in southern New Jersey and was home to 40 Russian immigrant families from the southern reaches of that distracted country. Labor on the farm was organized around units of four families who worked the land cooperatively, although some of the land remained common property of the entire colony. The colony also engaged in enterprises such as a sewing shop and a cigar factory.

Although the cooperative phase of the colony ended in 1908 in response to a desire for privatization by its members, a number of former colonists remained in the area.

ALPHADELPHIA PHALANX. This **Fourierist phalanx** was founded in the winter of 1843– 1844 by Dr. Henry R. Schetterly, a disciple of **Albert Brisbane** (1809–1890), on the Kalamazoo River in Kalamazoo County in southwest Michigan. It consisted of 2,814 acres and cost $32,000. Some 1,300 men, women, and children were initially enrolled in the Alphadelphia Association. Most were farmers, but the existing records show that a variety of mechanics also joined the Association. The actual project began with 200 members making the initial effort to create their perfected society. Plans were made to erect a two-story building for the residents, as well as a sawmill, a mill-race, and other structures necessary to assure the economic success and independence of the fledgling colony, but Schetterly assured those interested in joining the project that capital would not be allowed to encroach on personal liberty. However, by 1846, only two years after its founding, Alphadelphia was showing clear signs of internal discord over policy and finances despite the fact that a **phalanstery** 70 feet in length had been constructed the first winter and a school had been established on a part-time basis. Hard times and disagreements were apparently consuming the colony, and members began to leave one by one, leading to the demise of the phalanx by the end of that year. As with many other utopian projects and phalanxes in the 1840s, grandiose plans fell victim to economic realities and to personal benefits and concerns.

ALTNEULAND. *Altneuland* (Old-New Land) is a utopian work by the Hungarian Zionist Theodor Herzl (1860–1904), published in 1902, describing a future Jewish state, the New Society, established in 1923 in Palestine, the site of ancient Israel. In writing his utopian work, Herzl drew heavily from **Theodor Hertzka**'s *Freeland,* from his earlier *The Jewish State* (1896), and from his leadership in the founding of the World Zionist Organization. This new state as envisioned by Herzl would be marked by social justice; public ownership of land leased to individual farmers; public housing; social welfare agencies; a seven-hour workday; full political rights for women, including the right to vote; free education for children through the secondary level; a two-year service obligation in hospitals, retirement homes, or the like imposed on every citizen; urban planning; and a mass transportation system between cities. Furthermore, indigenous Arabs would enjoy equal rights in all respects with Jews as full participating members of the New Society. Although Herzl did not and could not anticipate the growth of Arab nationalism later in the century, his *Altneuland* marked an important step in the creation of a Jewish state in Palestine to escape the repression and anti-Semitism found throughout Europe in the early 20th century.

ALTRUIST COMMUNITY. This was one of five communes established by **Alcander Longley** (1832–1918) in Missouri. Longley began writing a periodical called *The Communist* in 1868, later renamed *The Altruist,* in which he promoted the idea of communistic living. For nearly 50 years, Longley attempted to interest his readers in sponsoring a succession of potential cooperative communities. A few were actually established for short periods of time, but they were decreasingly successful with each attempt. The Altruist Community, the last of the five, was established in 1907, and by the next year occupied eight-and-a-half acres of land near Sulfur Springs, Missouri, south of St. Louis. The Altruist Community did not have many long-term members, Longley being very good at writing up lists of rules for the residents to follow but decidedly lacking in interpersonal skills. The colony failed in 1908, although Longley continued to publish *The Altruist* until 1917, a year before his death.

ALTRURIA. In 1894 **William Dean Howells** (1837–1920) published his novel *A Traveler from Altruria.* In it he described a utopian community in which the people worked cooperatively during their three-hour workday and spent the remainder of their time developing their talents or doing housework. There was no crime, perhaps because there was no money; there were no class divisions; and everyone was given equal access to education. The novel so inspired its readers that a group of Christian Socialists from Berkeley, California, most of them Unitarians led by their ex-Congregationalist minister Edward Biron Payne, purchased 185 acres of farmland at Fountain Grove in Sonoma County for nearly $9,000. A constitution for Altruria was drafted in 1894, which described the ideals of the new community: all goods were to belong equally to all, every member could vote, and each member was to be given a labor check that could be redeemed for goods at the company store. In October of that year, 18 adults, including six bachelors, and eight children moved onto the property. Each member was required to pay a $50 fee, and many donated their worldly wealth to help with the purchase of the property. They began at once to build seven cottages to supplement the three houses that came with the property. These were completed by April 1895, and the community began to build a hotel. The colony was financially supported to a small extent by the many chapters of the Altruria Clubs that had sprung up across California. It also published a weekly journal called *The Altrurian,* which kept the club members up to date on the colony's progress, advertised the many craft items produced there, and reported on similar communities across the continent. Payne wrote most of the articles, although he remained a Unitarian minister in Berkeley, visiting Altruria often but never living there. Membership grew to 56, but by the summer of 1896 it became apparent that there were financial troubles in the colony. In an effort to save the community each member was required to donate his property and personal possessions, and the group was split into three smaller communities. None of the three survived beyond a year.

ALWAYS COMING HOME. This novel by **Ursula Le Guin** (1929–) was published first as an audiocassette of "Music and Poetry of the Kesh" in 1985, then as a book in 1987. Le Guin, a novelist, science fictionist, poet, essayist, and creator of short stories and children's books, is also the author of *The Dispossessed: An Ambiguous Utopia* (1974). *Always Coming Home,* combining poetry, prose stories, legends, and an "autobiography," deals with a people called the Kesh, who are agrarian, pacifist, and egalitarian and who live in northern California after a nuclear war in a new Stone Age with no gods and no faith in a postcatastrophe natural utopia. In this situation, the people have again become one with nature where being poor is being wealthy, the animals are also people, and songs are sung for every insect. Although not utopian in that it does not portray a perfected future and is not really reformist, the novel is essentially an examination of a possible distant tomorrow when civilization has been eradicated and is a spur to the conscience of those who would consider the march of events in modern times.

AMANA SOCIETY, *or* **EBENEZER SOCIETY,** *or* **THE SOCIETY OF TRUE INSPIRATION.** This religious communal society was founded in 1843 by 800 German Separatist-Pietists at Ebenezer (which means "Hitherto hath the Lord helped us"; 1 Samuel 7:12) in Erie County, six miles from Buffalo, New York, on 5,000 acres of former Seneca Indian land, and within 10 years the society numbered 1,200 persons. In 1854 the "Inspirationists" agreed on common ownership of all their property, sold their land at Ebenezer (now totaling 8,000 acres and including four villages: Middle Ebenezer, Upper Ebenezer, Lower Ebenezer, and New Ebenezer), and began a move to a 26,000-acre tract west of Davenport, Iowa, along the Iowa River. The Amana Society was incorporated by the State of Iowa in 1859. By the time their transplantation from Ebenezer had been completed in 1864, the Inspirationists had established six villages there: Amana (from the Song of Solomon signifying "believe faithfully"), West Amana, South Amana, High Amana, East Amana, and Middle Amana, plus the village of Homestead on the railroad nearby, each with its own cooking, eating, and prayer houses plus a bakery, dairy, sawmill, general store, and shoemakers', carpenters', and tailors' shops for self-sufficiency.

Each family in the Amana villages lived in its own house, although meals were eaten in common. Required dress was very plain, and the sexes were separated at all times other than within the home. Children attended school between the ages of six and 13, emphasis being placed on the "3 R's" and religious readings from the Bible or the catechism. No card playing, games, or other amusements were allowed. The religious precepts followed by the Inspirationists were contained in their 21 Rules for Daily Life, religious services were usually held every evening, and a general meeting was held in the church each Saturday morning. Christmas, Easter, and Holy Week were their great religious holidays, and once a year a general inquisition was held at which all members of the community were to publicly confess their sins, faults, and shortcomings. The Lord's Supper was celebrated only when the "inspired instrument" while in a trance directed that it be done. The Society was governed by 13 trustees chosen annually by the male members, each village being led by elders named by inspiration, who made the day-to-day decisions for the community. The Amana community thrived in Iowa on the basis of its members' hard work in agriculture plus the manufacturing of woolens and other products; it numbered some 1,800 persons by 1900.

The spiritual head of the society, God's chosen "instrument," was Christian Metz until his death in 1867, aided by **Barbara Heynemann** (1795–1883), another "chosen instrument," who led the society from Metz's death until her death in 1883, after which no inspired leader emerged to lead the society. The Amana Society as a utopian, communal society lasted from 1843 to 1932. In 1932 the society was reorganized into a joint-stock company with the property being divided among the remaining 1,400 members. In 1936 Amana Refrigeration began operations within the Society and enjoyed considerable success in the manufacture of home appliances. In 1950 the company dissolved all ties with the Society and then became part of the Raytheon Corporation in 1965. The Amana Society's existing villages remain popular tourist attractions, being designated National Historical Landmarks and visited by a million persons per year.

AMAURIANS. This 13th-century offspring of the teachings of **Joachim of Fiore** (1135–1202) and the **Free Spiritists** was made up of "prophets" operating primarily in the flourishing commercial centers of Europe, especially at Troyes in Champagne, France. Seeing themselves as followers of the pantheist philosopher Amaury, they professed that since all things are One and they themselves exist as parts of the One, they were, in fact, God the Father, the Christ, and the Holy Spirit. Like the abbot Joachim, the Amaurians saw history as developing in three stages corresponding to the three Persons of the Holy Trinity. From the beginning of time until the birth of Christ was the Age of God the Father, He being incarnated in Abraham and perhaps in other patriarchs of the Old Testament. From the birth of Christ to the present was the Age of the Son. And now the Age of the Holy Spirit, the third incarnation, was beginning with the Spirit taking on human flesh, the Amaurians (or "Spirituals," as they called themselves) being the first to do so.

As such, they were divinely charged with leading people to perfection as the world entered its highest epoch in which every person would know himself or herself to be divine. This last period would end with **millennial** catastrophes and tribulations, these in turn ending after five years with the overthrow of the Antichrist, that is, the Pope and the Church of Rome. Then would follow the reign of the king of France, who would never die but rule forever in the Age of the Spirit. The Amaurians were also antinomian in conduct, believing they, being God, stood above ordinary church-defined morality, neither sin nor divine punishment existing. This led to a lifestyle of total promiscuity, according to their critics. Amaurianism was condemned as heresy by the Roman Church at the Lateran Council in

1215, but its teaching of ascending stages of history leading to necessary perfection and its concomitant doctrine that sin does not exist for the morally enlightened would continue to be found in Christianity and utopianism in the centuries that followed.

AMENIA COMMUNITY, *or* **BROTHERHOOD OF THE NEW LIFE.** The Brotherhood of the New Life was a spiritual community led by **Thomas Lake Harris** (1823–1906), a Universalist minister who was born in England and emigrated with his parents to Utica, New York, at a young age. Harris's spirituality embraced Christianity and Eastern mysticism as well as the teachings of Emanuel Swedenborg, Baruch Spinoza, **Jacob Boehme**, and **Auguste Comte**. He governed his community in accordance with his own personal divine guidance. The community at Amenia in Dutchess County, New York, was a celibate patriarchal group established in 1861. In a letter to W. A. Hinds in 1877, Harris explained why his group remained celibate: "We think that generation must cease til the sons and daughters of God are prepared for the higher generation, by evolution into structural, bisexual completeness, above the plane of sin, of disease, or of natural mortality." The community maintained an orchard, a farm, and a vineyard, plus other industries. In the 1860s Harris traveled to England, where he received support from Lady Oliphant and her son. Their financial gifts enabled the community to move from Amenia to establish the **Brocton Community** near Lake Erie in western New York in 1867.

AMERICAN PHALANX. *See* OHIO PHALANX.

AMERICAN SETTLERS ASSOCIATION, *or* **DUKE COLONY.** Organized in Dayton, Ohio, by a group of impoverished farmers, this colony located in Ware County, Georgia, was inaugurated in 1898. It was not originally communal in outlook or practice; this came about only when it became necessary to clear 760 acres of timberland. Several families from Indiana subsequently joined. In 1899 it ended its independent existence by merging with the **Ruskin Colony**.

AMERICAN WOMAN'S REPUBLIC. When Edward G. Lewis formed the American Woman's League in 1908, his intent was to boost sales of his daily newspaper, *Woman's National Daily,* and his several magazines, while at the same time supporting women in their quest to win the vote. Those who wished to join the League were required to sell $52 in subscriptions to Lewis's publications; half of this money would go to the publications, and half would sustain the League. By 1910 the League had 100,000 members, according to Lewis. In 1906 he had also established a People's University on land he owned outside of St. Louis. The main purpose of this university was to educate women so that they could use their vote wisely once it was granted. The American Woman's Republic was born from a restructuring of the American Woman's League in 1912. The Republic declared itself a separate nation until such time as the U.S. government granted women the vote; at that time, the republic would be dissolved. Lewis and his wife, Mabel Wellington Lewis, spent the next few months searching for a suitable location for this new colony-country, eventually finding it in California at a property known as Rancho Atascadero. On July 4, 1913, opening ceremonies were held, and colonists began to buy lots and build houses. The colony produced dehydrated food products for government contracts during World War I, created its own flag (with six stars, each representing a state that had adopted women suffrage), and had one foreign consulate (in Scotland). Thousands of men and women joined the community over the years, and when the 19th Amendment was passed in 1920, the republic "rejoined" the United States. The site of the republic became the city of Atascadero.

AM OLAM, *or* **AM OYLOM.** This is the name (Hebrew for "Eternal People") of a Jewish society formed in Russia in 1881 by young idealistic utopian-**millennialists** who wanted to form socialist agricultural colonies in the United States. During that year and the next, they sent more than 175 Jewish refugees to the United States, the emigrants attempting to escape the anti-Semitism that swept Russia following the assassination of Czar Alexander II in 1881. During the 1880s, the Am Olam movement founded 26 agricultural colonies in eight states, primarily in the West. The first was **Sicily Island** in Louisiana. This was followed by the **Cremieux** and **Bethlehem Yehudah Colonies** in South Dakota. The longest-lived colony was **New Odessa** in Oregon under the leadership of **William Frey** (1839–1888), a non-Jewish disciple of **Auguste Comte**. New Odessa lasted only until 1887.

ANABAPTISTS. A radical offshoot of the Protestant Revolution, Anabaptism consisted of about 40 independent sects in German-speaking areas of Europe but was also found in Alsace, the Netherlands, and

Switzerland, areas beset by social unrest and religious reformism in the 16th century. Generally speaking, all rejected infant baptism and placed little importance on formal religious observances such as attending church services. They relied instead on literal observance of the precepts they gleaned from the New Testament with the assistance of personal divine inspiration to create a religion of brotherly love as practiced in the early Christian church. Anti-intellectual in the extreme and appealing to the semiliterate, the radical militant Anabaptists in the city of Münster in Westphalia, Germany, in 1534 were ordered by their first leader-dictator Jan Matthys (or Matthijs), who claimed direct revelation from God, to collect all books except the Bible and burn them before the cathedral. This was carried out without hesitation. And 2,000 non-Anabaptists were expelled from Münster as about 2,500 Anabaptists entered the city from surrounding territories. Matthys died shortly thereafter in a suicidal attack on the city's besiegers under the bishop of Münster, Franz von Waldeck, on Easter Sunday, April 1534.

The mantle of leadership among the Anabaptists in Munster was assumed by Jan Bockelson (ca. 1509–1536), also known as John of Leyden, a young man gifted with uncommon personal magnetism. Bockelson came to the attention of the inhabitants of Münster by running naked through the town before collapsing into a three-day trance. When emerging from the trance, he announced that he had received messages from God and, on this basis, set up a new government of the town that exercised complete authority over all matters spiritual and temporal. This included the power of life and death over all the town's inhabitants. Under the new code of laws decreed by Bockelson and the town's rulers (the "Twelve Elders of Israel"), death was imposed on any person guilty of murder, theft, slander, avarice, adultery, fornication, quarrelling, or insubordination, the last including the young against their parents, wives against their husbands, and, above all, anyone against God or His government in Münster. Bockelson, however, subsequently decreed that polygamy was demanded by God. Following his own advice, he soon acquired a harem of 15 or 16 wives, and, marriage with the "godless" being declared invalid, women engaged in such marriages were forced into unfaithfulness to their husbands. Bockelson in short order also revealed that God had made him king of the world as king of the **New Jerusalem**. As king, Bockelson thereafter dressed in rich robes, adorned himself with expensive jewelry, mounted a throne in the town marketplace, and demanded support to the last coin from the people of the town under pain of death, their homes being sacked and anything of value being confiscated to support the king and his luxurious retinue.

All of this was a reflection of Bockelson's "inspired" belief in the evolution of the world to perfection in three stages or ages. The first was the Age of Sin and lasted until the Flood. The second was the Age of Persecution and the Cross and lasted down to the present, these centuries marked by Christendom being subjected to the rule of Rome, the Babylonian Captivity. The third stage of vengeance and triumph of the Saints was now coming into being in which Christ would return to establish His kingdom in the city of Münster, preparation for this Second Coming having been made by setting over it the new David, Jan Bockelson. Incumbent upon the people in this new age was that they go out and establish God's kingdom throughout the whole world by wielding the Sword of Justice, killing all persons not marked with the "Sign" of the Anabaptists. Only then would Christ descend in his Parousia (Second Coming), inaugurating a new heaven and a new earth in which the Saints would live without want or sadness with all goods held in common. Throughout the months of Bockelson's reign, the town was under siege by its enemies and finally succumbed to these forces in June 1535. Subsequently the messianic Bockelson was publicly tortured to death with red-hot irons in 1536, his dead body and those of two of his associates thereafter being suspended from the tower of St. Lambert's Church. With his death, this radical **millennial** phase of Anabaptism came to an effective end.

The pacific forms of the Anabaptist creed that never followed Bockelson's extreme beliefs survive to the present day in the form of the Mennonites, Brethren, and the **Hutterites**, none of which hold to the dogma of a perfected heaven on earth to be established in time.

ANANDA ASHRAM. *See* VEDANTA SOCIETY.

ANANDA COOPERATIVE VILLAGE, *or* **ANANDA COOPERATIVE COMMUNITY,** *or* **ANANDA WORLD BROTHERHOOD VILLAGE.** Swami Kriyananda, born Donald Waters (1926–), had dreamed of living in a commune since the age of 15. He studied with Swami Paramahansa Yogananda, author of *Autobiography of a Yogi*, from 1948 to 1962, following his guru to monasteries in India and the

United States. In 1962 he was the vice president of Yogananda's organization, the Self-Realization Fellowship, but he was expelled from the organization that same year because of his decentralizing and schismatic opinions. Undaunted, he began to teach yoga and spirituality on his own. From 1967 to 1970 he bought land in Nevada City, California, which he developed into two communities: a 72-acre meditation retreat center, the Expanding Light Retreat Center, with meeting facilities and cabins, tents, and campsites where visitors could sleep; and a cooperative community on a nearby farm. Visitors are allowed to stay at the retreat center to meditate, take classes, attend workshops, and explore a variety of New Age topics. The permanent residents live in the cooperative community, meditating and practicing yoga as they remain celibate. Alcohol, marijuana, and dogs are forbidden (and young children are discouraged) on both properties as these interfere with the peace required for meditation.

In the first few years, they experienced financial difficulties. In addition, the young people who joined the community found that they disliked hard work, and a fire in 1976 destroyed most of the homes. However, by 1979, 87 permanent residents lived at the farm, which also had its own schools and businesses. In 1992 there were 356 residents and six other communities worldwide. In recent years, the community has faced several lawsuits. The Self-Realization Fellowship was unsuccessful in its claim that the Ananda group had violated the Self-Realization Fellowship's copyrights on Yogananda's likeness and writings. However, a former member did win a case against the commune relating to charges of fraud and sexual battery. Walters and the Ananda organization were ordered to pay more than $1 million in damages. As a result of this lawsuit, Walters resigned as leader of the Ananda Community and as of 1998 was in Italy avoiding prosecution, but the community continues in existence to the present time.

ANATOMY OF MELANCHOLY, THE. Written by **Robert Burton** (1577–1640) under the pseudonym Democritus Junior, *The Anatomy of Melancholy* was first published in 1621, five more editions appearing before his death and 60 additional editions thereafter. The work, primarily concerned with melancholia—seen at the time as a mental illness—included a section suggesting utopianism as a solution to the malady. Melancholia, Burton argued, has afflicted all humanity from the time of the Garden of Eden, all men being subject to selfishness, aggression, and so on since that time. These, in turn, have led to religious disputes, wars, political divisions, and the like. The cure, as he saw it, lay in changing the environment in which people functioned. Thus a perfected state, a utopia, was the cure for society's problems. As Burton described this ideal state, it would be isolated from Europe, have a salubrious climate, and include cities laid out symmetrically with uniform houses and public buildings such as churches and hospitals. Each city would be ruled by a governor and bureaucrats drawn from the city's aristocracy of merit. The central government would be headed by a limited monarch, and the state would subsidize scientific research, maintain a military force for defense, and provide aid for the poor unable to work as well as health insurance and old age pensions. State regulation would cover banking, weights and measures, and prices, all for the best use of resources. In the social realm, education would be available to all, crime would be severely punished, dress would be uniform, and marriage would be allowed for men only at age 25 and for women at 20, although the mentally defective would not be allowed to marry and reproduce. Burton's 17th-century utopian idea represented a step toward the modern theory of creating a good and just society by perfecting the circumstances within which its citizens live.

ANDREAE, JOHANN VALENTIN (1586–1654). Johann Valentin Andreae, Lutheran pastor, mystic, and influential contributor to the Rosicrucian Society, was born in Württemberg in southwestern Germany, the son of the Lutheran pastor of Herrenburg. He received two degrees from the University of Tübingen, where he displayed an interest in mystical theology as well as in drama and alchemy, avocations that continued throughout his life. In 1610 Andreae visited Geneva, where he was impressed by John Calvin's rule of the city and, after visiting Austria, Spain, France, and Italy, was ordained in 1614 in the Lutheran Church. Thereafter he continued to write mystical, alchemist, and reform works, including *Fama Fraternitatus* (circulated in manuscript), in which he argued that the only Christian basis for a society was on the cooperative activity of the group. In 1619, inspired by **Tommaso Campanella**'s *City of the Sun,* he published his utopian work *Reipublicae Christianopolitanae Descriptio* (Description of a Christian Republic).

In this work, one Cosmonexus Christianus, sailing on the ship *Fantasy*, is shipwrecked on the beautiful and bountiful island of Caphar Salama and is accepted by the inhabitants of the walled city of Christianopolis only after a successful moral examination. He is then taken on a tour of the mythical city based on true Christian principles. At the first level, he sees the agricultural and public works foundations of the city. In Christianopolis there is neither private property nor luxuries, but it is marked by material satisfaction. In the inner circle of the city, dedicated to education, justice, and religion, is a library that contains all writings that have been hitherto lost or destroyed in the world. Here Cosmonexus Christianus learns that the study of the physical world is a form of divine worship. This being so, the most important class in the city is made up of the scientist-artisans dedicated to understanding nature as the key to freedom from the unsanctified world of the time. The inner circle also contains a laboratory for scientific experiments to make life easier and more abundant for the city's citizens. Additionally, Andreae also proposes in *Reipublicae Christianopolitanae Descriptio* an educational system that does not rely on corporal punishment as an ingredient in scholarly excellence and in which both male and female students are instructed in the classical languages.

Although subsequently caught up in the horrors of the Thirty Years' War, Andreae continued his pastoral work in the Lutheran Church and his writing until his death in 1654. However, it was his *Reipublicae Christianopolitanae Descriptio,* in which he pictured an idyllic community founded squarely on Christian ideals, that brought Andreae literary fame and placed him among those writers keeping alive utopian ideas in the late Reformation period.

ANDREWS, STEPHEN PEARL (1812–1886). *See* MODERN TIMES.

ANDROGRAPH, THE. See RESTIF de la BRETONNE, NICHOLAS-EDME.

ANIMAL FARM. **George Orwell**'s satirical novel *Animal Farm* (1945) and his later *Nineteen Eighty-Four* (1949) are two of the major **dystopian** novels published in the 20th century. *Animal Farm* is a warning against revolutionary change as represented by the Bolshevik revolution and the repressive government thereafter imposed on the Soviet Union by Lenin and then Stalin. In the story, Mr. Jones, a farmer, is guilty of mistreating his animals, resulting in a boar, "Major," heading a successful revolution in which the animals take control of the farm. As the novel proceeds, leadership falls to the totalitarians "Snowfall" (Trotsky) and "Napoleon" (Stalin), who proceed to demonstrate to the reader how power can corrupt. Class struggles ensue, and a new despotism is imposed on the farm, the original ideas behind the revolution being changed to serve the government by deceptive propaganda. The novel ends when the chastised pigs arrange a deal with their former master, Mr. Jones. Extremely popular, along with *Nineteen Eighty-Four,* during the Cold War, Orwell's chilling dystopian work still ranks as one of the great works of literature in its genre.

ANTANGIL. This first French utopia was written anonymously in Saumur in 1616 and lay undiscovered until uncovered in 1922 by Frederic Lachevre. It describes a kingdom divided into 120 provinces with 100 cities and parishes within each. Houses in the cities and towns would be grouped by multiples of 10, that is, by tens, then hundreds, thousands, ten thousands, and hundred thousands according to the size of the city or town. Over each ten houses would be a chief charged with keeping the peace and keeping track of the financial affairs of each house and its inhabitants. In case of disputes, his decisions could be appealed, starting with other chiefs-of-ten, then to the chiefs-of-hundreds, then all the way up to the chief-of-hundred-thousand who, in consultation with the chiefs-of-ten-thousand, would make a final decision. Each province would elect three men, and the resulting 360 (each in suitable raiment to identify his province) would constitute the Estates General, which, in turn, would advise the king and his Council. The Council would be made up of 100 "great and wise personages" 40 years of age or more; the Council of senators, meeting in the capital city of Sangil, would have every sovereign power including choosing the king. In the matter of religion, the temples would be cleansed of all images of idols and replaced by passages from Scripture, and a bishop would be placed in the capital city of each of the 120 provinces to conduct "divine services" and supervise the clergy under him through one archpriest over every 10 parishes. Although the existing description of Antangil is clearly incomplete, the visionary state remains important in the story of utopia because it was the first to emerge in France.

ANTHEM. This gripping **dystopian** novel by **Ayn Rand** (1905–1982), the leading objectivist of the late 20th century, was published in 1937 and is reflective of Yevgeny Zamyatin's ***We*** and **Aldous Huxley**'s ***Brave New World.*** In *Anthem,* people have been depersonalized and dehumanized by the collectivist state. The robotized characters in the novel have been depersonalized to the point of having numbers attached to their names. The chief character in the novel, Equality 7-2521, is a near solitary voice of protest against state indoctrination, carried out by its banishing all previous knowledge through its program of Unmentionable Times and its system of eugenics and mind control through its Council of Vocations. Working secretly, Equality 7-2521 invents an electrical generator, only to have it rejected by the Council of Scholars, forcing him and his female companion, Liberty 5-300, to flee to the Uncharted Forest. Here they discover the pronoun "I" and produce an offspring, having found individual freedom and dignity. *Anthem,* then, remains one of the leading dystopian novels of the century alongside **George Orwell**'s ***Animal Farm*** and ***Nineteen Eighty-Four,*** Huxley's *Brave New World*, and Zamyatin's *We*.

ANTICHRIST. By general definition, one identified as the Antichrist is any person or creature who opposes Christ. More specifically, it refers to a great antagonist (Satan) expected to fill the world with wickedness until conquered by Christ at His Second Coming (the Parousia) as revealed in the **Apocalypse**, the Book of Revelation, the last book of the New Testament. Reference to the Antichrist was a key component in the **millennial** tradition, and at various times was used as an indictment against the clergy, the pope, and the Roman Catholic Church, especially during the Middle Ages and the Protestant Revolution.

APOCALYPSE, *or* **THE BOOK OF REVELATION.** The Apocalypse refers to a portion of the prophetic Book of Revelation in which St. John tells of a vision of things to come. In dramatic passages filled with earlier prophets, trumpets, vials, seals, angels, plagues, falling stars, fire, fantastic beasts (Gog and Magog, Satan's helpers), and various other happenings, the account moves to the vision of the Second Coming of Christ mounted on a white horse (the Parousia). Christ smites the **Antichrist**, who has assembled his legions for a great battle called Armageddon, and casts him into a lake of burning fire, hell. Then an angel comes down from heaven to chain the dragon, Satan, binding him for a thousand years. After this time, the **millennium**, Satan breaks free to inflict torment on humans once again before he is finally defeated and cast back into hell for all eternity while the present world ends with the Last Judgment. Blessedness with God is now assured for Christ's faithful followers, both the living and the dead, as the **New Jerusalem** descends from heaven while the condemned are cast into hell for all eternity.

APOSTOLIC BRETHREN. This religious sect first appeared in Parma, Italy, in 1260. Its founder was Gerard Segarelli (?–1300), who had been denied admission into the Franciscan Order of the Friars Minor and who was clearly influenced by the ideas of **Joachim of Fiore** (1135–1202). After Segarelli's death by burning in 1300, leadership fell to Fra Dolcino, who claimed the inspiration of the Holy Spirit in interpreting the Scriptures and revealing the future. He also preached that the history of humankind fell into four stages. The first was the pre-Christian stage of the patriarchs and prophets of the Old Testament. The second stage was instituted by Christ and His apostles and carried life to an elevated spiritual plane in which chastity was more meritorious than marriage and poverty was greater than riches. This stage ended with St. Silvester and the Emperor Constantine. The third stage saw the conversion of the Gentiles and the emergence of religious perfection through the influence of St. Benedict, St. Francis, and St. Dominic. The fourth stage was the present, when it became necessary to return to the apostolic way of life founded on poverty; this stage to last until the end of time. Dolcino also divided the history of the Church into four mutations. During the first it was pure and chaste. During the second it was rich but good. The third was the present in which the Church was in decline, but it would end in three years when all the clergy and members of religious orders would be killed. The fourth would then begin when the Church would return to its true self, being good, pure, and reformist.

At the same time that they viewed the history of Christianity as occurring in stages and mutations and ending in perfection, the Apostolic Brethren also repudiated all Church authority because its authority from Christ had ended because of the present evil leaders of the Church, and all Petrine authority had been passed to the Apostolic Brethren. This transfer of authority would be accomplished by a revolution in which the pope, the hierarchy, the clergy, and all members of religious orders would be exterminated by the sword of God wielded by a new emperor, King Frederick of Sicily. Thereafter a new and holy pope chosen by God would govern the Church with the outpouring of grace from the Holy Spirit; this new, truly apostolic Church would last until the end of time. The Apostolic Brethren came to a bloody end in 1306 when Dolcino's followers resisted to their deaths a crusade against them preached by Pope Clement V, but their teachings continued to be discovered and eradicated in the religious orders for the next decade and a half. Formed under the influence of Joachim of Fiore with their belief in the stages of history leading to perfection, the Apostolic Brethren, despite their brief history, stand as examples of utopian-**millennial** thought persistent in the Middle Ages.

APPLEWHITE, MARSHALL (1931–1997). *See* HEAVEN'S GATE.

AQUARIAN FOUNDATION. In the summer of 1926, the British metaphysical journal *The Occult Review* published several articles that described the visionary experiences of Edward Arthur Wilson (1878–1934), also known as Brother XII. Wilson claimed that he had been visited by 11 Masters of Wisdom who told him that he was to prepare the way for a coming world teacher, due to arrive in about 50 years. While touring England, he gathered together more than 100 **Theosophist** followers and brought them to Vancouver Island, British Columbia, Canada, where he formed a community near Nanaimo in 1927. Many American Theosophists joined the group after announcements of Wilson's vision were published by The Sun Group, an independent Theosophical community in Akron, Ohio. Brother XII demanded that each of his followers donate to him all of their worldly possessions; because many of them were very wealthy and because the community also received gifts from others in the range of tens of thousands of dollars, the community never experienced financial difficulties.

Brother XII's remarkable rise to power can be partially explained by other events occurring within the Theosophical community. Many Theosophists were dissatisfied with **Annie Besant**'s insistence that Jiddu Krishnamurti was their long-awaited world teacher. According to Brother XII, the world teacher would not appear until the mid-1970s. Wilson also won followers by advocating that the Theosophists should return to the teachings of **Helena Petrovna Blavatsky** rather than following the innovative leadership of Annie

Besant and Charles Leadbeater. As the colony became established, Brother XII had a new vision from his Masters and a new task for his followers. It turned out that Brother XII had been Osiris in a prior incarnation, and the one who had been Isis was a member of the Aquarian Foundation, Myrtle Baumgartner. The two, he said, were destined to have a child in this lifetime who would become the much-anticipated world teacher (who had been Horus in his past life). Meanwhile, it was important that certain colony females mate with Brother XII up to nine times each in order to produce the beginnings of the sixth root base. A section of Valdes Island was designated as safe haven for these highly evolved children.

In about 1930 Mabel Skottowe (also known as Madame Zee) joined the community and soon became Wilson's favorite and the community's coleader. Myrtle Baumgartner had not produced a son and eventually had a mental breakdown. The community fell apart when several former members sued the foundation, hoping to get their money back and claiming that they had been abused. When the two lawsuits came to trial in 1934, the court ordered the Aquarian Foundation to pay the former members a large sum of money and to give them most of the property owned by the Foundation. Mysteriously, community property was damaged and Brother XII, Madame Zee, and the colony's funds, in the form of gold, disappeared.

ARDEN. This single-tax community was formed in 1900 by the Philadelphia enthusiasts of **Henry George** (1839–1897) in New Castle County, Delaware, six miles north of Wilmington. Financial help was furnished by Joseph Fels, the soap manufacturer, a supporter of the ideas of George. By 1915 there were about 130 leaseholders and about 100 dwellings. At the present time, 72 acres of residential land are owned by the trustees; the remaining 90 acres are owned communally through the village of Arden. The idea of a single-tax community was extended in 1922 with the creation of Ardentown and in 1950 with the establishment of Ardencroft, an integrated community.

ARISTOPHANES (ca. 445–ca. 385 B.C.). Aristophanes, the dominant poet-genius of the Old Comedy, authored a comedy, *Ecclesiazusae,* or *Women in Parliament,* about the year 393 B.C. that envisioned a *polis* without private households or private property and with sexual equality. The plot of the play involves the women of Athens who decide to take over the city by disguising themselves as men, packing the assembly, and passing a resolution turning all affairs over to women, thereby creating a gynecocracy. Succeeding in this, under their leader Praxagora ("Busy in the Marketplace") they decree that all things are to be held in common to ensure that all citizens have an equal way of life, all property is to be held in a common store, all households will live in a common dwelling, all citizens will eat together, all slaves will be publicly owned and do all the work, and so on. Thus the ideas of community of property, no permanent marriage, communal living, communal raising of children, and complete and total sexual equality—the basic Greek concept of utopian communism— were introduced by Aristophanes through his comedy. These utopian communist ideas were picked up by **Plato** thereafter and moved into the mainstream of Western thought.

ARISTOTLE (384–322 B.C.). Whether or not this great Greek philosopher and student of **Plato** was in fact utopian in thought remains a matter of debate. Nevertheless, it is beyond question that Aristotle was a firm believer in reason as the highest faculty with which humans have been endowed and that reason (the result of speculative examination, knowing the causes of things, and living the theoretical life) properly applied can lead human societies to higher levels of development. He clearly believed and taught that progress can and does exist in time, indeed, that civilization is the result of men cooperating throughout history, all helping one another and bound together as in a chain of development toward a more perfect end. As with his mentor Plato, Aristotle viewed human advancement in terms of the Greek *polis,* but he saw possible improvements not in terms of a movement toward a perfection existing beyond human reality but as a perfection inherent within it. Additionally, whereas Plato in his *Republic* presents a highly structured, stratified, and fixed *polis* as an ideal, Aristotle in his *Politics* (350 B.C.) sees the city as a living, evolving organism marked by variety and capable of improvement. It would include such concerns as health, education, economic sustenance, a political structure made up of the rulers and the ruled, natural beauty, and urban planning. Through proper development and arrangement of these institutions its citizens, according to their individual talents, would be better able to realize to one degree or another an ideal life, a life permeated by virtue. Although Plato's ruminations on attaining perfection in time represent utopianism by another name and thus were reflected in Western thought for centuries thereafter,

Aristotle's concept of humanity's movement upward through applied speculative reasoning also became part of the West's utopian heritage in the centuries that followed (being blended with faith and moving into the Christian mainstream through the theology of Thomas Aquinas) and thus persists to the present day.

ARIZONA COMMUNITY. *See* APPENDIX.

ARKANSAS COMMUNITIES. *See* APPENDIX.

ARMSTRONG, PETER (ca. 1800–1892). As a Millerite, Armstrong was not discouraged by the failure of **William Miller**'s prophecy about Christ's Second Coming in 1843–1844. Rather, in 1852 he purchased 2,400 acres in the Allegheny Mountains to prepare a place for the 144,000 elect who would be gathered in prior to the **millennium**. Armstrong, his family, and a few followers (about 20) settled at **Celesta**, Pennsylvania, in Sullivan County in 1863, Armstrong having been planning this community for 11 years while clearing some 1,000 acres for his town site for the 144,000. He deeded the land to God in 1864, not to his children, but he eventually gave up on his project sometime around 1880 in the face of large-scale desertions arising from his own overbearing fanaticism. He and his family then moved to Philadelphia.

ARYAN THEOSOPHICAL SOCIETY. *See* JUDGE, WILLIAM Q.

ASSOCIATION OF ALL CLASSES OF ALL NATIONS (AACAN). One of many offshoots of the failed projects of **Robert Owen** (1771–1858) in Britain in the 1830s, the short-lived Association of All Classes of All Nations to form a New Moral World was the governing body of the First Lodge of the Order of the New Moral World. A branch was established in the United States on May 1, 1835, by delegates sent to Cincinnati from the Manchester and Salford Community Company to purchase land for a new community, the purpose, as in all AACAN branches, being to form an entirely new society "on the Owenite plan" through the reorganization of government and of the production and distribution of goods. According to its announcements, it would be governed by a "Social Father of the New Moral World," a senior council (those 35 and older), and a junior council (those 25–35 years of age). The established government of the Order was to be "paternal and one of unity." The New Moral World would allow no private property, and its membership would consist of three classes by progression with no priests, lawyers, military, buyers or sellers, or moneylenders allowed to join. There is no record of the Association ever becoming active in the United States, although 32 branches were in existence in England in 1838.

ASSOCIATION OF BENEFICENTS, THE. *See* DOMAIN.

ATASCADERO. *See* AMERICAN WOMAN'S REPUBLIC.

ATWOOD, MARGARET (1939–). Margaret Eleanor Atwood, novelist, poet, short story writer, and literary critic, was born in Ottawa, Ontario. The recipient of numerous awards and 13 honorary degrees for her writing, she is best known for her **dystopian** novel *The Handmaid's Tale,* published in 1985.

AUGUSTINE (AURELIUS AUGUSTUS) (354–430 A.D.). Augustine, the greatest theologian of the early Christian Church and canonized by the Roman Church as St. Augustine, was a Roman intellectual born in Algeria who gave up a professorship in Milan to become bishop of Hippo, not far from Carthage. It was here that he wrote his *The City of God,* arguing that the description of the Last Days as portrayed in the **Apocalypse** must be read as a spiritual allegory, as a picture of good versus evil, not literally, an argument that already had been made in the third century by the theologians Hippolytus and **Origen**. In his magisterial work, *The City of God,* Augustine argued that the struggle between good and evil was taking place in time with the triumph of the City of God as the end of history, and that Christians should struggle toward it by praying and doing good, on the one hand, and by avoiding evil, on the other. True bliss and perfection would be attained only in the afterlife. Parousia (the Second Coming) and the **millennium** had already come with the birth of Christ, and his Church *was* the kingdom of God on earth moving humanity toward the Last Judgment. The Apocalyptic promises did not refer to the coming of some Garden of Eden on earth, Augustine argued, but to individual salvation after death in unity with God. In 431, a year after Augustine's death, the Church at the Council of Ephesus adopted Augustine's allegorical interpretation of the Book of Revelation as its official interpretation and, as a result, visions of an earthly Armageddon, millennium, and final perfection in time were not to be interpreted literally. Still, partially fed by Augustine's necessary acceptance of progress over time, utopian millennial beliefs, reinforced by popular attitudes, visions, and simplistic faith, continued in the West and at times broke out in major ways to keep the literal millennial dream alive into modern times.

AUGUSTUS, AURELIUS. *See* AUGUSTINE.

AURORA COMMUNITY. The Aurora Community, which existed from 1856 to 1881 at Aurora in the Willamette Valley in Oregon, was led by **William Keil** (1812–1877). In 1855 Keil moved some 300 of his German American followers to Aurora after becoming unhappy with their previous location at Bethel in Shelby County, Missouri. The colonists enjoyed some financial prosperity from a hotel they built in 1863. Homes were also built for the members, and by 1872 the colony owned 23,000 acres of land and boasted 1,000 members. In 1872, however, Keil was forced to deed over the lands to individual colonists. After his death in 1877 the communal organization was dissolved, and the land and holdings were divided among the remaining colonists.

AUSTRALIA AND NEW ZEALAND COMMUNITIES. *See* APPENDIX.

AUSTRALIANS. This 17th-century description of people living in a more perfect society in the South Seas was the imaginative creation of **Gabriel de Foigni** (ca. 1630–1692). It was published a year after his death in England under the title *A New Discovery of Terra Incognita Australis, or the Southern World, by James Sadeur, a French-man.* The book tells of a 35-year sojourn in the South Seas by a shipwrecked sailor, where he discovers a nation of androgynes living in an ideal society. Goods are held in common, religious practices approximate natural religion, all persons are healthy without sickness or disease, members are educated in stages until the age of 30, and death without languishing is their happiness.

– B –

BABEUF, FRANÇOIS NOEL (GRACCHUS) (1760–1797). As an activist during the French Revolution under the assumed Roman name "Gracchus Babeuf," this radical thinker from Picardy attacked the caste system in the army and argued for an assembly of the people that would hold the king accountable to them. Of greater importance, Babeuf advocated social equality through common ownership of land and possessions. In his *Manifesto of the Equals* in 1790 during the early stage of the Revolution, he contended that inequalities in the lives of the people arose from individual ownership of property. Accordingly, in the newspaper *The Tribune of the People,* which he founded, he advocated absolute equality for all through common ownership of all possessions. This, he asserted, would result in people working willingly, and through their work they would attain happiness and tranquility. Involved in a plot in 1796 known as the "Conspiracy of Equals" to overthrow the Directory during the third and reactionary stage of the Revolution, he was arrested and executed after attempting suicide. Babeuf's utopian idea of absolute communist egalitarianism was important in the rise of 19th-century advocacy of socialist utopias guaranteeing universal equality of incomes and property.

BACK TO METHUSELAH. This antideterminist **dystopian** play of 1921, the work of the Irish playwright George Bernard Shaw (1856–1950), begins in the Garden of Eden and ends in the 32nd century. In the first of five parts, Shaw shows how the loss of the utopian Garden was a matter of choices made by individuals. In the second part, he moves to the 20th century in which a group of men are discussing World War I and Adam and Eve's choice of life over death, death being the end of the human race. The third part jumps to the 22nd century to show how greater human longevity has been gained by scientific advances, and the fourth discusses the ability of humans to live as long as Methuselah. In the fifth and last part of the play, which takes place in the 32nd century, human beings have advanced to a **millennium**; all is bountiful and peaceful, and they live to the age of 800 years. But this Golden Age has also produced life forms dominated by vanity and selfishness with the ability to kill. **Darwin-**

ian evolution, then, Shaw asserts through this play, is capable of producing wonders, but human will and wise judgment are necessary to prevent science-based utopian projects from degenerating and moving full circle back to primitivism.

BACON, FRANCIS, VISCOUNT ST. ALBANS (1561–1626). Sir Francis Bacon is best known as a philosopher of modern science on the basis of his *The Advancement of Learning* (1605) and *Novum Organum* (1620), but as a true Renaissance man he was also a historian, lawyer, political reformer, lord chancellor of England, and utopianist. His unfinished *New Atlantis* (1626), published after his death by his chaplain, was his sole utopian work. Coming from an aristocratic family and educated at Cambridge and Gray's Inn, Bacon served in Parliament and became lord chancellor in 1618. Throughout his life, Bacon strove for the promotion of the new science and for political and educational reform, although he was constantly aware that science, despite its ability to improve humanity, could also be a source of corruption. Despite its limitations as a utopian treatise, *New Atlantis* thereafter served as an inspiration for those wishing to create a more perfect society through knowledge and technology.

BAKER, GEORGE (1879?–1965). *See* FATHER DIVINE'S PEACE MISSION MOVEMENT.

BALLOU, ADIN (1803–1890). *See* HOPEDALE COMMUNITY.

BARMBY, GOODWYN (1820–1881). Barmby was one of the most prominent reformers in Britain during the 1840s. He set out to establish a communist utopian community utilizing his Central Communist Propaganda Society to bring it about. In his monthly publication *Educational Circular and Communist Apostle,* he urged the formation of a communitorium, or social house, for people marked by love, intelligence, and beauty. The central council of the Society met in November 1841 to establish the Universal Communitarian Association with five regional branches to build support for the project. All of this planning and organizing was a reflection of Barmby's philosophy of history in which he saw humanity evolving through four ages. The first age was that of pastorialism and clanism; the second was of feudalism and then the emergence of cities; the third was marked by monopolism (negative association) and association (positive association) but was transitory; and the fourth and last age was that of "communization." In this final age, communist communities would evolve in four stages: the club or lodging house stage, the common production and consumption stage, the complete city community stage, and the country community stage. On this framework he established the Moreville, or Hanwell, Communitorium in 1841 with an emphasis on adult and juvenile education and industrial training. From this start, he believed, the world would be emancipated from mercantile competition and spiritual and material discord. A mark of his profound belief that he was inaugurating a new **millennial** world order was his creation of a new calendar beginning with 1841 as the year 1. Barmby spent the remainder of the decade attempting to convince reformers throughout Britain and on the Continent of the efficacy of his vision, with no results. Thereafter, he converted to Unitarianism in 1848 and held more moderate views for the remainder of his life.

BAXTER, RICHARD (1615–1691). Richard Baxter, 17th-century English cleric, nonconformist theologian, and **millennialist**, came to his conclusion regarding human perfectibility only later in life. In an early tract, *A Holy Commonwealth* (1659), he asserted that a good state could not come about by ordinary human means alone; this was a wishful delusion. Baxter further asserted that a perfect utopian kingdom described in **Thomas More**'s *Utopia* or **Tommaso Campanella**'s *City of the Sun* could never be realized given human nature. Yet it is clear from his *The Glorious Kingdom of Christ, Described and Clearly Vindicated*, written years later (1691), that he had become a confirmed millennialist in the interim. God's Kingdom on Earth will indeed come about, but it will be by stages within history, God working through human nature, not through miraculous occurrences. Baxter, the author of more than a hundred religious works, was one of the modern precursors to the idea of progress occurring in time and through human development, a concept that would become increasingly secularized and dominant in the 18th and 19th centuries.

BEADLE COLONY. This **Hutterite** colony was established between 1905 and 1908 in Beadle County in eastern South Dakota, just south of the **Spink Colony**, to accommodate the growing population at **Bon Homme**, the first of the Hutterite colonies in the United States. Members of the **Wolf Creek Colony** also settled there. However, the local communities in the area were hostile to the Hutterites, and by 1922 the colony had relocated to West Raley, Alberta, Canada.

BEAVER ISLAND COLONY, *or* **THE KINGDOM OF ST. JAMES.** This kingdom, which lasted from 1851 to 1856, was established on Beaver Island in northern Lake Michigan. Its economic bases were fishing and trading. It was founded and ruled autocratically by James Jesse Strang (1813–1856), who practiced a variant form of **Mormonism** including polygamy. Upon the assassination of Joseph Smith in 1845, Strang, then living in Wisconsin, asserted that he was the prophet who was to succeed Smith and that he had seen angelic visitations and had unearthed additional golden tablets. Accordingly, he established the communal holy city of Voree near Burlington, Wisconsin, that same year. In 1847–1848, he established a new holy city, the City of St. James, on Beaver Island (called The Great Corner Stake of Zion by Strang) in 1850, proclaiming his new colony the Kingdom of God on Earth with himself as king and God's vice regent charged with establishing His kingdom throughout the world. The colony grew in numbers to include several thousand subjects, but Strang was murdered by disaffected members of the Kingdom of St. James who were unhappy with his benevolent theocracy, and his followers were driven from the island in 1856 by an angry mob, some of the displaced members moving to Utah to join the main body of Mormons.

BEERSHEBA COLONY. Established in 1882 and located on Pawnee Creek in Hodgeman County in western Kansas, the Beersheba Colony was the product of colonizing efforts by the Cincinnati Hebrew Union Agricultural Society. Twenty-four Russian Jewish families were brought to the site as the first settlers. Progress was marked for two years, but then disputes between the farm manager and the colonists emerged, and the manager confiscated some cattle and farm implements. Lacking funds to continue, the colony was disbanded in 1885.

BEGHARDS. The late Middle Ages were marked by spontaneous movements against the existing Roman Church, the devotees of the

Beghards movement convinced that voluntary and total poverty was the true Christian and perfect way of life. Made up largely of the intelligentsia, these persons moved from town to town and gained such a following that the Church in the early 13th century, disturbed by these "holy beggars" and their tendency to adopt heretical stands, took action against these **Free Spiritists** not only by officially condemning their doctrines in 1259 and again in 1310 but also by encouraging the new mendicant orders of Franciscans and Dominicans to also practice poverty and go out as wandering preachers to the people to convince them of the true faith. But in time these orders too lost their ardor and dedication to poverty. As a result, a movement back to superpoverty and superasceticism arose again. This took the form of the Franciscan "Spirituals" and the *Fraticelli* in northern Italy and southern France. In northern Europe, it led to a revival of Free Spiritism. This new Free Spiritism was marked by **millennialist** assumptions advanced by men commonly called "Beghards." Wearing distinctive costumes and raising the cry "Bread for God's sake," they moved throughout Europe displaying contempt for the regular friars, clergy, and bishops and disturbing church services. By the beginning of the 14th century, the heretical Beghards came to be known as the Brethren of the Free Spirit, who challenged the Roman Church for dominance but whose influence was thereafter expeditiously suppressed by the Church through persecution, thereafter to fade away slowly.

BEGUINES. *See* FREE SPIRITISTS.

BEHAVIORISM. This school of psychology founded by **John Broadus Watson** (1878–1958) and promulgated by **B. F. Skinner** (1904–1990) is, strictly speaking, not utopian as such. However, its basic assumptions and scientific approach to human conduct and, therefore, to the formation of human societies played an important role during the 20th century in keeping alive the idea of creating a perfected society through behavior modification. Behaviorism emphasizes environmental influences on human conduct and values, and it argues that behavior is, at base, a matter of training, of stimulus and response. This theory, developed in the first decades of the century, fit in well with Progressive and reform movements in the religious, social, and political arenas and was widely accepted in the United States' universities, especially in the social sciences and education. As such, its basic assumptions have become an integral part of the "**soft utopianism**" pervading the nation's education system, especially its colleges and universities, and have had a direct impact on the United States' continued belief that a perfected society can be created in time.

BEILHART, JACOB (1867–1908). Founder of the **Spirit Fruit Society** in 1899, Jacob Beilhart believed that a utopian society could be created that combined **Transcendental** spirituality and anarchistic ideals. Born in Ohio into a large family with strong religious traditions, Beilhart blended these with the ideas of **Ralph Waldo Emerson** and Walt Whitman. Moving to Kansas, he was converted to the Seventh-Day Adventist faith, attended an Adventist college, and began preaching in Ohio and Kansas. He then enrolled in a nursing program at the Seventh-Day Adventist Sanitarium in Battle Creek, Michigan, in 1890 and upon completing it he accepted a position in a sanitarium operated by natural health enthusiast Dr. Harvey Kellogg. Breaking with the Adventists, Beilhart moved to faith healing through the influence of C. W. Post, another cereal manufacturer, and then joined the Christian Scientist Church, which he soon abandoned.

In time, Beilhart developed his own religious movement called Universal Life, drawn from his previous religious experiences. Within it he advocated socialism to replace competitive capitalism and materialism and the granting of women's rights. Determined to try out his ideas, in 1899 he founded the Spirit Fruit Society outside Lisbon, Ohio, for the purpose. Within two years of its founding, however, the colony began receiving bad publicity over Beilhart's liberal sexual views, his advocacy of free love, and his alleged abduction of a Chicago physician's wife. Faced with threats of violence by local residents, Beilhart and a dozen members fled to Illinois and during 1904–1905 purchased land for a new colony at Wooster Lake, near Ingleside, north of Chicago in Lake County. Here they built a grand "Temple House" of 18 bedrooms and a massive barn. Beilhart died of a ruptured appendix in 1908. His Illinois colony continued in existence for a few more years, some of its members migrating to California to begin another colony near Santa Cruz. Beilhart's utopian

Free Spirit and Illinois colonies, although never very successful in their day, anticipated many utopian social and sexual ideas and practices that would come into prominence in the 20th century.

BEISSEL, JOHANN CONRAD (1690?–1768). Beissel was born in Germany and iemigrated to the United States in 1720. Already heavily influenced by the **Anabaptist** and pietist traditions, he planned to join **Johann Kelpius**'s Woman in the Wilderness Community at Coxsackie, Pennsylvania, near Germantown, but by the time he arrived it had ceased to exist. Instead, he became part of a nearby German Baptist Brotherhood settlement, and in 1721 joined with other pietists to form a celibate brotherhood dedicated to following the law of Moses. Within four years he had assumed leadership of the group, in part because of the messages he was convinced he had received from God. He was baptized into the Dunker faith in 1724 but fell out with his coreligionists over the question as to when the Sabbath should be celebrated. In 1732 he established Ephrata in Lancaster County, also known as the Solitary Brethren of the Community of the Seventh-Day Baptists, with two women and three men joining him.

At Ephrata the members, eventually reaching 300 in number, lived monastic, celibate lives in communal dormitories (one for the tonsured men, the Zionite Brotherhood, and the other for the shorthaired women, the Spiritual Virgins) and practiced community of goods and common worship. All of this occurred under Beissel's mystical and sometimes autocratic leadership. Among other things, the members were directed by Beissel to record their sins so that he could read these spiritual confessions aloud to all the members of the community. He renamed himself "Friedsam," meaning "Peaceful," as a symbol of his baptism into his new life; his followers called him "Father Friedsam." Tending toward drunkenness and senility in his old age, he died in 1768. Ephrata ended as a communal entity in 1770 with private ownership being allowed, but it continues in existence as a tourist attraction to this day.

BELL, ARTHUR L. (?–1951). *See* MANKIND UNITED.

BELLAMY, EDWARD (1850–1898). Undoubtedly the most famous and influential utopian novelist of the late 19th century, Bellamy was born in Chicopee Falls, Massachusetts, and attended school there until enrolling at Union College in Schenectady, New York, before studying for the law. During the 1870s he worked for the New York *Evening Post* and served as editor of the Springfield *Union* before traveling to the Sandwich Islands to regain his health. In 1880 he founded the *Springfield Daily News* and became an international celebrity with the publication of his ***Looking Backward: 2000–1887*** in 1888 describing a humane and successful utopian Boston after peacefully converting to socialism. The book sold 300,000 copies in two years. Almost overnight, Bellamy Clubs were established to discuss the work (the first in Boston), Nationalist Clubs were founded to implement the ideas Bellamy described in the novel, and a number of colonies were subsequently organized to put his ideas into practice. When the Nationalist Party failed in its quest for political power, many of its members joined the Populist Party, the most prominent reformist political party in the 1890s. Bellamy also published *Equality* in 1897 as a sequel to *Looking Backward.* It portrayed a United States now transformed into a tension-free and egalitarian nation. Bellamy's dream, cooperative organizations dedicated to peaceful political change bringing about a socialist perfected society, continued to inspire reformers long after his death in Chicopee Falls in 1898.

BEND SINISTER. This antitotalitarian **dystopian** novel was published in 1947, the work of Vladimir Nabokov (1899–1977), best known for his novel *Lolita.* Nabokov is a dystopian of major stature whose *Bend Sinister* in many respects is similar to **George Orwell**'s ***Nineteen Eighty-Four***. Nabokov, a refugee from Russian, then Nazi, totalitarianism, came to the United States in 1940, fleeing the Germans as they occupied Paris. This novel tells of an eastern European country in which a revolution overthrows an existing republican government under the leadership of a man named Paduk (meaning "toad" in Russian). Paduk's government institutes "Ekwilism" to standardize thought and action, "spiritual uniformity," within the people of the new state. As a result, nonsense in word and thought becomes habitual and logical. Paduk is challenged by the academic philosopher Adam Krug, but when Paduk tortures Krug's acquaintances and his son, Krug gives in. Then, when his son dies in a state-sanctioned medical experiment, Krug has a breakdown and dies. Although not as well known as other dystopian novels in the mid-20th century, the tragedy *Bend Sinister* established Nabokov as an antiutopian novelist of the first order.

BENEFITS. This 1976 futuristic **dystopian** novel is the work of Zoe Fairbairns (1948–), the English feminist writer, and deals with the inequalities and difficulties women face in the contemporary world. *Benefits* tells the story of late-20th-century society in which women are subject to compulsory birth control as the post-1984 **Orwellian** government attempts to institutionalize and improve motherhood by selective breeding, thereby reducing a woman's right to choose or not choose motherhood, those not chosen resorting to backstreet doctors to become pregnant. The government also pays women substantial salaries or "benefits"—thus the title of the novel—for rearing their own children. This, in turn, excludes mothers from the job market, but, of greater importance, leaves a woman's right to choose in the hands of the government.

BENEVOLENT ASSOCIATION. *See* REFUGEE HOME SOCIETY.

BENNETT CO-OPERATIVE COLONY. Little is known of this colony north of Long Lane, Dallas County, Missouri, except that it was begun in 1873 by **William H. Bennett** (1855–1920), who withdrew from the **Friendship Community** over dissatisfaction with **Alcander Longley**'s leadership. It probably ceased to exist in 1877. Bennett made a second attempt to establish a communitarian colony in 1894 with the **Home Employment Co-operative Company** in Dallas County, Missouri, but Bennett and his wife liquidated their holdings sometime between 1904 and 1906 and moved to Arkansas.

BENNETT, WILLIAM H. (1855–1920). *See* BENNETT CO-OPERATIVE COLONY; HOME EMPLOYMENT CO-OPERATIVE COMPANY.

BERGERAC, SAVINEM CYRANO de (1619–1655). Cyrano de Bergerac served as a military officer until, wounded at the Siege of Arras, he abandoned the military profession for literature. In his *History of the States of the Moon* (1657) and *Comic History of the States of the Sun* (1662), published after his death, Cyrano satirized the institutions of 17th-century French society by telling a tale about the lunar and solar worlds, where institutions and mores are superior to those found on earth.

BERLIN COMMUNITY, *or* **CHRISTIAN REPUBLIC.** Little is known about this community composed of 12 adults and six children that existed from 1865 to 1866 at Berlin Heights in Erie County, Ohio. It was similar to the colonies established at Berlin Heights by the **"Free Lovers at Davis House"** and the **Berlin Heights Community**, but it is not known if it was directly related to either of them.

BERLIN HEIGHTS COMMUNITY, *or* **POINT HOPE COMMUNITY.** This community was a continuation of the **"Free Lovers at Davis House"** after they left their original site due to their neighbors' hostility. Established in 1860 on a farm outside Berlin Heights, Ohio, the community of 10 men and 10 women was reorganized in 1861 and became the Industrial Fraternity.

BESANT, ANNIE WOOD (1847–1933). This prominent British-born **Theosophist** lecturer and writer during her lifetime moved from mainline Christianity as a pastor's wife to radical freethinking, to atheism, to social reform, to leading the Theosophical Society, to being an Indian activist. Born Annie Wood of middle-class parents, at age 19 she married the Reverend Frank Besant, a marriage that ended when she broke from Christianity and became an advocate for birth control. During the 1880s, she also became a crusader for women's rights and against unhealthy factory conditions. Converted to Theosophy after meeting Helena Petrovna Blavatsky (1820–1891), Besant became president of one branch of the Theosophical Society after Madame Blavatsky died in 1891 at her home. She later moved to India to study Hindu ideas and became involved in agitation for Indian home rule, a stance that led to her being interred during World War I. She died in Madras (now Chennai), India, in 1933.

BETHEL (*or* **BETH EL) COMMUNITY.** *See* KEIL, WILLIAM.

BETHLEHEM YEHUDAH. This Russian Jewish colony was established in 1882 in South Dakota on government land in Aurora County about three miles northwest of **Cremieux**. It was made up of 32 members of **Am Olam** ("Eternal People") known as the Sons of Freedom, a group inclined toward activist socialism. All were unmarried men who refused support from American Jewish philanthropists because of their desire to distance themselves from traditional Jewish petty trades and religious practices. They worked the land on a communal basis and lived as members of one family. Faced with a rigorous frontier existence, lack of farming experience, and crop failures, the colonists after a year and a half agreed to divide the land into individual holdings and distribute all shared property among themselves. Bethlehem Yehudah was liquidated in 1885, most colonists moving to New York.

BETTINA, *or* **DARMSTAEDTER KOLONIE.** With the aid of the Society for the Protection of German Immigrants to Texas, 33 radical students from Darmstadt, Germany, established this colony in 1847 in Gillespie (now Llano) County in eastern Texas. Their high ideals regarding freedom, friendship, and equality soon fell victim to internal chaos, and the experiment ended in 1848.

BEYOND FREEDOM AND DIGNITY. *See* SKINNER, B. F.

BIMELER, JOSEPH (1778–1853). *See* SEPARATISTS OF ZOAR.

BISHOP HILL COLONY. Established in 1846 at Bishop Hill in Henry County, Illinois, this communal settlement was made up of Swedes, called the "Readers" or "Janssonists," under their leader **Erik Jansson** (1808–1850). By 1850, the year Jansson was murdered, there were over 1,000 colonists on the 14,000-acre site. More member immigrants continued to arrive from Sweden until 1855, swelling the population of the prosperous colony. However, it was dissolved in 1862 because of discontent among the younger members over imposed celibacy plus financial malfeasance by one of its leaders. Some members had already left to join the **Shakers** at **Pleasant Hill** in Kentucky in 1854.

BISHOP, WILLIAM HENRY (1847–1928). *See THE GARDEN OF EDEN, U.S.A.: A VERY POSSIBLE STORY.*

BLACK UTOPIAS. In the mid-19th century, a number of utopian communities were established to aid blacks, both free and runaway slaves, in their plight. Unlike most utopian schemes, these black utopias were intended to be temporary, not permanent. Although they were designed to be communal and cooperative, they were to be transitory stages for the blacks who were thereafter to take their rightful and productive place in a free and self-reliant society. In Canada there were four black utopian communities: **Wilberforce**, **Dawn** and the British-American Institute, the **Elgin Association**, and the **Refugee Home Society**, all in Ontario. The United States had two: **Nashoba** in Tennessee and the **Port Royal Experiment** on the South Carolina Sea Islands.

BLAIR, ERIC ARTHUR. *See* ORWELL, GEORGE.

BLAVATSKY, HELENA PETROVNA (1820–1891). *See* THEOSOPHISTS.

BLESSED ISLES OF PRESTER JOHN. *See* BRAGMANS.

"BLOOMERTOWN." *See* RISING STAR ASSOCIATION.

BLOOMFIELD ASSOCIATION. Little is known about this commune of 500 acres that began in 1844 east of Honeoye Falls in western New York with 148 members. It apparently came to an end the following year in a number of legal disputes over property titles.

BLUE SPRINGS COMMUNITY. This offshoot of the attempt at communal living inspired by **Robert Owen** (1771–1858) was located near Bloomington, Indiana. It was established in 1826 and was said by **A. J. Macdonald** (?–1854) to be "harmonious and prosperous" in 1827, but no record of its existence can be found after that year.

BOCKELSON, JAN, *or* **JOHN OF LEYDEN.** *See* ANABAPTISTS.

BOEHME, JACOB (1575–1624). Jacob Boehme was a German cobbler turned metaphysician, cosmologist, and theologian who, though virtually unlettered and expressing his thoughts (gained through periodic visions) in a writing style very difficult to comprehend, gained attention with his works *Aurora* (1612) and *Way to Christ* (1623). Basically he argued that God was striving for self-revelation and self-actualization in time through a dialectic process of the positive and negative, which had its material manifestation in the evolution of all things, including humans, into God completed as fully known to himself. Obscure as Boehme's philosophy may seem, it had an effect on **Johann Andreae** (1586–1654) in his own time and on the Quakers, **Theosophists**, **Johann Kelpius** (1673–1708) and the Woman in the Wilderness colony, and **Georg W. F. Hegel** (1770–1831) in the centuries that followed. Resonances of his thought continue today among Theosophists, Christian mystics, and dialectical theologians.

BOHEMIA MANOR. *See* LABADISTS.

BOHEMIAN BRETHREN. *See* MORAVIANS.

BOHEMIAN CO-OPERATIVE FARMING COMPANY. Established by a group of Bohemian immigrants suffering from the Panic of 1907, this 5,300-acre colony was set up in 1913 on the Cumberland Plateau in Cumberland County in eastern Tennessee. Attempting to restore the village life they had experienced in their native country, their houses were grouped village style. But all the land was held in common, and a common treasury and common storehouse were maintained. With the return of prosperity, the project was abandoned in 1916.

BOISSIERE, ERNEST VALETON de (1810–1894). De Boissiere, a French reformer of noble birth, became a radical member of the Republican Party opposed to Louis Napoleon. When the Revolution of 1848 failed, de Boissiere immigrated to the United States and settled in New Orleans. In 1868 he met **Albert Brisbane** (1809–1890), the American disciple of **Charles Fourier** (1772–1837), and the two agreed to form a community based on Fourierist ideas. They bought 3,500 acres in Franklin County, Kansas, near Williamsburg, and 40 Frenchmen immigrated there. Most of the immigrants were silk makers, so 250 acres of mulberry trees were planted. But silk making did not prove to be successful and was abandoned in 1882 as unprofitable, after which de Boissiere returned to France. The colony was originally named the Kansas Co-operative Farm, but it soon came to be called "Silkville." It ended in 1886 when de Boissiere deeded the property over to the Odd Fellows Lodge for use as an orphanage.

BON HOMME COLONY. This first of the **Hutterite** colonies in the United States was established by Russian immigrants on 2,500 acres along the Missouri River in 1874, in Bon Homme County in southeastern South Dakota. When the members found themselves in financial difficulties a year later, the elders successfully applied for a $6,000 loan from the **Harmony Society** of Butler County, Pennsylvania. This enabled them to construct a flourmill. The Bon Homme colonists maintained friendly relations with the Harmonists and with the settlers at nearby **Amana**, Iowa. When the colony had outgrown its land in 1878 it received financial assistance from both Amana and Harmony, and the colonists at Harmony allowed the Hutterites to inherit and occupy their property in Pennsylvania as a daughter colony. The offer was accepted, but the Hutterites were not able to adapt to the new economy and unfamiliar neighbors, so they eventually moved back to South Dakota, establishing a colony at **Milltown**. The Bon Homme colonists were the only Hutterites who did not move to Canada in the years 1918 to 1922 under the pressure of anti-Germanism during World War I and thereafter, so for a time Bon Homme was the only Hutterite settlement in the United States. In 1936 it had 3,400 members and had purchased the facilities of the Hutterite **Rockport Colony** for a daughter colony two years before. It continues to exist today.

BOOK OF A HUNDRED CHAPTERS. See REVOLUTIONARY OF THE UPPER RHINE.

BOOK OF MORMON, THE. See MORMONS.

BOOTH, WILLIAM (1829–1912). See SALVATION ARMY FARM COLONIES.

BOOTH-TUCKER, FREDERICK (1853–1929). See SALVATION ARMY FARM COLONIES.

BORSODI, RALPH (1886–1977). This social philosopher and activist was influenced at an early age by the writings of both European and American intellectual reformers, resulting in his becoming active in the Single Tax party and serving as the editor of its publication, the

Single Taxer. In 1919 he moved his family from New York City to Suffern, New York, where he established a decentralist homestead away from the limitations of city life and their dependence on others. Here he experimented with labor-saving devices, and the family took steps to become self-sufficient. In the years that followed, Borsodi also published a number of works including *The Distribution Age* (1926), in which he examined why distribution costs were more than production costs; *This Ugly Civilization* (1928), which examined the factory system and its deleterious effects on the nation; and his best-known work, ***Flight from the City*** (1933), in which he recounted his homesteading efforts at Suffern. Borsodi also cooperated with the Farm Resettlement Agency, which settled families on one-and-a-third acres of land near Dayton, Ohio, on which they could grow their own food, raise animals, and supplement their income with nearby cash-paying jobs. This experiment only lasted from 1933 to 1935.

With the failure of the Dayton project, the Borsodis established the School of Living at Suffern. Here they experimented with many types of more efficient home production, keeping records of their work and issuing bulletins on their findings. Borsodi also played a role in the establishment of Bayard Lane Community, a decentralist homestead town, plus other projects at Nyack and Stillwater, New York, and Ringwood, New Jersey. All failed to thrive. In the 1940s he continued to write, turning his attention to commodity-based currency, and in the 1960s he spent four years in India. Although he enjoyed little success as a community organizer, his writings on home economy and quality decentralized living made him a well-known figure in his time.

BOURNVILLE. George Cadbury (1839–1922), of the Cadbury family chocolate business, in 1893 decided to build the garden village of Bournville four miles away from Cadbury's major works at Birmingham, England. Influenced in part by the ideas of **Robert Owen** (1771–1858), he wanted to avoid the slums and evils he saw in Birmingham. He, therefore, bought 330 acres of land between 1893 and 1900 and founded the Bournville Village Trust to carry out his scheme to provide decent living conditions for laborers. Cadbury supervised the construction of 313 compact but adequate houses, Ruskin Hall for social activities, a school, and shops on the site. In

1901 about 80 percent of the homes were occupied by Cadbury workers from Birmingham or Bournville. The model village continued to grow both in size and value and still exists today as part of the city of Birmingham.

BRADBURY, RAY (1920–). *See FAHRENHEIT 451.*

BRADLEY, RACHEL (?–1893). *See* OLIVE BRANCH.

BRAGMANS. Sir John Mandeville (ca. 1300–1373) was an English traveler who supposedly made a trip to the East in 1322 and composed a work entitled *Mandeville's Travels.* It included the 32nd chapter that was entitled "Of the Goodness of the Folk of the Isle of Bragman; of King Alexander; and Wherefore the Emperor of India Is Clept Prester John" and that described a good society of the "Bragmans." On this Isle of Bragmans, the people live good, moral lives without personal faults (even though they are not Christians), so there is no theft, murder, prostitution, and other crime found outside the island, nor is there war or hunger. The island sees neither snow nor any other form of bad weather. And because of living and eating temperately, the Bragmans usually die of old age. Their king is only their high teacher, and they have no judges because there is no crime or wrongdoing. Indeed, so good was their island that, on being informed about it, Alexander the Great refused to conquer it. Nearby are other "Blessed Isles of Prester John": Oxidrace, Gynoscriphe, Pytan (its inhabitants being dwarflike), a fifth where the people are amphibians and live 400 to 500 years because of their abstemious eating habits, and many others. All are under the rule of a king who has taken the name "Prester John" (Priest John), having witnessed and been impressed by the ordination of priests by a bishop. Whether this travel tale is a true account by Mandeville, which is doubtful, or a collection of tales derived from various French sources, the story of the fabled land of the Bragmans enjoyed a persistent hold on European minds in the centuries that followed.

BRANCH DAVIDIANS. The Branch Davidians are a splinter group of Seventh-Day Adventists founded by Bulgarian immigrant **Victor Houteff** (1885–1955) in 1934, who separated from the mother church and created what was called Shepherd's Rod. After 1942 they called themselves the Davidian Seventh-Day Adventists (the Seventh-Day Adventists having renounced any connection with the sect during the 1930s). Houteff and his followers believed that the Kingdom of David would soon be restored in Palestine and that they should live communally to prepare for this **millennial** event. They settled on 189 acres west of Waco, Texas, called Mt. Carmel, where they raised their own food, operated their own school, held religious services daily, and concentrated on producing literature and sending out missionaries to proselytize to gain the 144,000 souls to be saved at the Second Coming. At Houteff's death in 1955 his wife, Florence (1917–), assumed leadership of the colony, but splinter groups arose, convincing the main body of Davidians to move to a new Mt. Carmel east of the city where they built homes and other buildings on the 941-acre site. In 1955 the Davidians suffered a major crisis when Florence Houteff predicted that on April 22, 1959, the Kingdom in Palestine would be established. When it did not despite some 900 persons arriving at the colony to witness the event, hundreds left the movement, leaving only about 50 at Mt. Carmel. Thereafter, when Mrs. Houteff left the area, an existing splinter group led by Benjamin and Lois Roden took control of Mt. Carmel.

Arriving on the scene in 1981 was a guitar-playing Adventist named Vernon Howell (1960–1993), who subsequently changed his name to David Koresh ("David" for the monarchy to be established in Palestine and "Koresh," the Hebrew for "Cyrus," the messianic Persian king of the Bible) and took charge of the colony in 1988. As the patriarch of Mt. Carmel, Koresh took several wives. He was, he preached, the Lamb, able to open the seven seals, loose catastrophe on humankind, and lead the Davidians to heaven. Some members built up a substantial arsenal during these years. The Bureau of Alcohol, Tobacco, and Firearms launched a raid on Mt. Carmel on February 28, 1993, and four agents were killed by Davidians. As a result of this raid, the Davidians holed up and withstood a 51-day siege, Koresh having taught his followers that when the end of the world arrives some of the soldiers of Satan will be civil authorities. On April 19, 1993, the Federal Bureau of Investigation, now in charge of the siege, fired gas shells into the building after shots were fired. Somehow a fire broke out, incinerating 74 Davidians, including 21 children, within. The 50 or so survivors of the Waco siege and fire have not regrouped, and splinter groups of Davidians that broke off prior to April 1993 still exist, most notably in Missouri and South Carolina. Many critical questions regarding Koresh, his Branch Davidian followers, and what happened in 1993 remain unanswered, and recriminations continue, but there is no question that the Davidians of Waco were premillennialists dedicated to their communal ideas and ready to live by them and die for them.

BRAVE NEW WORLD. This antitotalitarian, **dystopian** novel published in 1932 was the work of **Aldous Huxley** (1894–1963). Huxley viewed totalitarianism as founded on the misuse of science and technology by government, which uses thought and action control to maintain what it holds to be the correct social, economic, and political order. This brave new world, set in the seventh century A.F. ("After Ford") is dominated by a figure named Henry Ford, who calls himself "Our Freud" when speaking of psychological matters. Ford oversees all activities in a state dedicated economically to unending production and consumption under the slogan "Ending is better than mending." Technology is highly valued even to the point of genetic engineering, which produces a class system based on cloning ("decanting," not normal birthing; one egg according to "Bokanovsky's Process" produces up to 96 identical human beings). Through the work of the Central London Hatchery and Conditioning Centre, the "Alphas," having been genetically engineered to ensure high intelligence and proper conditioning, are the governors and scientists; the "Deltas" and "Epsilons," at the bottom of the intelligence and social scale, have been bred and conditioned to do physical labor.

Technology is also used to condition people to accept the state's rules and values, thereby creating automatons who are without frustration because they are unaware of possibilities in thought and action otherwise available to them as humans. Contraceptives are always available to eliminate frustration and remove the possibility of unauthorized pregnancies, fertile women wearing "Malthusian belts" filled with contraceptives at all times (although the majority of women are prenatally sterilized), and frequent copulation is urged and widely accepted for all, the typical family structure and its mores having ceased to exist (the word "mother" has become an obscenity).

If anxiety still exists despite sexual gratification, drugs are available on demand, especially soma, which is distributed regularly and is frequently used by the citizens as their opiate, especially at their solidarity service held every other week, which features hymns to Ford and to death and ends with sexual consummation. A knowledge of history through books and museums is denied the people to eliminate questioning the government or the status quo; all are taught that the past is irrelevant, the new and the material being of greater value than the old and the spiritual. The World State is governed by 10 Controllers, who keep the people satisfied with their basic necessities provided and with entertainments. Huxley's *Brave New World,* a protest and a warning against **scientism** and rationalism from earlier centuries and against totalitarianism arising in the 1920s and 1930s, still stands as one of the most influential dystopian novels of the 20th century.

BRETHREN OF THE FREE SPIRIT. *See* FREE SPIRITISTS.

BRIDE OF CHRIST. This early 20th-century Oregon grouping was the creation of the German immigrant Franz Edmund Creffield, who arrived in Portland in 1903. Sent by the Salvation Army down to Corvallis that year, he soon proclaimed himself to be the second Christ— "Joshua." Several dozen women coalesced around him, and he instituted afternoon meetings in their homes where, at his urging, they abandoned their clothing. This led to his selecting some of them as special wives, who gained an exalted place in heaven by copulating with him on earth. Thrown out of his house by a wealthy businessman, Creffield established a colony outside the town where he and his female followers continued their practice of nudity. When a photograph of the unclad group appeared in the local paper, Creffield was tarred and feathered and driven from Corvallis. He sneaked back into town and, when caught with one of the women, was arrested and sentenced to two years in prison. After a year there, he again gathered a gaggle of female followers, bought land near Waldport, Oregon, on the coast, and urged others to come in order to escape the Lord's forthcoming destruction of Corvallis—foreshadowed by the San Francisco earthquake of 1906, he said. But the Bride of Christ grouping came to an end on May 7, 1906, when George Mitchell, the brother of a woman who was one of Creffield's devoted followers,

shot him dead—the sister subsequently shooting Mitchell in the head
for his foul deed! When Creffield's naked followers found out about
his death, they disbanded and returned to society.

BRISBANE, ALBERT (1809–1890). Born to a wealthy family in
Batavia, New York, as a young man Brisbane toured the intellectual
centers of Europe, studying under **Georg Hegel** (1770–1831) and the
Comte de Saint-Simon (1760–1825). His search for intellectual guidance ended when he read **Charles Fourier**'s book *L'Association Do-
mestique Agricole* in 1832 while in Germany. He subsequently gave
lectures on Fourier's heretical ideas until the German police deported
him to France. Here he met Fourier (1772–1837) and became his devoted disciple. Brisbane returned to the United States in 1834 and in
1837 began to spread the word about Fourierism, which he considered
the cure for all of society's problems. In 1840 Brisbane published *The
Social Destiny of Man,* an Americanized and somewhat simplified
version of Fourier's theory (excluding, for example, his mentor's
views on women, morality, and marriage); the book enjoyed great success. This book and the articles he published in **Horace Greeley**'s
New York Tribune condemned capitalism for worsening the lot of the
working class and society in general. He described how to establish
model communities, which again were simplified versions of
Fourier's ideal where everyone did the same work, received the same
wages, and enjoyed the same living conditions. In Brisbane's version,
each **phalanx** should have a minimum population of 400 persons,
who should invest at least $1,000 each (or otherwise raise at least
$400,000) to be used in part for the purchase of arable land. Thou-
sands of people attended meetings to hear about these ideas, and
dozens of settlements were planned and executed in 10 stages. None
of them met all of these conditions, not even the **North American
Phalanx**, which Brisbane cofounded in 1843. Brisbane also wrote *The
Doctrines of Charles Fourier* and was editor of *The Phalanx* from
1843 to 1845. During the 1860s he was associated with **Ernest Valeton de Boissiere** and was associated with the American Social Science Association in its efforts to promote rational and scientific planning. After 1877 Brisbane moved to France, where he invented a
system of transportation in pneumatic tubes, a system of underground
fertilization, a compressed wood pavement, and an oven designed to

cook in a vacuum. He returned to the United States in 1889 and died the next year in Richmond, Virginia, during a tour of the South.

BRITISH-AMERICAN INSTITUTE, THE. *See* DAWN COLONY.

BRITTANICUS, MERCURIUS (1574–1656). *See MUNDUS ALTER ET IDEM*.

BROCTON COMMUNITY. This community, also known as Salem-on-Erie, was established at Portland in Chautauqua County, New York, in 1867. It was led by **Thomas Lake Harris** (1823–1906), who moved his Brotherhood of the New Life from **Amenia** in Dutchess County to this 1,600-acre site near Lake Erie thanks to the financial generosity of **Laurence Oliphant** (1829–1888) and his mother, Lady Oliphant. The community prospered on winemaking (19,000 gallons annually); growing fruit, grapes, and other crops; processing and shipping hay; and operating a restaurant, hotel, general store, and steam-powered grist mill. Membership fluctuated between 75 and 100. Following a vision (Harris claimed to be divinely chosen as leader), Harris took a few selected members to **Fountain Grove** in California in 1875; those who remained behind had joined them by 1881 as the community fell into disrepair.

BROOK FARM. In 1841 **George Ripley** (1802–1880), a former Unitarian minister and **Transcendentalist**, decided to convert his 200-acre country home nine miles from Boston at West Roxbury into a community where all would share equally in the domestic and agricultural chores necessary to run a farm. They would receive equal wages for this work, thus allowing everyone a maximum amount of free time for intellectual and social pursuits. It was financed by a joint stock company with shares valued at $100 each with a guaranteed interest rate of 5 percent per year. Twenty members, most of whom were intellectuals, including Nathaniel Hawthorne (who wrote about his experiences in *The Blithedale Romance*), began the experiment. Eventually 115 members lived at Brook Farm, although the total population did not exceed 80 at any given time. **Ralph Waldo Emerson** and David Thoreau were frequent visitors. Although life at Brook Farm was filled with social events and various cultural endeavors, many found the physical workload to be somewhat daunting. Their most successful undertaking was their school, which attracted students from the surrounding cities by its emphasis on developing creativity and on student self-determination with regard to the subjects they studied. Eventually the framers' goal to keep the work to a minimum resulted in financial difficulties.

In an attempt to rescue their way of life, Ripley and Charles A. Dana, among others, embraced **Fourierism** in 1844. Brook Farm was renamed The Brook Farm Phalanx, and construction began on a large **phalanstery** that would house 150 new members. **Albert Brisbane** and **Horace Greeley** visited, giving long lectures on Fourierism and morality, and the Fourierist journal *The Harbinger* was published at the phalanx from 1845 to 1847. Thousands of people applied for membership, but it soon became apparent that the joy had gone out of life at Brook Farm. Work became more structured as new industries were added, but there were not enough members to allow for the rotation of job duties that they had enjoyed in the past. When the phalanstery was destroyed by fire days after it had been completed, no one had the funds or the energy to rebuild it. The property was sold off a year later in 1847.

BROTHER XII (EDWARD ARTHUR WILSON) (1878–1934). *See* AQUARIAN FOUNDATION.

BROTHERHOOD, THE. *See* SPIRITUALIST COMMUNITY.

BROTHERHOOD OF THE COOPERATIVE COMMONWEALTH. *See* EQUALITY.

BROTHERHOOD OF THE NEW AGE. *See* SOUTHERN CO-OPERATIVE ASSOCIATION OF APALACHICOLA.

BROTHERHOOD OF THE NEW LIFE. *See* AMENIA COMMUNITY; HARRIS, THOMAS LAKE.

BROWN, JOHN MACMILLAN (GODFREY SWEVEN) (1846-1935). *See LIMANORA, THE ISLAND OF PROGRESS.*

BROWNE, CARL (1846–1914). *See* FREEDOM COLONY.

BRUDERHOF. This 20th-century communal movement, also known as the Society of Brothers, began in Germany in 1920 when Eberhard

Arnold and his wife rented a farmhouse in Hesse and opened a Christian commune there. In 1926 Arnold and his followers purchased their own farm in the Rhon Mountains, where they began to read the works of the early **Anabaptists** and became interested in the history of the **Hutterites**. Then in 1930 Arnold traveled to the United States and Canada and visited the Hutterite colonies in these countries. While there, he was ordained a Hutterite minister. Facing opposition from the Nazis in Germany in the 1930s, they moved to England, although Arnold died in 1935. When World War II broke out and the members of the Bruderhof faced internment in England, they moved to Paraguay in 1941 after the United States and Canada refused to give them sanctuary. They purchased a 20,000-acre ranch they named Primavera and on the land developed three *hofs,* or colonies. By 1950 they numbered 600 persons.

Then in 1954 they established Woodcrest, the first American Bruderhof, near Rifton, New York. Membership expanded rapidly with nine colonies being established by 1956. In the meantime, the Macedonia Cooperative Community in Georgia decided to join them. Undergoing a leadership crisis between 1959 and 1961, some of the members were expelled or resigned, and all the South American colonies, plus one each in England and Germany, were closed by 1962. Since that time a number of breakaway members have been openly critical of the members of the Bruderhofs, commenting on their lack of the spirit of Christian love and their intolerance of any ideas or actions contrary to their own. And contacts with the western Hutterites have been at times stormy, the Hutterites accusing the Bruderhof members of acquiescing to immorality within their ranks. Still, the Bruderhof movement has experienced both growth and prosperity down to the present time.

BRUDERHOFS. *See* HUTTERITES.

BUFFALO COLONY. This granddaughter **Hutterite** colony was an offspring of **Milltown** in Hutchinson County and was founded in Beadle County, South Dakota, in 1907. It moved to James Valley Junction within the county in 1913 and became the **James Valley Colony**.

BUILDING OF THE CITY BEAUTIFUL, THE. This mystical, intensely religious novel written by **Joachim Miller** (1839–1913) in

1893 tells the story of a mysterious, spiritually insightful Russian Jewish woman named Miriam and "a stranger," John Morton, who first meet in Jerusalem and commiserate about the evils of the world. They agree that humans, not God, are responsible for the misery they see around them, humans being basically good and beautiful but dragged down by their environment. The stranger is fascinated by Miriam and reveals to her his plan to build a beautiful city in the United States. After a number of miraculous visions and adventures with Miriam, Morton attempts to build his city above San Francisco Bay but fails. Miriam, as promised, returns to him after five years, and, after more visions and insightful conversations, they conclude that any perfect society can only be built on the words of Christ in the Sermon on the Mount and in the blending of all religious beliefs. Thereafter, the stranger returns to his task and the novel ends.

BULWER-LYTTON, EDWARD (1803–1873). *See COMING RACE, THE.*

BUREAU COUNTY PHALANX. This small **Fourierist** association existed in 1843 in Bureau County, Illinois, west of Chicago. It lasted only one year; no record of its history exists.

BURLEY COLONY. *See* CO-OPERATIVE BROTHERHOOD.

BURNET, THOMAS (1635?–1715). This **Cambridge Platonist**, disciple of **Joseph Mede**, and student and theologian at Christ's College did not reject religion, the Scriptures, and **millennial** progress. Rather, Burnet viewed them as complementary. He argued that nature and human history are worked out in parallel according to natural law and that increasing and unfolding knowledge (both scriptural and natural) is but a preparation for the millennium to come when the earth will be transformed as humankind in its totality moves steadily toward a New Eden. Thus Burnet transferred the work of Divine Providence to nature, seen as a series of causes and effects set in motion by God at the time of creation. God, then, according to Burnet, becomes immanent (inherent or indwelling) in nature, a concept that would play a major role in intellectual and utopian trends to come. For Burnet, natural progress meant redemption for all of humankind in which every soul will progress to a union with the divine mind and share God's goodness.

BURNING BUSH, THE, *or* **THE METROPOLITAN INSTITUTE OF TEXAS.** A group of Free Methodists in Chicago, dissatisfied with formalism in their congregations, in 1913 purchased 1,520 acres of land with a plantation-style house a mile outside Bullard in Smith County in east Texas. Arriving on a chartered train, they established The Burning Bush, more formally The Society of the Burning Bush, on the site, adding a large tabernacle and a number of small houses and dormitories to the property. It consisted of 375 members from various occupational backgrounds who gave all their worldly possessions to the movement. They rejected predestination and believed in humankind's moral freedom, even to the point of apostasy. They believed in the gift of the Holy Ghost and the second blessing, after which a person lived without sin, had trances and visions, and could heal by faith. They agreed that all property would be held in common and all would eat from a common table. Life was gloomy in the colony, and the members were expected to spend their spare time in Bible study. Although referred to as the "Holy Jumpers" by their neighbors because of their Pentecostal, enthusiastic religious rites (including speaking in tongues), they nevertheless prospered on the land and operated a cannery and a sawmill for many years. However, when their major financial backer, Duke M. Farson, lost his investment business in Chicago, the colony came to an abrupt end in 1919 with Farson's creditor acquiring the land for only $1,000 from the sheriff. Several other similar communal settlements were established in Virginia, West Virginia, and New Orleans.

BURTON, ROBERT (1577–1640). The author of *The Anatomy of Melancholy*, Burton was born in Leicestershire to a genteel English family and received his B.A. degree from Christ Church, Oxford in 1602, followed by his M.A. in 1605 and his Bachelor of Divinity degree in 1614. Clerical duties in the Church of England and scholarly residence at Oxford followed thereafter. Following limited success in writing two comedies, Burton produced *The Anatomy of Melancholy* in 1621, followed by four more editions during his lifetime A sixth edition was published posthumously in 1651, and another 60 editions were published during the 19th century. At his death, he was buried at Christ Church Cathedral.

– C –

CABET, ETIENNE (1788–1856). Cabet, the son of a cooper and in his day the leading French propagandist for utopian socialism or communism, attained a law degree in 1812. In the years that followed, he became a member of a secret antigovernment society, the Carbonari, and took a number of steps in opposition to the Bourbon monarchy, for example, in 1827 publishing a pamphlet *Un Exposé d'une révolution nécessaire dans le gouvernement de France* in defense of republican government. After the Revolution of 1830 he served as attorney general in Corsica, then ran for and was elected to the Chamber of Deputies. In 1833 he published *La Révolution de 1830,* condemning the monarchy, and founded a working-class journal named *Le Populaire.* Indicted for publishing articles opposed to Louis Philippe in *Le Populaire* in 1834, Cabet chose to accept a five-year exile to avoid two years in prison and a 4,400-franc fine. Moving to England for these five years, he came under the influence of **Robert Owen** (1771–1858) and in 1839 published his utopian *Voyage en Icarie* (Voyage to Icaria), which displayed **Fourierist** influence too. Thereafter Cabet returned to Paris for 10 years to direct the resulting Icarian movement, preaching fraternity, equality, and a just legal system.

Between 1848 and 1858, three Icarian communities were established in the United States, which was to be the envisioned Icarian "model nation." Cabet in December 1848 sailed to the United States to attempt to salvage the first colony, Icaria, established in Fannin County, Texas, by 69 of his disciples earlier that year. This colony having failed miserably within four months, the remaining 280 Texas Icarians relocated in **Nauvoo**, Illinois, on the properties being vacated by the **Mormons**, Cabet in the meantime having returned to France to agitate against the government of Louis Napoleon. In 1854 Cabet returned to the United States and became a citizen, holding the presidency at Nauvoo until ousted by some dissidents there. Cabet then left with 180 followers and established a new Icaria at **Cheltenham** six miles west of St. Louis, Missouri. He died there shortly afterward.

CAESAR'S COLUMN. This utopian novel was written by **Ignatius Donnelly** (1831–1901), reformer, politician, and Populist, to point out the evils of the United States' disorderly and unjust capitalist-industrial society in the late 19th century and to direct Americans to the Golden Age, which was to be found by returning to the nation's agricultural past. The plot of *Caesar's Column: The Story of the Twentieth Century* (1890) is simplistic and far-fetched. It is developed by means of a series of letters in 1888 from one Gabriel Welstein in New York City to his brother back in Uganda, Africa. Gabriel, coming from a democratic community, is shocked at what he finds in the United States, especially the living conditions of the workers. In response to these conditions, he becomes involved in a secret society planning a popular rebellion by the oppressed. It is called the *Brotherhood of Destruction,* and is led by Caesar Lomellini, with a Russian Jew as "the brains of the organization." When it occurs, the rebellion becomes an orgy of uncontrollable violence and revenge. Eventually the rebels even destroy themselves, but not before erecting Caesar's Column, a giant cement column covering the bodies of a quarter million "human beings, who were once the rulers, or the instruments of the rulers" of New York. The monument is to stand as a "commemoration of the death and burial of modern civilization." Gabriel, along with some friends and a girlfriend, escapes in a balloon from the crushed modern civilization to create a utopia in Africa. The major features of this new utopia are apparently as he envisioned them earlier: no charging of interest on money, equality of wealth of all by law, the abolition of all corporations, an international paper money system, and a government to supply all its citizens' basic needs. Additionally, treason is the highest crime, but it includes not only attempting to overthrow the government but also politicians corrupting their office or selling their vote. Education is free and compulsory; only paper money is used as currency; and the state owns the roads, telegraph and telephone lines, railroads, and mines.

Donnelly's *Caesar's Column,* a reflection of his Populist views, won him instant renown. The book and his Populist crusading led him to pen *The Golden Bottle: The Story of Ephraim Benezet of Kansas* two years later in 1892. Its plot is even more simplistic and convoluted than any of his previous works, the hero ending up as president of the United States and founder of a new Universal Republic of prosperity and justice. Disappointed at not receiving the Populist Party nomination for president in 1896, having been one its leading figures for years and having written its platform, Donnelly faded from public interest until his death in 1901.

CALIFORNIA COMMUNITIES. *See* APPENDIX.

CALLENBACH, ERNEST (1929–). *See ECOTOPIA.*

CAMBRIDGE PLATONISTS. English intellectuals of the 17th and 18th centuries who espoused **millennial**-progressive ideas and helped revive utopian thought. *See* BURNET, THOMAS; EDWARDS, JOHN; MEDE, JOSEPH; MONBODDO, JAMES BURNETT; MORE, HENRY.

CAMPANELLA, TOMMASO (1568–1639). Born in Calabria in southern Italy, Tommaso Campanella was baptized Giovanni Domenico. He entered the Dominican order in 1582, but turning against the Aristotelian approach to philosophy that dominated that order, he was briefly imprisoned by the Dominicans for his beliefs. He was imprisoned a second time in Padua in 1594 for heresy, then in 1599 charged again with heresy and instigating political insurrection against Spanish rule over Italy by aiding the Turks. Feigning insanity, he was sentenced to life imprisonment and, while in prison, wrote his famous utopian work *Civitas Solis Poetica* in 1602, published as *The City of the Sun* in Latin in 1623 and in Paris in 1637, two years before his death. In 1629 he was released and fled Rome for Paris, where he spent his last years.

CANADIAN COMMUNITIES. *See* APPENDIX; BLACK UTOPIAS.

CANTERBURY COMMUNITY. This **Shaker** community was established in 1792 in Merrimack County, New Hampshire, and was composed of three spiritual groups known as "families." The founders and early members were Free Will Baptists in the Canterbury-London district who had converted to Shakerism. At one time, the community numbered 300 Shakers who lived on 3,000 acres of land. It was governed less strictly than most Shaker communities, members being allowed to eat meat and read newspapers, girls to take gymnastic exercise, and boys to play ball and go fishing. A washing machine was invented here. The last brother at Canterbury died in 1939, and by the 1960s there were only 11 women left in the community. These women caused a rift with the **Sabbathday Lake** Shakers when they refused to allow new members to join, suspicious that these youngsters were only interesting in the community's wealth, estimated to be about $3 million. Canterbury is no longer in existence, its last eldress having died in 1990, and its last member having died in 1992.

CANTON PHALANX. This **Fourierist phalanx** consisting of 15 members and their families was established in Fulton County in western Illinois in 1845 by John F. Randolph, a prosperous farmer and stock raiser in the county. Most were apparently Swedenborgians. It lasted only a short time.

CARDSTON COMPANY. This **Mormon** settlement was established in northern Alberta, Canada, receiving its charter from the governor of the Northwest Territories in 1890. Its founders, John Taylor and Charles Ora Card, envisioned a rural village built around a communal and business center. Its members secretly practiced polygamy. The colony was originally financially successful, but it declined rapidly after 1895, being overwhelmed by massive migration into the area of Cardston.

CARYL, CHARLES W. Little is known about this author except that he was in business in Chattanooga, Tennessee; saw firsthand the slums of the eastern cities; and moved to Denver about 1893, where he was president of the Gold Extraction, Mining and Supply Company. In 1897 he published a book entitled *New Era* (full title: *New Era: Presenting the Plans for the New Era Union to Help Develop and Utilize the Best Resources of This Country*) outlining in great detail a model city to be created to ameliorate the lives of the workers.

CEDAR VALE. *See* PROGRESSIVE COMMUNITY.

CEDARVALE COMMUNITY, *or* **CEDAR VALE BENEVOLENT AND EDUCATIONAL SOCIETY.** Located at Cedar Vale in Chautauqua County, Kansas, some four miles from the **Investigating Community**, the 160-acre Cedarvale Community was founded in

1875 by 15 young Russian revolutionaries led by Alexander Kapitonovich Malikov. When it was merged with the Investigating Community, the radicals objected, and the community ended in 1877. Thereafter, some of the members joined the **Shakers** at **Groveland** in New York State and at **South Union** in Kentucky.

CELESTA. This short-lived religious commune arose directly out of the prophecies of **William Miller** (1782–1849). Located at Celesta in Sullivan County, Pennsylvania, it was founded in 1863 by **Peter Armstrong** (ca. 1800–1892), a Second Adventist preacher from Philadelphia. He set out to establish a grandiose Heavenly Celestial City of 144,000 saints at the top of the Allegheny Mountains in 1852, pursuing his dream, with the help of his wife and children, only after 11 years of preparation. Despite interest in the project thanks to the publication of 3,000 copies of his paper *The Day Star of Zion,* few members arrived and stayed for any length of time in Armstrong's primitive colony. There were rarely more than 20 colonists present at Celesta at any time. In 1864, he deeded Celesta to God and obtained a special dispensation from President Abraham Lincoln allowing members of Celesta to be exempt from military service. But Armstrong lacked the charisma to convince prospective members that their only hope of salvation lay in taking up residence at Celesta; many of them believed they were already saved and counted among the 144,000. The project folded in 1864, and the Armstrong family moved to Philadelphia—leaving God to pay the taxes.

CENTRAL COMMUNIST PROPAGANDA SOCIETY. *See* BARMBY, GOODWYN.

CHAMBLESS, EDGAR (1871?–1936). In 1910 this architect authored a book entitled *Roadtown,* in which he asserted that all of the nation's inhabitants should be housed in a series of two-story buildings stretching all the way from New York to San Francisco. These linear settlements would include three levels of underground railways for transportation and promenades on the roofs. These dwellings, Chambless argued, would allow the people to all live a fulfilling communal life while also enjoying the undisturbed natural countryside.

CHARNAS, SUZY McKEE (1939–). Suzy McKee Charnas, fantasy fiction writer, is the author of two **feminist dystopian** novels, *Walk to the End of the World* (1974) and *Motherlines* (1978). In the first, the men of Holdfast maintain their anxiety over any differences in society by utilizing their masculine purity and strength. They have completely eradicated the "unmen" of all dark-skinned races, these "unmen" as inhuman as the "fems" they must tolerate in Holdfast for their ability to reproduce. From this first novel there emerges the character Alldera, who appears as the protagonist in the second, *Motherlines.* In this sequel, Alldera, a "fem," walks away from Holdfast into the Wild. Here she encounters two societies made up entirely of women. In one, the women simply refer to themselves as "women"; the other is made up of free fems. The "women" are the result of genetic engineering whereby they are complete with full sets of reproductive genes. When one of them is old enough to bear children, pregnancy is accomplished by mating with a horse, this carried out once a year at a celebration called the *Gathering*—which is why the free fems refer to the women as "mares." The horses provide no genetic material; as a result, each of the motherlines consists of clones from the mother alone, resulting in genetic duplication being carried through the generations. Thus, the society becomes stagnant and is doomed to eventual extinction. More recently, Charnas has published *The Furies* (1994), a dystopian novel in which women are held as slaves by men in Holdfast, the setting for her other novels, leading to a bloody war of violence and rivalry. A fourth volume in the series is planned by the author.

CHELTENHAM COLONY. After **Etienne Cabet** (1788–1856) was expelled from his colony at **Nauvoo** in October 1856, he traveled to St. Louis, Missouri, accompanied by 180 loyal followers. When Cabet suffered a fatal heart attack the next month, his followers vowed to keep his ideals alive by continuing to live communally. They were supported in this venture by the Icarian Society in France, which considered Cabet's followers to be the true **Icarians**. While in St. Louis they lived in three large houses, sharing their meals and earnings, joining together for musical and theatrical events, and publishing a newspaper, *Nouvelle Revue Icarienne.* In 1858 they moved to Cheltenham, a 28-acre farm six miles outside of St. Louis, which enabled their employed members to keep their jobs in the city while other members ran the farm and continued to publish Icarian works. However, the area was infested with malaria, the water caused dysentery and cholera, and it was difficult to expand their farm due to the high price of land so close to the burgeoning city. By 1859 membership had dropped to about 100, and discussions on drafting a constitution turned violent when a minority suggested that the process be done democratically. The minority left, taking with them some of the most intelligent colonists and skilled craftsmen. This departure effectively ended the community's ability to survive, particularly when the Icarian movement in France ceased to exist in 1860, along with the financial support they had been giving to the Cheltenham colony. In 1864, the mortgage was foreclosed and the property was abandoned.

CHERNYSHEVSKY, NIKOLAI G. (1828–1889). The author of the novel *What Is to Be Done?* N. G. Chernyshevsky won fame in his native Russia as a political and social critic and as a novelist. Seen as an enemy of the Romanov dynasty for criticizing Czar Alexander II's emancipation of the serfs in 1861 as incomplete, he was arrested and imprisoned in the Fortress of Peter and Paul. While in prison in 1863, he wrote *What Is to Be Done?* After his two-year imprisonment, he spent 25 years in hard labor and exile in Siberia before being allowed his freedom several months before his death. *What Is to Be Done?* remained unpublished because of the czarist censors and was not published until the Revolution of 1905. Nevertheless, it was widely circulated in manuscript form and had a great influence on late 19th-century reform thought in Russia. Vladimir Ulyanov Lenin, the Russian leader in the Revolution of 1917, said that he read it a number of times and was fired by Chernyshevsky's ideas.

The utopian socialist novel (which most agreed was poorly written) tells the story of Vera Pavlovna Rozalskaia, a "new woman," who succeeds at reform despite the many obstacles she faces. Through the novel, Chernyshevsky paints a picture of how Russia could be reformed when socially responsible and enlightened, unfettered "new people"—few in number now but destined to become a majority—are allowed to develop their reason and talents in a cooperative socialist state consisting of agricultural communities resembling **phalanxes**, an obvious borrowing from **Charles Fourier**. The centerpiece of the agrarian commune he pictures is a giant crystal palace (modeled after the Crystal Palace at the London Exhibition of 1851) that provides shops, homes, and cultural affairs in a workable blending of private and public efforts. *What Is to Be Done?* extolled knowledge and science, equality between the sexes, the goodness inherent in people removed from a corrupt environment, and communal property and labor. It achieved great popularity, especially among young Russian radicals who took it as their Bible and guide to an enlightened, fully human future for Russia.

CHILIASM (pronounced ki-le-a-zm). From the Latin *chilias,* meaning one thousand; an alternative term for **millennialism**, that is, the belief in a thousand years of peace as revealed in the **Apocalypse** or Book of Revelation.

CHING-BUA YUAN (FLOWERS IN THE MIRROR). *See* LI JU-CHEN.

CHRISTIAN CATHOLIC APOSTOLIC CHURCH IN ZION. *See* ZION CITY.

CHRISTIAN COMMONWEALTH COLONY. In 1896, some 25 families led by **Ralph Albertson** (1866–ca. 1926) settled on an old 934-acre former cotton plantation in Muskogee County in west central Georgia to inaugurate this Christian colony, which was to be a model of practical Christianity where all would live according to the law of love. Some had come from the **Willard Co-operative Colony** in North Carolina, others from **George Howard Gibson**'s **Christian Corporation** in Nebraska. There were 64 adult members, including 33 unmarried men and women. All Christian denominations were honored by the colony, and women were considered equal to men. Families lived together in separate homes, and eventually most colonists shared their meals in a communal dining room. Despite their efforts, the colony lasted only until 1900, being plagued by primitive living conditions, the usual problems of members' lack of job skills for their nascent industries, financial difficulties, and a typhoid epidemic in 1899. After its demise, some 17 members joined the **Southern Co-operative Association** at Apalachicola, Florida.

CHRISTIAN CORPORATION. This colony was founded in 1896 or earlier by **George Howard Gibson** at Lincoln in Lancaster County in southeast Nebraska. Gibson believed that earlier communities had failed because they were not sufficiently Christian. In 1897, he and his 26 followers joined the **Christian Commonwealth Colony** in Georgia after an arduous, three-month journey by prairie schooners to their new home.

CHRISTIAN GERMAN AGRICULTURAL AND BENEVOLENT SOCIETY OF ORA LABORA. *See* ORA LABORA COMMUNITY.

CHRISTIANOPOLIS. See ANDREAE, JOHANN VALENTIN.

CHRISTIAN REPUBLIC. *See* BERLIN COMMUNITY.

CHRISTIAN REPUBLIC, A. See LEIBNIZ, GOTTFRIED WILHELM von.

CHRIST'S CHURCH OF THE GOLDEN RULE. *See* MANKIND UNITED.

CHURCH OF JESUS CHRIST OF LATTER-DAY SAINTS. *See* MORMONS.

CICERO (106–43 B.C.). *See ON THE REPUBLIC*.

CINCINNATI BROTHERHOOD. *See* SPIRITUALIST COMMUNITY.

CINCINNATI HEBREW UNION AGRICULTURAL SOCIETY. *See* BEERSHEBA COLONY.

CINCINNATI PHALANX. *See* CLARMONT PHALANX.

CITYLESS AND COUNTRYLESS WORLD, A; AN OUTLINE OF PRACTICAL CO-OPERATIVE INDIVIDUALISM. This science fiction utopian novel published in 1893 was written by Henry Olerich

(1852–1926). Olerich's cityless and countryless world is the planet Mars, which has already passed through the evolutionary stages that Earth is currently undergoing. Here the Martians live in large buildings (the smallest housing 1,000 persons) located in beautiful parks alongside farms from which all wealth is produced. The Martians have large families to give them social and domestic advantages; these lead to their better health and happiness. There is no marriage, and the woman chooses her mate freely, living with him when she will, but only as long as they love one another. Everyone on Mars works according to his or her abilities, and no work, usually limited to two hours a day, is considered demeaning. The impact of Olerich's tale on his times cannot be ascertained, but the equality of women is surely one of the strong themes of his utopian story.

CITY OF GOD, THE. *See* AUGUSTINE.

CITY OF ST. JAMES. *See* BEAVER ISLAND COLONY.

CITY OF THE SUN. This classic utopian novel, originally titled *Civitas Solis Poetica,* was written by **Tommaso Campanella** (1568–1639), a sea captain from Genoa, in 1602. In the book, which proposes an ideal republic, a Genoese sea captain describes in a dialogue a humanistic and scientific society that he claims to have seen in his travels. This city on the island of Taprobane in the South Seas is ruled by a virtuous monarch, the Sole, assisted by three lieutenants: Power, Wisdom, and Love. Here the all-powerful state supersedes the individual and is technologically advanced; there are even flying machines. Scientific knowledge being of paramount importance, one third of the ruling body of the city is made up of scientists. This scientific knowledge is projected to the citizens by means of seven concentric walls in the circular city, and at the center stands the Solarian temple with seven candles named for the planets.

All property is held in common, all work happily for the common good, and marriage is for reproduction in the interest of the state, not for love, the young being supervised to assure that the republic's interests come first. The Ministry of Love requires that young persons copulate between the ages of 19 and 21, but with the permission of the First Master of Reproduction young men may copulate with older, younger, or pregnant women since they are unlikely to bear children. Sodomy is condemned, and if repeated often the sodomist is executed. Children live in communal residences after being weaned at the age of two, and they study the sciences at least four hours every day. Women have equal rights with men, including service in the military, defense being necessary because there are four different and sometimes hostile states on the island. Resembling in many ways **Francis Bacon**'s *New Atlantis,* **Johann Andreae's** *Christianopolitanae,* and **Thomas More**'s *Utopia,* Campanella's *The City of the Sun* played a major role in keeping the utopian vision alive in Europe in the centuries that followed.

CIVIL MILLENNIALISM, AMERICAN. This widespread belief, which could also be labeled "America's civil religion," emerged in the first half of the 19th century. It tended to blend **millennialism** and the course of American history to give sense and direction to the events occurring in the young republic. This phenomenon has sometimes been attributed to existing multidenominationalism, arguing that the people felt a need for commonly shared religious beliefs that had been shattered by denominational factionalism. According to this explanation, the people's need for a common identity encouraged them to look to the nation as a substitute. A second explanation attributes this civil millennialism to a desire to see Americans as the defenders of godliness in a world dominated by revolution, bloodshed, and heathenism. A third explanation argues that the basic cause of this civil millennialism was that the church leaders allowed themselves to be captured by romantic optimism, national republican idealism, and the cult of progress. Whatever the cause or causes, civil millennialism fit neatly into the Christian concept of redemptive, millennial history and urged its people to make the United States the Christian-republican pattern to follow, to be the primary agent in the redemptive history of humankind. This belief in the United States' divine mission has remained a part of the nation's religious-intellectual heritage since that time.

CIVITAS SOLIS POETICA. See CITY OF THE SUN.

CLARKE, ARTHUR C. (1917–). *See 2001: A SPACE ODYSSEY.*

CLARKSON INDUSTRIAL ASSOCIATION (*or* PHALANX), *or* **WESTERN NEW YORK INDUSTRIAL ASSOCIATION.** This **Fourierist** communal society founded "to establish justice and judgment in our little earth" existed during 1844–1845 in Monroe County, New York, about 30 miles from Rochester, as a successor to the **Ontario Phalanx** of Rochester. All members over 18 years of age were voters. No religious or political qualifications were required of members, although "decent character" was demanded. It began in February 1844 with 350 members, but before the summer was over half of the members had left, victims of lack of experience and financial problems, some joining the **Oneida Community**.

CLERMONT PHALANX. Located on 1,140 acres of land some 35 miles up the Ohio River from Cincinnati in Clermont County, Ohio, the **Fourierist** Clermont **Phalanx** (earlier called the Cincinnati Phalanx), was founded in 1844 and lasted two years before being dissolved with financial problems and plagued by waning enthusiasm for accepting the deprivations necessary in creating a utopia. Part of the site was subsequently purchased by the **Spiritualist Community**. Some of the remaining members formed the **Utopia Community**.

COAL CREEK COMMUNITY AND CHURCH OF GOD. This community was organized by William Ludlow in 1825 on the Wabash River at Stonebluff, Fountain County, Indiana, and was composed of 60 families. Ludlow withdrew from Coal Creek in 1827, and the community was finally dissolved the same year, the victim of internal disagreements.

COALSAMAO. The name for this never-implemented cooperative commonwealth was taken from the first letters of Canada's western provinces: British **Co**lumbia, **Al**berta, **Sa**skatchewan, and **Ma**nitoba plus **O** for Ontario. It represented the ideas of Edward Partridge (1862–1931) as spelled out in his *A War on Poverty* (1926) and required the secession of the Canadian west from Lake Superior to the Pacific Ocean. In Partridge's commonwealth, all production would be used for the members; all members would work or starve; the state would own all natural resources; monetary contracts would not exist; lawyers, landlords, and businessmen would be no more; there would be no class conflict, poverty, or shortage of capital; the basic social unit would be encampments of 3,500–7,000 residents; the commonwealth would be governed by 25 elected administrators, one from each of the 25 regions; all houses would be similar, with all homes having the same domestic equipment such as phones, sewage, and heating; clothing would be the same for all; one phonetic language would be used; intellectuals would control teaching, civil services, and administration; and the sexes would be separated and taught to appreciate each other through social interaction, not dancing. In time, Partridge asserted, members would develop an immutable, humane ego, and some would be reincarnated. Needless to say, Partridge's ideas were never adopted.

COCKAYGNE, LAND OF. During the Middle Ages and after, a popular myth stretching back to **Hesiod**'s **Golden Age of Kronos** and beyond told of an ancient time of happiness that existed in the Land of Cockaygne, "cockaygne" meaning "small cakes." It was very popular among the lower classes burdened by their hard life. Cockaygne literature and myth told of a land of plenty in food and drink where the peaceful peasants never had to work and lived in perfect health unrestrained by traditional customs and laws. In Cockaygne, there was no private property because it was a classless society where social justice reigned at all times. Although not a true utopia, Cockaygne represented a popular dream world of physical pleasure for the medieval peasants. It lived on in the popular mind of the socially downtrodden, both then and in the centuries to come, and fed into later utopian literature.

COHEN, JOSEPH (1878–1953). *See* SUNRISE COMMUNITY— MICHIGAN.

COLLINS, JOHN ANDERSON (1810–1890). *See* SKANEATELES COMMUNITY.

COLONY OF EQUALITY. *See* EQUALITY, SOCIETY OF.

COLORADO COMMUNITIES. *See* APPENDIX.

COLORADO COOPERATIVE COLONY. This colony that existed from 1894 to 1906 in Pinon, Colorado, was organized by 300 to 400 socialists; some were residential and some were nonresidential. It embodied a "single-tax" system of land ownership. Each shareholder was allowed to own only one share. A common rate of 20 cents per hour was paid to all workers regardless of their jobs, but the wage could only be "cashed" at the colony's communal store and dining room. Any surplus wage credits were pooled for purchase of more land and the building of a great irrigation ditch. At one time, the colony owned 30,000 acres of land. It was disbanded in 1906.

COLUMBIAN PHALANX. This communal society existed briefly in Franklin County, Ohio, on the Muskingum River seven miles above Zanesville in the mid-1840s. Brief mention of it in a **Fourierist** publication in 1845 indicates that it had a membership of 32 families and 250 acres of corn and grains under cultivation, plus other subsistence crops. The members were preparing to build a flourmill at Zanesville and a sawmill on their grounds. It apparently failed that year.

COLUMBUS, CHRISTOPHER (1451–1506). Despite the assumption generally accepted by intellectuals and churchmen during the Renaissance that human movement to perfection in time was not possible because of humans' fixed and fallen nature, the idea of finding a perfect world, a **Garden of Eden**, remained alive to those who explored the New World. Christopher Columbus, for example, sailed west, he said, under the inspiration of the Holy Ghost and was familiar with the travels of Marco Polo and the legend of Prester John (*see* **Bragmans**). He accepted the popular legend that the Garden of Eden lay to the farthest point of the East (as found in Genesis) at the highest point of the earth. Accordingly, when he reached the New World he was convinced that he had found the location of the Garden of Eden. When he discovered the Orinoco River in present-day Venezuela on his third voyage in 1498 and found its waters were running downhill from a high place, aided by the discovery of peaceful naked natives and reports of gold in the vicinity, he was convinced that he was at the foot of the Holy Mountain, the Garden of Eden to be at the summit like a nipple on a woman's breast. But frightened by his nearness to a terrestrial paradise and unwilling to enter it except by the will of God, he fled back to Hispaniola in the West Indies.

Columbus was also convinced that the district of Veragua in Panama was the place where David and Solomon had found the precious stones to rebuild the temple in Jerusalem. He had also seen the prophecies of **Joachim of Fiore** (1135–1202) and believed that his journeys to the Indies were a fulfillment of the prophecies in Isaiah. And since Joachim had predicted that the Redeemer would come from Spain and that the world was in the last stage, Columbus saw himself as a messenger of the **millennium** bringing to fruition God's plan as revealed in the **Apocalypse**. Columbus, then, stands as clear evidence of the continued widespread belief in the existence of a perfect place reachable by humans in time.

COMBE, ABRAM (?–1827). *See* ORBISTON.

COMING NATION, THE. See WAYLAND, JULIUS.

COMING RACE, THE. This novel written by Edward Bulwer-Lytton (1803–1873), English playwright and novelist most famous for his *The Last Days of Pompeii,* was published in 1871, two years before his death. A firm believer in scientific progress and evolution, Bulwer-Lytton was convinced that through social engineering a more perfect human race was possible. In the novel, a wealthy American descends into a mineshaft and discovers a world beneath the earth known as *An.* Here the residents are tall and have wings; disease does not exist; the liberated women are more intelligent than men; extended families exist; members employ "vril," an electrical-charge-like device that can destroy or restore; laws and traditional government do not exist, no longer being necessary; robots do most of the manual labor; and death is seen as a normal passage to another realm. Whether *The Coming Race* is utopian or **dystopian** is a matter of dispute since the state of An contains many flaws in its makeup; regardless, the novel had an influence on both **George Bernard Shaw** and **H. G. Wells**.

COMING REVOLUTION, THE. See GRONLUND, LAURENCE.

COMMONWEALTH COLLEGE. Originally established at the **New Llano Co-operative Colony** in 1923 to produce labor leaders for the working class, in 1925 it was moved to an 80-acre site west of Mena in Polk County in western Arkansas. The students and faculty agreed that education was the key to the improvement of the United States and that cooperation should supplant competition. Together they farmed, erected buildings, cooked and ate meals, and studied together, with classes in the morning and work after lunch (20 to 24 hours of manual labor per week being the norm). Maximum membership grew to 55 (including the son of Orval Faubus, who later, as governor, would resist school integration); this did not include African Americans out of fear of offending Southern sensibilities. Gradually moving to the left in its political orientation, Commonwealth College became the target of preachers and patriots. It was convicted of a number of "crimes" against the state in 1940 (such as failing to display the American flag) and, as a result, closed its doors, its property being auctioned off to pay the fines the court had levied.

COMMONWEALTH OF ISRAEL COLONY. This Baptist commune was situated on a 900-acre site in Mason County in central Texas. Little is known about it except that it was established in 1899, had a membership of 150 in 1901, and probably ended in 1902. The **Israelites** of Polk County may or may not have been part of the same movement.

COMMONWEALTH OF OCEANA, THE. *See* HARRINGTON, JAMES.

COMMUNIA. Founded by the German socialist expatriate Wilhelm Weitling (1808–1871) in 1847 on 1,240 acres of land in Clayton County in northeast Iowa, the colony was made up of revolutionary Germans who had recently emigrated from their native country. It was formalized in 1853 as the Communia Working Men's League with Weitling as its administrator. Weitling ruled the colony with an iron hand. Financial setbacks and factional disputes led to its demise in 1856 or 1857.

COMMUNIST MANIFESTO, THE. *See* MARX, KARL.

COMMUNITARIAN NETWORK. Located in Washington, D.C., the Communitarian Network is not a utopian organization but, rather, a contemporary movement based on the philosophy that individual liberties depend on bolstering American families, schools, and neighborhoods as the most important factors in restoring the spirit of community in the nation. Its key principle is that public policies should seek a balance between individual rights and the responsibilities of individuals to society at large. Founded by Amitai Etzioni of George Washington University, it is made up of individuals and organizations interested in improving the moral, political, and social environment of the United States by a careful examination of issues in these areas facing the nation.

COMMUNITY SERVICE, INC. *See* MORGAN, ARTHUR E.

COMPLEX MARRIAGE. Introduced into the **Oneida Community** by its founder **John Humphrey Noyes** (1811–1886), complex marriage taught that every member of the community, male and female, had the right to have sexual intercourse with a member of the opposite sex. In other words, all males were married to all females in the community. It was based on Noyes's teaching as part of "Bible Communism" that the Second Coming of Christ had occurred in 70 A.D. and that the "Perfectionists," as they were called, were, therefore, living in the **postmillennial** period of history where exclusive marriage between a man and a woman no longer exists according to the Bible. Complex marriage had already been practiced at Putney, Vermont, between Noyes, his wife, Harriet, and George and Mary Cragin before his move to upstate New York in 1848. This practice, however, was under the control of Noyes as the head of the community, a couple wishing to copulate had to obtain Noyes's permission before doing so. Noyes prescribed that a young man would have sex only with an older woman (young men tending to be too enthusiastic and possibly too unfeeling toward young women, older women tempering their enthusiasm) and that a young woman would have sex only with an older man (older men being less enthusiastic and more tender toward the young women). "Special love" between a man and woman was considered antisocial, and members were urged to change sex partners frequently. Complex marriage led to charges from the outside that Oneida was a free-love colony, leading to the suspension of the practice in 1852.

COMTE, AUGUSTE (1798–1857). The founder of sociology and the leading exponent of Positivism (the theory that theology and metaphysics having been superseded, knowledge must be based on natural phenomena and their properties alone as verified by the empirical sciences), Auguste Comte was also a utopian because he designed and described his reformist Religion of Humanity. The Positivist state that will necessarily come, will have a Positivist calendar of 13 months, each named after a great philosopher or scientist, and Positivist holidays and festivals to take the place of Christianity; industrialism will be embraced as the goal of scientific training to thereby elevate persons to the higher arts; the family and state will be patriarchal, although as women rise to their natural intellectual preeminence they will come to dominate; and stability will be attained by a rule of the "intellectuals," the mass of the people being treated humanely and allowed to rise socially and economically, but authority resting with those at the pinnacle of the Religion of Humanity, the sociologists, the priest-scientists of the state. The Religion of Humanity having been adopted, humankind will have risen to its highest form, having moved, argued Comte, in four stages: from polytheism, to monotheism, to fetishism, and finally to Positivism and a more perfect society. Whether recognized or not, the impact of Comte's Positivism on Western thought in general and on utopian schemes in particular has been tremendous.

CONCORDANCE OF THE OLD AND NEW TESTAMENTS. See JOACHIM OF FIORE.

CONDORCET, MARQUIS de (1743–1794). Marie-Jean-Antoine-Nicolas Caritat, the marquis de Condorcet, was a French nobleman, mathematician, contributor to the *Encyclopédie,* political reformer, and victim of the French Revolution. In 1794, he published **Anne Robert Jacques Turgot**'s idea of the stages of the cultural development of humankind all the way to ultimate perfection through expansion of human intelligence in his *Esquisse d'un tableau historique de progrès de l'esprit humain* (Sketch of a Historical View of the Human Mind), making this concept a dominant influence on Western thought. Condorcet also argued in his *Esquisse* for the necessary creation of a new man in 10 stages from the agricultural to the scientific and technological, this new man not needing God for salvation. He further suggested that as man is improved to "une perfection plus grande," even death may be postponed indefinitely.

Condorcet was convinced that humankind stood at one of the turning points of history, on the verge of a great leap forward, and that he was under an obligation to accelerate the rate of obtainable progress. One way in which this could be done was by creating an organization of the world's elite scientists to carry out coordinated research for the perfection of humankind. This body was to assure the production of scientists, thereby to create a society of peace, equality, and plenty. Compelled to action by these ideas, Condorcet became involved in the French Revolution, and when the Girondists fell from power he was forced into hiding for eight months. Finally arrested, he took poison and died. Condorcet's contributions to the idea of secular, scientific progress to a perfected world remain of major importance to utopian thought.

CONFUCIANISM. The great Chinese philosopher Confucius (551–470 B.C.) stated in *The Evolutions of Li* that when in bygone days the great *Tao* was in practice (the process of nature by which all things change, which is to be followed for a life of harmony), the world was common to all with leaders selected according to talent, virtue, and ability. At that time, sincerity was honored and friendship was cultivated. Accordingly, all persons were treated with love and consideration; the aged were provided for until death; kindness and compassion were shown to the helpless and disabled; the hoarding of wealth was unknown; selfish schemes were repressed; and robbers and traitors were not present, leaving no need for gates or walls in the cities and the countryside. But, said Confucius, the great *Tao* has fallen into disuse and the world lacks harmony and peace. It can be argued, however, that the social and political ideas of the Taoist school were present in modern Chinese history in the persons of **K'ang Yu-wei** (1858–1927) and Sun Yat-sen (1866–1925), the Nationalist party leader and founding father of modern China, and may be reasserting themselves at the opening of the 21st century as China moves toward modernization.

CONNECTICUT COMMUNITIES. *See* APPENDIX.

CONSIDÉRANT, VICTOR PROSPER (1808–1893). Educated at the Ecole Polytechnique, Considérant served in the French army until he gave up his military career in 1830 to publicize the theories of **Charles Fourier** (1772–1837), becoming his leading publicist. With Fourier's death in 1837, Considérant became the leader of the French cooperative movement. After the Revolution of 1848, he was elected to the Constitutional Assembly, but, with Louis Napoleon coming to power, he was forced to flee France in 1849. After an 1852 visit to the United States where he met with **Albert Brisbane** (1809–1890), Considérant returned to France to promote a Fourierist colonization scheme for Texas, especially with his *Au Texas.* In 1855, the first émigrés settled at **Reunion** within the city of Dallas. But after two successive droughts and attacks by the Know Nothings (the Native American political party), the colony began to fall apart. Considérant moved to San Antonio, where he received American citizenship. In 1859, he returned to Paris and died there in poverty in 1893.

CO-OPERATIVE ASSOCIATION OF AMERICA. *See* SOUTHERN CO-OPERATIVE ASSOCIATION OF APALACHICOLA.

COOPERATIVE BROTHERHOOD. This 294-acre socialist colony, also known as Burley, was organized in 1898 at Burley, Kitsap County, Washington, north of Seattle, to encourage the collective ownership, distribution, and manufacture of goods. By 1901 its membership stood at 115, a mix of unemployed miners from Colorado and middle-class utopians who had studied the teachings of **Edward Bellamy** and **Laurence Gronlund**. There were also nonresident members, at one time numbering over 1,000, who paid $1 a month and could become regular members after 10 years. Labor was based on a time-check system, and vouchers were issued that could be used in the company store and in the common dining room. Communal living was only for bachelors in dormitories, but all meals were taken communally. Its major industries were agriculture and lumbering, supplemented by cigar manufacturing. In 1904 the colony was reorganized; thereafter, much of its communalism disappeared as it was converted into a cooperative. One of its founders, **Cyrus F. Willard** (1858–1935), and some of the members who were **Theosophists** later joined the Theosophists at **Point Loma**. By 1906 it had ceased to function as a cooperative, and it finally ended in 1913 when the properties were distributed among the remaining members.

CO-OPERATIVE BROTHERHOOD OF WINTERS ISLAND.
This colony was founded by Erastus Kelsey on 640-acre Winters
Island, which he owned, in Contra Costa County, California. Incorporated in 1893, it was formed on the pattern of the **Kaweah Cooperative Commonwealth** of Tulare County, California, and was to
be limited to a maximum of 100 members, each of whom was to pay
a $5 membership assessment for 100 months. But only 86 signed up,
and only 22 members were present in 1896. With the members being
unable to pay the monthly fee during the Panic of 1893, the colony
had collapsed in failure by 1898.

COOPERATIVE COMMONWEALTH, THE. See GRONLUND,
LAURENCE.

**COOPERATIVE PLAN FOR SECURING HOME AND OCCU-
PATIONS AT PORT ANGELES, WASHINGTON.** *See* SMITH,
GEORGE VENABLE.

CORNING. In 1854 **Etienne Cabet** (1788–1856), the leader of the
Icarian movement, purchased 3,000 acres of land in Corning, Adams
County, Iowa, and sent 18 colonists from **Nauvoo** to prepare the land
for occupation. Some years later, after Cabet had been expelled from
Nauvoo, taking with him the deeds to the Iowa property, the colonists
remaining at Nauvoo ran into financial difficulty and decided to
move to Iowa. The land in Illinois was sold, and the colonists relocated. They found themselves in an isolated part of the country,
which prevented them from finding adequate markets for their produce. But they constructed a flourmill, a steam sawmill, and a printing shop. Living conditions were harsh, and many fell ill. By 1863,
most of the settlers had deserted the colony and only 35 remained, including children. However, the Civil War, which dramatically raised
the price of farm produce, proved to be a saving grace. They escaped
bankruptcy by giving their lands back to their creditors and repur-
chasing 1,900 acres. The community flourished in the 1870s, constructing spacious houses for families and a large building that
housed a communal kitchen, a dining room, and living space. In 1877
there were 83 members. When the Icarian commune in Paris failed in
1871, many of its members immigrated to Corning. But these new

members brought with them radical new ideas that resonated with Corning's younger members, such as voting privileges for women and an end to private vegetable gardens. Disputes between the older and younger members became violent, and eventually the colony split when the courts ruled that Corning's charter had been violated and therefore was forfeit. In October 1878 the radical young minority was given the farm and central buildings at Corning, which then became known as *Jeune Icarie*, while the older majority established itself as the **New Icarian Community** on 1,000 acres on the eastern end of the original Corning property.

COSME COLONY. Founded by the young Englishman William Lane (1861–1917) in 1894 after failed attempts to establish a colony in Australia and another called *New Australia* in Paraguay, Cosme Colony was established at the fork of the Piraop and Tebicuari Rivers in Paraguay. Thereafter, the Cosmeans cleared the forest and prepared the land for cultivation amid horrible living conditions. Lane devised a new constitution in which women lost the suffrage, and the colony was divided into villages with each village governed by committeemen, an executive officer, and a chairman. There was also a central authority over all the villages to assure the upholding of Cosme principles and to hold the common funds. Members came and went with some regularity. In May 1898 there were 99 members, but many of them were looking to the Paraguayan government for relief. In that same year, William Lane resigned and went back to Australia, leaving his brother John in charge. John Lane changed the ideological basis of the colony by employing native labor. This caused defections, some seeing this as slave labor, others fearing eventual miscegenation. Finally the Paraguayan government stepped in, divided the lands of both New Australia and Cosme into individual holdings, and assimilated the remaining members into Paraguayan life.

COUNCIL OF EPHESUS. *See* AUGUSTINE.

COXSACKIE COMMUNITY. *See* KELPIUS, JOHANN.

CREFFIELD, FRANZ EDMUND (?–1906). *See* BRIDE OF CHRIST.

CREMIEUX COLONY. Located on the line between Davison and Aurora Counties in South Dakota, about 25 miles southwest of Mitchell, Cremieux was founded in 1882 by young, well-educated, secularized Russian Jews, victims of the liquidation of the **Sicily Island Colony** that same year. Part of the **Am Olam** ("Eternal People") Movement, which aimed to establish cooperative colonies on the model of **Charles Fourier** (1772–1837) and **Robert Owen** (1771–1858), it was named in honor of Adolphe Cremieux, the French Jewish philanthropist and president of the Alliance Israelite Universelle. Each colonist lived on his own 160-acre farm, but agricultural implements, lumber for housing, and livestock were owned communally. Thoroughly secular in orientation, Cremieux had no synagogue and included no religious leaders. Although membership at one time had climbed to 200, a number of natural disasters, a lack of knowledge of farming techniques on the harsh Dakota frontier, and inadequate financial resources led to the liquidation of the colony in 1889.

CRIDGE, ANNIE DENTON (?–pre-1884). Annie Denton Cridge was a prominent 19th-century suffragist, critic of patriarchy, and, she believed, a "psychometer" (a person having the power to see all that ever happened to any piece of matter placed in contact with him or her). Her novel *Man's Rights: or, How Would You Like It?,* consisting of five satiric dreams and published in 1870, featured a dreamlike voyage to Mars where it is discovered that women rule and men are second-class citizens. Women are strong, beautiful, and condescending toward men. As a result, the men hold a "men's rights" meeting in which they protest that they are paid less than women, are consigned to housework, and are denied educational opportunities. This role reversal theme, a criticism of the popular "cult of true womanhood" accepted at the time, would appear often in later feminist utopian novels.

CRITIQUE OF PURE REASON, THE. *See* KANT, IMMANUEL.

CRONUS (*or* KRONOS), KINGDOM OF. *See* COCKAYGNE, LAND OF; GOLDEN AGE, MYTH OF THE.

CRYSTAL BUTTON. *See* THOMAS, CHAUNCEY.

CSI. *See* MORGAN, ARTHUR E.

– D –

DAMON, WILLIAM (1838–?). *See* WILLARD CO-OPERATIVE COLONY.

DANIEL, BOOK OF. This book of the Old Testament was written in the second century B.C. during the Babylonian captivity of the Jews. Daniel is a prophet who sees visions and has the power to interpret dreams. Chapters 2 and 7 describe the destruction of four great world empires (Babylon, Media, Persia, and Hellenistic Greece) personified as terrible beasts. This comes after a period of suffering by God's people and is accomplished through His divine power. In the last scene, "the ancient of Days," God appears and the last of the four beasts is slain, along with the Antichrist, its body destroyed in fire. The Book of Daniel was a cherished part of the Jewish belief of the events leading up to the end of the world with God's justice being triumphant. It was also a powerful complement to the Christian New Testament account of the last days, climaxed by the Second Coming of Christ, as described in the **Apocalypse**.

DARKNESS AT NOON. See KOESTLER, ARTHUR.

DARMSTAEDTER KOLONIE. *See* BETTINA.

DARWIN, CHARLES (1809–1882). Although not utopian, the work of the English naturalist Charles Darwin, especially his *The Origin of the Species* (1859), played a major role in advancing the idea of human progress in the late 18th and 19th centuries, his theory of natural selection marked by the survival of the fittest giving a scientific gloss to the emerging belief in social evolution, a theory already propounded by the **Marquis de Condorcet**, **Auguste Comte**, **Georg W. F. Hegel**, and others and contemporarily advanced by Alfred Wallace.

DAVIDIAN SEVENTH-DAY ADVENTISTS. *See* BRANCH DAVIDIANS.

DAVIESITE KINGDOM OF HEAVEN. This community was formed in 1867 by a breakaway group of 40 **Mormons** from Utah led by

William W. Davies (1833–1906) near Walla Walla, Washington. Davies claimed that here they had found the Kingdom of Heaven. Some 70 new members joined from San Francisco and Portland. When Davies's two sons (the elder was known as "Walla Walla Jesus"—Christ reincarnated) died of diphtheria, the community fell into chaos and ended in 1881.

DAWN COLONY, *or* **THE BRITISH-AMERICAN INSTITUTE.** This **black utopia** near Dresden in western Ontario grew out of a desire by three Americans, abolitionist Hiram Wilson, Quaker philanthropist James Cannings Fuller, and escaped slave Josiah Henson, to establish schools for blacks in Canada. After a year of raising money in England, the British-American Institute was opened in December 1842 as a manual labor school with 12 students. The Dawn community grew up around the Institute as an adjunct to its functions. It included a sawmill; a gristmill; a rope factory; a brickyard; 1,800 acres of land on which they raised corn, wheat, oats, and tobacco; Baptist and Methodist churches; and four elementary schools as part of the juvenile division of the British-American Institute. By the early 1850s, some 500 blacks had settled in the vicinity of Dawn. Despite its short-term success, continued economic problems and a running feud between Henson and the appointed manager, John Scoble, led to the abandonment of the project in 1868. The Institute was closed, the land was sold, and the money raised was used to endow the Wilberforce Educational Institute in nearby Chatham.

DAY OF YAHWEH. *See* MESSIANIC KINGDOM OF THE JEWS.

DEBS, EUGENE VICTOR (1855–1926). Although best known as the organizer of the American Railway Union (ARU), which played a major role in the Pullman Strike in 1894, and as the presidential candidate of the Socialist party five times between 1900 and 1920, Eugene V. Debs was also the author of a utopian scheme to benefit the working class. Having earlier taken part in a brotherhood of railroad workers' plan for a cooperative colony and unhappy over the victory of William McKinley and the Republicans in 1896, at the annual convention of the ARU in 1897 Debs proposed the creation of a community called the Social Democracy of America. Thereafter a colonization department was established within the ARU to find a suitable site for the colony, and a number of sites were investigated. However, the project fell through because most members of Debs's Social Democracy party were more interested in finding political solutions to the workers' problems than in avoiding them by some utopian scheme.

DELAWARE COMMUNITIES. *See* APPENDIX.

DEMOCRITUS JUNIOR. *See ANATOMY OF MELANCHOLY.*

DESCARTES, RENE (1596–1650). This French mathematician and philosopher was the leading advocate of deductive reasoning from self-evident principles, all doctrines to be tested according to mathematical principles and logic (deduction) rather than by experimentation (induction). In his *Discourse on Method* (1637), he argued that through the use of the deductive method beginning with the simple and moving to the complex, all of nature, including persons, nations, and even God, could be understood. Eventually the core ideas of **Francis Bacon** and Descartes (inductive and deductive reasoning) were accepted as basic to Enlightenment thought, leading, in turn, to the belief in the natural and necessary progress of humans.

DESCRIPTION OF A CHRISTIAN REPUBLIC. *See* ANDREAE, JOHANN VALENTIN.

DESCRIPTION OF MILLENNIUM HALL, A. *See* SCOTT, SARAH.

DESERET. *See* MORMONS.

DES MOINES SINGLE TAX CLUB. *See* GASTON, ERNEST B.

DEWEY, JOHN (1859–1952). Best known for his pedagogical theories of child-centered education, John Dewey, perhaps the most important American philosopher of the 20th century, was utopian, in fact, if not in name. Assuming that a more perfect society can be achieved on the basis of individual autonomy and governmental intervention, Dewey's ideas, clothed as they were in the appearance of being rational, scientific, self-fulfilling, and workable, found a wide audience among all classes in society, especially among the modernist, secularist intellectuals already imbued with a belief in necessary progress. Dewey based his philosophy not on speculation regarding metaphysical, discernible truth but on a positivistic technique to best serve the people and thereby lead them to freedom, that is, achievable human perfection. Progress, he argued, depended on human effort to be achieved through unceasing investigation to secure the best methods of gaining improvement, these methods to be found in open-ended scientific experimentation and inquiry. For Dewey and his disciples, this meant that people must think in modern, scientific terms alone, not in prescientific moral terms, in order to confront and solve the problems facing them. The proper answers must be based on whether or not proposed solutions "worked" or not.

The result of this pragmatic type of investigation and problem solving, Dewey argued, would be the self-realization of themselves properly functioning in an interdependent community based on common, realizable values. This type of pragmatic investigation, in turn, rested on the education of children and their being taught to think in this way. If adopted, this rational, pragmatic type of investigation would assure the open-ended progress of society through the accumulation of scientific, workable knowledge. Thus John Dewey made a major contribution to the acceptance of utopian thought in the United States not by openly advancing utopian ends and means, but by the acceptance of his pragmatic approach to the accumulation of knowledge, this aggregation leading to a more perfect society.

DICAERCHUS (ca. 355–285 B.C.). *See* GOLDEN AGE, MYTH OF THE.

DIDEROT, DENIS (1713–1784). One of the literary and artistic giants of 18th-century Paris, Denis Diderot was the principal editor and author of the *Encyclopédie,* an attempt to record all rational, scientific, and technological knowledge of the ages in one set of volumes. His utopian outlook was revealed in his description of life in the South Seas, part of the *Supplement to Bougainvillea's Voyage* (1772), a description of happy, felicitous, and natural life in Tahiti as opposed to the unnatural and corrupt values and mores of his native France; it was published in 1796 after his death. Life on Tahiti, as he described it, was perfect because of complete sexual freedom (including what Christians would label adultery, fornication, and incest) as the natural way of life for humans that led to a cooperative and caring lifestyle among the natives of the island. *See also NATURE'S CODE.*

DIEDERICH, CHARLES (?–1997). *See* SYNANON COMMUNITY.

DIGGERS. In the aftermath of the English civil war of 1642–1648, there was much devastation in the land. When local church services were disrupted by the military at Walton in Surrey in April 1649, a handful of men led by the tailor and mystical **millennialist** Gerrard Winstanley (1609–1676) left the estates of their masters and began digging in the common fields at St. George's Hill, Weybridge, to prepare them for seed as a gesture of their discontent. They were soon joined by other poor and depressed persons from nearby London, leading to protests against their presence in the form of beatings by the local citizens, followed by their being driven off the land and then having their settlements destroyed by the Commonwealth government. Other settlements of Diggers (or, as the called themselves, "True Levellers") in the realm were also destroyed, and the people were scattered and forced to live in little hutches during the winter before again being dispersed. In the aftermath of these events, Winstanley wrote a treatise entitled *The Law of Freedom in a Platform or True Magistracy Restored* in 1652. Addressed to Oliver Cromwell (1599–1658), it contained all the elements of a utopian community. Private property was forbidden; work and play were communal; money was nonexistent (thereby precluding commerce); relief for the needy was provided without charge from communal storehouses; laborers would no longer work for their masters but on common fields; marriage was a civil ceremony only in this secular realm; government was patriarchal, with officials being elected by the males 40 years of age or older; a complete educational system would be established; hanging, whipping, and imprisonment would no longer be used; and there was no state church. In *The Law of Freedom,* Winstanley was primarily interested in advocating a society free of hunger and want, not one of abundance and self-indulgence, as would be found in many later utopian visions. Still, the Diggers are often properly regarded as the first genuine communist-utopian actors in modern times.

DISCOURSE ON POLITICAL ECONOMY. *See* ROUSSEAU, JEAN-JACQUES.

DISPOSSESSED: AN AMBIGUOUS UTOPIA, THE. This 1974 science fiction novel by **Ursula Le Guin** (1929–), also the author of *Always Coming Home* (1987), was written early in her career and does not display a perfect society. As its title indicates, the society pictured, Annares, is an ambiguous utopia. On the one hand, it does possess sexual equality and has eliminated patriarchal and matriarchal qualities in persons; on the other, human beings remain flawed.

DISTRICT OF COLUMBIA COMMUNITIES. *See* APPENDIX.

DODD, ANNA BOWMAN (1855–1929). *See REPUBLIC OF THE FUTURE: OR, SOCIALISM A REALITY.*

DOMAIN. Also known as *Harmonia,* the *Kiantone Community,* and *The Association of Beneficents,* this 123-acre utopian colony was established in 1853 at Kiantone in Chatauqua County in western New York by a group of spiritualists led by **John Murray Spear** (1804–1877). The colony had two springs, which the members believed had special magnetic and healing qualities. This belief arose after a local blacksmith in 1850, while in a trance, was told that one of the springs had once been the site of a perfect society that practiced free love. The blacksmith sent water from the spring to leading spiritualists, including Spear, who decided to build a city of universal harmony on the site. Ten small homes were built for the original harmonists (most members spent the winter away from the colony), and a hotel was built later. Membership fluctuated between 20 and 40 persons. All female members were feminists. A convention of 1858 featured lectures on the abolition of marriage and the family, elevating women to freedom, and creating a society of perfection and order. In 1859 the colonists sailed down the Mississippi to New Orleans to promote a congress to bring peace to the world. On the way they established a colony at Patriot, Indiana, in 1860. Both Domain and Patriot were dissolved in 1863.

DONI, ANTON FRANCESCO (1513–1574). *See I MONDI.*

DONNELLY, IGNATIUS (1831–1901). A prominent late 19th-century social reformer, politician, and agrarian utopian author, Ignatius

Donnelly was born in Philadelphia, trained as a lawyer, and moved to Minnesota in 1856 to promote a self-sufficient land development scheme known as Nininger City. When it failed in the Panic of 1857 he moved into farming and politics, abandoning the Democratic Party, joining the Republican Party as an abolitionist, and serving in the U.S. House of Representatives from 1863 until 1869. Thereafter he switched parties and reform causes with great rapidity in his attacks on capitalist-industrial exploitation of the masses. He became serially a Radical Republican, a Liberal Republican, a Greenbacker, and a Farmer-Labor Party member while also forming the Independent Anti-Monopoly Party in 1877 and the Populist Party in 1891. He also ran for Congress again, agitated for a graduated income tax, and sought the Populist Party nomination for president in 1896. In the meantime Donnelly published a number of works including *Atlantis: The Antediluvian World* (1882), in which the Garden of Eden is buried in the Deluge; *Ragnarok: The Age of Fire and Gravel* (1883), in which he argued that the earth's mineral deposits are the result of a huge comet colliding with the planet in prehistory; *The Great Cryptogram* (1888), a polemic against fraud and deception that also argued that Shakespeare's plays were actually written by **Francis Bacon**; and his very popular utopian novel *Caesar's Column* (1890) that told of a great revolution against the rich and powerful in the United States during the 20th-century. He also penned *The Golden Bottle, or, The Story of Ephraim Benezet of Kansas* (1892), a second utopian novel, nine years before his death in 1901.

DOOR INTO OCEAN, A. This science fiction utopian novel was written by Joan Slonczewski (1956–), a biology professor at Kenyon College since 1984. *A Door into Ocean* (1986) tells of the affairs on Shora, an ocean-covered moon around the planet Valedon, and of the desire of the Patriarch, the ruler of a hundred scattered planets, to have Valedon take control of Shora. Within this broad framework, Slonczewski examines the basic questions as to what it means to be human and what would separate us from humanity. These questions are brought to light through the interplay of the novel's major characters: Merwen the Impatient, a Shoran; her daughter, Lystra; Realgar, the army officer sent to invade Shora; and the young Valan boy, Spinel. In the process of developing these troubling concepts, Slonczewski discusses the importance of rational ecological practices. She also depicts how Shoran women reproduce by merging genetic information and, over time, how they have evolved to the point that normal heterosexual sex is impossible, in the process arguing that love is not a matter of anatomy. Since the publication of *Door,* Slonczewski has written four other science fiction novels. These include *The Wall around Eden* (1989), in which teenagers face the environmental consequences of nuclear war, and *Brain Plague* (2000), in which intelligent microbes invade human brains, giving them unlimited power—at a price.

DOWIE, JOHN ALEXANDER (1847–1907). *See* ZION CITY.

DRUMMOND ISLAND. This Finnish cooperative colony located in Lake Huron off the eastern coast of Michigan's Upper Peninsula was founded in 1905 by Maggie Walz (or Waltz), the spearhead of a drive to establish a Finnish colony in the United States since her immigration to the United States in 1881. In short order, four settlements and 900 residents could be found on the island. They worked the lumber camps, sawmills, and sugar beet farms there, leading to reports of general prosperity. However, life in the remote island community was hard, and the socialists among the members led a revolt against Walz's leadership in 1914. Thereafter, all communal features on Drummond Island quickly vanished.

DUCHY OF JERUSALEM. *See* MULLER, BERNHARD.

DUKE COLONY. *See* AMERICAN SETTLERS ASSOCIATION.

DYNAMIC SOCIOLOGY. See WARD, FRANK LESTER.

DYSTOPIA/DYSTOPIAN/DYSTOPIANISM. The word "dystopia" (or "distopia") is derived from the Greek *dus* (diseased, faulty, difficult, unfavorable, or bad) + *topos* (place), meaning a bad or faulty place. It is the opposite of "utopia" (or "eutopia") from the Greek *ou* (no or not) + *topos* (place), meaning literally "no place" but commonly accepted as meaning "a good place." "Dystopia" is used in literature or common parlance to designate or describe a would-be perfect society that is, in fact, a very bad, unfavorable, or faulty place or society. "Dystopian" (or "distopian") is the adjectival form of the noun "dystopia." "Dystopianism" (or "distopianism") refers to a body of judgments or beliefs that would-be utopias (good places) are, in fact, dystopias (bad places).

DYSTOPIAN NOVELS (MAJOR). The following is a list of important dystopian literature:

Title	Author	Year
Mundus Alter et Idem	Joseph Hall	1605
The Last Man	Mary Shelley	1826
The Coming Race	Edward Bulwer-Lytton	1871
Republic of the Future	Anna Bowman Dodd	1887
Looking Further Backward	**Arthur D. Vinton**	1890
The Isle of Feminine	Charles Niswonger	1893
Limanora, The Island of Progress	John Macmillan Brown	1903
The Iron Heel	**Jack London**	1907
"The Machine Stops" (essay)	E. M. Forster	1909
Back to Methuselah	George Bernard Shaw	1921
We	Yevgeny Zamyatin	1921
Last and First Men	William Olaf Stapleton	1930
Brave New World	**Aldous Huxley**	1932
It Can't Happen Here	Sinclair Lewis	1935
Anthem	**Ayn Rand**	1937
Darkness at Noon	**Arthur Koestler**	1940
Bend Sinister	Vladimir Nabokov	1947
Animal Farm	**George Orwell**	1945
Nineteen Eighty-Four	**George Orwell**	1949
Player Piano	**Kurt Vonnegut**	1952
Fahrenheit 451	Ray Bradbury	1953
One	**David Karp**	1953
"Love among the Ruins"	Evelyn Waugh	1953
Lord of the Flies	**William Golding**	1954
2001: A Space Odyssey	Arthur C. Clarke	1968
Walk to the End of the World	**Suzy McKee Charnas**	1974
Benefits	Zoe Fairbairns	1976
Motherlines	**Suzy McKee Charnas**	1978
The Handmaid's Tale	**Margaret Atwood**	1985
The Furies	**Suzy McKee Charnas**	1994

– E –

EBENEZER. *See* AMANA SOCIETY.

ECCLESIAZUSAE. *See* ARISTOPHANES.

ECKERLIN, ISRAEL (1706–1758?). Born in Germany to a family known for its radicalism, Eckerlin, with his mother and three brothers, moved to Pennsylvania in 1725, where he fell under the influence of **Johann Conrad Beissel** (1690?–1768). Along with his brothers, he joined the Ephrata Colony and soon became an influential member of that community. He left Ephrata, however, in 1745 in a dispute with Beissel and, with two others, established a colony they called Mahanaim on a 900-acre site at New River, Virginia. With the failure of this venture, he returned to Ephrata in 1750, but stayed only seven months before Israel and his brothers settled at Dunkard Bottom in Preston County, Virginia (now West Virginia). They remained there during the violence of the French and Indian War, and, as a result, Israel was captured by the Ottawas as a spy. Sent to Quebec, he probably died in jail in 1758, although there is some evidence he died in France sometime after 1757.

ECONOMY. In 1814, the members of the **Harmony Society** founded by **George Rapp** (1757– 1847) sold their 6,000 acres of land in Butler County, Pennsylvania, and moved to a 30,000-acre site on the banks of the Wabash River in southwest Indiana. Their new town of Harmony prospered, but in 1825, their settlement being too far from the markets for their goods, they sold the site to **Robert Owen** (1771–1858) for $125,000 (who established **New Harmony** in its place) and moved back to Pennsylvania, this time to a site in Beaver County on the Ohio River 20 miles north of Pittsburgh. The "Harmonists" or "Rappites" called their new colony Economy. It, too, prospered, but in 1832 a large number of members broke off under **Bernhard Muller** (1787–1834), or Mueller, who called himself "Count Leon." The dissidents moved to the **New Philadelphia Colony** in Pennsylvania 10 miles northwest of Economy and then to Louisiana. Rapp died in 1847, but

Economy continued to prosper with silk and woolen manufacturing, a cutlery shop, ownership of coal mines and oil wells, and a grand hotel for vacationers until the end of the century, when legal problems and financial difficulties ended the colony in 1898. It was legally dissolved in 1905.

ECONOMY IN THE PARISH OF HARMONY. *See* QUEEN-WOOD.

ECOTOPIA. This novel by Ernest Callenbach (1929–) published in 1975 described a future materialistic near-utopian state in the Northwest that seceded from the United States because of the latter's anti-ecological policies and practices. Ecotopia, its capital located in San Francisco, did not allow private ownership of property, and all economic units were small to eliminate class consciousness. The influence of bureaucracies and technology was minimal, and the workload for its citizens was light so that they could enjoy the beautiful environment. Dominated by females, Ecotopia relied heavily on contraceptives and abortion to control population growth, and the closest the state came to religion was the near-worship of trees. The Ecotopians believed they would be recycled at death. Callenbach penned a sequel in 1981 entitled *Ecotopia Emerging.*

EDWARDS, JOHN (1637–1716). One of the **Cambridge Platonists**, leader of the Restoration Calvinists, and minister of St. Sepulchre's, Cambridge, John Edwards argued for a **millennium** as the culmination of advancing stages of human progress, human knowledge progressing hand in hand with human piety according to God's divine plan to attain a utopia here on earth.

EDWARDS, JONATHAN (1703–1758). Remembered as the greatest preacher and theologian of American Puritanism and an activist in the Great Awakening of the 1740s and 1750s, Jonathan Edwards was one of the strongest believers in the **millennium** in his day. As he saw it, the Protestant Revolution represented the Fifth Vial of Revelation and the world was now in the Sixth (and last) Vial. Through prayer, rededication to God, and missionary proselytizing, the Age of Grace would surely come on earth. As a **postmillennialist**, he believed that after a thousand years of virtue in which the church will flourish in the United States—Protestantism being purified, the papacy being destroyed, the Jews being converted, and the heathens being enlightened—the earth will ultimately be destroyed by fire from heaven and from the bowels of the earth after the completion of the millennium and the saints' removal to heaven. Linking religion and intellectual growth, the Puritan divine argued that by the grace of God and their own efforts humans could achieve a perfected world within history, making him the most prominent utopian of the 18th century in colonial America.

ELGIN ASSOCIATION. This most successful of the **black utopias** in the pre–Civil War era was founded by **William King** (1812–?) just south of Chatham, Ontario, in December 1849 as a result of his determination to act as the blacks' civil and religious leader by providing them with religious training and education while also overseeing their physical needs. Building on 4,300 acres of land, expanding the settlement to 7,000 acres by 1853, and receiving financial help from church collections and gifts from individuals, King's efforts to provide each black family with 50 acres of agricultural land were very successful; by the late 1850s at least 200 families, over 1,000 persons, made up the community. Reflecting King's careful planning and oversight, the community was laid out with the houses of the families, individually owned and built, constructed according to a minimum model with each house, some of finished lumber or brick, no smaller than 18 feet by 24 feet by 12 feet. Each house also had a garden enclosed by a picket fence. The Elgin Association continued to function until 1873, coming to an end not because of the racial opposition to it by its neighbors but by the Civil War and the emancipation of blacks that followed. Its members returned to the United States, where they served in various private and public leadership roles thereafter.

ELGIN, SUZETTE (1936–). Author of *Native Tongue (1984)* and *The Judas Rose* (1988), Suzette Haden Elgin is a science fiction writer and linguist. In *Native Tongue,* she makes clear her conclusion that female oppression is based on male-dominated linguistic mechanisms. The **feminist utopia** she reveals at the end of *Native Tongue* is maintained by means of a female-created language. This language, Laadan, expresses a number of phenomena that are not perceived by men. The women spend their time secretly defining their unique perceptions, making up words for them, and building a grammatical structure for their own unique language. Over time, Laadan becomes the native tongue of all women. This, in turn, leads the men to separate themselves from the women, even to the point of building separate women's residences, thus creating for the women a sort of feminist utopia free from male domination. This line of argument for Laadan as a means of protecting feminine reality is continued in *The Judas Rose,* the sequel to *Native Tongue,* although this second novel reveals the women suffering from sexual frustration without the company of men but on occasion enduring the inept sexual fumblings of men for the sake of reproduction, even faking orgasms. But Elgin has not resorted to parthenogenesis as a means of perpetuating her all-female utopia, as found in a number of feminist utopian novels ever since **Mary Bradley Lane**'s *Mizora* in the 19th century. Thus Elgin, while attempting to build an all-female utopian model in these two novels, has created a nonperfect society with women still dependent upon men for reproduction.

ELIJAH MUHAMMAD (1897–1975). *See* NATION OF ISLAM.

ELIOT, JOHN (1604–1690). *See* PRAYING TOWNS.

ELMSPRING COLONY. Later known as Old Elmspring, this colony was established in 1878 near Parkson, Hutchinson County, in southeastern South Dakota, about 20 miles west of the **Wolf Creek Colony**. Its founders were 13 families of **Hutterite** emigrants from Russia who adopted communalism upon their arrival at the 5,440-acre site. The **Rockport Colony** of Hanson County six miles to the north was its first daughter colony. **New Elmspring** was another spin-off from Elmspring. Elmspring continued in existence until 1929.

EMERSON, RALPH WALDO (1803–1882). As one of the leading philosophers, lecturers, and spokesmen for **Transcendentalism** during the 19th century, Ralph Waldo Emerson delved deeply into the human condition and a person's ability to affect it personally and collectively. A good friend of Henry David Thoreau, Emerson was closely tied to **Brook Farm**, an outgrowth of William Ellery Channing's Transcendental Club of reformers. Brook Farm was established by **George Ripley** (1802–1880) at West Roxbury, Massachusetts, in 1841. Transcendentalists, including Emerson, attempted to blend advancing human knowledge with Christian evangelical enthusiasm based heavily on individual experience. They believed and taught that the instincts of every person spoke for both God and Nature, all reality being part of the evolving Great Oversoul, making God immanent (indwelling) in nature and humanity, both moving to perfection in time by harmonious living.

EMIGRATION TO THE TROPICAL WORLD. *See* ETZLER, JOHN ADOLPHUS.

EMPEDOCLES (ca. 490–430 B.C.). Empedocles, Greek poet, philosopher, and statesman, added to the myth of the **Golden Age of Kronos** in describing the primordial period in human history when Strife was unborn and Kupris (Aphrodite, the goddess of love) reigned as the solitary goddess in the world.

ENFIELD COMMUNITY—CONNECTICUT. Established in the Town of Enfield in Hartford County, Connecticut, in 1790, this 3,300-acre **Shaker** community based its existence on farming and became known for its garden seeds. By 1823 it had some 200 members, mostly American with a few Scots and Englishmen, a number still present in 1848. It recruited many converts to Shakerism from a religious revival among the Baptist Christians in Rhode Island in the 1830s. The community enjoyed significant prosperity. However, its large-scale trade with the South was ruined with the outbreak of the Civil War. It continued in existence, however, until 1917.

ENFIELD COMMUNITY—NEW HAMPSHIRE. Three spiritual families formed this **Shaker** community in 1793 on 3,000 acres of land at Enfield, Grafton County, New Hampshire, the first to be established through **Mother Ann Lee**'s personal influence. It was visited by President James Monroe in 1817. The colony was marked by its granite and brick architecture. Its population reached its maximum number, 330 persons, in 1845. Its economic base was agriculture plus the manufacturing of spinning wheels, rakes, pitchforks, scythes, linen, cotton, and woolen goods, brooms, and patent medicines, especially "Shaker anodyne." It continued to thrive throughout the 19th and early 20th centuries, and when it was dissolved in 1923 the seven remaining members moved to **Canterbury** in Merrimack County, New Hampshire.

ENQUIRY CONCERNING POLITICAL JUSTICE. This work is but one produced by William Godwin (1756–1836), the prodigious English writer, reformer, Deist, social and political critic, and father of Mary Wollstonecraft Shelley (1797–1851). It is his most famous publication and the only work in which he presented a utopian vision for the future. Despite his pointed and scathing criticism of the England he saw around him, Godwin was a firm believer in the eventual triumph of reason and the perfectibility of human society. Accordingly, in his *Enquiry Concerning Political Justice, and Its Influence on General Virtue and Happiness* (2 vols., 1793), he argued that persons are all equally perfectible and that society must be based on utility and private judgment, not on government strictures. In his conclusion, he asserted that a perfected society based on minimal government, cooperation, the abolition of marriage, no religion, and the termination of private property was realizable.

EPHESUS, COUNCIL OF. *See* AUGUSTINE.

EPHRAIM—DOOR COUNTY. Abandoning the original **Ephraim—Green Bay** colony in 1853 over a dispute over land titles, A. M. Iverson and his congregation withdrew and formed a second Ephraim of 400 acres on the western shore of the nearby Door County, Wisconsin, peninsula. But when Iverson left the colony for Illinois in 1864 on a new pastoral assignment, the communal features of Ephraim came to an end. Still, the area became a locus of extensive Norwegian settlements in the years thereafter.

EPHRAIM—GREEN BAY. This **Moravian** commune was founded in 1850 by a wealthy Norwegian convert to Moravianism named

Nills Otto Tank at Tanktown in Brown County, Wisconsin. The members were 25 poor Norwegian families from the congregation of A. M. Iverson's church in Milwaukee. Three years later, when Tank refused to grant legal title to their land, Iverson and his followers withdrew and formed a second, **Ephraim—Door County**. The original Ephraim is now part of the city of Green Bay.

EPHRATA COLONY. *See* BEISSEL, JOHANN CONRAD.

EPICURUS (341–270 B.C.). The Greek philosopher Epicurus taught that peace of mind can be reached in a quiet life away from the multitude, especially if this solitude can be enjoyed in a community of likeminded friends, this community being not unlike that of the gods. Therefore, the wise person will not marry or engage in affairs of state and will attempt to secure an income that will not make him dependent on others or be beyond his simple needs. In effect, the wise person will be a secular mendicant living in pleasant serenity. Dependent not on the gods for a peaceful life, the Epicureans were dependent on themselves as individuals to perfect themselves and live a happy life. Although not utopian in the usual sense of the word, the teachings of Epicurus are important to utopian thought because of their emphasis on perfecting oneself by oneself without depending on some higher power, an idea that would loom large in secular utopianism as it emerged in the 17th and 18th centuries.

EQUALITY, *or* **BROTHERHOOD OF THE COOPERATIVE COMMONWEALTH.** Named after **Edward Bellamy**'s novel, this was the first of many colonies the Brotherhood established in Washington. Located near Edison in Skagit County, it was established in 1897 and existed until 1907. It was supported by over 3,000 nonresident members of the Brotherhood who paid membership fees of 10 cents or more per month. Equality's economic base consisted of farming, livestock raising, shoemaking, blacksmithing, tailoring, and operating a sawmill. All profits were shared among the members equally, and the colony was administered by elected committees. Each family lived in its own house. The members were in frequent contact with nearby colonies, especially with the **Cooperative Brotherhood** at Burley. Equality faced declining membership and a disastrous fire in 1904, and then the colony fell under the influence of anarchists newly arrived from New York, who revised the constitution to reflect the ideas promulgated in **Theodor Hertzka**'s *Freeland*. This divided the members into two factions, resulting in court battles and the colony being dissolved by court order in 1907.

EQUALITY, SOCIETY OF, *or* **HUNT'S COLONY.** This group of 21 persons led by Thomas Hunt bought 263 acres of land in 1843 at Spring Lake in Waukesha County, Wisconsin. Followers of the ideas of **Robert Owen** (1771–1858), they had turned to the United States after the failure of **Queenwood**, England, to meet their aspirations for communal life. They soon found that they were not prepared for the difficult tasks confronting them on the frontier in the form of clearing the land, putting in crops, and so on, and many members began to leave. Although 16 more enthusiasts arrived in 1845, by 1847 the colony had failed and the land had been sold off, a victim of personal conflicts within the community and the lure of a better life outside the community either as individual farmers or as tradesmen in Milwaukee.

EQUITY. See LOOKING BACKWARD: 2000–1887.

EROS AND CIVILIZATION, A PHILOSOPHICAL INQUIRY INTO FREUD. This 1955 work by the German-born social and political philosopher Herbert Marcuse (1898–1979) was a synthesis of the doctrines of **Karl Marx** and Sigmund Freud and played an important role in the emergence of utopian enthusiasm in the 1960s. Marcuse argued that with the development of an advanced economy, instinctual repression (as documented by Freud) as demanded by the capitalist, labor-based economy had been replaced by nonrepressive instinctual development. This, in turn, provided for the release of the energies of Eros and the pleasure principle, freeing the libido for full expression. The body was now being resexualized and the entire human personality was being eroticized. This will result, he said, in a new realm of freedom from pain, strife, and even fear of death. In the end, total human fulfillment will be achieved through eroticization, including the individual now being reconciled with the whole. Marcuse's subsequent writings, however, contained fears that this new freedom would lead to a new enslavement via blind permissiveness, the instinctual being separated from the intellectual, and physical pleasure being separated from thought. Still, his earlier *Eros and Civilization* had made him the guru of the 1960s student counterculture and a major factor in the resurgence of communal utopian attempts during that decade and the 1970s.

ESCHATOLOGY/ESCHATOLOGICAL. Eschatology, from the Greek *eschaton* meaning "ultimate" or "last," is a branch of theology dealing with the final events in the history of the world or humankind. In Christianity, it is specifically concerned with the events preceding the Second Coming of Christ, the resurrection of the dead, and/or the Last Judgment. "Eschatological" is the adjectival form of the noun.

ESOTERIC FRATERNITY. This group was founded in the 1870s in Boston by Hiram Erastus Butler. In the late 1880s they purchased 500 acres near Applegate, California, northeast of Sacramento in Placer County, and developed a commune there. The community, which included both male and female members, was celibate and promised its members immortality, or at least resurrection, after death. Butler and his successor, Enoch Penn, wrote and preached a doctrine of reincarnation and a belief that the Fraternity would grow to a **millennial** 144,000. By the time of Butler's death in 1916, the communal property was extensive and a number of successful businesses had been established, especially publishing. Although decline set in thereafter, the Fraternity is apparently still in existence.

ESOTERIC SECTION OF THE THEOSOPHICAL SOCIETY. *See* OLCOTT, HENRY S.

ESPERANZA. Little is known about this colony located in Neosho County in southeastern Kansas, except that it was formed in 1877 after the **Friendship Community** of Dallas County, Missouri, disbanded. A dozen families led by N. T. Romaine established the community. It was reported in the commune's newspaper in 1878 that some 61 applications for membership had been received. The colony probably died that same year.

ESQUISSE D'UN TABLEAU HISTORIQUE DE PROGRES DE L'ESPRIT HUMAIN **(SKETCH OF A HISTORICAL VIEW OF THE HUMAN MIND).** *See* CONDORCET, MARQUIS de.

ESTERO. *See* KORESHAN UNITY.

ETZIONI, AMITAI (1929–). *See* COMMUNITARIAN NETWORK.

ETZLER, JOHN ADOLPHUS (ca. 1796–?). Born around 1796 in Germany, Etzler immigrated to the United States in 1831. After failing to establish a utopian community near Cincinnati, he moved to Pennsylvania the next year and edited a German-language newspaper. During the 1830s he published two works outlining his vision of a possible future for the United States, *The Paradise within Reach of All Men, without Labour by Powers of Nature and Machinery* (1833) and *The New World: or Mechanical System to Perform the Labours of Man and Beast by Inanimate Powers, That Cost Nothing, for Producing and Preparing the Substances of Life* (1841). In *The Paradise,* he proposed the use of "re-acting power" (by which he meant that natural forces, once harnessed, could be utilized while needing very little supervision), for example, using the heat of the sun concentrated in great "burning mirrors" to create steam to power the nation's industries. The burning mirrors would also provide power for large apartment houses 1,000 feet long, 200 feet high, and 100 feet wide with each inhabitant having a private room with hot and cold water, air conditioning, artificial lighting, pleasant scents, and "boxes that move up and down" to carry them to the upper floors. Etzler also envisioned windmills 200 feet high, coastal devices to harness the waves to create power, huge rafts on the oceans and lakes covered with soil to produce food, the building of a ship to be powered by the waves themselves (it sank when he attempted this in the Thames in 1842), and a mechanism known as "the Satellite," capable of clearing the ground of trees and stones, then sowing and harvesting any crop. The Satellite would be driven by a stationary source of power, either a windmill or a waterwheel utilizing water from a reservoir.

To carry out his plans for the use of these mechanical devices to supplant human labor and to make people prosperous with ample time to cultivate the arts and sciences as they lived to 110, or even

170, years without avarice and covetousness, Etzler proposed the formation of an association to raise funds and create a pilot community on the Atlantic coast. Following this, the lands on the Mississippi would be divided into communities of 1,000 to 3,000 persons; 100 communities would then constitute a state. Then more communities of the same type would be started on the Pacific coast (where the winds, tides, waves, and sun would be more readily available) to move eastward. Finally, these communities would be linked by roads where mechanical vehicles would travel at the rate of 40 miles per hour. Etzler argued that this Paradise could be created in five to 10 years from the founding of an association to carry out his ideas. When these ideas elicited little interest, he moved to the West Indies, then back to the United States, and finally to England, in the process picking up the support of fellow German immigrant and publisher C. F. Stollmeyer, who became his major backer thereafter. Also receiving support from the **Owenites** and **Fourierists**, who published his *Emigration to the Tropical World* and *Two Visions of John Adolphus Etzler* in 1844, Etzler formed the Tropical Emigration Society that same year. Venezuela being the chosen land for their tropical utopia, 56 members sailed for that country in 1846 with another 140 following soon thereafter. The emigrants soon found that little land had been set aside for them by the Venezuelan government, and their troubles multiplied thereafter. The project soon failed from defections, sicknesses, and death, resulting, with the failure of other such schemes, in the British socialists looking to home-based projects rather than those across the seas. John Adolphus Etzler, one of the most colorful characters in the history of the 19th century, thereafter returned to Germany. The year of his death has not been ascertained.

EUPSYCHIA. *See* MASLOW, ABRAHAM.

EUROPEAN COMMUNITIES (MAJOR). *See* APPENDIX.

EUTOPIA VS. UTOPIA. Eutopia means "the good place." Utopia, as used satirically by **Thomas More** in his *Utopia,* means "nowhere" or "no place" but has come to designate an ideal society attainable on earth and in time. *See also* DYSTOPIA; *UTOPIA*; UTOPIANISM.

EVANS, FREDERICK W. (1808–1893). Born in England, Evans immigrated to the United States with his father and elder brother in 1818, settling first at Binghamton and later at Ithaca, New York. He displayed a marked concern about various social issues, including women's rights and the negative impact of monopolies and land ownership. He joined **New Harmony** in 1828, and when that colony failed he traveled to England before returning to New York, where he joined a group of freethinkers led by **Frances Wright** (1795–1852) and **Robert Dale Owen** (1801–1877). During 1830, he visited the **Shaker** community at **Mount Lebanon** and experienced a series of visions that converted him to the Shaker faith. He joined the Mount Lebanon colony and became an elder in 1843, continuing in that capacity for 57 years. Under his influence, the Shakers began to interact with the outside world. Flowers, music, magazines, and newspapers appeared within the colony, and hygienic conditions were established in the kitchens. Evans wrote two seminal works on the Shaker lifestyle, *The Shakers: Compendium of the Origin, History, Principles of the United Society of Believers* (1859) and *Auto-Biography of a Shaker* (1869), and was instrumental in shaping the journal *The Shaker and Shakeress* (1871–1899), which he edited from 1873 to 1875. He toured England in 1871 and was well received as a speaker, but he was unable to gain converts to the Shaker faith. When the U.S. chapter of the World Peace Movement was established, Evans ensured that the Shakers were founding members. He died in 1893 at Mount Lebanon.

EXPANDING LIGHT RETREAT CENTER. *See* ANANDA COOPERATIVE VILLAGE.

EZEKIEL, BOOK OF. This Old Testament account was written in the sixth century B.C. It contains the visions and prophecies of Ezekiel during the Babylonian captivity of the Jews. The early part of the book tells of God's unhappiness and consequent wrath against His people for their unfaithfulness and transgressions. The last eight chapters (40–48) describe a utopia-like elaborate new society that will be ushered in with the rebuilding of the **New Jerusalem**, a city six miles in circumference and called "The City of God." The Book of Ezekiel, along with the **Book of Daniel**, kept alive in Jewish society the belief in a perfected state in time as a manifestation of the will and goodness of God.

– F –

FAHRENHEIT 451. This science fiction **dystopian** novel by Ray Bradbury (1920–) was written in 1953 during the Cold War as an expression of Bradbury's determination to protect free expression against a repressive state. It tells the story of Guy Montag, a "fireman" whose job is to burn illegally stashed books. As Montag gains recognition and promotion for his good work, he struggles with his curiosity about the contents of the banned books. He finally flees to join a group of rebels who keep the classics of literature alive by memorizing them verbatim. The novel illustrates how science and technology can be used to advance the techniques of social repression and control that tend to eliminate personal identity and freedom. The film version of the book appeared in 1966.

FAIRBAIRNS, ZOE (1948–). *See BENEFITS.*

FAIRHOPE COLONY. This 135-acre utopian community on the eastern shore of Mobile Bay in Alabama was begun in 1894 by the radical reformer **Ernest B. Gaston** (1861–1937), who hoped to combine cooperative living with greater individual freedom. Fairhope was so named by a member who said the experiment had a "fair hope of success." The basic idea of Gaston and his two dozen Des Moines, Iowa, Single Tax Club enthusiasts was that all of the land in the colony would be owned by the Fairhope Industrial Association (later renamed the Fairhope Single Tax Corporation) and leased to individuals, but every colonist would have equal access to the association's common property and would pay a fee to the association each year based on the value of the land, a reflection of **Henry George**'s single-tax idea. The colony would also own and operate all the utilities and public facilities to ensure low costs and maximum efficiency. This included not only water and telephone systems but also a library and a "progressive" school based on the ideas of **John Dewey** (1859–1952). The project was capitalized with 5,000 shares of stock totaling $1 million. The radical millionaire Joseph Fels, who had become wealthy from the manufacture of Fels Naptha Bar Soap, provided much of the capital for the single-tax experiment. New members could acquire land at Fairhope without cost as long as they agreed to pay the $100 (lowered from the original $200) association fee and the annual single tax or fee.

By 1907 the colony owned 4,000 acres around Fairhope, and by 1930 the population had risen to more than 1,500. Reflecting Gaston's idea of Fairhope as a true democracy, all adult males and females were voting members of the association and elected a governing council that answered to them. The colony's governance also included the Progressive ideas of the initiative, referendum, and recall. The colony featured a commercial town center with a cooperative store; a park overlooking Mobile Bay for recreation, social events, and fishing; and a steamboat for transportation across the bay to Mobile. After the city of Fairhope was incorporated in 1908 on 11,000 acres (40 percent of which belonged to the association), most of the community property was gradually taken over by the municipality and, accordingly, the original principles and practices of the Fairhope colonists slowly faded away. Hit hard economically by the Great Depression in the 1930s and Gaston's death in 1937, Fairhope became a traditional community, Gaston's dream of establishing a lasting model cooperative-individualistic community in the South having never been realized.

FAMA FRATERNITATUS. *See* ANDREAE, JOHANN VALENTIN.

FAMILISTS, *or* **FAMILY OF LOVE.** This offshoot of the **Anabaptists** appeared in England in the 1550s in the wake of governmental persecution of Anabaptists within the realm, including a number being burned at the stake. In reaction to this persecution, the Family of Love was formed by David Joris, who considered himself to be the "Third David." Joris then convinced a merchant and former Catholic named Henry Niclaes that he, too, was a prophet of God. Niclaes set about to establish the Kingdom of God on earth in communities, first in Kent in 1552 and then in Cambridgeshire in 1574. His new religion had no worship or sacraments, and Niclaes taught that the Bible was mere allegory, that Moses was the prophet of hope, that Christ was the prophet of faith, and that he, Niclaes, was the prophet of love. The Familists believed that perfection could be attained in this life and denied the resurrection of the body in the hereafter. By the late 1570s, it was obvious to the government that the Family of Love was spreading. This persuaded the Privy Council to employ a special agent to ferret them out, but there is evidence that their doctrines were still being spread 70 years later in the 1640s. Despite the limited effect of the Familists on English religion in the long run, Niclaes's life was immortalized in John Bunyan's *Pilgrim's Progress.*

FARM, THE. Shortly after the collapse of the **Christian Commonwealth Colony**, its founder, Congregational minister **Ralph Albertson** (1866–ca. 1926), and his second wife, Hazel, in 1909 bought a run-down farmhouse in West Newburyport, Massachusetts, on the Merrimack River. They were joined by a number of persons who came to stay either temporarily or permanently. Among these were Walter Lippman and Lincoln Steffens, both of whom would later reach national prominence by their reformist writing. Albertson never insisted that his guests pay for their upkeep on The Farm; consequently, he was perpetually in debt. When Albertson left his wife and moved to New York, Hazel kept the enterprise afloat and during the 1940s, the nonreligious gathering place for idealists attracted a number of younger residents. The voluntary colony continued into the 1980s, making The Farm one of the longest-lasting communes in the United States.

FARM ECO-VILLAGE, THE. This nonideological communal experiment was founded in 1971 by University of San Francisco teacher Stephen Gaskin (1935–), who led a group of Haight-Ashbury hippies in search of a better life to a 1,700-acre site at Summertown southwest of Nashville, Tennessee, in Lawrence County. In 1980 the number of residents reached a peak at 1,400. They built solar houses, utilized wind turbines for electricity, and engaged in organic farming. In the early 1980s, the undertaking experienced many defections because of economic problems and what the defectors considered poor administration on the part of Gaskin. Accordingly, the commune was reorganized to allow private ownership of property. Currently about 250 residents are in the colony, which has its own roads, schools, medical and recreational facilities, publishing house, and government. The Farm Eco-Village continues on the basis of its manufacture of electronic equipment and specialty foods, having adopted technology as the key to its continued success.

FARRAKHAN, LOUIS (1933–). *See* NATION OF ISLAM.

FATHER DIVINE'S PEACE MISSION MOVEMENT. This religious communal movement grew out of Minister George Baker's preaching in New York City in 1915. Baker (1879?–1965) was born near Savannah, Georgia, or Rockville, Maryland, and at a young age began preaching to poor blacks in the rural South, claiming he was God incarnate and being arrested several times for his claims. He migrated north and eventually established himself in New York City in 1915. Here he became known as "Father Divine." By the 1920s, Divine had purchased a house in Sayville on Long Island as a communal residence for his followers, who were forbidden to use tobacco, alcohol, and cosmetics. More and more they came to consider him God in human form. Being largely a black movement and thereby under pressure to leave white Sayville, Divine led his group to Harlem. Here the movement grew rapidly and soon had 500,000 followers of all races who embraced his doctrine of nonviolence, racial harmony, and inner tranquility, Divine ministering to his followers both spiritually and physically. He bought up hotels and apartment buildings that at one time numbered 170 as communal "heavens" for his followers, and he fed thousands daily and at lavish banquets both before and after he moved to Philadelphia in 1942. After the end of the Great Depression and World War II, the movement began to decline, and since Father Divine's death in 1965, his widow, Mother Divine (1925?–), the former Edna Rose Ritchings, has continued to guide the movement, now very much diminished but still in existence.

FEIBA-PEVELI. This colony was a subset of **New Harmony** formed in 1826 in Posey County, Indiana, by a group of English farmers discontented with life on **Robert Owen**'s colony on the Wabash River. The name is derived from the latitude and longitude of the site transformed into letters. Nothing else is known of this colony of dissidents.

FELLOWSHIP FARM ASSOCIATION. This communal society was located at Westwood, Massachusetts, about 12 miles southwest of Boston. Formed in 1907 by George E. Littlefield, a Unitarian minister, it consisted of 72 acres. One acre of land was assigned to each of the 40 members; the remaining land was held communally. It existed until 1918.

FELLOWSHIP OF INTENTIONAL COMMUNITIES (FIC). This loose confederation of intentional communities, known in its early years as the Inter-Community Exchange, was formed in 1940 under the direction of **Arthur E. Morgan** (1878–1976). As it evolved, it served as a link for the communication and exchange of goods between communities, as a refuge for pacifists appalled by the carnage of World War II and the hostility displayed toward them during the Cold War, and as an agency to encourage new communities in the United States. Among its member communities were Hidden Springs in New Jersey; Tangy Homesteads in suburban Philadelphia; Tuolumne Co-operative Farms near Modesto, California; Skyview Acres at Pomona, New York; Parishfield near Brighton, Michigan; Kingwood in New Jersey; Quest near Royal Oak, Michigan; **Canterbury** outside Concord, New Hampshire; May Valley near Seattle; The Valley near Yellow Springs, Ohio; St. Francis Acres/Glen Gardner in New Jersey; **Koinonia Farm** near Americus, Georgia; and the **Bruderhof**, or Society of Brothers. Despite its prominence during the 1950s, the Fellowship of Intentional Communities gradually weakened, its dissolution coming in 1961. A major reason for its demise was the withdrawal of the Bruderhof, its largest and most prosperous member. The FIC was revived in 1986 under the name of the Fellowship of Intentional Community, like its predecessor attempting to serve as a link between communities. In 1990 it published a directory of existing communities, listing more than 300 communities in the United States and 50 overseas.

FELLOWSHIP OF INTENTIONAL COMMUNITY. *See* FELLOWSHIP OF INTENTIONAL COMMUNITIES.

FEMALE MAN. *See* RUSS, JOANNA.

FEMINIST UTOPIAN NOVELS (MAJOR). The following is a list of important feminist utopian literature:

Title	Author	Year
Ecclesiazusae, or *Women in Parliament*	**Aristophanes**	ca. 393 B.C.
A Description of Millennium Hall	**Sarah Scott**	1762

Ching-bua yuan	**Li Ju-chen**	1828
Man's Rights	**Annie Denton Cridge**	1870
Mizora: A Prophecy	**Mary E. Bradley Lane**	1889
A Cityless and Countryless World	Henry Olerich	1893
The Garden of Eden, U.S.A.: A Very Possible Story	William H. Bishop	1895
Herland and *Our Land*	**Charlotte Perkins**	1915
Walk to the End of the World	**Suzy McKee Charnas**	1974
The Dispossessed: An Ambiguous Utopia	**Ursula Le Guin**	1974
The Female Man	**Joanna Russ**	1975
Woman on the Edge of Time	**Marge Piercy**	1976
Benefits	Zoe Fairbairns	1976
Motherlines	**Suzy McKee Charnas**	1978
Native Tongue	**Suzette Elgin**	1984
The Judas Rose	**Suzette Elgin**	1988
The Furies	**Suzy McKee Charnas**	1994

FERRER COLONY. This anarchist community, led by **Harry Kelly** (ca. 1871–1953), Joseph Cohen, and Leonard Abbot, was established at Stelton (now Edison) in Middlesex County, New Jersey, in 1915 after three years in New York City. It featured an experimental day school that emphasized the manual arts, nature study, and free expression. By 1918 the anarchists had built 51 homes on the 143-acre site. The colony ran a cooperative store in conjunction with Fellowship Farm, a neighboring communal settlement. The land was owned by individuals, not the colony. At the colony's peak more than 100 families lived at Ferrer, approximately three fourths of them Russian Jews. But conflict ensued between the anarchists and the communists within the community, and by the 1940s many colonists began to leave. By 1946 it had ceased to exist as a colony.

FERRIS, JEROME. Pen name of Alice Ilgenfritz Jones (1846–1906). *See UNVEILING A PARALLEL.*

FEW DAYS IN ATHENS, A. *See* WRIGHT, FRANCES.

FICHTE, JOHANN GOTTLIEB (1762–1814). Although usually not included in the catalog of modern utopians, the German philosopher and first rector of the University of Berlin Johann Gottlieb Fichte should be numbered among them. Above all a secular rationalist, Fichte argued that humanity proceeds necessarily—not accidentally—through five stages of understanding or reason. The first stage is that of instinctive rationality wherein persons accept community customs and laws without understanding them. The second is the stage of authority in which persons submit out of faith and obedience alone. The third stage is that of individualism in which the claims of rationality are rejected in favor of "unrestrained licentiousness" (through which humankind is passing during the Enlightenment, Fichte asserts, but which is coming to an end). The fourth stage now coming into being is the stage of reason in which persons consciously and deliberately place themselves completely at its disposal. The fifth and final stage is that of perfect freedom in which authority will wither away as unnecessary in the face of reason and persons will convert themselves into the very image of reason, humanity fusing itself into a unanimity in which all will be known to each other and all will possess a similar culture. Having attained this final stage of perfect freedom, nature will be conquered by spirit and will be fully understood and controlled, the necessary end of reason and history. Fichte's arguments in favor of ordered reason and science had a crucial effect on philosophy during the 19th century when secular perfectionism, that is, secular utopianism, was having a major impact on Western thought.

FIFTH MONARCHISTS. During the period of the Commonwealth (1649–1660) in England under Oliver Cromwell (1599–1658), the idea of a special mission of the English people took the form of the Fifth Monarchists. They combined political radicalism with a determination to return Christianity to its original and true form. These **postmillennialists** believed that the Fifth Monarch—the reign of King Jesus—was at hand. The thousand-year binding of Satan had begun with the Reformation, they preached, and the Fourth Kingdom described in the **Book of Daniel** was coming to an end. The personal reign of Christ was about to begin with all earthly powers being overthrown and the **New Jerusalem** being established in England. As they saw history, God was working through men and their institutions to regenerate His kingdom on earth. The Fifth Monarchists complemented the contemporaneous belief of the Levellers, who wanted to equalize all social and economic disparities; the **Diggers**, who advocated communal living and common ownership of the land; and the Quakers, who believed they would be guided to perfection by the Inner Light of God within them. The Fifth Monarchists played an important role in convincing the English and their American colonists of their divine **millennial** role in history.

FIRST COMMUNITY OF MAN'S FREE BROTHERHOOD. This short-lived colony was founded in 1833 near Covington in Fountain County, Indiana, by Isaac Romine after the nearby **Coal Creek Community and Church of God** was dissolved. It lasted only until 1835. Some of its members moved on to become members of the **Grand Prairie Community** in neighboring Warren County.

FIRST LODGE OF THE ORDER OF THE NEW MORAL WORLD. *See* ASSOCIATION OF ALL CLASSES OF ALL NATIONS.

FIRST PRINCIPLES. *See* SPENCER, HERBERT.

FISKE, JOHN (1842–1901). Fiske was a prolific writer, lecturer, librarian at Harvard University, and one of the most celebrated orators of his day. By his efforts, he added to the acceptability and popularity of the theory of evolution extending all the way to human perfection. In his *The Destiny of Man Viewed in the Light of His Origin* (1884), Fiske urged the adoption of human cooperation in all things and was convinced that cooperation was the key to progress and could be strengthened and transmitted through heredity. Fiske convinced a generation of historians of the validity of his ideas regarding human evolution and that they should be applied to the study of the affairs of societies politically, socially, and economically, thereby indirectly aiding in the acceptability of progressive evolutionism in American life.

FLIGHT FROM THE CITY: THE STORY OF A NEW WAY TO FAMILY SECURITY. This utopian work was written by **Ralph Borsodi** (1888–1977), the American decentralist economist and reformer who founded the School of Living colony in Suffern, New York, in 1919. *Flight from the City* was published in 1933. In the book, Borsodi advocated a "city-farmer" plan by which families in the city would grow enough food to be self-sufficient. He also described how he had moved from New York City to Suffern northwest of the city so he could work in New York but have suburban acres on which to raise vegetables, chickens, and goats for milking during the current depression. Along with other popular works like those of **James Hilton** (1900–1954) and **Upton Sinclair** (1878–1968), Borsodi's *Flight from the City* kept alive in the 1930s the utopian dream that would come back into prominence after World War II.

FLORIDA COMMUNITIES. *See* APPENDIX.

FLOWERS IN THE MIRROR. *See* LI JU-CHEN.

"FLYING ROLL." An alternate name given to the **Israelites** in east Texas around 1900.

FOIGNI, GABRIEL de (ca. 1630–1692). Foigni was a cleric who left the Franciscan Order, went to Switzerland and embraced Protestantism at Geneva and Lausanne, married there and fathered four children, returned to France to his Catholic order when his wife died, lived the remainder of his life as a penitent, and was the author of the utopian tale *A New Discovery of Terra Incognita Australis, or the Southern World* (1693). In this work, he tells of a 35-year sojourn in the "Southern World" by a shipwrecked man named Jacques Sadeur. There, Sadeur discovers a nation of rational androgynes who live in a society where all things are held in common and their religion contains no worship dogma, ritual, or ministers. Children are suckled for two years, speak at eight months, walk at 12 months, and reason at three years. For their formal education, the children are under the conduct of the first master before moving on to discipline of the second for four years; they proceed through stages of education until the age of 30, at this point having gained knowledge and skill in the arts and sciences. The people are strong and vigorous from eating fruits and never suffer ill health (unlike Foigni's world, he asserts, where illness is caused by intemperance and corruption of the blood). The Australians are also of the belief that, life being filled with troubles, death is the happiness they long for because it puts an end to their pain. Accordingly, they have a rite of suicide wherein a person by eating certain fruits will peacefully leave the world.

FORD, WALLACE D. *See* NATION OF ISLAM.

FORRESTVILLE COMMUNITY. This **Owenite community** located at Lapham's Mills in Coxsackie, Green County, New York, in the upper Hudson Valley was founded in 1826 and consisted of 60 persons engaged in farming and handicrafts. When it ended in failure the next year, half of its members journeyed to Ohio to join the **Kendal Community**.

FORSTER, E(DWARD) M(ORGAN) (1879–1970). *See* "THE MACHINE STOPS."

FORT AMITY COLONY. This second of the **Salvation Army farm colonies** was established near the town of Holly in southeastern Colorado in 1898 with 14 families from Chicago as the original settlers. It was planned that the 640-acre site would be occupied by the urban poor, who would work the land until they paid back the Army's purchase price of $20 per acre. The land would then be theirs. By the next year, the colony could boast of dwellings for its inhabitants, a school, a post office, an assembly hall, and various stores, plus over 100 residents. Fort Amity relied heavily on the growing of cash crops such as cantaloupe and sugar beets. But by 1905 it was obvious that salt buildup from irrigation was ruining the crops and even the buildings. As a result, the colony was abandoned by the Army, and in 1910 the property was sold off, ending the experiment.

FORT HERRICK COLONY. This third of the **Salvation Army farm colonies** was founded in 1898 outside Cleveland, Ohio, with the financial support of Mark Hanna, the Ohio politico who led a campaign to raise money for the project. Settlers were allowed plots of five to 10 acres; artisans received less. As with the other Salvation Army colonies, cottages were built for the residents, and a school, post office, and store were constructed for the convenience of the 10 families living there. Small-scale market gardening was the mainstay of the colony. But the land was unsuitable for this, so the Army converted Fort Herrick into an "industrial colony" and home for recovering alcoholics. Sometime later, the colony was turned into a summer camp for children; this Army activity continued until the property was sold in 1974.

FORT ROMIE COLONY. This initial **Salvation Army farm colony** was begun in 1898 near Soledad, California, on land bought from Charles T. Romie. The colony ran into early difficulties with making mortgage payments and had an inadequate irrigation system. However, in 1900 and 1901 new colonists arrived at the site, a new irrigation system was built, and the colony began to prosper. By 1904 definite progress was being made in the colony's financial situation, but Fort Romie was abandoned a few years later as the Salvation Army turned its attention back to relief for the urban poor.

FOUNTAIN GROVE. This last settlement of **Thomas Lake Harris** (1823–1906) and the **Amenia Community** was established in 1876 on 1,700 acres north of Santa Rosa in the wine country of Sonoma County, California. Although it started as a dairy farm, Fountain Grove soon became famous for its wine, producing 70,000 gallons of wine per year by 1886. Harris described the community as being theosocialistic and regularly interfered with family life in the colony. Despite the prescribed belief in the practice of celibacy among the 39 colonists, a widely publicized sex scandal involving Harris and one Alzine A. Chevaillier, who accused Harris of making advances toward her, led to his leaving Fountain Grove for New York in 1892 with his third wife. Thereafter, the community moved away from its communal beginnings and evolved into a commercial venture, being legally dissolved in 1896.

FOURIER, FRANÇOIS MARIE CHARLES (1772–1837). Along with **Robert Owen** (1771– 1858) and **Etienne Cabet** (1788–1856), Charles Fourier was one of the most prominent European utopian socialists of the early 19th century. With experience in business, banking, and the military, he became convinced that a study of Western society would reveal the problems in administration that appeared endemic within it. His examination of the problems led him to conclude that society was burdened with competitiveness and waste. This, in turn, led him to settle on the idea that a reorganization of society into socialist communities would solve its problems. Convinced that human identity developed through eight separate stages and that at the highest stage persons would live in harmony with one another, Fourier advocated

phalanxes (or phalansteries) as a means of effecting this highest stage, which would last for 35,000 years. Each agrarian phalanx would consist of 5,000 persons working at occupations they enjoyed, with cooperation replacing competition. A number of phalanxes would come together to form a socialist nation, and in time the whole world would be a federation of phalanxes with Constantinople as the capital. Fourier's highest stage also included a number of bizarre ideas: persons living to the age of 150, the sea becoming lemonade, the North and South poles heated by an aurora borealis, animals being taught music, and wars being replaced by cake-eating contests.

Converts to his ideas, especially **Albert Brisbane** (1809–1890), established phalanxes in France and the United States. Most prominent among the American phalanxes were **Brook Farm** in Massachusetts, the **North American Phalanx** in New Jersey, and the **Wisconsin Phalanx** in that state. Some 31 Fourierist phalanxes were formed in the mid-1840s and thereafter; most lasted only one or two years, some even less. As in the case of most other failed utopian communities of that time, inequality of effort, little ground of common understanding among the heterogeneous membership, poor management, and lack of effective leadership contributed to the short life span of these Fourierist efforts.

FOURIERIST PHALANXES IN THE UNITED STATES.

Phalanx	State	Years
Brook Farm	Massachusetts	1841–1847
Social Reform Unity	Pennsylvania	1842–1843
McKean County Association	Pennsylvania	
(*or* Teutonia)	1842–1844	
Hopedale Community	Massachusetts	1842–1868
Sylvania Association	Pennsylvania	1843–1845
Bureau County Phalanx	Illinois	1843–1844
Jefferson County Association	New York	1843–1844
Morehouse Union	New York	1843–1844
North American Phalanx	New Jersey	1843–1856
LaGrange Phalanx	Indiana	1843–1846
Washtenaw Phalanx	Michigan	1843?
Alphadelphia Phalanx	Michigan	1844–1848
Bloomfield Association	New York	1844–1846

Clarkson Industrial Association
  (*or* Western New York Industrial

Association)	New York	1844–1845
Clermont Phalanx	Ohio	1844–1846
Iowa Pioneer Phalanx	Iowa	1844–1845
Leraysville Phalanx	Pennsylvania	1844
Mixville Association	New York	1844–1845
Ohio Phalanx	Ohio	1844–1845
One Mention Community	Pennsylvania	1844–1845
Ontario Union	New York	1844–1845
Sodus Bay Phalanx	New York	1844–1846
Skaneateles Community	New York	1844–1846
Trumbull Phalanx	Ohio	1844–1848
Wisconsin Phalanx (*or* Ceresco)	Wisconsin	1844–1850
Canton Phalanx	Illinois	1845
Columbian Phalanx	Ohio	1845
Philadelphia Industrial Association	Indiana	1845–1847
Integral Phalanx (absorbed by		
Sangamon Phalanx)	Ohio	1845–1846
Sangamon Phalanx (*see* **Integral**		
Phalanx)	Illinois	1845–1846
Pigeon River Colony	Wisconsin	1846–1847
Spring Farm Association	Wisconsin	1846–1848
Utopia Community	Ohio	1847–1850
Reunion Colony—Texas	Texas	1855–1859
Memnonia Institute	Ohio	1856–1857
Fourier Phalanx	Indiana	1858
Kansas Co-operative Farm (*see*		
Boissiere, Ernest)	Kansas	1868–1888
Reunion Colony	Missouri	1869–1870
Friendship Community	Missouri	1872–1877

FOURIER PHALANX. Located in Dearborn County, Indiana, this **phalanx** was founded in 1858 by **Alcander Longley** (1832–1918), who had resided at the **North American Phalanx** from 1852 to 1854. The phalanx lasted only a couple of months as Longley moved to Christian communism from his earlier espousal of Fourierist socialism.

FRANKLIN COMMUNITY. *See* HAVERSTRAW COMMUNITY.

FRATERNAL COMMUNITY NO. 1. *See* HOPEDALE COMMUNITY.

FREDERICK II (1194–1250). Soon after the death of Frederick Barbarossa, the Holy Roman Emperor, in 1190 during the Third Crusade, **eschatological** prophecies began to circulate in Germany of a future Frederick who, as Emperor of the Last Days, would liberate the Holy Sepulchre in preparation for the Second Coming and the **millennium**. When Frederick's grandson, Frederick II, assumed the imperial throne in 1215, the prophecies were applied to him. He was, it was believed, the Emperor of the Last Days, especially when he embarked on a crusade in 1229 and recaptured the city of Jerusalem, proclaiming himself king of the city. Because of his continued conflicts with the Church in Rome over its wealth (which he saw as the source of its corruption), Frederick was also seen as the cleanser of clergy prophesied in the Last Days, particularly by the pseudo-followers of **Joachim of Fiore** (1135–1202). Even a century after his quiet death in 1250, many in Germany continued to look forward to a resurrected Frederick returning by the will of God after a period of terrible warfare and suffering to bring peace and to assume his role as the Emperor of the Last Days, the Messiah of the Poor, and the persecutor of the corrupt Church for all Christendom. With his return, peace would reign, law would be restored, the Jews would be converted, the Greek Church would return to the fold of Rome, and monasteries would be closed and nuns forced to marry, both now to serve the people, in a renewed Church. The myth of Frederick II illustrates the persistence of apocalyptic-millennial thought among the populace during the late Middle Ages. *See also* REVOLUTIONARY OF THE UPPER RHINE.

FREEDOM COLONY. Located six miles northwest of Fulton, Kansas, and existing from 1898 to 1905, this utopian community was an outgrowth of the General Labor Exchange of Independence, Missouri, a work-bartering project. Situated on 60 acres with several buildings including residences and industrial structures plus additional farmland, it enjoyed short-run prosperity on the basis of its agricultural products and a sawmill. Among its 30 ex–Labor Exchange members in 1900 was Carl Browne (1846–1914), a former sideshow medicine man and believer in the reincarnation of souls, who had been a leader in Coxey's Army during its march of the unemployed on Washington in 1894 (his wife was Jacob Coxey's daughter). Browne built a meditation platform in a tree and, while perched there, noted the flying ability of crows. From this he conceived the idea of an airplane. He forthwith announced the establishment of an airplane factory that would produce inexpensive airplanes and would employ everyone in the Middle West who needed a job. Models of Browne's airplanes were built and displayed, but no prototype ever emerged. Browne also ran for Congress on the Populist Party ticket. Freedom, however, experienced declining membership and ended in 1905 when a fire set by an arsonist destroyed most of its buildings.

FREELAND, *or* **FREILAND.** *See* HERTZKA, THEODOR.

FREELAND ASSOCIATION. Disenchanted members from **Equality** in Skagit County, Washington, and the **Cooperative Brotherhood** in Kitsap County, Washington, started a less organized colony at Freeland on the eastern shore of Whidby Island, Washington, in 1900. More socialist than communal, it probably ended in 1906. Thereafter, some members joined the **Theosophists** at the **Temple Home Association**, or Halcyon, in California.

"FREE LOVERS AT DAVIS HOUSE." Established at Berlin Heights in Erie County, Ohio, in 1854, this group of free lovers, most of whom were spiritualists, were led by Francis Barry. They lived not as one family but rather on small farms on one side of the village of Berlin Heights. Because of their neighbors' hostility to their ideas and practices, they moved to a farm outside the village, where they lived together until 1858. Their official name is unknown.

FREE SPIRITISTS, *or* **BRETHREN OF THE FREE SPIRIT.** During the 12th through the 14th centuries when prosperity was resurgent in Europe, some pious persons, affected by the teachings of the **Amaurians**, viewed the new earthly enjoyments as temptations of Satan. As a result, these advocates of total poverty became a major heretical force in the Church. These voluntary poor, who saw themselves as the true imitators of the Apostles and even of the Christ of

Poverty, came from all classes, including the artisans and middle class and the lower clergy. They formed a restless intelligentsia often roaming from town to town preaching that the regular monks and higher clergy were damned for not observing a life of true and complete poverty. And although the great mendicant orders, the Franciscans and Dominicans, founded early in the 13th century to preach to the poor masses, for a period of time furnished nonheretical religion to the people, they, too, eventually fell into a loss of ardor and began to acquire property, opening the door once again to renewed influence by the advocates of extreme voluntary poverty.

Thus the Spiritual Franciscans emerged, primarily in southern France and northern Italy. They drew heavily on **Joachim of Fiore**'s idea of humankind moving through stages of development to the final Age of the Spirit, a **millennium** of supernatural bliss in which they would replace the Church of Rome with one all-embracing, poverty-loving church. Northern Europe, on the other hand, witnessed the emergence of the Free Spiritists or Brethren of the Free Spirit, as they came to be called, in the last decades of the 13th century. These male counterparts to the mendicant orders were called *Beghards,* or "holy beggars." Their female counterparts were called *Beguines,* who were often women of the towns from wealthy families, especially spinsters and widows who lacked function and prestige in medieval society. Some Beguines, who dressed in religious garb, lived with their families. Others supported themselves by working or attaching themselves to the wandering Beghards. Many, however, came together in unofficial and unsanctioned religious communities. The adepts of the Free Spirit, whether men or women, acknowledged no authority except their own consciences because they believed that in their poverty they had attained a perfection so absolute that they were incapable of sinning. They rejected the authority of the Church as an obstacle to full communion and perfection and believed in a new perfected church of themselves. In their conduct they were clearly antinomian moral anarchists, believing that it was morally permissible to do what was commonly regarded as sinful, indeed, that they had a duty to do so, especially in sexual matters. Here they indulged in promiscuity on principle, and sometimes in public nudity, as a sign of spiritual emancipation.

Theologically the Free Spiritists were pantheists, believing that they, the "subtle in spirit," were divine even in their bodies from all eternity and by proper training could be wholly transformed into God, at death being restored to their original state before they flowed forth from God. Both the Beghards and the Beguines were condemned by the Church in 1259 and again in 1310 but continued clandestinely throughout the High Middle Ages. In the late 14th century, the Free Spiritists were still preaching their doctrines, including a millennium as a re-creation of the lost Golden Age in which classes and private property did not exist. The Free Spiritists, then, like the Spiritual Franciscans, represent a clear continuation of the aspiration of a perfected society on earth in time during the High Middle Ages, despite the official Church's disapproval of literal apocalyptic millennialism stretching back to the time of **Augustine**. In a secularized form, Free Spiritualism would enjoy wide acceptance in the centuries that followed.

FREILAND. *See* HERTZKA, THEODOR.

FRENCH DAEDALUS, THE. *See* RESTIF de la BRETONNE, NICHOLAS-EDME.

FREY, WILLIAM (1839–1888). Born Vladimir Konstantinovich Geins in Russia in 1839 and educated there, William Frey was attracted to the ideas of **Charles Fourier**, **Claude-Henri Saint-Simon**, **Etienne Cabet**, and **John Humphrey Noyes** and might have been a member of the radical anarchist underground group known as *Land and Liberty* in the 1860s. In 1868 he and his new wife (calling themselves "William and Mary Frey") immigrated to the United States and joined **Alcander Longley**'s **Reunion Colony** in Missouri. In 1871 he formed the communistic **Progressive Community** at Cedar Vale, Kansas. The experimental colony lasted until 1875 with Frey withdrawing to form the **Investigating Community** nearby. In 1879 he then joined the Positivist movement and established "**complex marriage**" of voluntary sexual relations (as practiced at the **Oneida Community**) at Clermont, Iowa, the next year. In 1881 he became involved in a group within the **Am Olam** movement working for the immigration of Jews to the United States and in 1883 founded the **New Odessa Community** in Oregon. He left that group two years later and moved to London, where he served as a publicist for the Positivist and Ethical Culture churches. He died in London in 1888.

FRIEDSAM, FATHER. *See* BEISSEL, JOHANN CONRAD.

FRIENDLY ASSOCIATION FOR MUTUAL INTERESTS. *See* KENDAL COMMUNITY.

FRIENDSHIP COMMUNITY. This **Fourierist** communal society was established by **Alcander Longley** (1832–1918) in Dallas County, Missouri, in 1872, two years after the failure of his **Reunion colony**. Although the five original members were augmented by persons from the region joining them during the Panic of 1873, they were unable to sustain the community economically. Also aware of hostility from the neighbors because it was seen as akin to **Mormonism**, Longley closed the experiment in 1877.

FRUIT CREST. This short-lived cooperative colony was established at Independence, Missouri, in 1911 by several socialists. Consisting of 35 acres, it was modeled after the **Fellowship Farm Association** in Massachusetts. It ceased to exist in 1912.

FRUIT HILLS. Located at Foster's Crossing, Warren County, Ohio, Fruit Hills was a small colony on the Miami River north of Cincinnati established by Orson S. Murray, an enthusiast for **Owenism** and anarchism, in 1845. It functioned until 1852 and maintained close contact with the **Grand Prairie** and **Kristeen** communities in Indiana.

FRUITLANDS. *See* ALCOTT, BRONSON.

FULLERITES. *See* ADONAI-SHOMO CORPORATION.

FURIES, THE. *See* CHARNAS, SUZY MCKEE.

– G –

GARDEN CITY. The Garden City movement was an extension of ideas stretching back to the early 19th century regarding ideal urban life as it had been promulgated by **Robert Owen** (1771–1858), **Edward Bellamy** (1850–1898), **William Morris** (1834–1898), and other utopians. It emphasized the establishment of cities featuring self-sufficiency, good health, and population distribution. Building on the ideas of Dr. Benjamin Ward Richardson (1828–1898) and his projected city of Hygeia in which streets would be fashioned on a grid pattern and washed daily, plus no pubs or tobacco establishments would be allowed, Ebenezer Howard (1850–1928) described his ideal English city in his *Tomorrow: A Peaceful Path to Real Reform* (1898). According to Howard's plan, each city would contain 30,000 persons on 6,000 acres divided into six wards. It would feature public parks, contain schools, and be separated from any other cities by 3,000-yard strips of open land. The result would be good and healthy living for the inhabitants, equitable land holdings, limited government, and good relations between citizens, as well as between the inhabitants and God. A number of such planned cities were established in England during the 1880s and 1890s, and Howard's city of Wythenshawe was established in 1927. The movement had an impact on city planning in the United States, and after World War I enjoyed a resurgence in Britain and later spread to Australia.

GARDEN OF EDEN. This is the garden where according to the Book of Genesis, Adam and Eve, the first humans, lived in freedom and plentitude until expelled by God for the sin of disobedience. The ability of humankind to return to this idyllic place of existence is frequently found in utopian ideas and schemes, especially within a Christian context.

GARDEN OF EDEN, U.S.A.: A VERY POSSIBLE STORY, THE. This **feminist utopian** novel published in 1895 was the work of journalist, novelist, and sometime professor of languages William H. Bishop (1847–1928). Its main female characters, Stella Vernon and Alice Hathaway, are assertive egalitarian **feminists** sought by two men, Wayne and Stanley, for their planned utopian community. In their projected **Garden of Eden**, a guaranteed wage ensures unmarried women a home of their own, and centralized cooking and mechanical cleaning devices free them from housework. But as Bishop's melodramatic and essentially shallow story unfolds, Stella and Alice demand power and equality, not subordination, both sexual and otherwise. They have rejected the "Cult of True Womanhood," that is, the perception of woman as loyal and subordinate wife, mother, and sustainer of morality that was popular at the time. They have become liberated women, freed from patriarchy and at liberty to create a more idyllic society in equal competition with men.

GASKIN, STEPHEN (1935–). *See* FARM ECO-VILLAGE.

GASPER SPRINGS. *See* SOUTH UNION SOCIETY.

GASTON, ERNEST B. (1861–1937). Born in Illinois, raised in Des Moines, Iowa, and a business degree graduate of Drake University, Ernest Gaston became active in the agrarian reform movement in his adopted state in the 1890s. Influenced by his study of the attempted utopian settlement at **Topolobampo Bay** in Mexico and the single-tax ideas propagated by **Henry George** (1839–1897) in his *Progress and Poverty,* Gaston drafted a constitution for a single-tax colony in 1890, although he still looked to political action through the Peoples' Party in Iowa in 1892 through 1894 as the answer to the persistent farmers' problems, then the subject of widespread agitation in the Midwest. When this reliance on the Populists failed to bring about fundamental reform of the economic system as the party met with defeats at the polls, Gaston turned to communal living as the answer to the people's problems and with the Des Moines Single Tax Club established the **Fairhope Colony** in Alabama. Gaston's death in 1937 and other factors led to the eventual failure of the Fairhope experiment by the mid-20th century.

GEORGE, HENRY (1839–1897). Henry George, journalist, popular economist, contemporary of **Edward Bellamy** (1850–1898) and **Ignatius Donnelly** (1831–1901), and author of *Progress and Poverty* (1879), was one of the most prominent reform spokesmen of his day, his book selling in the thousands both in the United States and abroad. His solution to the economic problems of the time and the creation of a **millennium** came not through some governmental socialist scheme but by a fundamental change in taxation, specifically by the adoption of the Single Tax. As George argued, it was land speculation and high land rents resulting from economic progress that were the cause of poverty and injustice. The idle, monopolistic landowner was a parasite and a thief reaping unearned profits from the scarcity of land (the first factor of production) at the expense of capital and labor. Therefore, the cure to the nation's economic problems lay in taxing land as the only form of taxation. This would cause land prices to fall to near zero, giving laborers free access to land, assuring that unemployment would disappear, and creating a tax surplus for public works. To George, a firm believer in human progress as the world moved from inequalities to equalities, the adoption of the Single Tax was more than mere reformism. This was the path to a **Golden Age**, to a moral millennium where people would live by the precepts of natural justice and enjoy God-ordained equality.

GEORGIA COMMUNITIES. *See* APPENDIX.

GERMANIA COMPANY. Originally a colony of "Second Adventists" from Groton, Massachusetts, the Germania Company existed from 1856 to 1879 in Marquette County, Wisconsin. Led by one Benjamin Hall, in the colony all industries (a flourmill, a cooper shop, a wagon and blacksmith shop, a shoe making shop, and a general store) were owned and operated in common with each individual doing what he or she could for the common good. The colony also included a farm of 1,200 acres. Little is known as to the cause of its eventual failure.

GERMANTOWN. After **Count Leon Muller**'s death at **Grand Ecore** in Nachitoches Parish, Louisiana, in 1834, his followers moved to higher and healthier ground in the Red River Valley north of Minden in Webster Parish in 1836. They continued their communal life there until the colony was dissolved in 1871.

GERMINAL. This 1885 utopian novel by Emile Zola (1840–1902), French novelist known for his campaign for the acquittal of Captain Alfred Dreyfus, was written to suggest ways of instigating reforms in the modern urban industrial society of France and modern Europe. "Germinal" is the spring month in the revolutionary calendar of 1793. It was chosen as the title of the novel because the word signifies Zola's dedication to the necessary rebirth of sympathy for the plight of the worker. The novel, set in the mid-1860s and drawing on moderate reformism, **Marxism**, and anarchism, presents a vivid contrast between the values and living conditions of the workers and the managers, in the process deriding bourgeois values and the managers' use of God as an ally against the workers. He condemns the tendency toward overproduction and monopoly and presents reformist and even revolutionary proposals to enhance the condition of the workers and bring them and the nation to a just and internally peaceful society.

GIBSON, GEORGE HOWARD. This Christian Socialist founder of the **Christian Corporation** and cofounder of the **Christian Commonwealth** began his public career as a journalist and publisher. In 1896, or earlier, he formed the Christian Corporation in Lancaster County, Nebraska, in an attempt to put Christianity into practice by cooperative "farming, stock-raising, fruit-growing, manufacturing and love-educating." Its membership was made up of 23 families, who lived on 1,360 acres of land. These persons may or may not have lived communally on the site, but in 1895 Gibson convinced 26 of them to join the Christian Commonwealth, formally founded the next year by Gibson, **Ralph Albertson** (1866–ca. 1926), and William C. Damon (1838–?), its members moving in 1897 to the new colony at Muskogee County, Georgia. Gibson left the Christian Commonwealth in 1900, reportedly thereafter joining an "industrial community" in Illinois. Nothing more is known of his life.

GILLETTE, KING CAMP (1855–1932). Although best known as the inventor of a disposable razor blade in 1895 and founder of the Gillette Safety Razor Company in Boston, Massachusetts, Gillette wrote a number of utopian works based on his social theories. These included *The Human Drift* (1894), in which he blamed all social-economic-political problems on competition, arguing that the solution was a worldwide corporation to own and manage all means of production. He also proposed in this work that the whole population of the United

States, totaling 60 million at that time, should be housed in towering apartment buildings with 100 million rooms located near Niagara Falls, which would supply the electricity. This book was followed by *Gillette's Social Redemption* (1907); *Gillette's Industrial Solution* (1908); *The World Corporation* (1910), in which he announced he had formed a corporation in the Arizona Territory to achieve world consolidation, offering Theodore Roosevelt $1 million to serve four years as its president; and *The People's Corporation* (1924), written with the help of **Upton Sinclair** (1878–1968) and dedicated "To MANKIND." All of these works were reflective of Gillette's conviction that the industrial monopolies then existing under capitalism were but precursors to a utopian socialistic world corporation based on universal cooperation to come. Gillette died in near poverty in California in 1932, his fortune virtually wiped out by the 1929 stock market crash and lost investments in the California real estate market.

GILMAN, CHARLOTTE (STETSON) PERKINS (1860–1935). Gilman, science fictionist, novelist, feminist activist, editor and publisher of the feminist journal *Forerunner,* and cofounder of the Women's Peace Party, was best known in her time as the author of the chilling novella *The Yellow Wallpaper* (1899), which has been regularly reprinted since that time. She also wrote *In This Our World* (1893) in which she saw women as virtual economic slaves entrapped in the United States' male-oriented, capitalist society. However, her major contribution to utopian thought and literature is her **feminist utopian novel** *Herland,* originally published in *Forerunner* in 1915, although her earlier utopian novel, *Moving the Mountain,* had been published four years before. She also authored a utopian sequel to *Herland* entitled *With Her in Ourland: Sequel to Herland* (1916), but it is generally considered to be of lesser literary quality.

Herland is the story of three American men who, while exploring a faraway jungle, discover a hidden valley inhabited by white women alone. The athletic and seductive women lure them into a mysterious electric net, and they are subsequently led as prisoners into Herland. After months of reeducation and instruction in the Herland language, the men are released into the all-female society where women do all the tasks done by men in the outside world. They also wear comfortable, "nonfeminine" clothes, play noncompetitive sports, and reproduce asexually. The men learn that the free male citizens had been eliminated from Herland 2,000 years before when they were all killed by a volcano while fighting in a mountain pass. The volcano also sealed in the women from the outside. Subsequently a revolt by male slave noncitizens broke out, but the women slew all of the revolutionaries. All men having been killed, the women then had to learn to live without them, which they have done successfully.

Society in Herland is organized around motherhood ever since the first virgin mother founded an Aryan race of women capable of reproducing themselves by bearing female children, although eugenics determines which women are allowed to become pregnant. Now all masculine traits have disappeared in Herland, and the women live idyllic lives in their world closed to the outside. Sexuality having been tamed, the women of Herland are now free to maintain their perfect society. Gilman's story ends with the men being deported by the women because one of them has tried to rape his chosen "wife," such patriarchal attitudes of male domination over females no longer being tolerated in this female utopia.

GLENNIS COOPERATIVE INDUSTRIAL COMPANY. Little is known about this colony except that it was founded in 1894 at Eatonville, Pierce County, Washington, about 17 miles south of Tacoma. It was inspired by the Nationalist movement set off by **Edward Bellamy**'s *Looking Backward*. At one time, the colony had 30 members before failing in 1896.

GLORIOUS KINGDOM OF CHRIST. See BAXTER, RICHARD.

GNOSTICISM. Gnosticism was a religious and philosophical movement in Europe and the Middle East from the second through the seventh centuries. Gnostics believed they had secret knowledge about the universe and the origins and destiny of humanity. Salvation, they taught, was attained through *gnosis* (knowledge), and the world was created by the Demiurge and ruled by evil spirits. Through *gnosis*, the divine spark in human beings would be liberated from the evil world and united in perfection with the Supreme Being. Because the gnostic sects also taught that Jesus was only a divine messenger occupying a human body temporarily, thus denying His death on the cross and Resurrection, they were condemned as heretics by the Church, especially through the work of Irenaeus. The gnostic idea of knowledge as the key to perfection is reflected in many utopian ideas in modern times.

GODWIN, WILLIAM (1756–1836). *See ENQUIRY CONCERNING POLITICAL JUSTICE.*

GOLDEN AGE, MYTH OF THE, *or* **THE GOLDEN AGE OF KRONOS.** A myth is a sacred or secular story of what happened in the past, containing accounts of fabulous things that reflect deeper, fundamental, and crucial meanings about life that should be learned and emulated as a model for human behavior. Western myths can be found in earliest times with the Greeks. Among them is the Myth of the Golden Age, or the Myth of the Golden Age of Kronos. In the ninth century B.C., **Hesiod** in his *Works and Days* told of a generation of people who lived when Kronos was king in heaven and how they spent their days in feasting and merriment. In that Golden Age, food grew without cultivation, giving forth of itself without humans having to labor for it. There was no violence, pain, or grief in this pastoral land, and people glided into death as though falling asleep. The Myth of the Golden Age, no longer existing but always longed for, where people lived in a state of natural happiness, persisted through ancient times, especially in the works of **Empedocles** and Dicaerchus.

Ovid's *Metamorphoses* brought the myth to popularity in the Roman world. In Ovid's work, all persons did what was right without law or punishment, there were no wars, the earth gave forth food without human labor, streams of milk flowed through the land, and honey was distilled from the green oak. Of crucial importance, as the Myth of the Golden Age became part of the Western body of thought it was no longer seen, as in Hesiod, as an age gone by but, rather, as an age to be attained or hoped for, as kept alive, for example, in the popular legend of **Cockaygne**. Thus, in mutated form the myth of the Golden Age of Kronos was infused into the future-oriented utopian tradition of the West where its influence continued through the centuries.

GOLDEN BOTTLE, THE. *See* DONNELLY, IGNATIUS.

GOLDING, WILLIAM GERALD (1911–1993). Golding, British by birth, educated at Oxford University, a Royal Navy veteran, and an English literature teacher, is known worldwide for his **dystopian** novel *Lord of the Flies* (1954) and for other major works published since that date. These netted him a Nobel Prize in literature in 1983. Drawn from Golding's experience in the Royal Navy and as a teacher of young boys, *Lord of the Flies* tells the story of a group of schoolboys whose plane crashes on a deserted island during a nuclear war. Despite Golding's hint that this could be the beginning of a new start for human civilization, factions soon emerge among the boys. One faction is led by Jack, the totalitarian, the other by Ralph, the democrat. In time the boys become savage and vindictive, and Piggy, the fat boy, is tortured and killed, along with Simon, the symbol of Christ. Golding uses his novel to illustrate his belief in humankind's natural tendency toward aggression and depravity despite the modern rationalists' belief dating back to the Enlightenment that human societies can be perfected. To Golding, order in society derives only from the ethical fiber of the people, not from governmental or social structures as most utopians would argue. It ranks among the most powerful dystopian works of the 20th century and in 1963 was turned into a movie, thereby spreading its dystopian argument to an even wider audience.

GOOSE POND COMMUNITY. This **Owenite community** was located in the Pocono Mountains in Pike (now Monroe) County in eastern Pennsylvania and was situated on the abandoned site of **Social Reform Unity**, the first **Fourierist phalanx**. Established in 1843 with 60 people involved, it failed in only one year.

GORHAM COMMUNITY. This **Shaker** community was located at Gorham in Cumberland County, Maine. Established in 1807, it failed to prosper. In 1819 the members sold off the land, some moving to the nearby **Alfred community** and others to the **Sabbathday Lake** community.

GOULD'S FARM. This Christian communal undertaking was founded in 1913 at Monterey near Great Barrington in southwest Massachusetts by William Gould (1867–1925). This Congregational layman was dedicated to alleviating the problems of the world, to build, as he said, "the Kingdom of God Here and Now." At the farm, Gould and his wife, Agnes, brought care to persons in need of help, primarily alcoholics, sex offenders, convalescents, and the mentally and physically handicapped. The Goulds and the staff of Gould Farm lived economically in a communal manner in voluntary poverty as a Christian ministry. After William Gould's death in 1925, his wife assumed the leadership of the farm, and the project continued, although some of the communal practices were somewhat relaxed. In 1989, the community had 40 "guests" and a staff of more than 35 persons. It continues to function today as a center for psychiatric rehabilitation.

GRAND ECORE. Leaving the **New Philadelphia Colony**, **Count Leon Muller** (1787–1834) and a group of followers sailed down the Ohio and Mississippi Rivers and established a colony at Grand Ecore in Natchitoches Parish, Louisiana, in 1834. Muller died there the same year. His followers moved to **Germantown** two years later.

GRAND PRAIRIE COMMUNITY. Also known as the Grand Prairie Common Stock Company, the Grand Prairie Community existed from 1845 to 1847 in Warren County, Indiana. Made up of former members of the **First Community of Man's Free Brotherhood**, also in northwestern Indiana, some 20 families worked 230 acres of land. They disbanded after two years over disputes regarding a proposed constitution.

GRAND PRAIRIE HARMONIAL INSTITUTE. Not to be confused with the **Grand Prairie Community**, also in Warren County, Indiana, the Grand Prairie Harmonial Institute was begun by **John O. Wattles** (1809–1859) in 1853 after the failure of The Cincinnati Brotherhood, or **Spiritualist Community**, in Clermont County, Ohio, located on the site of the **Clermont Phalanx**. Wattles advertised his institute as an "association for educational and social reform purposes." **Horace Greeley** was one of the trustees, but the Institute failed after one year.

GREAT AWAKENING. This outbreak of religious enthusiasm swept through the American colonies between 1734 and 1745. Its most renowned personage was George Whitefield, who arrived in the colonies in 1739, gradually turning on the leaders of the established church for their beliefs and challenging their authority. It represented a major step in American religion in that it encouraged personal judgment in matters of faith and religious practice.

GREAT CORNER STAKE OF ZION. *See* BEAVER ISLAND COLONY.

GREAT EQUALITY, THE (TA T'UNG SHU). This description of an ideal society was authored by K'ang Yu-wei (1858–1927), a Chinese **Confucian** philosopher. Although it appeared in manuscript form in 1902, it was not published in its entirety until 1935 after K'ang Yu-wei's death. It represents a blending of Western ideas with Confucian traditions. Influenced by the evolutionary theory of **Charles Darwin** (1809–1882), K'ang envisioned a one-world society evolving from disorder to peace in three stages: the ancient pattern of disorder, a gradual movement toward peace, and finally ultimate human maturity in the Great Equality. When this stage was reached, there would be total equality among persons, no private ownership of property, and no social needs as these would be taken care of by governmental bureaucracies. K'ang also envisioned the gradual evolution of international limitations on weapons to end warfare and the merging of nation states into an international body divided into 20 massive bureaucracies for planning the application of resources to prevent the exploitation of workers. Many of K'ang's ideas were inspired by the non-class-based social system as found in the United States, and he advocated that the state play a major role in the education and welfare of the people. *The Great Equality* stands as one of the most important blends of Eastern and Western values and the most complete scheme for the creation of an ideal society that has ever appeared in China.

GREELEY, HORACE (1811–1872). One of the best-known journalists, politicians, and radical reformers in the 19th century, Horace Greeley founded the *New York Tribune* in 1841, a newspaper well known for expressing Greeley's liberal views, especially regarding abolitionism, Free Soilism, antimonopolism, capital punishment, and labor organizations. In 1872 he was nominated as the presidential candidate of the breakaway Liberal Republicans and was endorsed by the Democrats but was defeated by Ulysses S. Grant, who was seeking a second term of office. Greeley died completely insane soon after that. In the aftermath of the Panic of 1837, Greeley had urged people to join utopian communes, helped **Albert Brisbane** (1809–1890) draw up the constitution of the **North American Phalanx** (1843–1856) based on the ideas of **Charles Fourier** (1772–1837), and served as the phalanx's treasurer. He also gave Brisbane a weekly column in his *New York Tribune* to popularize Fourier's ideas. In the post–Civil War years, Greeley's agricultural editor, **Nathaniel Meeker** (1817–1879), organized the **Union Colony** in Weld County, Colorado in 1869. The colony was transformed from a communal basis within four years and became the town of Greeley, Colorado.

GREENING OF AMERICA, THE. This 1970 bestseller was the work of Charles Reich (1928–), attorney, social philosopher, and guru of the "new freedom" to be attained in the United States. In this book, Reich predicted the coming of a new, utopian nation with the emergence of a new stage of consciousness among its citizens. Consciousness I, as he saw it, reflected hardworking farmers, workers, and businessmen struggling against adversity in early American history. Consciousness II, he claimed, placed a premium on the corporate state and sacrificed humanity on the altar of material gain, leaving the nation's people exhausted and defeated. Consciousness III, a product of the mid-1960s, he pictured as a utopian stage of individual emancipation that will set persons free. Each will be at liberty to create his or her norms and values, nonjudgmentalism and tolerance of all being the bywords of this evolving new era in American history. *The Greening of America* convinced many persons in the aftermath of the turbulent 1960s that, indeed, a new and more perfect United States was on the horizon.

GRONLUND, LAURENCE (1846–1899). A native of Copenhagen, Denmark, Gronlund immigrated to the United States in 1869, where he made a name for himself with the publication of his *The Coming Revolution: Its Principles* (1879), an attack on American capitalism, followed by his *The Cooperative Commonwealth* (1884), the first book to explain clearly the doctrines of **Karl Marx** to an English-speaking audience. It was also the source of **Edward Bellamy**'s ideas on the virtues of socialism. Opposed to the establishment of co-operative colonies, Gronlund supported Bellamy's socialist ideas after the publication of *Looking Backward*. Although always luke-warm in his support of communal living, Gronlund's writings, particularly *The New Economy; A Peaceable Solution to Social Problems* (1898) and *Socializing the State* (1898), convinced many socialists of the value of separatist colonies and brought significant philosophical-economic support to the utopian movement.

GROVELAND SOCIETY. This **Shaker** community at Groveland, or Sonyea, was established in Livingston County, New York, in 1836 by Believers from **Sodus Bay**, some 60 miles away. It was located 37 miles from Rochester on almost 2,300 acres and boasted of a sawmill, a gristmill, a successful agricultural output, a school, and a library of 400 volumes. At one time, the community had some 200 members. It continued in existence for six decades despite major calamities in the form of floods and fires. When the community was dissolved in 1895, those members who remained moved to **Water-vliet**, the original home of the "Shaking Quakers."

GUNSBERG, JOHAN EBERLIN von (ca. 1470–1533). *See WOL-FARIA*.

– H –

HALCYON THEOSOPHISTS. *See* TEMPLE HOME ASSOCIA-TION.

HALL, JOSEPH (1574–1656). *See MUNDUS ALTER ET IDEM*.

HANCOCK, *or* **WEST PITTSFIELD.** Located on a 3,000-acre site in the Berkshire Hills three miles east of the **Mount Lebanon** community in upstate New York, this **Shaker** community was established in 1790 in Berkshire County, Massachusetts, and existed until 1960. It was one of the smaller Shaker communities with a membership of only 300 persons gathered in three "families." Many of the buildings at Hancock have been restored and are open for visitors during the summer months.

HANDMAID'S TALE, THE. This 1985 **dystopian** story by **Margaret Atwood** (1939–) tells of the United States being replaced by the Republic of Gilead and dominated by religious fundamentalists. In Gilead, sexual liberation has been replaced by a Puritanism that includes the degradation of women. Successful men are given "wives" to manage their domestic affairs, "Marthas" as their servants, and "handmaids" for sexual purposes. For the less successful, "econowives" play all these roles, "aunts" train and control the handmaids, and "Jezebels" service foreign dignitaries. The remaining women, "unwomen," work at the lowest and most hazardous occupations. All women are kept illiterate. Love is not allowed, and pleasure is not allowed in sex. Religion is dominated by the state with the Bible considered seditious and television dominated by religious broadcasting and distorted news reporting. The handmaiden in the story is Offred, who exists in this regimented state. Her manuscript, being discovered in 2195, gives the reader some hope that the future will not be as dark as portrayed in Atwood's gloomy tale.

HANWELL COMMUNITORIUM. *See* BARMBY, GOODWYN.

HARBINGER, THE. This was the weekly publication of **Brook Farm**. It served as the official organ of the **Fourierist** movement in the United States after 1845 and contained accounts of many communal activities in the country. Its editor was **George Ripley** (1802–1880), the **Transcendentalist** founder of Brook Farm, who continued to act in that capacity until the demise of the publication in 1849, two years after the dissolution of the community.

HARMONIA. *See* DOMAIN.

HARMONIAL VEGETARIAN SOCIETY. This utopian society was made up of 18 families from New York, Ohio, and the South who formed a commune in 1860 near Maysville in Benton County in the far northwest corner of Arkansas, to follow a vegetarian regimen and practice free love. Marriage was not recognized in the commune, and males and females chose their mates by lot. All children born were to be persons of the society, not of their parents. The colony ended in 1864, some of their buildings being used by the military during the Civil War.

HARMONY HALL. *See* QUEENWOOD.

HARMONY SOCIETY. This society was formed by some 300 families of dissenters from the established Lutheran Church from Württemburg, Germany, in 1805 under the leadership of **George Rapp** (1757–1847). The members based their faith on a literal interpretation of the Bible; common ownership of goods; and celibacy as the preferred state, although marriage was tolerated. The society's first settlement was at Harmony in Butler County, Pennsylvania, 25 miles northwest of Pittsburgh. In 1814 the "Harmonists," or "Rappites," sold their 6,000 acres in Pennsylvania and moved to a new 30,000-acre site in southeastern Indiana on the Wabash River. Here they prospered both in agriculture and in manufacturing. By 1817 they had more than 1,000 persons in the community. In 1824–1825, they sold about 9,000 acres of land and 130 buildings to **Robert Owen** (1771–1858) for $100,000 and returned to Pennsylvania, this time to a site on the Ohio River 20 miles north of Pittsburgh in Beaver County. Here they established a new settlement called *Economy*. In 1832 a splinter group under "Count Leon," or **Bernhard Muller** (1787–1834), left Economy, moving first to another site in Pennsylvania and then to Louisiana. Despite this defection and Rapp's death in 1847, this third settlement lasted until 1898 and served as a model for other communal experiments. Owen, having bought the Harmony property in Indiana, proceeded to establish his ill-fated **New Harmony** community on the site.

HARRIMAN, JOB (1861–1925). Harriman, the founder of the **Llano del Rio Company**, was trained for the ministry at Northwestern Christian University in Indianapolis but turned to the law, gaining admittance to the bar in Indiana in 1885. The following year he moved to California and joined one of the Nationalist Clubs in San Francisco inspired by the writings of **Edward Bellamy** (1850–1898). Active in the Socialist Labor party and associated with the **Altrurians** in Sonoma County, in 1898 he became the Socialist party nominee for governor of California, and in 1899 he became the state organizer for the Socialist Labor party. When the party merged with the Socialist Democrats, he became the vice presidential candidate on the ticket headed by **Eugene V. Debs** (1855–1926) in the election of 1900. In 1911 he served as the Socialist and labor candidate for mayor of Los Angeles. After that failed campaign, he turned to cooperation and in 1914 became president of the Llano del Rio Company, whose members were drawn from socialist and labor ranks. When the colony met an end in California in 1918, he left the community and led some of the members to **New Llano** in Louisiana. Two years later he moved back to California, and in the last five years of his life suffered from a number of debilitating illnesses.

HARRINGTON, JAMES (1611–1677). Harrington was a wealthy English landowner who composed *The Commonwealth of Oceana* (1656) in response to the English civil war. All in all, Harrington wrote more than a dozen utopian works during his lifetime. *Oceana* explained how the monarchy of Charles I had failed and why a republic was the only viable substitute form of government for the realm. Harrington hoped that Oliver Cromwell (1599–1658) would accept his ideas of governance, but the lord protector ordered the publication seized and never considered adopting Harrington's ideas.

Oceana, as Harrington hoped to see it adopted, was drawn from the author's knowledge of the Venetian republic, the Hebrew commonwealth, the Greek city-states, and the Roman and Dutch governments. In Oceana, the amount of property held by individuals would be limited to assure equality of power, and government would consist of an elective senate to propose laws, a popular assembly to vote on these laws, and an elective assembly to carry them out. The state would tolerate all faiths (except idolatry, Roman Catholicism, and Judaism), and there would be a national church with the priests elected by the people. All citizens would be classified according to age, fortune, quality, and residence. Residences would be divided into 50 tribes, each consisting of 20 hundreds of 10 parishes, for a total of 50 tribes, 1,000 hundreds, and 10,000 parishes. The chief magistrates (the knights, who would have the highest income) and tribal deputies would meet in the capital city of Emporium (London) to govern. Although Harrington's *Oceana* was utopian only in a literary sense, its ideas never being adopted, it was widely read during the period of the Commonwealth and, of greater importance, its ideas were subsequently taken up by reformers and revolutionaries in France and the United States. Many of its concepts, such as the separation of powers, rotation in office, and religious liberty, were adopted by utopian-minded political theorists in the centuries that followed.

HARRIS, THOMAS LAKE (1823–1906). This spiritualist leader and founder of the **Spiritualist Community at Mountain Cove**, the **Amenia Community**, the **Brocton Community**, and **Fountain Grove** was born in England and immigrated with his parents to Utica, New York, when he was four. He was converted to Universalism from being a Baptist and during the 1840s formed the spiritualist Independent Christian Congregation. In 1851 he led a group of followers to Mountain Cove, Virginia, to await the **millennium**. Harris worked with fellow spiritualist James Scott at the Spiritualist Community at Mountain Cove, but the colony failed in short order.

After a trip to England, Harris founded the spiritualist colony called the Brotherhood of the New Life in 1861 at Wassaic, New York, moving the entire colony to a 1,600-acre site near Brocton, New York, in 1867. Here Harris was the spiritual director of the celibate colony, relying on his communication with the spiritual world to govern his followers. This included spiritual breathing rituals in which the members breathed rhythmically with Harris, allowing him to become an energy portal for the divine and enabling them to breathe in a divine essence that warded off sin and the death spirits. When Harris split with **Laurence Oliphant** and Lady Maria Oliphant in 1875, he led his followers to Santa Rosa, California, where he established the Fountain Grove Community on a 700-acre site. Fountain Grove was financially successful because of its vineyards and other agricultural endeavors; in 1884 the members had 1,700 acres under cultivation. By 1894 Harris was convinced that he had attained immortality, but stories of free love at Fountain Grove led to its dissolution in 1896. Harris moved to England, where he died in 1906.

HARTLIB, SAMUEL (ca. 1600–1662). *See MACARIA.*

HARVARD SOCIETY. This **Shaker** community was established in 1791 the town of Harvard in Worcester County, Massachusetts, northwest of Boston. Its members were predominantly women, Americans by birth, and adult converts from other religions. The home farm of the society comprised 1,800 acres with another farm in Michigan and one other in Massachusetts. The society supported itself almost entirely in agriculture, employed a few hired laborers to aid in the work, and had a library and a school. In 1823 it had 200 members; by 1874 the number was down to 90. It continued to exist until 1918.

HAVERSTRAW COMMUNITY. This utopian society, also known as the Franklin Community, was formed in 1826 by a group of men from New York and Philadelphia. It was located at Haverstraw, New York, two miles from the Hudson River some 30 miles north of New York City in Rockland County and was described as having 120 acres of woodland, two mansion houses, 12–14 outbuildings, plus a sawmill and a rolling mill. Founded on the principles of **Robert Owen** (1771–1858), it was marked by common ownership of property. Its members, admitted by ballot, included various tradesmen. They formed a church called the Church of Reason and attended Sunday lectures on philosophy, morals, and scientific subjects, but there were no religious services or articles of faith. Although Haverstraw enjoyed some initial economic success, the community broke apart in only five months, apparently when its monetary affairs fell into disarray due to its weak leadership. Some of its members joined the **Forrestville Community**.

HEARD, HENRY FITZGERALD (*or* GERALD) (1890–1971). Born in London, Heard engaged in promoting agricultural cooperatives and wrote *The Agent of Humanity* (1928), espousing human evolution. His pacifism and his alarm at the rising wave of fascism caused him to move to California in 1928. Here he came under the influence of Swami Prabhawananda of the Vedanta Center in Hollywood and became a devotee of Eastern philosophy and religion. In 1942 he founded Trabuco College on 392 acres behind Laguna Beach southeast of Los Angeles as a pacifist, celibate meditation community, "college" referring to a *collegium* or community. Here he intended to train future leaders, neo-Brahmins, to lead humankind away from the violence and destruction of World War II and the world in general, which he believed was based on egotism, individualism, greed, and fear. Heard was convinced that only meditation and spiritual training could overcome human violence and greed, thus the community was structured on Vedantist religious philosophy and Benedictine-like monasticism that included three hours of meditation each day. **Aldous Huxley** (1894–1963) was associated with the project, although he never joined Trabuco College. The community lasted until 1947, when Heard announced that it was God's will that the project end. Thereafter Heard deeded over the property to the **Vedanta Society** and returned to Los Angeles.

HEAVEN CITY. This short-lived 1920s community was the work of Albert J. Moore. Established by Moore in 1923 near Harvard in McHenry County, Illinois, Heaven City was to be a refuge from the world catastrophe that was to occur between that year and 1927. In 1923, said Moore, the world would witness economic panic; 1924 would see widespread labor strikes; 1925 would see worldwide revolution; 1926 would be marked by a great war in which three fourths of the world's population would perish; and 1927 would welcome in a "new dawn." Moore's colony, established on 130 acres and beginning with a membership of 36, would be partly communal. Members were required to turn over their property to the colony before joining, and cooking and laundry facilities were communal. Yet each family was to have a private home. Moore's catchwords were "coordination" and "cooperation." Heaven City ended in 1927 with no "new dawn."

HEAVEN'S GATE. This **millennial** cult was begun in the 1970s by Marshall Applewhite (1931–1997) and ended in March 1997 at a spacious mansion near San Diego, California, when 39 members (21 women and 18 men, including Applewhite) committed ritualistic mass suicide. This was carried out by ingesting a phenobarbital mixture so that the members could link up with the comet Hale-Bopp, their bodies to be whisked away by extraterrestrials as the earth was about to be recycled in an **apocalyptic** event ushering in the millennium. As with many New Age cults, the utopianist Heaven's Gate members mixed Christian teaching regarding an afterlife and messianic deliverance with a belief in space aliens and human transmigration into a higher form of life after death.

HECKER, ISAAC (1819–1888). Largely self-educated, Hecker joined the Workingmen's Party in New York under the tutelage of Orestes Brownson and in 1843 became a member of **Brook Farm**. After only six months there, he left for Fruitlands and again stayed only a short time. Returning to New York, Hecker converted to Roman Catholicism in 1844 and was ordained a priest in London five years later. Then in 1851, as a Redemptorist missionary, he returned to the United States to minister to German immigrants. In 1858 he founded a new religious order, the Missionary Priests of St. Paul, or "the Paulists," and continued his missionary work, as well as publishing, directed toward both Catholics and non-Catholics until his death in 1888.

HEGEL, GEORG WILHELM FRIEDRICH (1770–1831). This major German philosopher is not usually identified with utopianism, but his system of thought (based on progress to perfection by steps from the imperfect to the perfect, an idea found in utopian schemes from the earliest centuries) served as a philosophic underpinning for many utopian constructs during the 19th and 20th centuries. Hegel adopted his worldview of humanity within history on the notion of freedom in the sense of persons living self-consciously in a totally rationalized community or state. He saw history as the movement toward progress through the dialectic process of a thesis (movement or force) being necessarily challenged by an antithesis (counter movement or counterforce). This, in turn, would produce a new thesis (movement or force), the process to continue over and over again until total consciousness-reality is achieved, that is, total knowledge of the Absolute when the mind finally knows itself totally. Hegel is especially important in the history of utopian thought because his dialectic materialism provided the basis for **Karl Marx**'s attack on the capitalist system (the thesis) by socialism (the antithesis) as a necessary step in the process of history moving to the final rule of the proletariat. At this point history will end, the final perfect (worldwide) state having come into existence. Hegel, then, like his disciple Marx, must be placed as well within the canon of utopianism.

HEIDEGGER, MARTIN (1889–1976). This German philosopher and professor at the University of Freiburg was a major figure in the emergence of existentialism in the 20th century. He argued that human beings, once realizing that they are bound by time and circumstance between nothingness (preconception) and nothingness (death), are then able to move forward toward the future rather than avoiding the future by being preoccupied with death and nothingness. In doing so, they must follow their authentic consciences to elevate themselves and achieve their potential as humans. In this way, humans can, indeed, elevate themselves and society in the time span allotted to them, although his philosophy can also open the door to existential moral chaos with its emphasis on individualism as the deciding factor in human affairs.

HELICON HALL COLONY. *See IT CAN'T HAPPEN HERE*; SINCLAIR, UPTON BEALL.

HELVETIUS, CLAUDE ADRIEN (1715–1771). This philosopher and major figure in the French Enlightenment drew from **Blaise Pascal** the idea of the essential nothingness of humans as morally neutral forces, neither good nor bad. This being the case, he argued, humans find their meaning only in the analyst-legislator because moral force is found only in society and the analyst-legislator gives necessary direction to a society as a substitute for grace and predestination. Power, therefore, belongs to the state (society), and human beings are but functional units within it rightly controlled by public planning. If progress—or perfection—is to be achieved, it will come about not through reasoning individuals but through the guidance of the analyst-legislators applying a higher state of reasoning, an idea that became prominent in the centuries that followed and was reflected in many, if not most, utopian schemes.

HERLAND. See GILMAN, CHARLOTTE PERKINS.

HERRNHUT COMMUNE. This was the first commune in Australia's white history. It was founded in 1853 by Johann Frederick Krumnow (1811–1880) close to Hamilton in Victoria. Along with his 12 followers, Krumnow was determined to care for the physical and spiritual welfare of his people and others. The members shared all money and property, but Krumnow reserved leadership for himself alone. After his death in 1880, the commune gradually declined from a lack of new members and the deaths of the original settlers. It was sold off in 1889.

HERTZKA, THEODOR (1845–1924). Although Theodor Hertzka did not consider his novel *Freiland* (Freeland) utopian, it is usually considered as such because of its contents. Hertzka was an Austrian economist and proselyte of **Karl Marx**'s socialism, John Stuart Mill's pragmatism, and **Charles Darwin**'s evolutionary theory. In his *Freiland: Ein Sociales Zukunftsbild* (Freeland: A Social Anticipation; 1890), he pictured an entirely new type of society that excluded the negative elements of both capitalism and socialism. Some of his enthusiastic disciples attempted to plant a Freeland on the island of Lamu off Kenya in 1894 but failed miserably in less than three months. Freeland, Hertzka's ideal colony, was to be located in Kenya where 200 workers would create the colony in four months. In the colony, there would be equal access to land by all the inhabitants; the state would care for those unable to work; and all adults would participate in democratic government, its powers divided between the executive and legislative departments. Freeland would also have planned schools, banks, libraries, theaters, and cultural academies, all housed in magnificent buildings. Peace and equality would reign, and there would be no police, judges, or military because "criminal" behavior would be treated as a medical problem. The state would also maintain the roads, canals, and railroads, and the workers would receive maximum benefits, yet the state would not own anything. Rather, it would serve only as the facilitator of the public good. Hertzka's principles served as the revised basis of **Equality**, or the Brotherhood of the Commonwealth, on Puget Sound, Washington. Despite his disclaimer, because of his *Freeland* and its sequel, *A Visit to Freeland* (1893), Hertzka must be included within the ranks of utopian theorists of the late 19th century.

HERZL, THEODOR (1860–1904). *See ALTNEULAND.*

HESIOD (9th century B.C.). The Greek poet Hesiod was the author of the epic *Works and Days* in which he pictured a pastoral age of old when food grew without human effort and humans were not forced to work. In this **Golden Age**, there was no violence, pain, or grief, and death held no terror. Living in a hard age when such idyllic conditions did not exist, Hesiod presented his alternative vision as a model for his contemporaries that was attainable if only they would strive to curb the injustices and hardships of their lives. This same message was contained in his rendering of the myth of Prometheus who, defying the wrath of Zeus, brought fire to wretched humankind, thus placing the human race on the road to progress and civilization, a significant theme in Greek literature thereafter.

HEYNEMANN (*or* HEINEMANN), BARBARA (1795–1883). The second great leader of the **Amana Society**, Heynemann succeeded Christian Metz after his death in 1867 and led the community until her death. An illiterate and worldly innkeeper's maidservant from Alsace, she became "inspired" in 1818 and joined with Metz and others in the Community of True Inspiration (separatists from the German Lutheran, or Evangelical, Church). She was expelled from the "Inspirationists" in 1833 for a period of time because of her interest in and subsequent marriage to a young schoolteacher named George Landmann, but immigrated to the United States with the group in 1842, settling first at one of the six villages of the Ebenezer Society in upstate New York and then in Iowa between 1854 and 1861 as the Amana Society moved to its new location. Heynemann was the last "inspired" leader of the Amana Society.

HIAWATHA VILLAGE. This socialist colony grew out of Walter T. Mills's *The Product Sharing Village* (1894). Located at Manistique in Schoolcraft County, in Michigan's Upper Peninsula, the idea originated with Abraham S. Byers, a homesteader, who, after reading Mills's book, offered his farm to Mills as the location for a cooperative colony. Mills (1856–1942) accepted, and in 1893 the Hiawatha Village Association was formed from several farms in the area. A membership fee of $100 was required, and a time-credit labor system (one time-credit for each hour's labor) was inaugurated for work and community exchange of goods. Hiawatha Village consisted of 1,080 acres of land, 125 cattle, and 25 horses. The 200 villagers operated a sawmill, farmed, and erected their own homes. After Mills resigned as president in 1895 the experiment disintegrated, and the next year the land reverted to private ownership.

HIGHLAND HOME. *See* PRAIRIE HOME COMMUNITY.

HILTON, JAMES (1900–1954). Although best known as the screen-writer of the 1942 Academy Award–winning movie *Mrs. Miniver* and his novels-turned-into-movies *Good-bye Mr. Chips* (1934) and *Random Harvest* (1941), James Hilton first achieved fame with the publication of his *Lost Horizon* in 1933. It depicts a utopian paradise called Shangri-La hidden in the mountains of Tibet in the Valley of the Blue Moon. Shangri-La is a Christian monastery whose inhabitants remain young and live beyond the life span of outsiders. In Shangri-La there are no economic problems, and moderation in all things is the basic rule, explains the monastery's leader, Father Perrault. Here the homicidal world never intrudes, and here the art, music, knowledge, and religion that the world has squandered are preserved. Shangri-La is discovered by four Westerners whose leader, Conway, decides to stay but is persuaded to return to the outside to lead one of the other men back to the external world. As the novel closes, Conway is attempting to return to Shangri-La. This was a comforting conclusion to Hilton's readers mired in the suffering of the Great Depression.

HIPPODAMUS OF MILETUS (5th century B.C.). This Greek philosopher has been called "the inventor of political utopianism" for his writings on planning colonies, specifically for laying out urban streets in a grid pattern (although octagonal street plans were found in Greek cities long before his time) and for designing imaginary laws and an imaginary plan for an imaginary city. His plan called for a city of 10,000 citizens and included *nomoi* (a written code of laws) governing the polis, raising political philosophy to a more ideal level. He also introduced the idea of a city with a distinct quasi-Spartan soldier class. One third of the public land was to be used for the support of this class; the other two thirds were to be shared by the other two classes, the farmers and the craftsmen. Hippodamus is important in early Greek thought not only because he introduced the concept of city planning but also because he introduced the question of the best constitution to be adopted to govern a Greek polis. Of equal or greater importance, he must be recognized as the first to write something that can be recognized as a utopia and to use a fictional literary form. This would subsequently be employed by philosophers of the ideal city, such as **Plato** and **Aristotle**.

HISTORY OF AMERICAN SOCIALISMS. See MACDONALD, A. J.

HISTORY OF THE KINGDOM OF BASARUAH. See MORGAN, JOSEPH.

HOFFMANN (*or* HOFMANN), MELCHIOR (ca. 1495–1543/1544). Hoffmann was one of the reformers during the Protestant Reformation who accepted and built upon the threefold stages of history of **Joachim of Fiore** (1135–1202). As Hoffman saw it, the history of the Church should be seen as three distinct steps leading to a perfected state: first, from apostolic times to the reign of the popes; second, the period of the unlimited power of the popes; third, the period of the Spirit, now underway, in which the popes would be deprived of all power and the letter of God's law would be transformed into the Spirit. Hoffmann, a convert to **Anabaptism**, saw himself as one of the witnesses in the **Apocalypse** and believed himself and his disciples to be the Israelites sent into the wilderness in the Old Testament. Over time, he came to view himself as the Woman Clothed in the Sun in the Apocalypse fleeing, as the bride of Christ, into the wilderness, also as either Elijah or Enoch in the final age. His native Strassburg was to be the spiritual Jerusalem from which 144,000 heralds of regeneration would go forth to cleanse and renew the world. He also predicted the end of the world in 1533 and that he would ride into Strassburg with Christ in the clouds to establish the New Jerusalem. Arrested in his native city in 1533, he eventually died in prison with his prophecy unfulfilled. His followers, the Melchiorites, persisted for a short time afterward.

HOLY BEGGARS. *See* BEGHARDS.

HOLY COMMONWEALTH, A. See BAXTER, RICHARD.

HOLY JUMPERS. *See* BURNING BUSH, THE.

HOLY MOUNT. *See* LEE, MOTHER ANN.

HOME COLONY, *or* **MUTUAL HOME ASSOCIATION.** This Puget Sound, Washington, anarchist colony was formed in 1898 on 26 acres on Von Geldern Cove (popularly known as "Joe's Bay") by dissidents from the remains of the short-lived **Glennis Cooperative Industrial Company** (1894–1896), which had been established south of Tacoma, Washington, on the basis of **Edward Bellamy**'s Nationalist movement. The original membership of 40 persons stood at 54 within a year and then climbed to 230 by 1910. Individualism and personal freedom were the hallmarks of the colony, including free love, free speech, and freedom of ideas—although some members engaging in nude swimming caused a serious rift in the colony. Members could own their own homes and buy small plots of land to be held in trust by the association until 1909; thereafter, members were allowed to buy land outright. Liberty Hall, a structure for social activities and schooling, was built cooperatively, as were their houses. The colony achieved notoriety via its anarchist newspaper, *Discontent: Mother of Progress,* and later, after *Discontent* had been closed down when the editors were arrested for publishing obscene material, it was replaced by *The Demonstrator.* The Mutual Home Association attracted colonists from a number of other colonies, including the **Ruskin Colony** and **Equality**, and visitors came from **Koreshan Unity** in Chicago and the **Roycrofters**. The colony received a great deal of criticism as a haven for radicals, especially after the turn of the century and the assassination of President William McKinley. Its always-limited cooperative base gradually withered away, and following World War I the Mutual Home Association became a typical rural community, being dissolved by court order in 1919.

HOME EMPLOYMENT CO-OPERATIVE COMPANY. Founded in 1894 by **William H. Bennett** (1855–1920), who had previously been a member of the **Friendship Community** of **Alcander Longley** (1832–1918), this association was located at Long Lane, Dallas County, Missouri. The approximately 20-member colony had a number of small industries, including a flourmill, a blacksmith shop, a shingle mill, and a cannery. The members also engaged in farming on their 180-acre tract. The eight-hour workday was standard, and the workers were paid by script or checks. Prospective members had to pay a $300 membership fee and owned their own household goods and clothing. The colony expired sometime between 1904 and 1906.

HOPEDALE COMMUNITY. Founded in 1842 by Adin Ballou (1803–1890) and patterned after **Fourierist** ideas, this joint-stock colony, also known as *Fraternal Community No. 1,* was located on 250 acres at Hopedale in the Town of Milford, Massachusetts, and capitalized at $4,000. It emerged in 1841 out of a group of Universalist church members at Mendon, Massachusetts, who believed in the brotherhood of man and the teachings of Christ and wished to put their Christianity to the test.

The 31 members of the group pledged to abstain from murder, hatred, lack of chastity, and liquor. They also opposed oaths, slavery, violence, war, and military service and refused to vote. Marriage was considered sacred, and divorce was allowed only for adultery. At Hopedale the members initially all lived in one house and sent their children to a common school, but individual households and individual ownership of land were adopted early in the group's tenure at the colony. Made up largely of liberal reformers, the colony enjoyed early success, expanding to 400 acres by 1845 and numbering 110 residents and 200 associates who supported them by 1852. In 1855 Hopedale established an offshoot at Union Grove in Minnesota, but it lasted only two years. As the colony became more business-oriented under the leadership of George and Ebenezer Draper, Ballou, believing the colony had lost its moral principles, withdrew from its affairs in 1862. In 1868 the community ended its independent existence when it merged with the Hopedale Parish, a Unitarian organization of which Ballou remained pastor until 1880.

HOREKILL. *See* PLOCKHOY, PIETER CORNELIUS.

HOUSE OF DAVID. This **Israelite** House of David was founded by "Queen Mary" (1862?–1953) and "King Benjamin" (1861–1927) Purnell east of the town of Benton Harbor in southwest Michigan for the gathering in of the elect 144,000. They ruled the colony autocratically until "King Benjamin's" death in 1927. Established in 1903 on the basis of Purnell's prediction of the coming of the millennium in 1905, the celibate colony numbered 500 by 1907 and close to 1,000 in the 1920s, some of the members coming from Australia and England. Their 1,000-acre land holdings included an auditorium, a cannery, a laundry, a coach factory, and an automobile house. They operated farms in the Benton Harbor area and also ran an amusement park and

Benton Harbor's streetcar company. After World War I they formed a baseball team of long-bearded members that barnstormed throughout North America and the world. They also had a barnstorming basketball team and a traveling band. But Jesus, "King Benjamin's" older brother, did not come to institute the **millennium** at the commune in 1916 as predicted, and the House of David was involved in a lawsuit in 1920 as a result of a break between the followers of Purnell and his detractors. Then in 1923 Purnell was charged with statutory rape for having seduced two minor sisters. The charges were true but were condoned by the members, who accepted his conduct as appropriate to his divine mission—although "Queen Mary" did not. After Benjamin's death in 1927, the colony was divided in 1930 between the followers of "Queen Mary," who set up the City of David Community in 1930, and a faction led by Thomas Dewhirst, which continued on as the House of David. Both movements continue to exist, although the membership of each is but a fraction of its former size.

HOUTEFF, VICTOR (1885–1955). Victor Houteff, a native of Bulgaria who immigrated to the United States in 1907, was the leader of a splinter group of Seventh-Day Adventists that broke off from the main body in 1934. The group called itself "the Shepherd's Rod" and, after 1942, the *Branch Davidians*. A convinced **millennialist**, Houteff believed that the Kingdom of David would soon be restored in Palestine. He also taught that his followers should live communally in preparation for the millennium. The group established itself on a 189-acre expanse of land west of Waco, Texas. They called the site *Mt. Carmel*. Here they grew much of their food, developed their own money system, operated a school, and held daily worship services. With the death of Victor Houteff in Waco in 1955, the group began to splinter despite the fact that his wife, Florence (1917–), then took over the colony. Thereafter the main group purchased property east of Waco. In that same year, Florence predicted a specific date in 1959 for the Establishment of the Kingdom of Palestine; when it failed to occur, most members left the colony.

In the meantime two leaders of one of the splinter groups, Benjamin and Lois Roden, had emerged, and when Florence left the colony the Rodens took over control of Mt. Carmel. However, Vernon Howell, in turn, seized control of the Waco community in 1988.

By this time Howell was calling himself "David Koresh," "David" signifying the Davidian monarchy to be set up with the millennium, and "Koresh," the Hebrew for "Cyrus," recalling the messianic biblical Persian king. The rule of David Koresh ended on April 19, 1993, when he and his followers died in a raid launched after a long siege by the Federal Bureau of Investigation, the rule of Victor and Florence Houteff being long forgotten in the controversy over Koresh's "Branch Davidians" and their fiery end.

HOWARD, EBENEZER (1850–1928). *See* GARDEN CITY.

HOWELL, VERNON (1960–1993). *See* BRANCH DAVIDIANS.

HOWELLS, WILLIAM DEAN (1837–1920). Howells, author of no less than 35 novels, including the familiar *The Rise of Silas Lapham* (1885) and *A Hazard of New Fortunes* (1890), was also a prominent literary critic, playwright, poet, and editor of the *Atlantic Monthly* and *Harper's* at the turn of the 20th century. In addition, Howells became a major—if passing—figure in American utopian literature with the publication of his popular romance *A Traveler from Altruria* (1893 serially, 1894 in book form) and its sequel *Through the Eye of the Needle* (1892–1893 serially, 1907 in book form), both quiet homilies on the devastation brought about by the new industrial-technological order. Having lived in a log cabin for a year in a communal settlement near Xenia, Ohio, in his youth as his family tried to convert a sawmill and a gristmill into a cooperative paper mill, Howells's reform instincts quickened toward the end of the 19th century as he observed the ethics of competitive industrialism and the transformation of American life during the Gilded Age. This is evident in his *The Rise of Silas Lapham,* where he questioned the optimism of the Gospel of Wealth, which argued that prosperity and financial success were somehow divinely related. By this time in his life, Howells had turned to social utopianism when he had associated with a group of Christian Socialists and had turned to the People's Party as an answer to the problems facing the American workers both rural and urban.

Howells's "Altruria" was an imaginary island in the Aegean Sea where altruism dominated both socially and governmentally. In *A Traveler from Altruria* an Altrurian man, Aristides Homos, journeys back from the future to visit the contemporary United States, and in its sequel, *Through the Eye of the Needle,* Homos returns to idyllic Altruria with Eveleth, his American bride. In both of these novels, Howells points out the gap between American ideals and the nation's harsh realities for the poor and unfortunate, emphasizing the superiority of the altruistic Altrurian way of life. Despite their lack of depth, both of these utopian novels gathered an impressive audience for Howells's ideas but resulted in no movement to implement them, as was the case with his contemporary **Edward Bellamy** (1850–1898) following the publication of his *Looking Backward.*

HUNT'S COLONY. *See* EQUALITY, COLONY OF.

HUNTSMAN, MASON T. *See* LORD'S FARM, THE.

HURON COLONY. This **Hutterite** colony, one of 16 Hutterite colonies established in South Dakota after 1874, was an offshoot of **Bon Homme** and was located in Huron in Beadle County, South Dakota. It was established in 1906, and in 1918 the site was sold off to a small *Dariusleut* group that came from **Spring Creek** near Lewiston in Montana via Canada, to settle there in 1920. The original Huron colonists resettled in Elie, Manitoba, Canada.

HUS, JAN (1372/1373–1415). *See* TABORITES.

HUTTERITE COLONIES IN THE UNITED STATES AND CANADA.

Name	Location	Years
Bon Homme Colony	South Dakota	1874–
Wolf Creek Colony	South Dakota	1875–1930
	Alberta	1930–
Elmspring Colony	South Dakota	1878–1929
Tripp Colony	South Dakota	1879–1884
Tidioute Colony	Pennsylvania	1884–1886
Jamesville Colony	South Dakota	1886–1918
	Alberta	1918–
Milltown Colony	South Dakota	1886–1907
Kutter Colony	South Dakota	1890–1918
	Alberta	1918–

Rockport Colony	South Dakota	1891–1934
	Alberta	1934–
Maxwell Colony	South Dakota	1900–1918
	Manitoba	1918–
New Elmspring Colony	South Dakota	1900–1918
	Alberta	1918–
Rosedale Colony	South Dakota	1901–1918
	Manitoba	1918–
Spink Colony	South Dakota	1905–1918
	Alberta	1918–
Beadle Colony	South Dakota	1905–1922
	Alberta	1922–
Huron Colony	South Dakota	1906–1918
	Manitoba	1918–
Richards Colony	South Dakota	1906–1918
	Alberta	1918–
Buffalo Colony	South Dakota	1907–1913
Milford Colony	South Dakota	1910–1918
	Alberta	1918–
Spring Creek Colony	Montana	1912–1919
	Alberta	1919–
Warren Range Colony	Montana	1913–1918
	Alberta	1918–
James Valley Colony	South Dakota	1913–1918
	Manitoba	1918–

HUTTERITES. This communal group originated within the **Anabaptists** of Germany in the 16th century. They were Protestants who believed in adult baptism, pacifism, the separation of church and state, and the primacy of individual conscience, all marks of the early centuries of Christianity, as they saw them. Suffering from persecution throughout western Europe and Russia, between 1874 and 1877 the entire Hutterite population, some 800 souls, moved to the United States. About 400 settled in the colonies, or *leuts* (German for "people"), of **Bon Homme**, **Wolf Creek**, and **Elmspring** in South Dakota; the remainder settled on individual homesteads in that state (where most became Mennonites and abandoned the Hutterite way of life). By 1917 Hutterite membership had grown to

1,700 and the number of *Bruderhofs* (dwelling places of brothers) had grown to 17.

Each *Bruderhof* is marked by communal dwellings and dining halls and a rejection of "worldly" distractions, although the Hutterites accept such modern laborsaving technologies as tractors and electrical devices. When a colony reaches 150 in number, it is split and a new colony is established, with lots being drawn over who will be members of the new community. Each colony is self-sufficient as far as possible regarding its food and personal necessities. The use of the German language, their strong religious beliefs regarding separation from the world, and their total community of goods hold the Hutterites together despite outside opposition, which arises from their refusal to support warfare and from their economically efficient agricultural operations, which tend to squeeze out traditional farmer-neighbors. As of 1980, there were 25,000 Hutterites in over 100 colonies in the upper Midwest and Canada, although splits over relations with competing **Bruderhof** colonies have been a continuing problem for them. Still, the Hutterites remain one of the fastest-growing communal groups in the United States and Canada.

HUXLEY, ALDOUS LEONARD (1894–1963). Huxley, the English novelist and **dystopian**, is probably one of the two best-known dystopians in the Western world (the other being **George Orwell**) largely due to his *Brave New World* (1932). Huxley turned from the utopianism of his mentor, **H. G. Wells** (1866–1946), to dystopianism largely from reading Zamyatin's *We* (1921), which clearly argued against Wells's one-world state. For Huxley, the modern worship of science and **scientism** can only lead to a society that is secular, crudely utilitarian, impersonal, drug-addictive, and rejective of the best of all past civilizations, giving no heed to governmental totalitarianism and its denial of human rights and dignity. He also foresaw the impact of the media and its ability to remove people from reality, with perception becoming reality. *Brave New World,* then, anticipated and warned against the creation of a "Brave New World" of big government, big media, and big business. However, in his last, more hopeful novel, *The Island* (1962), Huxley contended that a spiritual belief system can lead to an improved life for everyone.

– I –

ICARIA-CHELTENHAM. *See* CHELTENHAM.

ICARIA-CORNING. *See* CORNING.

ICARIA-SPERANZA. *See* SPERANZA.

ICARIANS. The first colony established according to the principles of **Etienne Cabet** (1788– 1856), the French utopian socialist who based his ideas on his novel *Voyage en Icarie* (Voyage to Icaria; 1839), was Icaria in Texas, established in 1848 with 88 persons. It failed in only three months, its Icarians moving on to **Nauvoo**, Illinois, in 1849. There the Icarians met with considerable success and were reported to have had 1,500 people in the colony, but they subsequently suffered a split. Some of the adherents moved to **Cheltenham**, a suburb of St. Louis, along with Cabet; others moved to **Corning**, Iowa, on 4,000 acres of land. Again, a split occurred. The conservatives within the Corning group formed the **New Icarian Community** in 1878 while the progressives formed **Jeune Icarie** (Young Icaria) that same year. Then a splinter group from Jeune Icarie split off and went to Cloverdale, California, and formed **Speranza** in 1881, which lasted only five years. Thus from their beginnings in Texas in 1848 until their demise in 1895, the various Icarian communities in the United States were marked by limited success and recurrent factionalism throughout their brief existence.

ICARIAN COMMUNITIES IN THE UNITED STATES.

Community	State	Years
Icaria (*see* **Icarians**)	Texas	1848–1849
Nauvoo	Illinois	1849–1859
Cheltenham	Missouri	1856–1864
Corning	Iowa	1860–1878
Jeune Icarie	Iowa	1879–1887
New Icarian Community	Iowa	1879–1895
Speranza	California	1881–1886

ILLINOIS COMMUNITIES. *See* APPENDIX.

I MONDI. This 1552 work (translated as The Worlds) by Anton Francesco Doni (1513–1574), the Italian Renaissance writer, journalist, critic, and popularizer of **Thomas More**'s *Utopia,* consists of a series of dialogues on seven imaginary worlds. The sixth is about the city of Mondo Savio, presented in the form of a dialogue between Savio, representing wisdom, and Pazzo, meaning folly. In Doni's imaginary utopian city, marriage has been abolished and free love has been instituted. This was a source of much controversy at the time of its publication. The city is designed like a star with a temple at the hub. The doors of the temple open onto 100 streets that reach to the gates of the city with a priest guarding each street. But in addition, the city includes many features common to utopian conceptions. For example, Doni's city features social equality and communal ownership of property. And in Doni's imaginary city, all the inhabitants live in simple houses and dress alike, and adequate food is available for all. Education consists of learning a skill or craft, and work is limited, allowing adequate time for leisure.

Doni did not provide for a governmental structure or a system of law enforcement since there would be no discord or crime in Mondo Savio, and there is no military because no state would attack the city since it contains no riches. Nor did he provide for organized religion. *I Mondi,* perhaps the first Italian book influenced by one in English, was very popular during the Italian Renaissance and served to keep alive the utopian tradition in the West.

IN DARKEST ENGLAND AND THE WAY OUT. See SALVATION ARMY FARM COLONIES.

INDIANA COMMUNITIES. *See* APPENDIX.

INDUSTRIAL FRATERNITY. *See* BERLIN HEIGHTS COMMUNITY.

INQUIRY INTO THE PRINCIPLES OF THE DISTRIBUTION OF WEALTH MOST CONDUCIVE TO HUMAN HAPPINESS. See THOMPSON, WILLIAM.

INSPIRATIONISTS. *See* AMANA SOCIETY.

INTEGRAL PHALANX. This **Fourierist** association was founded in 1845 by John S. Williams of Cincinnati in Butler County, Ohio, 23 miles north of the city on the Miami Canal. It contained 900 acres, 600 of which was farmland and the remainder of which was woodland. By the summer of that year, the **phalanx** had in operation a flourmill, a sawmill, a lathing factory, and a shingle-cutting machine, all driven by waterpower, and plans were being made to establish a newspaper as well as a lecture series on the "science" of this association. Despite the early statements of its founders that they would move with resolve and care, during August of that same summer the Integral Phalanx was merged with the 555-acre Sangamon Phalanx at Lick Creek in Sangamon County, Illinois, 14 miles southwest of Springfield. The secretary of the Sangamon Phalanx, reflecting on the failures of the Integral Phalanx, commented that those who made up the Integral Phalanx were "with us, but not of us" and were too willing to abandon the cause. The secretary also pointed out that families would stay separate for five years and that hired labor was being used, these arrangements being temporary and transitional until membership totaled 400 persons and the full principles of Fourier could be applied. Whatever the problems involved with the Sangamon Phalanx, no further record of its existence or of the Integral Phalanx can be found beyond 1846.

INTER-COMMUNITY EXCHANGE. *See* FELLOWSHIP OF INTENTIONAL COMMUNITIES.

INTERNATIONAL BIBLE STUDENTS. *See* JEHOVAH'S WITNESSES.

INVESTIGATING COMMUNITY. This community was formed near Cedar Vale, Chautauqua County, Kansas, in 1875 by **William Frey** (1839–1888), who withdrew from the **Progressive Community** because of the spiritualists in the commune and relocated his followers nearby. The secessionists, five adults and two children, all Russians, were given one third of the Progressives' land holdings. The commune soon dissolved, its few members joining another group of Russians in the **Cedarvale Community** nearby.

IOWA COMMUNITIES. *See* APPENDIX.

IOWA PIONEER PHALANX. This **Fourierist** experiment was organized at Watertown, New York, by Alanzo M. Watson, a Watertown lawyer, for the purpose of immigrating to the Iowa Territory to establish a **phalanx** there. Established in 1844 some nine miles west of Oskaloosa in Mahaska County, the community consisted of about 50 persons, mostly from Watertown. Within a year, all had left the phalanx to relocate on their own land.

IRON HEEL, THE. See LONDON, JACK.

ISAIAH, BOOK OF. This treasured book of the Old Testament, which inspired both Jewish and Christian believers to anticipate a more perfect world to come, contains "The Little **Apocalypse**" (24:1–27:13) in which the prophet speaks of the present world as doomed, Yahweh's magnificent victory, the Divine provision for the future, and ultimate redemption. Its final chapters describe "Yahweh's New People" (56:1–66:24), who witness God's judgment and redemption, the glory of God, and the new heavens and the new earth. It concludes with Mother Zion suckling her young, the gathering of the nations under the one God, and God's lasting reward for the virtuous and punishment for the wicked.

ISLAND, THE. This last novel of **Aldous Huxley** (1894–1963), published in 1962, continues his insistence on the insecurity of earthly happiness and the fragile position of any utopian island in the modern world. The rather convoluted plot is centered around one Will Farnaby, who deliberately shipwrecks his small boat on the "forbidden" South Seas island of Pala and there learns the story of this would-be perfect utopian society. The island and the Palanese way of life have a plethora of positive attributes, but Huxley brings out the persistent presence of evil in the form of the disease of cancer, his metaphor for the unchanging vulnerability of humans in time. The realization of this vulnerability, a spiritual insight, he argues, is essential for any society, no matter how perfect, to maintain itself. Spiritual values can at least make life tolerable in time.

ISLANDIA. This uncomplicated utopian novel, published in 1942, a decade after the author's death, describes an island in the South Seas. Penned by Austin Wright (1883–1931), a law professor at the University of California and the University of Pennsylvania, it portrays a simple agricultural society marked above all by brotherly love. It is important for the emphasis it places on the status of women on Islandia, women being the equals of males and enjoying a notable degree of sexual freedom. The island is seen through the eyes of John Lang, assigned to the island in 1907 as its first diplomatic consul, who soon learns upon his arrival of the two types of love practiced there. *Ania* is married love and is designed to produce a family; *apia* is sexual love based on physical attraction. Through his relationships with two island women, Dorna and Nattana, Lang comes to know the depth of each type of attraction between men and women. Three years later Lang returns to Boston and marries Gladys Hunter; they then move to Islandia. Here Gladys finds adjustment to Islandia's two modes of love very difficult but settles on *ania* in their new home. *Islandia* is important because of Wright's sensitive treatment of women and their emotions, a quality not found in the writing of most male novelists at that time.

ISLE OF FEMININE, THE. This 1893 **dystopian** novel by Charles Elliot Niswonger (1868–1918) is a parody on feminism that takes place on a Caribbean island ruled by asexual women. The narrator of the story is a New York stockbroker named Andy who is shipwrecked and finds himself on the remote Isle of Feminine. First concluding that he has arrived at a matriarchal island paradise, he soon finds out that here the men are dwarfed slaves, symbolically castrated and terrorized by a council of asexual virgins. The power of the women on the island hinges on their rejection of sexual intercourse, but the community is weakened when the virgins become attracted to the outsider. Andy meets Queen Diana, the immortal dictator of the isle, and persuades her to exchange her power, beauty, and immortality for eternal Protestant life. When Diana accepts and passionately embraces Andy, her face shrinks and is "made hideous by the wrinkles of three thousand years." The virgins attack Andy for destroying their queen, but he escapes and carries his favorite princess to safety on the old boat on which he reached the island from the doomed ship. As they enjoy their first passionate kiss, the Isle of Feminine disappears. Niswonger's novel stands as a powerful antifeminist warning to the people during a decade when women's rights and gender equality were becoming major issues in American life.

ISLES OF THE BLESSED. *See* BRAGMANS.

ISRAELITES, *or* **NEW HOUSE OF ISRAEL.** A vegetarian Canadian sect that followed the Mosaic Law known as the Israelites, or the "Flying Roll," in 1895 settled on a 144-acre tract of donated land in Polk County in eastern Texas in 1895, this site to be their Promised Land. The group included **Benjamin Purnell** (1861–1927), who would later found the **House of David.** They added some 75 local families sometime around the turn of the century. The male members sported long hair and beards. The members built a church they called the New House of Israel. But when their "high priest," "Prince" Michael Mills, died, the families began moving away, and the colony was totally abandoned by 1920. Another Texas religious group, the **Commonwealth Colony of Israel** (1899–1902) of Mason County northwest of San Antonio, may or may not have been part of the same movement.

IT CAN'T HAPPEN HERE. Sinclair Lewis (1885–1951), the author of such successful novels as *Main Street* (1920), *Babbitt* (1922), *Arrowsmith* (1925), and *Elmer Gantry* (1927) and a two-month resident at the utopian community Helicon Hall in 1906, hurriedly wrote *It Can't Happen Here* (1935) in reaction to the rise of Adolf Hitler in Germany and the popular demagogue Huey Long in the United States as a warning against totalitarianism in the guise of utopian promises to lift the nation out of its depression and malaise. It tells the story of the rise to power of Senator Buzz Windrip with his "15 Points of Victory," his subsequent election to the presidency, and his dismantling of the nation's democracy and its replacement by a dictatorship known as Carpo. All were made possible by the rise of big business, widespread cultural mediocrity, and the gullibility of the American people when promised schemes that would end their suffering and their feelings of frustration and helplessness. More of a warning against totalitarianism than a **dystopian** novel in the usual sense, *It Can't Happen Here* nevertheless falls well within the contours of antiutopian literature designed to bring readers to the reality of the human condition when confronted with unrealizable utopian promises of security and peace.

– J –

JAMES VALLEY COLONY. This **Hutterite** colony, a continuation of the **Buffalo Colony** formed in 1913, was located at James Valley Junction in Beadle County in eastern South Dakota. It was established in 1913 and continued in existence until 1918 when it moved to Elie, Manitoba.

JAMESVILLE COLONY. Located in Utica, Yankton County, in southeastern South Dakota, the Jamesville Colony was the second branch-off from the **Hutterite Wolf Creek Colony** of neighboring Hutchinson County. Founded in 1886, the colony suffered physical violence at the hands of its neighbors in 1918 during World War I when its members refused to buy Liberty Bonds. When its members also failed to obtain conscientious objector status, the colony moved to Alberta, Canada, that same year.

JAMES, WILLIAM (1842–1910). The Harvard psychologist and philosopher William James played a decisive though indirect role in the emergence of utopianism in American life insofar as he is the father of pragmatism, that is, the rejection of the ideas of "common-sense" philosophy in favor of an expedient approach to truth. The common-sense philosophers argued that individuals have the ability to arrive at reliable and fixed truth in politics, economics, and ethics through the natural faculty of common sense and reason. This philosophy had dominated American thought until James's time. Instead, pragmatism argued that there are no fixed absolute truths in an evolving society and that ideas and theories must be judged only in terms of their practical results. Pragmatism was later advanced by the writings of **John Dewey** (1959–1952), opening the way to a belief not only that society is evolving but also that truth is evolving and variable in time according to conditions and individual perceptions. This led to further acceptance of individual judgment and to social and political interventionism as practical means of attaining perfection or near perfection in time.

JANSSON, ERIK (1808–1850). This founder and temporal and spiritual ruler of the **Bishop Hill Colony** in Illinois was born of a peasant family in Sweden. Undergoing religious conversion at the age of 22, Jansson began to lead religious revivals, breaking with the Church of

Sweden when in 1840 he began to preach a doctrine of perfectionism without sin. By 1844 he had formed a congregation of followers, some of its members considering him to be a second St. Paul. His followers, called *"Janssonists,"* engaged in public book burnings to emphasize the Bible as the centerpiece of the Christian religion. These activities landed Jansson in jail for supporting such activities. The following year his followers forced his release and he fled to New York, 1,200 Janssonists following him between 1846 and 1849, 700 of whom joined him in forming the pietist community at Bishop Hill. In 1850 he blocked the marriage of his female cousin to John Root, an apostate, by demanding that she return to the colony. Root subsequently pressed charges against Jansson, sought him out at the courthouse in Cambridge, Illinois, and shot him to death.

JAPANESE UTOPIAS. Japanese culture has been and continues to be dominated by religious traditions, especially Shintoism, and by spiritual cooperation with nature rather than any scheme of life to be imposed upon nature (especially any secular scheme). In addition, Japan was opened to the West and Western ideas only in the 1850s. As a result, utopianism has not struck deep roots in that country. Nevertheless, it would appear that neo-**Confucian** concepts from China did have some effect on Japanese thought during the Tokugawa period (1615–1867). For example, Ogyu Sorai (1666–1728) argued that the *Tao,* the ideal way of life, must be in harmony with nature. And Hiraga Gennai (1728–1779), who had learned Western ideas from the Dutch merchants at Nagasaki, produced a precursor to Japanese utopias in his *Furyu Shidoken den* (The Dashing Life of Shidoken; 1763), an imaginary travel novel describing distant lands and, as such, a critique of Japanese society. Ando Shoeki (1701–1758) attacked the feudal caste system in his *Shizen shin'eido,* one chapter of the work outlining an ideal society, the *shizensei,* in which humans live in harmony with nature and in which class divisions and discord between persons have disappeared.

Japanese utopianism increased during the Meiji period (1868–1912) when the emperor encouraged contact with the West. During this period, a translation of an 1865 Dutch utopian novel by Pieter Harting (1812–1885), *The Year 2065,* appeared; two indigenous utopias by Takase Naokuni and Suehiro Shigeyasu were published in 1883 and 1886 respectively; a translation of **Thomas More**'s *Utopia* appeared in 1882; and Hattori Sei'chi wrote three popular utopian works between

1884 and 1887. In the 20th century, the works of the reformer and utopianist Kagawa Toyohiko (1888–1960), novelist and editor, had a major influence on Japanese thought, although the 1920s witnessed the military government attempting to repress utopian (as well as Christian) works in Japan. Some utopian-futurist thought has emerged in Japan in the post–World War II period, although its emphasis has been on spiritual regeneration rather than on social-economic-political reform to create a better society. It remains unclear whether or not Japan's continued contact with the West and Western ideas will have a major impact on that country. *See also* YAMAGISHI-KAI.

JASPER COLONY (*or* JASPIS KOLONIE). Organized by 20 German Swedenborgians of St. Louis in 1851, most of whom had fled Germany after the Revolutions of 1848, this communal colony of 1,000 acres was located at Jasper in Iowa County in eastern Iowa. Communalism, however, was abandoned in 1853 as the members opted for private ownership of property.

JEFFERSON COUNTY ASSOCIATION (*or* PHALANX). Located in Jefferson County, New York, on the eastern shore of Lake Ontario near the city of Watertown, this **Fourierist** association (also known as the Jefferson County Industrial Association) was formed in 1843 with 400 members and 1,200 acres of land. It lasted only about 12 months. It apparently failed from internal disagreements, a lack of organization and dedication to Fourierist principles, and inadequate capital to sustain its subscribers during its formative period. These were problems typical of the dozens of Fourierist **phalanxes** in the East and Midwest in the 1840s.

JEHOVAH'S WITNESSES. This religious group was born when an American named Charles Taze Russell (1852–1916) became convinced that Jesus would return in 1874. He spelled out his vision in a pamphlet entitled *The Object and Manner of Our Lord's Return,* which set off a **millennial** movement that came to be known as the Jehovah's Witnesses or, earlier, as Russellites, Millennial Dawn People, and International Bible Students. Five years later, in 1879, Pastor Russell began the publication of a magazine called *The Watchtower and Herald of Christ's Presence.* The next year, he organized the first formal group of followers in Pittsburgh and sent J. C. Sunderlin to England to organize the religion there. Russell taught that his followers, or "witnesses," were the nucleus of the blessed Kingdom of God that would soon be established on earth after Armageddon and Christ's Second Coming.

Following the death of Russell in 1916, Joseph F. Rutherford became president of the Witnesses. Accepting completely the teachings of God as found in the Bible and believing in a "triple alliance" of Satan's allies (the false teachings of the churches, the tyranny of human governments, and oppression by big business), the Witnesses refuse to salute the flag, bear arms in war, or participate in political affairs. They believe that the "triple alliance" must be destroyed at Armageddon before the new and perfect world can be born. During the 20th century, the Jehovah's Witnesses have become one of the best-known **millennial** sects worldwide with more than 4 million adherents in 211 countries (about 892,000 in the United States) and over 66,000 congregations in the world (over 9,000 in the United States) in the 1990s. Their creed and their publication *The Watchtower,* with a circulation of over 16 million, manage to keep the centuries-old millennial dream alive in the world.

JERONIMO DE MENDIETA (1525–1604). Jeronimo de Mendieta was a Spanish Franciscan very familiar with the prophecies of the three stages of **Joachim of Fiore** (1135–1202). Working in Mexico in the latter half of the 16th century, he viewed himself as a representative of the Spaniards, the people chosen by God to convert all races to Christ. Spain's *conquistadores* and armies were, as he saw it, sent to the New World as hosts of the new Israel, her rulers as the missionary-kings of the universal divine monarchy to come with the establishment of the New Jerusalem. Here all would live in peace and earthly poverty until the **millennium** ended with the Last Judgment. The New World was the City of God, in Jeronimo's view, with the native Indians the descendants of the 10 lost tribes of Israel. Jeronimo visualized the Indians he encountered as meek, gentle, uncorrupted, and instinctively practicing Christian virtues. These, combined with their natural reason, made them "soft wax" to be molded by proper discipline and education into perfected, angelic, and sinless Christians. Mendieta was but one of a number of Christian humanists of the Renaissance who clung to the idea of a millennial utopia to be established on earth according to the Scriptures.

JERUSALEM COLONY. Also known as the Society of Universal Friends, this colony was established in Yates County in the Finger Lakes region of upstate New York, by the disciples of Jemima Wilkinson (1752–1819). Convinced in 1788 that she had died of fever and had been reborn to preach a new gospel, the "Public Universal Friend," she traveled throughout New England preaching repentance and the avoidance of evil to all who would listen. During that same year, her followers established a celibate colony at Seneca Lake they called Jerusalem; in 1780 she joined them there. Its members, formerly either Quakers or New Light Baptists, numbered 260 in 1790. Wilkinson remained at Jerusalem until her death in 1819, receiving visions and dreams that she communicated to her followers. Thereafter the community gradually declined, but some members stayed on until 1863.

JEUNE ICARIE. Established in 1879 by the progressive **Icarians** who had broken off from the **Corning** colony the year before, Jeune Icarie (1879–1887) was set up on part of the site of the old colony in Adams County, Iowa. (The nonprogressives established the **New Icarian Community** nearby.) Composed of some 35 Icarians, mostly women and children, the members of Jeune Icarie adopted a new constitution abolishing the office of president and extending the suffrage to women. Despite the fact that new members joined the group and new industries were started, frequent withdrawals led to a weakening of Jeune Icarie and the eventual demise of the colony. Some of those who withdrew set up a new colony in 1881 called *Speranza* three miles south of Cloverdale in Sonoma County, California. Within five years, this new Icarian colony had also failed.

JEWISH COMMUNITIES.

Name	Location	Years
Sicily Island Community	Louisiana	1881–1883
Painted Woods	North Dakota	1882–1887
Beersheba Colony	Kansas	1882–1885
Bethlehem Yehudah	South Dakota	1882–1885
Cremieux Colony	South Dakota	1882–1885
Rosenhayn	New Jersey	1882–1889
Alliance Colony	New Jersey	1882–1908
New Odessa	Oregon	1883–1887
Temple of the Gospel of the Kingdom	Virginia & New York	1900–1920s

pt 4pt 4pt 4pt 4pt 4ght

New Jerusalem	Western Australia	?–1913
Ferrer Colony	New Jersey	1915–1946
Sunrise Community	New Jersey	1933–1936
Sunrise Community	Michigan	1933–1936

JOACHIM OF FIORE (1135–1202). Most prominent among the **Free Spiritists** of the 12th century was a former Cistercian abbot from Calabria named Joachim of Fiore who fled to that town in the "toe" of Italy. Here he established a breakaway order of monks at San Giovanni in 1196, his new order dedicated to following a stringent monastic rule. Drawing on his study of the Old and New Testaments, Joachim in his *Concordance of the Old and New Testaments* envisioned a utopia evolving on earth in time. As Joachim perceived human history, humankind was moving through three stages of progress corresponding to the three persons of the Blessed Trinity, each stage divided into seven periods named after persons in sacred history. The first stage was that of the Reign of the Father in which humankind was under the law; it was marked by submission, suffering, and fear. The second was the Reign of the Son in which humankind was under grace; this stage was marked by obedience, action, and faith.

The third stage, now dawning on the world, was the Reign of the Holy Ghost in which humankind received more ample grace; it was marked by freedom, contemplation, and love. During this third stage, the stage of the Heavenly Kingdom, the Christian Church was to be replaced in 1260 after a brief reign of the **Antichrist**. In this stage, too, love would rule the earth as all persons are absorbed into the One, the Old and New Testaments to be disposed of as obsolete. This third stage was held to be transitional by Joachim, with the Second Coming and the Judgment Day being postponed indefinitely. Although Joachim's teachings of the three stages were condemned by the Lateran Council of 1215 as heretical, his doctrines, especially his concept of history as three ascending stages leading to a **millennium** of peace and unity with God, represented a crucial point in the emergence of utopian millennialism and remained a powerful attraction in the late Middle Ages and during the centuries that followed.

JOHN OF LEYDEN (ca. 1509–1536). *See* ANABAPTISTS.

JONES, ALICE ILGENFRITZ (1846–1906). *See UNVEILING A PARALLEL.*

JONES, JAMES WARREN (1931–1978). James Warren (Jim) Jones, the founder and leader of the People's Temple, was born in Lynn, Indiana; attended local schools; and married Marceline Baldwin in 1949. The couple raised eight children, seven of whom were adopted. In 1953 he founded the Christian Assembly of God Church in Indianapolis, renaming it the People's Temple Full Gospel Church a decade later. In the meantime, in 1961, he received a degree in education from Butler University and worked for Belo Horizonte, a missionary project in Brazil, making a visit to Guyana in 1962–1963. In 1964, he was ordained in the Christian Church (Disciples of Christ). Announcing the following year that the world would perish in an **apocalyptic** nuclear war in 1967, he convinced 70 families to move with him to Ukiah, California, north of San Francisco. Then in 1971 he moved the People's Temple to the Fillmore district of San Francisco. Preaching a philosophical mix of Marxism, **millennialism**, faith healing, social protest, and evangelism to the poor, inner-city blacks of the city and to white radicals, the charismatic Jones soon had a congregation of about 5,000 members who relinquished all their goods to the Temple and permitted their sex lives to be altered by fiat of their leader. Jones also became an important political personage in San Francisco as chair of the city's housing authority.

By this time, Jones had rejected the Christian God and now presented himself as the living God of Apostolic Socialism, Savior, and Redeemer with the power to heal and resurrect the dead. In 1974 he took a lease on 27,000 acres of land in northern Guyana, and three years later made plans to build a model community there. In 1977 a large number of his followers (about 75 percent of them black) moved to Guyana, where his rural utopia carved out of the jungle named Jonestown was located. Despite the backing of many important political figures in California and the nation, complaints of brutalities and sexual irregularities by relatives of Jonestown members convinced California Congressman Leo Ryan to visit the site. Just prior to their departure from Jonestown, Ryan and most of his party were murdered by Jones's armed guards. Within hours, on November 18, 1978, on orders from Jones (now clearly paranoid, especially regarding the U.S. government), 913 members of Jonestown, including Jones, committed suicide by drinking cyanide-laced punch (having practiced the rite in mock suicide drills), having been convinced by Jones that they were about to be attacked by outsiders and would by their deaths enter into a better life beyond. Those who refused were shot.

JORDAN, CLARENCE (1912–1969). *See* KOINONIA FARM.

JUDAS ROSE, THE. See ELGIN, SUZETTE.

JUDD, SYLVESTER (1813–1853). A disciple of **Ralph Waldo Emerson**, Sylvester Judd was the author of a utopian novel, *Margaret, a Tale of the Real, Blight and Bloom,* published in 1845. It was a reflection of the ideas found in **Transcendentalism** and argued that any transformation of earth into heaven could occur only when people recognized their Christian belief in the worth of the self, the idea of God as punisher of sin being abandoned. In the novel, Margaret, impoverished and unlettered, intuitively comes to the knowledge of love and leads her community of Livingston toward a utopian society because love in practice allows humans to organize and create a more perfect society of ease and comfort.

JUDGE, WILLIAM Q. (1851–1896). Irish-born William Q. Judge at age 24 was one of the founders of the Theosophical Society in New York City in 1875, along with **Helena Petrovna Blavatsky** (1820–1891) and **Henry S. Olcott** (1832–1907). After two notable business failures in Latin America, he journeyed to the Theosophical headquarters at Adyar in India in 1884 but remained only a short time before returning to the United States. Resuming his law practice, Judge reorganized the **Theosophists** into The Aryan Theosophical Society of New York and in 1886 became the editor of *The Path* magazine, later to become the official organ of the American Section of the Theosophical Society. During that same year he was elected as general secretary and treasurer of the American Section, thereby becoming the chief spokesman for the Theosophy movement in the United States. After Blavatsky's death in 1891, Judge and **Annie Besant** (1847–1933) headed the American movement, Judge assuming a prominent speaking role on behalf of the Society not only in the United States but also in Europe. During these years before his death in 1896, he also converted **Katherine Tingley** (1847–1929) to Theosophy. She became the leading Theosophist of her day and the founder of the **Point Loma** community.

– K –

K'ANG, YU-WEI (1858–1927). *See GREAT EQUALITY, THE.*

KANSAS COMMUNITIES. *See* APPENDIX.

KANSAS CO-OPERATIVE FARM, *or* **SILKVILLE.** *See* BOISS-IERE, ERNEST VALETON de.

KANT, IMMANUEL (1724–1804). One of the most important propagators of the idea that utopia can be reached through evolving reason was Immanuel Kant. This Königsberg University professor of logic and metaphysics, father of German idealism and the moral imperative, and important figure of the Enlightenment penned *The Critique of Pure Reason* (1781) to spell out his notion of idealism. Idealism to Kant meant that Truth can be arrived at only by examining the ways in which ideas are formed in the mind. Truth can be acquired not just by information revealed through the senses but also by mental concepts such as time and space, these being nonsensory, nonsupernatural, and located entirely in the human mind. Thus the basic questions of life— Does God exist? Is there life beyond the grave? Do humans have free will?—are not answerable by reason alone. Kant, therefore, concluded that God's existence, the immortality of the soul, and human free will cannot be demonstrated because they are beyond rational proof.

But Kant was also a utopian, as is revealed by his speculations regarding the history of the world. As he examined the *telos* (end) of human history, he concluded that it was the development of human reason that enabled people to know and dominate the physical world and human passions and to fashion an ethical society in which moral imperatives are honored and obeyed and in which evil is thereby repressed. Reasoning that this is impossible given humans' incomplete mental development, Kant argued that humanity's full development will be realized only in the distant future after many trials and hardships, these afflictions arising out of the conflict between the desires of flawed individuals and the greater common good. Thus Kant, although usually not included in the catalog of utopians, is clearly among the adherents of intellectual utopianism arising out of the Enlightenment and bequeathing to the modern world its faith in eventual if not immediate perfection on earth in time.

KARP, DAVID (1922–1999). Karp, a novelist, screenwriter, and television producer and writer, was born in New York City the son of Russian Jewish immigrants. He began writing while still in his teens and continued through his education at City College of New York. Among his serious novels is his first, the **dystopian** *One* (1953). Often compared to **George Orwell**'s *Nineteen Eighty-Four* and described by one reviewer as "chilling and as full of warning as any recent volume," it tells the story of a man's struggle against the obliteration of his identity by a totalitarian state that does not permit nonconformity to its dictates.

KAWEAH COOPERATIVE COMMONWEALTH. This colony was established in 1885 by James J. Martin and Burnette Haskell, two labor leaders of the International Workingmen's Association in San Francisco, near Visalia in northeastern Tulare County, California. As socialists, the men were inspired by **Laurence Gronlund**'s book *The Cooperative Commonwealth* (1884), a treatise that attempted to apply the writings of **Karl Marx** to American life. They and their followers formed the Cooperative Land Purchase and Colonization Association of California, and in 1885 some 53 of them, taking advantage of the Timber Act of 1878 and the Homestead Act of 1862, went to the Visalia land office and claimed 600 acres in the newly opened Sequoia Forest area. They named their colony Kaweah after the river that ran through the property.

During the next six years, between 150 and 400 persons were in residence at Kaweah. Membership in the community required a $500 payment, and a time-check system was established for work done in the community. Socialists from across the country supported the venture without taking up residence by paying a membership fee. Living conditions were somewhat primitive for the families living there, but classes were organized and social functions were held. Naming the larger sequoias after famous socialists, the men spent much of their time constructing a road into the timber forests. In 1890 the federal government challenged the colonists' right to the land. Then, the following year, about half of the residents protested against the time-check system of pay and took possession of the land. Kaweah ended in 1892 amid legal disagreements over ownership of the land and the government's charges that the colonists had used the mails illegally. By that time, most of the colonists had simply left Kaweah. The lands of the now-defunct colony became part of Sequoia National Park.

KEIL, WILLIAM (1812–1877). A native of Austria who immigrated to the United States in 1831, Keil worked as a tailor in New York City before turning to medicine. Although he had no medical education, through his self-education in chemistry he concocted exotic medicines and developed a sizeable practice. Abandoning the Methodist church, he formed a religious sect based on his own belief that he was one of the witnesses mentioned in the **Apocalypse**. Then in 1844 he and his German American followers established Beth El (or Bethel), named after the biblical city, a 2,560-acre Christian community located in northeastern Missouri with Keil as its paternalistic, benevolent dictator.

Beth El had no clear religious or social tenets other than common ownership of property because Keil refused to adopt any theories, believing that living by the Bible would spontaneously result in the members living communally. By the early 1850s, the now 4,000-acre colony had grown to 1,000 members and was enjoying prosperity based on its agriculture and various other enterprises. Single, elderly, and infirm members lived communally. In 1853 certain members of Beth El traveled to Oregon and chose land on the Willapa River in the Washington Territory as their new home. Two years later, Keil followed with half of the Bethel members. Dissatisfied with the chosen location in the Washington Territory, he moved his followers to the Willamette Valley in Oregon and named the new settlement *Aurora* after his daughter. The colony prospered and eventually encompassed 23,000 acres of prime land. Keil remained a force at Aurora until 1872, when he was compelled by the members to relinquish the colony's lands to individual owners. After his death in 1877 no new leader emerged, and Beth El was dissolved in 1880 with its property being divided among the 175 to 200 members who remained. Aurora was dissolved in 1881.

KELLOGG, DR. JOHN HARVEY (1852–1943). *See* BEILHART, JACOB.

KELLY, HARRY (ca. 1871–1953). A printer by trade and wanderer by inclination, Harry Kelly was a radical anarchist who, along with Leonard Abbott and **Joseph Cohen** (1878–1953), was one of the **Ferrer Colony**'s first organizers in 1915. In 1925 he founded the Mohegan Colony at Lake Mohegan, New York, and the Mount Airy Colony at Harmon, New York.

KELPIUS, JOHANN (1673–1708). Born in Germany and recipient of a doctor of philosophy degree at the University at Altdorf, Kelpius became a follower of Johann Zimmerman, the Württemberg mathematician who made plans to lead 16 families to Pennsylvania to separate them from the confused life they were experiencing in Germany. With Zimmerman's death just prior to their departure to the United States, 20-year-old Kelpius assumed the leadership of the group. Upon their arrival in Pennsylvania, the mystical, pietistic group established a colony, The Society of the Woman in the Wilderness (named after a person in the **Apocalypse** who was to announce the **millennium**), on 175 acres at Coxsackie, on Wissahickon Creek near Germantown. There the 40 members erected a central building for religious services and schooling, although they lived in separate cell-like rooms. Kelpius lived in a small cave where he read and contemplated, hoping to unite all German sects in Pennsylvania into one Christian church. They called their neighbors to repentance in view of the coming millennium in 1694 and to seek God in the wilderness as they had done. Although the Woman in the Wilderness Community attracted a number of converts, marriages and defections led to its weakening, and it declined rapidly after Kelpius's death in 1708.

KENDAL COMMUNITY. This temporarily successful **Owenite community** (its official title was The Friendly Association for Mutual Interests) was founded on over 2,000 acres in June 1826 in Kendal, now within the city limits of Massillon, near Canton in Stark County in northeastern Ohio. Its purchase price was $20,000. Its numbers reached some 150, mostly neighborhood farmers and mechanics, and a woolen factory was built and put into operation. But the community was plagued by indebtedness; its members were attacked by a fever the following summer, seven heads of families becoming victims; and its leaders abandoned the project. Accordingly, the experiment was officially disbanded on January 3, 1829, its members losing their investment in the Kendal Community.

KENTUCKY COMMUNITIES. *See* APPENDIX.

KIANTONE COMMUNITY. *See* DOMAIN.

KIBBUTZ MOVEMENT. The kibbutz agricultural communal movement originated in Israel in 1909, even before the Balfour Declaration of 1917 by which Britain pledged to support a Jewish national homeland there, in an attempt to deal with the plight of refugees entering the country, the modern-day problems of alienated workers, and the relationship between individuals and the common good. The *kibbutz* ("gathering" or "group" in Hebrew; plural, *kibbutzim*) sought to alleviate these problems through decentralized authority, mutual cooperation, and individual initiative and creativity. In the early kibbutzim there was no private wealth, and each kibbutz was responsible for the needs of its members.

The creation of the kibbutzim was a part of Zionism, a movement stretching back to ancient times and the Davidic monarchy with its capital in Jerusalem. In postexilic literature, Zionism attached itself to the Land of Israel, the "holy land" promised to the ancient Israelites and their descendents. It became a special unifying religious symbol to Jews living outside Palestine after the Babylonian exile and the Muslim conquests in the seventh century. Zionism continued to exist during the Middle Ages with an emphasis in some, but not all, of the body of Hebraic literature on the coming of the Messiah and his primary task of gathering all Jews in Palestine. By the end of the 19th century, partially fueled by European anti-Semitism, especially in Russia, traditional messianism had fused with advanced secular nationalism to create the modern Zionist movement and, with it, a renewed interest in communal, agricultural societies. After the creation of Israel in 1948, young, religious Zionists saw the establishment of this state as the fulfillment of traditional Jewish messianism, adding a strong religious dynamic to the growing movement.

There were originally three types of cooperative agricultural societies created in Israel: the *kibbutz* was a settlement in which property was owned collectively by the members and was worked with greater cooperation than in the *moshav ovdim*; the *moshav ovdim* ("labor settlement") was a settlement in which the land was owned by the Jewish National Fund (established in 1901 as part of the World Zionist Organization to purchase land in Palestine) but each family retained the income from the land it worked; and the *moshav shittufi* ("communal settlement") communities provided cooperative work but individual ownership.

Most kibbutzim were marked by children living together in a dormitory away from their parents during their formative years and being schooled together, this arrangement designed to build a closer relationship between themselves than with their families; families having very few worldly possessions, other necessities being provided by the kibbutz; all members of the kibbutz eating together in common dining rooms with the cooking done communally; joint decision making regarding specific job assignments within the kibbutz decided by weekly general meetings of the members, these tasks being periodically rotated; and a democratic choice of the leaders of various committees, these posts being rotated every year or two. The other forms of communal living, the *moshav ovdim* and the *moshav shittufi,* were marked by less communal life and a greater emphasis on the family structure. There were also federations formed among the member villages beginning in 1927. These offered financial assistance to the individual kibbutzim as well as technical advice; central purchasing and marketing services; industrial production; courses in technology, agriculture, and kibbutz management; and federation-wide choirs and orchestras and adult education courses for interested members.

Between 1948 (the year in which Israel was declared to be an independent state) and 1954, 227 kibbutzim made up of 76,000 participants were established, most along socialist, but non-Marxist, lines. By 1960 the numbers had grown to 239 kibbutzim and 176,000 participants. In 2002 the numbers stood at 268 kibbutzim and 117,300 members, some kibbutzim numbering less than 100 people, others having a membership of over 1,000. Yet there are clear signs that major changes are taking place within these communities. The average age of their members is increasing, the concept of total equality within the kibbutzim is almost extinct and differential wage systems have been adopted, workers have the right to refuse to undertake certain tasks, rotation of jobs has come to a virtual end, members are allowed to work off the kibbutz, the industries run by the kibbutzim have a workforce that consists of 66.7 percent nonkibbutzim laborers, only 15 percent of the members work in agriculture, and children are being raised by their parents and live at home.

Clearly, the kibbutz movement is being challenged and eclipsed by Israel's development as a nation under Western influences, specifically by centralization replacing decentralization and class consciousness replacing nonclass outlooks and by the nation's moves toward industrialization and exporting that began in the 1960s and continues to the present time. Accordingly, the kibbutzim since the 1990s have been fading from a central position in Israel's social, economic, and political life and in the process are losing their original utopian characteristics. Still, although never conceived theoretically as utopian, the kibbutz movement can still be credited as being one of the most successful and longest-lived communal experiments of the 20th century.

KINDER LOU. This colony was established in 1900 in Lowndes County, Georgia, by Ruskinites who realized that the **Ruskin Colony** in Ware County was not located on a healthy site. They, therefore, established their own Ruskin-type colony on a communal basis. However, when they obtained employment in the local lumbering industry, they abandoned the idea of formalizing a cooperative colony. As a communal enterprise, it ended in 1902.

KING, WILLIAM (1812–?). Founder of the **Elgin Association**, William King was born in Ireland and after attending the University of Glasgow came to the United States in 1834, where he became rector of an academy in Louisiana. He returned to Scotland in 1843 to study theology and, after the death of his wife and child the next year, completed his studies and journeyed to Canada as a missionary for the Free Presbyterian Church of Scotland. In 1848 he freed his slaves and moved them to Canada, where he established the Elgin Association in 1849 on 4,300 acres. It was the most successful black colonization effort in the antebellum period, at its height totaling 1,000 persons. King's plan was to make Canadian blacks self-sufficient and landowners. Despite racial prejudice by Canadians who opposed black settlement, Elgin lasted until 1873, 70 former members returning to the United States that year. *See also* BLACK UTOPIAS.

"KINGDOM OF HEAVEN COLONY." *See* DAVIESITE KINGDOM OF HEAVEN.

KINGDOM OF KRONUS, *or* **CRONUS.** *See* COCKAYGNE, LAND OF; GOLDEN AGE, MYTH OF THE.

KINGDOM OF MATTHIAS. *See* MATTHEWS, ROBERT.

KINGDOM OF ST. JAMES. *See* BEAVER ISLAND COLONY.

KINKADE, KATHLEEN (1931–). *See* TWIN OAKS COMMUNITY.

KIRKLAND COMMUNITY. Founded in 1830 by Sidney Rignon in Lake County in northeastern Ohio as an attempt to restore the primitive Christian church based on common ownership of property, Kirkland was initially made up of some 100 individuals. But in the fall of that year, the members of the community were visited by four young **Mormons** and subsequently adopted Mormonism. In 1831 Joseph Smith (1805–1844) moved to Kirkland, where he established the church's headquarters. Following a revelation experienced by Smith that same year, the communal holding of goods came to an end, although the Mormons remained at Kirkland until 1835.

KOESTLER, ARTHUR (1905–1983). Hungarian-born novelist Arthur Koestler rose to immediate fame with the publication of his **dystopian** novel *Darkness at Noon* in 1940. A dedicated Communist in his early years, Koestler became thoroughly disillusioned with Josef Stalin and the totalitarian Soviet state during the Moscow Trials of 1938, in which many Bolshevik revolutionaries were put to death. Often compared to **George Orwell**'s *Nineteen Eighty-Four*, *Darkness at Noon* illustrates through the story of its main character, Rubashov, how men break down others by prolonged interrogation, sleep deprivation, refusal of medical treatment, and torture. Although Koestler concentrated less on political writing beginning in the 1950s, his *Darkness at Noon* remains his best-known work.

KOINONIA FARM. Founded near Americus in Sumter County, Georgia, in 1942 as an experimental interracial commune by Clarence Jordan (1912–1969), a Georgian with a doctorate from a Baptist seminary, Koinonia Farm exists to this day. Jordan believed that the gospel of Jesus was meant to be lived whatever its demands. He also believed that blacks had to be educated in modern agricultural techniques. The members of the commune were given homes and tools with which to farm, and the goods produced were marketed cooperatively. Proceeds went into a common treasury, from which the members could draw to care for their needs. Any profits went into a "Fund for Humanity" to finance a number of self-help projects. Hostility soon developed toward the integrated project. It became the victim of violence and a boycott of its products in 1956 when Jordan supported two black students attempting to enroll in a white state college. During 1956 and 1957, the violence escalated to the point where not only was property destroyed but also shootings at persons and property occurred. With the help of northern supporters and with courage and determination by the members of Koinonia, the colony managed to survive despite continued problems and Jordan's death in 1969. Its interest-free mortgages and homebuilding projects for the homeless served as a prototype for Habitat for Humanity under the leadership of Millard Fuller, a member of Koinonia Farm. Koinonia Farm must not be confused with Koinonia near Baltimore, Maryland, which moved away from its original 1950s communal lifestyle in the 1960s to concentrate on education on vital issues of the day and whose property was sold in 1985.

KORESHAN UNITY. This movement was founded as a utopian community in Chicago by a visionary doctor, Cyrus R. Teed (1839–1908), in 1888. Teed rechristened himself "Koresh" (Hebrew for Cyrus) in 1894 and outlined his community philosophy, called Koreshanty. According to Koreshanty, an astronomical and religious system (called cellular cosmology) by which persons should live, the earth is a hollow sphere with humans living inside it with their feet pointing outward from the center. Koreshanty also incorporated celibacy, reincarnation, communism, and a belief in Teed's visionary leadership. Gathering a number of followers, Teed decided to establish his New Jerusalem at Estero, Florida, a few miles south of Fort Myers. The group migrated there in 1894 and continued to grow. At one time, Teed claimed that Koreshan Unity had 10,000 members in the United States; some 200 lived on 6,000 acres at Estero. Other Koreshan groups were established in San Francisco (1890–1891), Washington, D.C. (1908), and perhaps in other major cities (the record is unclear). When Teed was injured by a Fort Myers marshal in a political dispute in 1906 and died two years later (some of his followers keeping a futile vigil around his remains waiting for his resurrection, which he had predicted), dissension split the Estero colony, some following Victoria Gratis, Teed's coleader, and others founding a new church, the Order of Theocracy at Fort Myers. Accordingly, the movement began to fade. In 1961 the surviving members transferred the property to the state of Florida, where it is maintained as Koreshan State Park. This community has no connection with David Koresh (1960–1993) and the **Branch Davidians**.

KORESH, DAVID (1960–1993). *See* BRANCH DAVIDIANS.

KRISTEEN COMMUNITY. Located on the Tippecanoe River in Marshall County, Indiana, this 376-acre community was established in 1845 by Charles Mowland and others who had previously been associated with the **Prairie Home Community**. The community existed on its timber and lumber trades until 1847.

KRIYANANDA, SWAMI (1926–). *See* ANANDA COOPERATIVE VILLAGE.

KRONOS, *or* **CRONUS, KINGDOM OF.** *See* COCKAYGNE, LAND OF; GOLDEN AGE, MYTH OF THE.

KROTONA COMMUNITY OF ADYAR THEOSOPHISTS. This community originated as a branch of the Theosophical Society, India. It was organized in 1912 by Albert Powell Warrington, a close friend of **Annie Besant** (1847–1933), in Hollywood, California. By the next year, it had 45 members and was carrying out a number of educational and spiritual programs. Because of pressing financial problems, the land was sold off and the colony of **Theosophists** moved to the Ojai Valley north of Los Angeles, in part because it was the home of Jiddu Krishnamurti, the Indian theosophy leader who was identified by Besant as the World Teacher who would bring into being a new age. Today the community operates a school of theosophy with branches in more than 50 countries.

KRUMNOW, JOHANN FREDERICK (1811–1880). *See* HERRNHUT COMMUNE.

KUTTER COLONY. This **Hutterite** colony was established in 1890 near Mitchell in Hanson County, South Dakota, northwest of Sioux Falls, as a branch of the **Wolf Creek Colony**. As was the case with other Hutterite colonies that faced clear public opposition because of its pacifism during World War I, it moved to Redlands, Alberta, Canada, in 1918.

– L –

LABADIE, JEAN de (1610–1674). Jean de Labadie was educated by the Jesuits from an early age and entered the order as a novice in 1625. In 1628 he was ordained a subdeacon. For the next three years, he studied at the Jesuit College at Bordeaux. Then in 1630 he left the Jesuits and became a wandering preacher, traveling all over France. In 1650 he joined the Reformed Church and continued to proselytize throughout Europe, especially in Holland, and settled in Herford, Westphalia, Germany, with 55 disciples. Accused by the Catholic Church of heresy, he converted to Calvinism and preached his controversial gospel throughout Europe. He died in Germany in 1674. *See also* LABADISTS.

LABADISTS. These followers of **Jean de Labadie** (1610–1674) reformed their community in Holland in 1675, the year following their leader's death. This first Labadist community, Wieuwerd, was modeled after the church in Jerusalem after the time of Pentecost. Membership was divided into three classes: visitors, who were welcomed; probationers, who lived in austerity; and the elite, numbering 250, who lived in comfort. The Labadists believed that only those who were inspired by the Holy Spirit could understand the Bible, a Pietist view. The Eucharist was only occasionally celebrated, and marriage to an outsider was not considered binding. Those who wished to join the Labadists were required to divest themselves of all property and special affections in order to do the will of the Lord. Members wore simple clothing with no jewelry. Women attired themselves in habits of coarse wool, their hair pulled back and covered like that of a nun. Men wore rough smocks and were allowed to worship only in dark clothing. All worked communally at Wieuwerd, their cloth-processing cottage industry becoming very successful. They also farmed and ran a bakery, a brewery, a tannery, a printing press, and a soap manufactory, as well as a successful manufactory of pills to counteract fever (Labadie Pills). Wieuwerd was dissolved in 1732 when their last spiritual leader died.

Meanwhile, the Labadists established a 3,750-acre community under the leadership of Peter Sluyter (1645–1722) called Bohemia Manor at the head of Chesapeake Bay in 1683 in what is now Cecil

County, Maryland. The members, totaling 125 men, women, and children, donated their personal wealth and possessions to a central fund knowing that if they left the colony they would leave their wealth behind. In their pursuit of the coming **millennium**, they denied themselves physical comforts such as adequate heating and appetizing food. Marriage was allowed if both partners belonged to the community, but it was considered less pure than the celibate life. Both sexes shared equally in all work and spiritual activities, spending most of their days in the fields tending to crops of corn, hemp, and tobacco and producing linen from the flax purchased from nearby plantations. Despite the fact that smoking was forbidden in the colony, Sluyter instigated the growing of tobacco. The colony also owned slaves, whom Sluyter treated savagely. Beginning in 1690, their finances and spiritual vitality were adversely affected by the dogged hostility of the Reformed Church and by the more widespread acceptance of Pietism, a religious belief close to their own. This resulted in defections from the community. It was then hit by an epidemic of major proportions in 1691. Still, the Labadists continued to survive communally for the next half-century before disappearing from the scene, Bohemia Manor continuing to exist until 1727.

LABOR COPARTNERSHIPS. *See* LLOYD, HENRY DEMAREST.

LAGRANGE PHALANX. Located in LaGrange County, Indiana, about 40 miles from Fort Wayne on the Wabash and Erie Canal, this **Fourierist phalanx** was established in 1843 on about 1,500 acres of land (half prairie, half timbered) purchased at $8 per acre. By the following year, the phalanx had about 150 members from surrounding Springfield Township, about half being children and the remainder being farmers, mechanics, and a few professional persons. By 1846 the phalanx could boast a large community building, three barns, a blacksmith shop, a school, and a dining facility. Although the membership had been augmented by transfers from the **Alphadelphia Phalanx** in Michigan, the LaGrange Phalanx failed that same year, apparently from mismanagement of its finances and a lack of organizational skills by its hardworking farmer members.

L'AN 2440. *See* MERCIER, LOUIS SEBASTIEN.

LANDMANN, BARBARA. *See* HEYNEMANN, BARBARA.

LANE, CHARLES (1800–1870). Little is known of the life of this co-founder of **Bronson Alcott**'s Fruitlands except that he was the editor of a business journal. The colony was established with the aid of Henry Wright on the basis of Lane's belief in the "consociate family," meaning a group who possessed a certain intellectual rapport and could help one another develop their spiritual life. After leaving Fruitlands in 1844, Lane briefly joined the **Shakers' Harvard Society** before returning to England. Nothing is known of his later life.

LANE, MARY E. BRADLEY. Mary E. Bradley Lane, about whom very little is known, even the years of her birth and death, in her *Mizora: A Prophecy* (1889) created an all-female utopia of beautiful Amazon-like women where men had been extinct for several thousand years. Religion was a form of pantheism; scientific knowledge was the key to the women's happiness; and no crime, suffering, or disease occurred because no men existed in Mizora. First published anonymously in the *Cincinnati Commercial* in 1880–1881, *Mizora*, the second known **feminist utopian novel** written by a woman (the first being **Annie Denton Cridge**'s *Man's Rights,* 1870), tells of an all-woman society under the North Pole whose children are produced by parthenogenesis and who by technology have eliminated brunettes and all men. They have thereby produced a race of blond superwomen.

Males are considered a separate race and "impure," as are "unmen" of the dark-skinned races. Both have been filtered out by selective breeding. Technology has enabled the women of Mizora (meaning "happiness") to discover the "secret of life," that is, parthenogenesis, which produces genetic duplicates. Undesirable "fems," the product of genetic experiment by which human beings with full sets of genes result, produce female children by mating with horses once a year in a celebration known as *The Gathering.* Although Lane's *Mizora* displays a decided lack of knowledge of biology, and specifically genetics, on the part of its author, it remains important as a path-breaking feminist novel centered around what the main character, Vera Zarovitch, a Russian princess, learns, namely that "motherhood is the only important part of life." At least in a very limited way, Lane opened the door to feminist utopian writing that would reach considerable dimensions in the 20th century.

LANE, WILLIAM (1861–1917). *See* COSME COLONY; NEW AUS-TRALIA.

LAST AND FIRST MEN. William Olaf Stapleton (1886–1950), the author of this novel, was not only a science fictionist but also had a profound influence on the writing of **dystopian** science fiction. From his early experiences, he became convinced that the world was in need of radical social solutions to cure its many problems. *Last and First Men,* published in 1930 in the midst of a worldwide depression, spans 2 billion years, in the process detailing 18 human species struggling for existence and happiness. Stapleton's theme throughout the novel is clear: How can humankind accept its fate?

Dealing with the First Men, 200 million people, he portrays them destroying themselves except for 35 survivors at the North Pole because they were unable to coordinate their technological triumphs. Eventually the survivors developed a Second level, a utopian existence, but a Martian assault over thousands of years resulted in the Second Men resorting to force and suffering internal wars. In the process they exposed the Martians to a virus that destroyed them, but it also infected humans, resulting in an atrophy of brain power over millions of years thereafter. Only when the Fifth Men arrived did humankind achieve the same level of existence as the Second Men, creating a world with high standards of living with no social divisions or international conflicts.

When the moon's orbit began to inch closer to the earth over millions of years, the Fifth Men prepared for an evacuation to Venus. But to make it livable, they had to kill off the existing life forms on Venus. Eventually the Fifth Men succumbed to guilt over what they had done and began to mutate into semihumans, blending with birds and animals to produce Sixth Men, who lacked many human qualities. Eventually the Seventh Men appeared, a species of carefree, flying artists. They were succeeded by the Eighth Men, who were faced with the sun beginning to shrink. The only alternative was to move to Neptune, so the Eighth Men bred a smaller human version, Ninth Men, to make the trip.

When Stapleton moves the story rapidly to the Fifteenth Men, he sees them as taking positive steps toward eliminating disease, work, aging, social division, and conflict, resulting in the Sixteenth Men, closely resembling the Fifth Men in their physical and mental capacities. But even the evolved Seventeenth Men could not solve the mysteries of the universe. This became possible only with the Eighteenth Men, who had longevity, sexual freedom, and a telepathic psychological unity with all the species. Still, Eighteenth Men faced disaster from the dissolution of the sun and sought to plant the human species on another planet. This resulted in chaos and scarcity, leading to the use of force and the threat of war. Facing the end of humankind, a mysterious messianic figure, "the last born of the Last Men," appears to end Stapleton's, and humankind's, story.

LAST MAN, THE. This 1826 **dystopian** novel by Mary Wollstonecraft Shelley (1797–1851), famous for having penned the fantastic science fiction tale *Frankenstein* eight years before, is a powerful critique of utopian values. It was written at a time in the early 19th century when attempts at turning utopian dreams into actual experiments were coming into vogue. Perhaps affected by the deaths of her husband, Percy Bysshe Shelley, in 1822 and her friend Lord Byron in 1824, Mary Shelley's dystopian novel of high ideals gone wrong is set in the 21st century. At this time, a plague obliterates the human race despite myriad attempts at reform and revolution aimed at forestalling the inevitable end. Each attempt fails, and the **Apocalypse** arrives to end humankind on earth. This repudiation of the belief in progress by Shelley represented a rejection of the Enlightenment's evolutionary-rationalist-scientific view of humankind. Nature, in her view, had become disordered and humans had lost control of their own destiny in their confused and futile longing to achieve perfection on earth.

LATE GREAT PLANET EARTH, THE. *See* LINDSEY, HAL (1929–).

LATIN AMERICA COMMUNITIES. *See* APPENDIX.

LAW OF FREEDOM IN A PLATFORM. *See* DIGGERS.

LEDOUX, CLAUDE-NICOLAS (1736–1806). Ledoux began his career as an architect for the aristocracy of the French ancient régime.

In that capacity, he designed and had built a number of handsome palaces and residences in Paris and elsewhere, few of which remain. However, his major project was the buildings of the Royal Salt Works in Arc-et-Senans near Besancon, which were erected in part from 1774 to 1779. More than just an industrial establishment, Ledoux planned an "ideal city" that would also include suitable housing for the workers. It was laid out in a circle with the director's office in the center and the workers' houses on the periphery. With the approach of the French Revolution, construction ceased, and the salt works themselves were closed in 1895.

Having been in the employ of the state and aristocrats, Ledoux was no longer trusted or given serious commissions, but he continued conceiving model cities and structures, most composed of simple geometric forms. Through these models, he also sought to express a deeper meaning and raise the aesthetic and social awareness of those who used them, whether they were temples of a secular religion or meeting places for artisans in different trades. Like the salt works, they were all on a massive scale with the later designs being doubtlessly difficult to construct at the time but foreshadowing architectural trends of one and even two centuries to come. Engrossed in this activity, Ledoux philosophized on the relationship between people and their habitation and sought to advance the human race through improved environments. Much of his later conceptual work was summed up in a book published in 1804, *l'Architecture considerée sous le rapport de l'art, des moeurs et de la législation* (Architecture Considered from the Angle of Art, Mores and Legislation). Meanwhile, more than two centuries later, the salt works of Arc-et-Senans stand as a monument to his thought, which should remain influential many centuries more.

LEE, MOTHER ANN (1736–1784). Born in Manchester, England, the daughter of a blacksmith, "Mother" Ann Lee was the founder of the **Shakers**, or the Society of Believers in Christ's Second Appearing. She received little education and worked in a textile mill and as a cook in her early years, in 1758 joining two dissenting Quakers in a religious society, often called the "Shaking Quakers" because of their demonstrative and clamorous worship services. Married in 1762, she bore four children, all of whom died in infancy. Mother Ann believed that their deaths were the result of her sinfulness, specifically indulging in sexuality. Sex, she came to believe, was the greatest sin the world, stemming from Adam and Eve lusting after one another in the Garden of Eden and leading to The Fall. By 1770 she had assumed leadership of the group, now preaching against sexual intercourse and worldliness within the churches. She and her Quaker followers refused to take oaths and to observe the Sabbath. For her efforts, she was jailed in 1772 and again in 1773. She claimed that during her imprisonment Christ appeared to her and that she was Jesus Christ in the female form. During 1774 Lee and seven members of the sect sailed to New York City in response to a vision she had received commissioning her to preach the Gospel in the United States.

Two years later the group moved to a small farm outside Albany, where they established **Mount Lebanon**, also called New Lebanon or the Holy Mount. It would develop into the center of Shakerism. In 1780 Mother Ann and her followers began to hold public meetings. Mother Ann promised her listeners salvation by abstaining from sex. She also continued to hold that she was Christ in female form, the "woman clothed with the sun" described in the **Apocalypse** with the **millennium** to follow. From that year until her death in 1784, she spread her gospel throughout New England, seeing the Shaker society grow and prosper. After her death Shakerism under the leadership of **Joseph Meachem**, **Lucy Wright**, **James Whittaker**, and **Frederick W. Evans** became organized in the East and spread to Kentucky, Ohio, and Indiana. By 1826 19 Shaker communities had been established in the Midwest. By the time of the Civil War some 6,000 Shakers were living in their communities, only to see a decline in the movement in the years after 1875.

LEINHARD UND GERTRUD: EIN BUCH FUR DAS VOLK, or ***LEINHARD AND GERTRUD: A BOOK FOR THE PEOPLE.*** *See* PESTALOZZI, JOHANN HEINRICH.

LE GUIN, URSULA KROEBER (1929–). One of the best-known science fiction novelists of the 20th century, Ursula Le Guin is the author of *The Dispossessed: An Ambiguous Utopia* (1974), *Always Coming Home* (1987), and numerous other novels, plus children's fiction and poetry. She always attempts to portray the troubled situation of contemporary humanity in the light of the possible future without, however, offering any social programs or panaceas. Thus she cannot strictly be classified as a utopian writer but rather one who, like utopianists, examines for her readers the world and society in terms of their limitations and the possibilities for improvement given greater human insight and effort.

LEIBNIZ, GOTTFRIED WILHELM von (1646–1716). This German utopian, writer, and inventor of differential calculus played a major role in the Enlightenment not so much as a creator of a utopia but as a propagandist for science as the key to progress. Leibniz spent much of his time describing a utopia called *Pansophia* (meaning "holder of wisdom") to be established throughout the entire world. He called upon the rulers of Europe to serve as God's agents in bringing about his grand design for humankind under the leadership of the king (which king depending on his audience) and the pope in a resurrected Holy Roman Empire. In his utopia, called *Republica Christiana* (Christian Republic), the cohesive force of the society would be science. The religious orders would become scientific communities, the scientific academy would replace the monastery, and priests and monks would become scientists. In the academies, linked together throughout the world, the arts and sciences would be taught with special emphasis on applied science in the fields of agriculture, industry, and commerce. They would also propagate the Christian religion and institute stable governments and customs among all peoples. Finally, reason as the natural voice of God in men would lead all humanity to a natural religion that, aided by revelation, would bring all peoples of all creeds together before one God. Leibniz's idea of a great utopian world was, of course, never realized—and rarely taken seriously—during his lifetime, but his vision of science and knowledge as the keys to progress to a constantly perfected universe represented a major step toward a full-blown faith in **scientism** during the 18th century and since.

LEON, COUNT. *See* MULLER, BERNHARD.

LERAYSVILLE PHALANX. This **Fourierist phalanx** was established at Leraysville, Bradford County, in northern Pennsylvania in 1844. Its leader was Lemuel C. Belding, a preacher in the Swedenborgian

Church of New Jerusalem. Most of the original 40 members were also Swedenborgians in the vicinity of Leraysville, although some members came from Maine and nearby New York. Apparently the phalanx lasted only eight months because of conflicts between the original members and those who came in from the outside.

LEVELLERS. *See* DIGGERS; FIFTH MONARCHISTS.

LEWIS, SINCLAIR (1885–1951). *See IT CAN'T HAPPEN HERE.*

LI JU-CHEN (1763–1830). The distinguished Chinese writer Li Ju-chen began writing his utopian novel *Ching-bua yuan* (Flowers in the Mirror) when he was 50 years of age and eventually spent more than a decade on the work. In this novel published in 1828, the protagonist, T'ang Ao, frustrated by the cruel reign of Empress Wu of the T'ang dynasty, sails away from China with his brother-in-law and an old sailor and visits several "strange lands." One of these is a matriarchal society where females keep males in their harems and otherwise subject men to repression common in patriarchal societies. The other is the Land of the Great where people walk on clouds of various colors growing out of their feet, the colors signifying the person's disposition and character. Rainbow clouds signify the most honorable persons; yellow signify the less honorable; and other colors are equal except for black, which signifies the least honorable. The king demands that those who have grayish-black clouds sprouting from their feet (which they attempt to hide) either repent of their evil deeds, in which case their honorable-colored clouds will reappear, or be punished by him. The work of Li Ju-chen marks him as a predecessor of other utopian works that appeared in China later, the numbers increasing somewhat after the opening of the country to the West in the 19th century.

LIMANORA, THE ISLAND OF PROGRESS. Corresponding in time to the popularity of utopian novels in the United States in the late 19th and early 20th centuries, John Macmillan Brown (1846–1935), a New Zealand academic writing under the pseudonym Godfrey Sweven, wrote the satirical utopian novel *Limanora, the Island of Progress* (1903). On Limanora, located far across the ocean and inaccessible behind a dense wall of mist and fog, wrote Brown, the elders have concluded that no progress can be made in curing vices or establishing a proper social order until those people possessing major vices are removed from their society. Accordingly, the Limanorans have designated separate islands in their archipelago of Riallo for the practitioners of certain vices: Tirralaria for socialists, Meddla for intellectual propagandists, Wotnekst for people who think they can accomplish anything by passing laws, Foolgar for snobs, Awdyoo (the foulest of all islands) for journalists, Jabberoo for constant talkers, Witlingen for practical jokers, Meskeeta for censors, and Kloriole for those who would deify the senses and sex. Furthermore, on Limanora children are raised by the most capable persons, not necessarily by their parents; most women are given work that requires continuous effort and little in the way of creative powers; men are given more strenuous work and are the inventive ones; children with evil or negative passions are taken to an ethical laboratory to discover scientifically the cause of their disease in their bodily tissue; and research is being done on violations of the moral code such as devotion to the past, superstition, and belief based on unreason or ignorance. All of this is undertaken to allow the human system to progress by putting Limanorans on the "scale of energy" through which the cosmos is necessarily climbing to perfection. And because nothing retrograde can end in progress on Limanora, politics and political projects are not allowed there.

LINDSEY, HAL (HAROLD L.) (1929–). Lindsey is the author of *The Late Great Planet Earth* in which he predicted the Bible-recorded end of time, the Second Coming, and the advent of the **millennial** kingdom. Born in Houston, Texas, Lindsey dropped out of the University of Houston to serve in the Korean War, then worked as a Mississippi River tugboat captain. Contemplating suicide, instead he was converted to Christianity after reading the Bible. He entered Dallas Theological Seminary in 1958 and, after graduating, became a missionary for Campus Crusade for Christ with his second wife. His *The Late Great Planet Earth,* published in 1970, became one of the best-selling books of the decade and was translated into more than 50 languages. This premillennial tract reviewed the "end-time" events, such as the creation of the Jewish state of Israel, the rise of Russia, an Arab confederation arrayed against Israel, European integration, the rise of military power in East Asia, the revival of dark occult practices, and the apostasy of Christian churches. He then prophesied that the **Antichrist** will emerge to lead a revived Roman Empire composed of the European community, an Arab-African confederacy will assault Palestine, the European alliance will be attacked by an army of 200 million Asians in an Armageddon-type battle in which nuclear weapons will kill a third of the world's population, and finally Christ will appear in His Second Coming to bring peace on earth. Lindsey predicted that Christ would return in 1988, but in his 12 sequels to the book he has assured his readers that these events would occur in the 20th and 21st centuries. Lindsey remains the best known of the prophetic teachers at the turn of the 21st century.

LIU SHIHP'EI (1884–1919). Liu, a Chinese anarchist living in Japan, was the editor of the journal *Natural Justice*. As an agricultural utopianist, Liu urged that labor should be organized to integrate its theoretical (satisfying moral needs) and its practical dimensions. He also argued that women should be leaders in the anarchist revolution. A brief experiment based on Liu's ideas emerged in China in the aftermath of the overthrow of the Manchu monarchy in 1911. It was known as the New Village Movement, but it, along with Chinese anarchism, remained virtually stillborn as China was overwhelmed by nationalism and eventually by communism under **Mao Zedong** in the 20th century.

LLANO DEL RIO COMPANY. This cooperative colony was established in 1914 on some 2,000 acres of desert land northeast of Los Angeles by **Job Harriman** (1861–1925) for socialists and labor unionists. Harriman had been **Eugene V. Debs**'s vice presidential running mate in 1900. Originally consisting only of Harriman and five families, within the year the colony's membership was augmented by the arrival of 100 families. By 1917 its membership stood at 1,100, most of the new members being recruited through the colony's promotional magazine *The Western Comrade*. Life in the colony was convivial and featured lectures, readings, musical concerts, sports, and dances. But Llano del Rio came to an end the next year because of primitive living conditions, loss of vital water rights, internal conflicts, and lawsuits against the colony. Meanwhile, Harriman and most of the membership had moved to a new location in Louisiana called *New Llano* to continue their cooperative way of life.

LLANO DEL RIO COMPANY OF NEVADA. This socialist colony, also known as *Nevada City,* was founded by C. V. Eggleston in 1916 in Churchill County, Nevada, to demonstrate the possibilities of practical cooperation. Eggleston had formerly been a promoter and fiscal agent of the **Llano del Rio Company** in California. The Nevada colony embraced 1,640 acres scattered over many square miles. At its peak it had a membership of almost 200 persons. Mismanagement of its finances brought about its downfall in 1918. Eggleston had resigned from the controlling board the year before, but he regained partial control of the association in 1919 and was elected vice president of the Nevada Colony Corporation, later reorganized as the United Development Company. With this reorganization, the socialist colony became a regular capitalist land company.

LLOYD, HENRY DEMAREST (1847–1903). Active on the American intellectual scene during the decades after the Civil War when the nation was undergoing major economic and social changes with the advent of industrialization, Henry Demarest Lloyd was a prominent advocate for utopian communes. Drawing on his background as a lawyer, journalist, and writer on economic questions, Lloyd was the first of the "muckrakers," exposing abuses by Standard Oil. He produced three major works: *A Strike of Millionaires against Miners: The Story of Spring Valley* (1894), *Wealth against Commonwealth* (1894), and *Labor Copartnership* (1899). From his studies of the problems of labor, he came to advocate cooperation between employers and employees and governmental control of industry. As a communal anarchist, he looked to self-sufficient communes, advocating personal equality and freedom of expression. It was his authorship of *Wealth against Commonwealth,* a scathing condemnation of business monopolies, that made him a major figure on the American economic scene and an ally of those who advocated communal organization as an alternative.

LOCKE, JOHN (1623–1704). Seventeenth-century England, important for engendering a number of **millennial**-perfectionist schemes such as those of the **Fifth Monarchists** and the **Cambridge Platonists** such as **Joseph Mede**, is also important for its protests against political absolutism. Foremost among the political philosophers who charted the course of modern liberalism was John Locke. Locke is chiefly remembered for his anti-absolutism as set forth in his *Two Treatises of Government* (1690), but he also reflected a utilitarian belief in the improvement if not perfectibility of society through education, as spelled out in his *Some Thoughts Concerning Education* (1693). Thus Locke is important in Western thought, not only because of his political ideas that, when put into practice, would revolutionize the nature of governments thereafter but also because of his ideas regarding education. This places him well within the mindset of the modern utopians because by arguing that progress toward perfectibility was attainable through secular, not religious, and governmental means, he was advocating the major thrust of Western utopian thought.

LONDON CO-OPERATIVE SOCIETY. *See* THOMPSON, WILLIAM.

LONDON, JACK (JOHN GRIFFITH) (1876–1916). Known primarily for his tales of adventure such as *The Call of the Wild* (1903), *The Sea Wolf* (1904), and *White Fang* (1906), Jack London, prolific novelist, socialist, and devotee of such avant-garde thinkers as **Karl Marx**, **Charles Darwin**, and **Herbert Spencer**, was also a noted **dystopian**-utopianist. After an early life of adventure and misadventure, London completed his university education, then made a trip to England, where his socialistic ideas matured. During these years, he wrote of the struggle between the capitalist class and the proletariat, as in "A Curious Fragment" (1908), in which a ruling oligarch is confronted by his industrial slaves; "Goliah" (1908), in which a "scientific superman" masters the ultimate energy source, Energon, becomes master of the world, and inaugurates a millennium of international socialism; and "The Dream of Debs," (1909) in which a general strike brings the capitalist class to its knees.

But London's *The Iron Heel* (1907) is his dystopian-utopian masterpiece. Set in the 27th century, it tells of events in the early 20th century through the memoirs of Avis Everhard, the widow of socialist Ernest Everhard, crushed by a fascist dictatorship seven centuries before. The memoirs reveal that Everhard challenged the unjust 20th-century economic-social-political system. When he ran for Congress, having given up on religious leaders as agents of reform because they accommodated the existing unjust system, Everhard frightened the middle class with his forecast of the inevitable victory of socialism. But in the ensuing economic chaos the people turned instead to the fascists, to the Iron Heel. Everhard, elected to Congress, challenged the ideas and principles of the bourgeois fascists, and, as a result, was tried and imprisoned as a subversive by them. Freed by socialist rebels, Everhard and other congressmen of like ideas led an underground movement against the Iron Heel. The incomplete memoirs hint at the failure of the underground movement, but London concludes the work with socialism eventually triumphing over the fascists and their imagined utopia, leading to a true utopian era of peace and plenty. *The Iron Heel,* for all of its pessimism and gloom, ends on a positive note, a reflection of London's belief in the justice and inevitability of the triumph of the proletariat and his attachment to the ideas of Marx, Darwin, and Spencer.

LONGLEY, ALCANDER (1832–1918). Drawn to utopian communitarianism by his father, who had help establish the **Clermont Phalanx**, Longley at age 21 joined the **North American Phalanx**. In 1854 he moved to Cincinnati, where with his four brothers he established a printing firm for reform literature and between 1857 and 1865 attempted to form **phalanxes** in Indiana, Michigan, and Ohio. Then in 1867 he became a follower of the ideas of **Etienne Cabet** (1788– 1856) and joined his followers' settlement at **Corning** in Iowa. But he soon moved on to St. Louis, where he began the publication of *The Communist* (later called *The Altruist*) in early 1868. In 1869 Longley, attracted to the ideas of the **Fourierists**, established a successful colony called the *Reunion Colony* in Missouri, and, when that faltered, Longley proposed the **Friendship Community** near St. Louis. Then in 1877 he tried unsuccessfully to establish a community called Principia in Missouri. In 1883 he again tried to establish a successful colony called the *Mutual Aid Community,* again in Missouri, but this effort also failed, as did another in Randolph County in the same state. Undeterred and still enthusiastic, Longley in 1907 at age

77 established the **Altruist Community** at Sulphur Springs south of St. Louis, but this effort was soon added to his list of failures. Successful as a propagandist for utopianism but also a man who labored in vain in his attempts to work out his communitarian dreams in reality, Longley died in Chicago in 1918.

LOOKING BACKWARD: 2000–1887. This path-breaking utopian novel written by the socialist **Edward Bellamy** (1850–1898) and published in 1888 recounts the story of Julian West, a wealthy Bostonian, who falls into a hypnotic sleep in 1887 and awakens in 2000. He is then taken on a tour of the city led by his betrothed, her father, and her friends and discovers that the United States has been transformed into a utopian commonwealth. Private ownership is no more, and the people freely contribute to the good of the nation by their membership in the Industrial Army. Cooperation has been accepted in place of compulsion because there is no scarcity, crime has been reduced in the wake of the end of poverty, and the general culture has improved appreciably in the last 113 years. All of this has come about without suffering or revolution because people, being basically good and needing only to be released from the economic inequality that holds them down to attain a humane and rational social order, have peaceably evolved to this more perfect way of life. The impact of the book was enormous with over 300,000 copies sold within two years and 500,000 copies by 1900. Bellamy Clubs were formed to study the work, and some 165 Nationalist Clubs were forthwith established to implement the economic-political-social principles outlined in the novel. Bellamy spent the remainder of his life furthering social reform in the United States. He died in 1898, his *Looking Backward* and its sequel, *Equity* (1897), having made Bellamy's ideas the subject of discussion and enthusiastic embrace not only in the United States but also in Europe, especially in Russia.

LOOKING FURTHER BACKWARD. See VINTON, ARTHUR DUDLEY.

LOPEZ ISLAND COMMUNITY. This Pentecostal community was founded in 1911 by the itinerant preacher Thomas Gourley (1864?–1923) and 150 of his followers on Lopez Island in the San

Juan Islands of Washington state as a place where Pentecostal Christians could separate themselves from the corruption of the world. Gourley had earlier opened a successful Pentecostal mission on the Seattle waterfront in 1908. On Lopez Island the colonists constructed homes and other structures, including a dining hall and a school, but their communal life was difficult and their foodstuffs were monotonous. Gourley even forbade the eating of the plentiful seafood available in the area because it came from killing. Epidemics of typhoid and tuberculosis took a number of lives, but most residents stayed on because of the dominance of their Bible-based faith (worship services being held daily and twice on Sunday) and their trust in Gourley. When World War I began and Gourley advised his followers—the neighbors referred to them as "Holy Rollers"—against serving in the military and was subsequently charged with violating the Espionage Act, the reputation of the colony suffered. Gourley's prediction of the Second Coming of Christ in November 1918 also hurt his credibility when it failed to occur. He left the struggling community in 1920, possibly started a new colony somewhere in the South, and died on February 26, 1923, in a train wreck near Calhoun, Georgia, being decapitated while attempting to jump from a careening car. He was buried in St. Louis. The remaining members divided the property and reentered the world from which Gourley had tried to save them.

LORD OF THE FLIES. See GOLDING, WILLIAM.

LORD'S FARM, THE. The Lord's Farm was a religious commune founded in 1889 by Mason T. Huntsman (who had taken the name *Paul Blaudin Mnason* after his conversion to Christianity) and a group of supporters in Woodcliff, New Jersey. Mnason, who at one time apparently claimed to be the "New Christ," preached a version of Christianity based on the Sermon on the Mount but imposed no doctrines or rules of conduct on his followers. Accordingly, the commune of some 40 persons soon gained a reputation as a place without private property, an open-door policy, and consensual nude group dances (their neighbors referred to the members as "Angel Dancers"). The colony was beset by troubles from the beginning. These included welcoming freeloaders and even criminals into their midst and stringent opposition from their neighbors because of widespread rumors that they practiced nudity and sexual promiscuity. The Lord's Farm was dissolved in 1910, and Mnason lived out the remainder of his life in New York City.

LOST HORIZON. *See* HILTON, JAMES.

LOUISIANA COMMUNITIES. *See* APPENDIX.

"LOVE AMONG THE RUINS: A ROMANCE OF THE NEAR FUTURE." This **dystopian** short story that appeared in 1953 was written by Evelyn Waugh (1903–1966), the English novelist and prominent man of letters best known in the United States for the media adaptations of his *A Handful of Dust* (1934) and *Brideshead Revisited* (1945, rev. ed. 1960). "Love among the Ruins" was penned in criticism of the semisocialist welfare state into which his country was falling in the post–World War II years. In this short story, England is now dominated by dinginess, inefficiency, and ineffectual government bureaucrats. This is personified in Miles, made a national hero for burning down an air force base with great loss of life. He is sent to a country-club-like house of correction for rehabilitation by experts skilled in the new penology. Thereafter, he is assigned to work at the flourishing Department of Euthanasia where crowds line up for self-extermination. He meets and falls in love with a ballet dancer named Clara, who has been sterilized but, by surgical error, has a full beard. Clara longs for death, but Miles persuades her to live. They become lovers, and, despite being sterilized, she somehow becomes pregnant. But medical science comes to the rescue; she has an abortion and plastic surgery removes her beard. She then returns to the ballet, leaving Miles rejected and alone. In depression over this event, he burns down the house of correction. Finally he is given a job in the Ministry of Rest and Culture whereby he is to travel around the country delivering lectures on the success of the new penology with himself as the example (his setting of the second fire with great loss of life has not been discovered). Waugh's England of the future represents contradiction and chaos. The ministers of culture are uncultured, the industry of death flourishes while all others deteriorate, and criminals are national heroes. His "Love among the Ruins" is a satirical reminder that what is labeled as progress and governmentalism can lead instead to stagnation and depersonalization.

LUCRETIUS (ca. 96–ca. 55 B.C.). The Roman poet and philosopher Lucretius endorsed the idea of progress by introducing the idea of necessary advancement through stages of human development. In his *On the Nature of Things,* which revealed Lucretius to be a pure naturalist and an enemy of religion, he argued that humans and society evolved in increasingly more perfect stages because some forms of life were inadequate and, as a result, died off while other forms of life generated higher species. In the beginning, he said, humans lived as solitary beings driven only by individual will until they developed families. These families eventually joined together to form societies and developed a common language. Within these societies absolute kingship evolved, only to be followed by anarchy. This, however, gave way to genuine government and law based on agreed-upon principles of life. Lucretius, then, was one of the exponents of the idea that human advancement was not only desirable but also natural and evolutionary.

LUDLOW, WILLIAM. *See* COAL CREEK COMMUNITY AND CHURCH OF GOD.

LUTHER, MARTIN (1483–1546). Martin Luther was an Augustinian priest and theologian at the University of Wittenberg. He first came to public notice in 1517 when he published his Ninety-Five Theses calling for open debate and discussion of certain Church doctrines and practices. Subsequently, in his *Freedom of a Christian,* his *To the Nobility of the German Nation,* and his *On the Babylonian Captivity of the Church* he developed his doctrines, heavily influenced by the **Apocalypse** story with Babylon being the Church of Rome and the Antichrist the pope. As a **postmillennialist**, Luther also believed that the **millennium** had already begun, probably when St. John wrote the Book of Revelation, with the end of the world occurring with Christ coming again to pass judgment on the pope and his followers before Christ's kingdom not of this world would be established. In the meantime, he urged all true believers to strengthen themselves against the trials to come in the Last Days.

– M –

MACARIA. This 1641 utopian work (its full title is *A Description of the Famous Kingdom of Macaria*) is usually associated with Samuel Hartlib (ca. 1600–1662), the English publicist for the use of science to establish human domination over creation, but it was probably written by his associate Gabriel Plattes. It is sometimes classified as a "full employment" utopia because it argues for a full utilization of scientific knowledge and organization to solve the problem of limited resources available to a society to correct its ills, such as ridding it of poverty, rather than the more austere programs advocated by such utopians as **Thomas More** (1478–1535).

Macaria, written in the form of a discussion between a traveler and a scholar, describes the kingdom of Macaria. In Macaria agriculture is managed to assure maximum production, taxes are low because the king avoids expensive wars, the king is made aware of the needs of his people through subordinate officials, and the duties of government are divided into economic categories such as fishing, trade, and colonies. These assure the utopian kingdom's economic, political, and social success. In the kingdom of Macaria, too, there is no state religion; there are no disputatious religious groupings, as was found in 17th-century England; and the government is strong and active in planning the lives of its citizens. *Macaria* inspired a number of reforms in England during the next century, culminating, it can be argued, in Adam Smith's *Wealth of Nations* in 1776.

MACDONALD, A. J. (?–1854). This Scotsman by birth and printer by trade immigrated to the United States in about 1842 and subsequently spent the dozen years until his death from cholera in 1854 visiting American utopian and communal societies, such as various **Owenite**, **Shaker**, and **Fourierist** communities, and collecting materials on them and many others. These materials and Macdonald's personal observations on the colonies are now preserved in the Yale University Library. After his untimely death, his collection was examined by **John Humphrey Noyes** (1811–1886), who used Macdonald's findings to write his valuable *History of American Socialisms* (1870).

MACEDONIA COOPERATIVE COMMUNITY. This community near Clarkesville in Habersham County in northern Georgia, was founded by Morris Mitchell, who believed that many of society's problems could be solved by communitarianism. The first two families moved onto the site in 1937. In philosophy and outlook the colony was predominantly nonsectarian, although there were liberal Protestants among the members. The members were also pacifists, which created some problems during World War II in this Southern community. Economically, Macedonia was very communal with common ownership of property and communal cottage industries. It attained commercial success in the late 1940s with the manufacture of wooden children's furniture and toys under the name Community Playthings. The community was badly split in the early 1950s when half of its approximately 50 members joined up with the members of the **Bruderhof**. Although the division was patched over temporarily, in 1957 it broke open again, and the decision was made to terminate Macedonia. The property was sold off in 1958.

"MACHINE STOPS, THE." This **dystopian** essay was first published in the *Oxford and Cambridge Review* in 1909 by E. M. Forster (1879–1970), best known for his books *Howard's End* (1910) and *A Passage to India* (1924). It was written as a warning to his intellectual colleagues against utopian thinking, specifically against the writings of **H. G. Wells** (1866–1946) with their optimistic view of the future because of improving technology. Forster, like **Aldous Huxley** (1894–1963), asserted that man was not made for technology but technology for man. He feared the emergence of a faceless bureaucracy determining the fate of humankind with the capitalist profit motive hindering if not precluding humane decision making regarding those things created by technology. In his essay, humans live in an isolated underground state where all decisions are made by The Machine. The Machine regulates everything in this regimented state; the people are subjects of The Machine. The Machine has convinced the people that they should not even think about contingencies or decision making. And mechanical devices have become so common that human muscles have atrophied. Babies who display the slightest inclination to independence are killed off. Human weakness has become a virtue. Forster then raises the question: What if The Machine stops? The answer he makes clear: Since the population has become completely reliant on The Machine, they cannot survive if it fails. Forster did not produce a solution to the dangers of technology out of control in "The Machine Stops," but he did sound a warning that the technological utopian state being proposed by some was in fact a society fully capable of dehumanizing its subjects.

MACLURE, WILLIAM (1763–1840). Born in Scotland, Maclure at age 19 entered employment at a mercantile house in London and by dint of hard work became a partner in the firm. He then retired in 1799 to devote his life to science and philanthropy. Following a second visit to the United States, in 1803 he became an American citizen, thereafter traveling throughout the country studying natural history and geology. In 1824 he visited **Robert Owen**'s projected site for **New Harmony** and bought a tract of land there to establish a school for the colony based on the utilitarian **Pestalozzian** method of education. By 1826 the school enrolled 300–400 children. When New Harmony began to disintegrate despite Maclure's efforts to keep it afloat by loaning money to Owen, one of the splinter groups named their settlement **Macluria** in his honor. Maclure moved to Mexico because of failing health in 1827. He died en route back to the United States in 1840 after suffering heart failure. He is still honored as the father of American geology, and his School of Industry at New Harmony introduced the trade school to the United States.

MACLURIA. This was a spin-off colony from **New Harmony** in Indiana. Formed in 1826, it was named in honor of **William Maclure** (1763–1840) and its members stood in opposition to **Robert Owen**'s deistic beliefs, not knowing that Maclure was opposed to any organized religion. Like the other spin-offs, it failed in short order.

MAGNALIA CHRISTI AMERICANA: OR, THE ECCLESIASTICAL HISTORY OF NEW-ENGLAND . . . *See* PURITANS AS UTOPIANS.

MAHANAIM. *See* ECKERLIN, ISRAEL.

MAINE COMMUNITIES. *See* APPENDIX.

MALCOLM X (1925–1965). *See* NATION OF ISLAM.

MANCHESTER UNION. *See* ONTARIO PHALANX.

MANDEVILLE, SIR JOHN (ca. 1300–1373). *See* BRAGMANS.

MANIFESTO OF THE EQUALS. See BABEUF, FRANCOIS NOEL.

MANKIND UNITED. This utopian movement first appeared in California in 1934. In 1942 its mysterious "Speaker" or "Voice of the Right Idea" was identified as Arthur L. Bell (?–1951), who emerged to warn of a plot against human freedom. He asserted that an enclave of mysterious Hidden Rulers had been developing plans for decades to enslave the human race but that a top-secret countereffort had been in place since 1875 to thwart them. These secret defenders of the human race, said Bell, had now decided to reveal their work and put their own plan into action. These early and faithful members of Mankind United were to usher in a Golden Age in which each member of the sect would be given guaranteed employment, a four-hour workday, a four-day workweek, an eight-month work year, a $3,000 per year salary, retirement at 40 years of age with full salary, bountiful necessities of life, and a luxurious home. These benefits would be possible because of secret technological innovations already developed by their saviors, the secret defenders.

When 16 leaders of the movement were arrested by the Federal Bureau of Investigation in 1942 on charges that they were impeding the war effort, and when most of them were convicted the next year, most members of the movement left. But to those who remained, Bell promised a new communal Christ's Church of the Golden Rule. It was organized in 1944 with 850 members, all of whom gave up their right to personal property and real estate. But life was hard in Bell's new community, and dissidents began to leave the movement. Bell vanished in 1951. Christ's Church, however, survived and in the early 1960s its scattered membership merged into a new utopian community on a site near Willits, California, north of San Francisco. The new colony thrived, and through the 1990s its 100-plus members continued their efforts to make the world a better place based on love of God and one another.

MAN'S RIGHTS. See CRIDGE, ANNIE DENTON.

MAO ZEDONG (1893–1976). As the totalitarian leader of the People's Republic of China from 1949 until his death, Mao Zedong rejected Western ideas and values and attempted to create a Chinese utopian society based on the nation's historical rural, peasant orientation. Maoism evolved from the Great Leap Forward in the late 1950s to the Cultural Revolution of the mid-1960s. During both programs, Mao relied heavily on authoritarian control of the media and the military to convert the social-economic-cultural Chinese way of life into pure communism. In the 1960s with the implementation of the Cultural Revolution, Mao manipulated the 13-million-man Red Guards, motivated by the little red book of published "Quotations" of Chairman Mao, to carry out his program. Mao's "Quotations" contained four basic principles: In a time of tyranny and injustice, a person must be a rebel; the true and great struggle is itself a liberating good; violence on behalf of the historic cause is both necessary and desirable; and the revolution will begin all things anew, for its face is set toward the white shining blankness of the future. When the Red Guards fell into factionalism in the late 1960s, Mao dissolved them but continued to impose his Cultural Revolution on the country. Yet even before Mao's death in 1976, China had begun to move toward allowing some Western ideas and techniques into the country, and economic progress was becoming evident. The scuttling of utopian Maoism in China marked a major change in that nation's economic, political, and foreign policy positions as it looked more toward the West and embraced economic modernism by the end of the 20th century.

MARCUSE, HERBERT (1898–1979). *See EROS AND CIVILIZATION.*

MARGARET, A TALE OF THE REAL, BLIGHT AND BLOOM. See JUDD, SYLVESTER.

MARLBOROUGH ASSOCIATION. This community, many of whose members were Freethinkers, was located in Stark County, Ohio, about 45 miles southeast of Cleveland on some 500 acres of land, and existed from 1841 to 1845. The Marlborough Association, also called the Marlboro Community, was founded by two brothers, Edward and Abram Brooke, and featured a community mansion wherein each family had a separate apartment. When dissension broke out over the principles upon which the colony should be based, the association was dissolved in late 1845. Abram Brooke had earlier withdrawn and had attempted to form a second colony called Abram Brooke's Experiment, in Clinton County, Ohio. It, too, failed.

MARQUIS DE SADE. *See* SADE, DONATIEN ALPHONSE FRAN-COIS, COMTE de.

MARX, KARL (1818–1883). Karl Marx, the creator of Marxism, was born at a time in German history in which romantic nationalism and idealist philosophy were dominant. As a journalist he spent some time in France, then toying with utopian ideas. He also engaged in a partnership with his socialist conationalist Friedrich Engels, who had spent time in England and knew the utopian **Robert Owen** (1771–1858) and who was also a disciple of the ideas of **Charles Fourier** (1772–1837). Marx was also familiar with the writings of **Saint-Simon** (1760–1825) and of **Georg W. F. Hegel** (1770–1831). As a "Young Hegelian," he accepted the master's view that history is the contradictory unfolding of reason to ultimate thought, that is, to God, the Absolute Mind, and that the duty of the philosopher was to find truths in events and then participate in advancing these truths to the goal of the progress of the human race. And from Ludwig Feuerbach (1804–1872) in his *The Essence of Christianity,* he came to accept the argument that there is no God, only humans and material things being in existence.

From these teachings of Hegel and Feuerbach, Marx developed his own philosophy and view of history, spelled out in *The Communist Manifesto* (1848), where he argued that the end of human existence is not God, but perfected real men in time. This was the inevitable end of the Hegelian dialectic of thesis versus antithesis between classes taking place throughout history. It would result in the temporary dictatorship of the proletariat in which state confiscation and redistribution of property on an equal basis would take place after the final clash between the bourgeoisie and the workers. This would then be followed by a perfect classless society, a **millennial** heaven on earth. Man, then, according to Marx, was creating his own perfection and progress throughout history with all reality in a state of constant flux with no truths, no essences, to live by but only constant change. This change, Marx argued, was eternal and would end only with human perfection in the classless socialist state.

The task, then, for true humans was to engage in a Promethean struggle for truth and change, which lies buried under a gigantic superstructure of economic, religious, and political tyranny. Within this, the worker had a duty to tear down the existing economic-political-social structures and free humans to create an earthly utopia in which all will work for all and not for the self. Adopted by the Bolshevik revolutionaries under Lenin (Vladimir Ulyanov) in Russia in 1917 and imposed upon the peoples of the Soviet Union under the name "communism," Marxism held sway for decades both there and in many other countries both on the Soviet borders and in the Third World. But Marxism as a utopian dream began to fade in the 1980s, culminating in the final collapse of the Soviet Union in 1991 and of its satellite system thereafter. However, it still enjoys support in many parts of the globe, especially in the Third World.

MARYLAND COMMUNITIES. *See* APPENDIX.

MASLOW, ABRAHAM (1908–1970). Regarded as the founder of humanistic psychology, Maslow enjoyed a distinguished teaching career both at Brooklyn College and Brandeis University. His *Motivation and Personality* (1954) and *Toward a Psychology of Being* (1962) advanced his new humanistic model and introduced and explicated the psychological concepts of the ascending need hierarchy, self-actualization, and peak experience in humans. He concluded that persons who have reached self-actualization and peak experience could well be suited to become part of a special utopia called *Eupsychia*. Here people in their ideal state of human existence would be freed from notions of sin and most social restraints, be able to achieve their potential by going beyond sexual and social oppression, become more spiritual, and able to witness new human dimensions via drugs and Eastern philosophy.

MASSACHUSETTS COMMUNITIES. *See* APPENDIX.

MATHER, COTTON (1663–1728). *See* PURITANS AS UTOPIANS.

MATTHEWS, *or* **MATTHIAS, ROBERT** (1787–1841?). Matthews, the leader of the Zion Hill Community, also called "the Kingdom of Matthias," was originally a member of the Presbyterian Church. In 1816, however, he became involved in the religious revivalism of the United States' Second Great Awakening and adopted temperance and vegetarianism. In 1830 he prophesied that Albany would be destroyed and revealed that in a vision he had been informed that all true Christians were to be unshaven. Wandering throughout Albany with his messages, the now-bearded Matthews began calling himself Matthias the Prophet of the Jews, denying that he had ever been a Christian and asserting that he was a Jew. After journeying through New York State and Pennsylvania, he gathered his disciples, including ex-slave Sojourner Truth (known as Isabella Van Wagenen at that time), in New York City, convincing them that he was both the Messiah and God. Matthews then moved his sect to Zion Hill near Ossining (also known as Sing Sing), New York, where, as "The Spirit of Truth," he established a communal lifestyle with them. Zion Hill soon evolved into a free love colony with "spiritual marriages" taking place. Matthews was arrested in 1835 for having murdered his chief disciple, Elijah Pierson, the year before. He was found not guilty but was imprisoned on an assault charge. Little is known of him thereafter, although he probably died in 1841.

MAXWELL COLONY. This **Hutterite** colony was a spin-off from **Bon Homme** and was located in Hutchinson County in southeastern South Dakota. Established in 1900, it was moved to Headingly, Manitoba, in 1918, one of 10 of the 16 Hutterite colonies in South Dakota that moved to Canada at this time because of their neighbors' hostility to their "Germanism," although some of the original Hutterites from Maxwell Colony returned to South Dakota in 1936.

MCKEAN COUNTY ASSOCIATION. Formed by a large number of Germans in 1842 in McKean County in northern Pennsylvania under the leadership of the Reverend George Ginal, a Lutheran minister from Philadelphia, on 30,000 acres, the McKean County Association, also known as *Teutonia* and as the Society of Industry, enjoyed only a brief existence according to information available. At its peak it numbered 400 inhabitants, but because of large financial losses incurred, this **Fourierist** colony ended after only two years.

MCLEOD, NORMAN (1780–1866). Born in the Highlands of Scotland, McLeod at an early age underwent a religious conversion and decided to become a minister of the established Church of Scotland. But while at the University of Edinburgh, he became disillusioned with the Church's teachings and corruption and became a lay preacher, drawing converts away from the established Church. In 1818 he immigrated to Pictou, Nova Scotia, undergoing a hazardous voyage in the process. Here he again drew large crowds but made many enemies for criticizing the people for their sinful ways. Deciding to move to Ohio on the invitation of a group of Highlanders, he built a ship, the *Ark,* and, with his followers, set out in 1822. But the ship was blown into St. Ann's harbor on Cape Breton Island, and here McLeod stayed and built a community, determined to create a paradisiacal society in Canada in this place marked by good land and bounteous fishing.

But when economic hard times caused by severe winters and crop failures hit St. Ann in the 1840s and the people were reduced to starvation, McLeod began to think of leading his followers elsewhere. The next year he received a letter from his son Donald, who had immigrated to Australia, urging him to come to that continent. Accordingly, McLeod and his followers built two ships to make the journey, the *Margaret* and the *Highland Lass,* using local wood for the body of the ships and selling their lands to purchase sails, rigging, and food for the journey. The *Margaret* sailed from Cape Breton in October 1851 and arrived in Adulate, South Australia, in April 1852. The *Highland Lass* followed six months later. Altogether they carried 300 immigrants. But here they ran into a typhoid epidemic; exorbitant land prices; and, some said, the Australians' fondness for drink, so they decided to move on to New Zealand.

The first group arrived at Oakland on the North Island in September 1853 and received land from the government for their community. In addition, four shiploads of people arrived from Nova Scotia between 1856 and 1858, and eight families came directly from Scotland. In all, more than 800 persons joined McLeod in New Zealand. Most settled at Waipu south of Auckland, with sister communities nearby. Still nourishing his dream of isolating his followers from the sinful world in a more perfect setting, at his death in 1866 McLeod's last words to his followers were reported to have been: "Children, children, look to yourselves; the world is mad." Waipu remains today as a popular tourist site.

MCWHIRTER, MARTHA (1827–1904). Born in Tennessee, McWhirter joined the Methodist church at age 16 and became active in church work. In 1855 she moved to Belton, Texas, with her husband. With the death of her brother and two of her children in 1866, she became convinced that she was suffering God's punishment. Thereafter she received a Pentecostal baptism and believed she was now sanctified in the perfectionist tradition. She began to hold prayer meetings for the mostly well-to-do women of the town, forcing some to leave their unsanctified (having had no Pentecostal vision) husbands. In 1876 the women, officially the Women's Commonwealth but known locally as the "Sanctificationists," set up a communal, celibate household dedicated to the interpretation of dreams, personal holiness, visions, and community property. To support themselves they worked as domestics, and in 1886 they opened a hotel in Belton. Despite their economic success in owning the hotel plus several other businesses in and around Belton, in 1899 the women, under the leadership of McWhirter, sold the hotel and moved to Mt. Pleasant in Washington, D.C. They also owned a farm in suburban Maryland. When McWhirter died in 1904, the commune began the process of disintegration. It ended in 1906, the remaining sisters moving to the farm where they operated a nursing home and a restaurant. The last surviving member of the Women's Commonwealth died at the farm in 1983.

MEACHEM, JOSEPH (1741–1796). Born and raised in a religious Baptist family, Meachem was a lay preacher at the Baptist church in New Lebanon, New York, outside of Albany, when, in 1779, he led a revival among the New Light Baptists in the area. While preaching there, he was converted to the **millennial** doctrines of **Mother Ann Lee** (1736–1784) and the **Shakers** and joined them at nearby **Mount Lebanon**, the first utopian community of native-born, English-speaking persons in the United States. When Mother Ann died in 1784 leadership passed to **James Whittaker** (1751–1787), but when he died in 1787 Meachem became one of the leaders of the Shaker community at New Lebanon. Under his tutelage, the Shakers became organized with rules set forth for their relations with the outside world and for conduct between men and women; these were later codified and published in 1821 as the *Millennial Laws.*

Meachem also appointed **Lucy Wright** (1760–1821) to lead the Shaker sisterhood and establish a separate order for women. He called upon all Shakers to come out of the world and be gathered at New Lebanon, also known as "the Holy Mount." It became the center, the "Mother-Church," of Shakerism. At New Lebanon he supervised the erection of buildings and gave the society a business-like foundation to enable its member societies to succeed economically. Under his guidance the number of Shaker communities was expanded, and ministers were trained to support the fast-growing religious sect. At Meachem's death in 1779, Lucy Wright assumed the leadership of the New Lebanon Shakers.

MEDE (or MEAD), JOSEPH (1586–1638). While England was witnessing radical, popular **millennialist** enthusiasm in the 17th century, the **Cambridge Platonists** led by the eminent Biblical scholar Joseph Mede of Christ's College were also adding a deeper dimension to millennialism. Influenced by the Protestant reliance on Scripture alone as the guide to faith and, therefore, the necessity of subjecting it to intense textual criticism, Mede (sometimes spelled Mead) and his followers accepted it literally and concluded that the **Apocalypse** clearly implied a millennium to come on earth with the binding of Satan yet to occur. This meant that the story of humankind was ultimately the story of both religious and secular progress, the golden age of the church yet to come. The pouring out of the seven vials described in the Book of Revelation, Mede argued, could be traced historically: the first the rising of the Albigensians and Waldensians, the second the work of **Martin Luther**, the third the anti-Catholic laws of Elizabeth I, the fourth the Thirty Years' War, the fifth to come with the destruction of the papacy, the sixth the conversion of the Jews, and the seventh and last the final judgment and millennium. All of these represented linear progress. The ideas of the contemporary Enlightenment, as Mede saw it, were a predestined foreshadowing of the millennium, the final step in humankind's inevitable spiritual and material progression from Eden to a new heaven and a new earth, from utopia to utopia. The ideas of this Cambridge don as espoused by himself and his disciples, such as **Thomas Burnet**, **Henry More**, **John Edwards**, and **James Burnett Monboddo**, played a major role in resurrecting the idea of a millennium arising from lineal progress through history.

MEEKER, NATHANIEL COOK (1817–1879). Little is known of the early life of this founder of the **Union Colony** from Euclid, Ohio, except that in the 1840s he became an enthusiast for the ideas of **Charles Fourier** (1772–1837) and began to lecture on his philosophy. He lived at the Fourierist **Trumbull Phalanx** in his native state for a brief period of time before returning to Euclid. In 1865 he joined **Horace Greeley**'s *New York Tribune* as its agricultural editor. Four years later he founded the Union Colony with the support of Greeley and the *Tribune.* It was located near the Platte River in Weld County, Colorado. Union Colony was based on private ownership of land but its members shared community responsibilities. It boasted a school, a library, and a lyceum, but no saloons or billboards were allowed. As president of the community Meeker was known to be lacking in tact, but his newspaper, the *Greeley Tribune,* urged moderate reform. As the Union Colony developed into another Colorado commercial center, its members voted in 1871 to opt for an elected town government to replace the officers governing them. In 1878 Meeker accepted an appointment as an Indian agent on the White River Reservation in Wyoming. The next year, again displaying his lack of tact, this time toward his Ute charges, he set off an uprising in which he and two other white men were killed.

MEGAPATAGONIA. *See* RESTIF de la BRETONNE, NICHOLAS-EDME.

MELCHIORITES. *See* HOFFMANN, MELCHIOR.

MEMNONIA INSTITUTE. The Memnonia Institute was founded in 1856 by Thomas Low Nichols and Mary Sargeant Neal Gove Nichols, a pair of reformers and **Fourierists** advocating women's rights and free love, at Yellow Springs, Ohio, after they had left **Josiah Warren**'s **Modern Times** on Long Island. Their free love views had forced them to move to Cincinnati in 1855 where they published *Nichols Monthly* and promoted hydropathy. The next year they leased the Yellow Springs Water Cure and founded the Memnonia Institute, named after the goddess of waters. They were strenuously opposed by Horace Mann, the president of Antioch College, for their free love beliefs. Undaunted, they opened their "School of Life" in September 1856, emphasizing instead asceticism, fasting, and spiritual penance. Within a year the Nicholses converted to Catholicism, claiming that one of them had been visited by Ignatius Loyola and Francis Xavier during seances. Thus the 20-member Memnonia Institute ended in March 1857 when both Thomas and Mary Nichols were baptized into the Roman Catholic faith, following three other Memnonians who had been baptized a month earlier.

MENDENHALL, HIRAM (1801–1852). *See* UNION HOME COMMUNITY.

MENDIETA, JERONIMO de. *See* JERONIMO de MENDIETA.

MEN LIKE GODS. *See* WELLS, H. G.

MENNONITES. *See* ANABAPTISTS.

MERCHANT, ELLA (1857–1916). *See* UNVEILING A PARALLEL.

MERCIER, LOUIS SEBASTIEN (1740–1814). Mercier was a Parisian man of letters who in his major work *L'An 2440* (The Year 2440; 1771) lamented the intellectual debasement that the ancient régime's tyranny had fostered in France. In this **utopian novel**, he pictured a new and better France marked by justice and true fidelity to the arts and sciences. Of major significance, in *L'An 2440* Mercier created a new literary device for depicting an ideal society, one taking place in future time instead of in some faraway place. The protagonist in this work sinks into a deep sleep and awakes 672 years later. As he walks out of doors, he beholds a transformed Paris marked by broad avenues, amiable and orderly people, carriages reserved for the elderly and the officials only, and no prostitutes or crowding in the streets. The Louvre has been completed, and the Bastille has been torn down. In the center of the city are hospitals, theaters, and houses. The very temper of the city has been progressively perfected in the years since the protagonist's sleep began. Mercier's use of the literary device of a futurist utopia would be emulated many times thereafter.

MERRILL, ALBERT ADAMS. Nothing is known about this American writer beyond the fact that he wrote the utopian novel *Utopia, The Great Awakening: The Story of the Twenty-Second Century* (1899). In it, a reincarnated 19th-century American is escorted through the technological wonderland that the United States has become 200 years in the future. The nation is now marked by electric cars and television, all persons are paid the same wage, all property belongs to the state, and happiness reigns supreme.

MESSIANIC KINGDOM OF THE JEWS. Among the Jews of ancient Israel there was a story of Paradise, or the Golden Age, as described in Genesis wherein the first man and the first woman were found in a beautiful garden where God walked in the evening and where they lived in innocence until the Fall and their expulsion. But hope for humankind to regain access to the beautiful garden and God remained within Jewish literature, as is revealed in a number of passages in the **Book of Isaiah** wherein Yahweh turned the deserts back into Eden, to a Golden Age with Jerusalem restored.

Some time thereafter, at least by the eighth century B.C., there emerged among the Jewish people the expectation of "The Day of Yahweh," signifying the triumph of God's chosen race in a restoration of the Golden Age in time when all would be light and joy with no war and abundance for all. This concept led to the belief in the establishment of the Kingdom of God to be inaugurated and administered by the Messiah (meaning "the anointed One," the "Christ" in Greek) who would be born of the house of David. When this occurs, the Messiah will establish a reign of justice and peace, as made clear in the Book of Jeremiah. At this **apocalyptic** stage, the New Covenant between God and humankind will be written in people's hearts, it will be universal and all-embracing, and its culmination will be experienced not in the world as known but in a transformed and perfected universe. From this base in Jewish literature and belief, the concept of a future millennial transformed world of perfection, of utopia, passed into Christianity in the form of the Second Coming, then into the Western world.

METAMORPHOSES. See GOLDEN AGE, MYTH OF THE.

METROPOLITAN INSTITUTE OF TEXAS. *See* BURNING BUSH, THE.

METZ, CHRISTIAN (?–1867). *See* AMANA SOCIETY.

MEXICAN COMMUNITIES. *See* APPENDIX.

MICHIGAN COMMUNITIES. *See* APPENDIX.

MILFORD COLONY. This **Hutterite** colony was founded in Beadle County, South Dakota, in 1910 as a branch of the Old Elmspring colony. Facing local opposition during World War I because of their stand against military service and their "Germanism," the members moved to Raymond, Alberta, Canada, in 1918.

MILLENNIAL DAWN PEOPLE. *See* JEHOVAH'S WITNESSES.

MILLENNIAL LAWS. See MEACHEM, JOSEPH.

MILLENNIUM, MILLENARIANISM, MILLENNIALIST. Following are definitions of these terms:

Millennium: Literally 1,000 years; also the 1,000 years mentioned in the Book of Revelation, or the **Apocalypse**, during which holiness is to prevail with Christ reigning on earth for a 1,000-year period of great earthly happiness *or* any 1,000-year period of earthly happiness.

Millenarianism: Belief in the millennium of Christian prophecy *or* belief in a coming 1,000-year ideal society.

Millennialist: A person who accepts the existence of the millennium in time, either in a religious sense or in a nonreligious sense; also referred to as a millenarian.

MILLER, JOAQUIM (1839–1913). Born Cincinnatus Hiner (or Heine) Miller in Indiana, this poet and writer drifted around the West until he became a lawyer and, in 1866, a judge. He divorced his wife, abandoned his children, and moved to London in 1870. He remained there for a year before embarking on more travel, finally settling in California in 1887. His plays, novels, and poetry drew heavily on stories from the American West. Miller's importance to utopianism rests on his *The Building of the City Beautiful* in 1893.

MILLER, WILLIAM (1782–1849). This farmer and militia veteran of the War of 1812 underwent a religious conversion around 1816 and became convinced that the Second Coming of Christ as predicted in the **Apocalypse** was imminent. He gathered thousands of enthusiastic followers in the years thereafter. Miller became a licensed Baptist preacher in 1833 and predicted that Christ would appear between March 1843 and March 1844. When this failed to occur, his Millerite (Adventist) disciples rapidly deserted his movement. However, his remaining followers subsequently organized the Seventh-Day Adventist movement in 1863.

MILLS, WALTER T. (1856–1942). *See* HIAWATHA VILLAGE.

MILLTOWN COLONY. This **Hutterite** colony was founded in 1886 at Milltown, Hutchinson County, in southeastern South Dakota. It consisted of the 19 families of the **Tripp Colony** who had attempted to start a new colony called the **Tidioute Colony** in Warren County in northwestern Pennsylvania in 1884. With its failure, they moved back to South Dakota to Milltown on the James River. They moved again in 1896 to a new location to the north in Beadle County and continued in existence until 1907.

MINNESOTA COMMUNITY. *See* APPENDIX.

MISSOURI COMMUNITIES. *See* APPENDIX.

MIZORA: A PROPHECY. See LANE, MARY E. BRADLEY.

MODERN TIMES. This community, based on the idea of the sovereignty of the individual, was established by **Josiah Warren** (1798–1874) at Brentwood in Suffolk County on Long Island in 1851 some 26 miles from New York City with the help of another reformer, Stephen Pearl Andrews (1812–1886). It advocated a cooperative and nonprofit system of labor and commodity exchange with each member owning his own house and land. The community numbered some 200 persons, including a number of former members of **Brook Farm**; some practiced free love. Warren left Modern Times in 1863 and never returned, but it continued to exist until after the turn of the century.

MODERN UTOPIA, A. See WELLS, H. G.

MODJESKA'S COLONY. This short-lived colony—sometimes referred to as the "Polish Brook Farm"—was established near Anaheim in the Santa Ana Valley in California in 1877 and collapsed in 1878. It was made up of some 20 Polish immigrants, mainly intellectuals and artists, including Henry Sienkiewicz, who later wrote *Quo Vadis* (1896). They came to the United States to escape censorship in their homeland. The colony was named after one of its members, Helena Modjeska (1840–1909), a celebrated actress. Basing their 1,165-acre colony on **Brook Farm**, they expected to set up an agricultural utopia, thereby to ensure a good, civilized life. Lacking both sufficient financial backing and knowledge of farming skills, within six months the colony had failed. Most of the colonists returned home, but Modjeska resumed her stage career, making a national tour with the noted Shakespearean actor Edwin Booth and advocating rights for Polish women.

MOHEGAN COLONY. *See* KELLY, HARRY.

MOLOKAN COMMUNITIES. The Molokans, Spiritual Christians from the Russian Transcaucasus, split from the Doubkhobors in the

18th century over whether final spiritual authority resided in a leader or in the Bible, the Molokans arguing the latter. When the pacifist Molokans resisted the tsarist draft in the latter 19th century and thereby suffered repression by the Russian government, they immigrated in 1904, first to Canada and then to southern California. They initially settled in East Los Angeles, then around Potrero Hill in San Francisco and on agricultural enclaves in the Guadalupe Valley near Ensenada, Baja California. At the Guadalupe Valley site they bought 13,000 acres, and 50 families moved there. Here they attempted to reestablish a traditional village surrounded by communally tended fields. Problems with Mexican squatters prompted them to return to the United States in the 1950s. Meanwhile, a group of Molokans had established a colony near Glendale, Arizona, in 1911 made up of four village settlements. Things went very well on this site with their cash crop of cotton, cotton growing in the area thanks to irrigation of the land. But when the cotton boom ended in 1921 and the postwar depression in cotton prices caused the colony's income to fall precipitously, most Glendale Molokans returned to Los Angeles. Another group of Molokans had established a colony near Potter Valley, near Ukiah, California, sometime around 1910; this lasted until 1918 when they returned to San Francisco. Still another group had established a colony in 1915 near Kerman, California. It remains in existence as a religious community. Ethnic enclaves of Molokans still exist in a number of locations, but their rural communal enterprises have expired.

MONBODDO, JAMES BURNETT (1714–1799). Lord Monboddo was a Scottish judge, philosopher, anthropologist, and cultural evolutionist and is usually considered a member of the **Cambridge Platonists**. He agreed with his namesake **Thomas Burnet** [*sic*] that humankind proceeds in history by stages to a union with God, redemption being the process of gradual development of the mind from the time of the Fall to fulfillment in knowledge in the "true religion" with God, that is, to a utopia with a new heaven and a new earth inhabited by a new race of righteous men properly called "saints."

MONTANA COMMUNITIES. *See* APPENDIX.

MONTANISM. This movement emerged from the preachings of one Montanus in Phrygia in central Asia Minor, who in 156 A.D. declared himself to be the Holy Spirit who was to reveal things to come. He and his disciples believed in the visions they experienced that told of the coming of the Kingdom with the impending descent of the New Jerusalem to take place in Phrygia. Montanus and the close adherents who gathered about him invited their followers to witness this Second Coming. The Montanist movement spread not only around the region of Asia Minor but also into Africa, Rome, and Gaul and even counted among its supporters the foremost theologian in the West, Tertullian. Montanism did not persist in the West much beyond the second century, but it did help to keep alive the idea of a blessed **millennium** and **apocalyptic** dreams, whether occurring soon or in a time to come.

MOORE, ALBERT J. *See* HEAVEN CITY.

MOORE, DANIEL (1764–1822). *See AN ACCOUNT OF COUNT D'ARTOIS AND HIS FRIEND'S PASSAGE TO THE MOON.*

MORAVIANS. The "Renewed Church" of the United Brethren (Unitas Fratrum), more commonly known as the Moravians, was formed in 1722 when fugitive remnants of the Bohemian Brethren, fleeing from religious persecution in Bohemia and Moravia, found refuge on the estate of Count Nicholas Ludwig von Zinzendorf (1700–1760) at Bethelsdorf in Saxony, Germany. The Brethren, a religious sect dating back to the 15th century and Jan Hus, developed an exclusive social and economic structure on Zinzendorf's estate. Additionally, they sent out emissaries to establish colonies of missionaries abroad. In 1742, with Zinzendorf as their leader, they established a colony at Bethlehem in Pennsylvania, having made communitarian arrangements called "Sea Congregations" on their passage across the Atlantic. In Pennsylvania their communitarian tendencies resulted in the establishment of the "General Economy" at Bethlehem in 1744 under which each member gave his time and labor to the General Economy, receiving no wages in return but being provided with food, clothing, and shelter by the congregation. All of the economic output of the colony, including its buildings, industries, and abundant agricultural yields, belonged to the General Economy, that is, the church, in this theocratic society. This arrangement lasted until 1762. Other Moravian colonies were established at Lititz and Nazareth, Pennsylvania, and at Wachovia (now Winston-Salem) and Bethabara, North Carolina.

MORE, HENRY (1614–1687). The **Cambridge Platonist** Henry More, **millennial**-utopianist, Anglican clergyman, theological writer, and poet, was in fundamental agreement with **Joseph Mede**, **Thomas Burnet**, **John Edwards**, and **James Burnett Monboddo**, arguing that the function of religion and knowledge was to make men better and better, redemption of humankind consisting of regaining the divine life lost by Adam and Eve in the **Garden of Eden**.

MORE, THOMAS (1478–1535). Sir Thomas More, a leading light of the English Renaissance, a devout Christian humanist, lord chancellor to Henry VIII after 1529, and martyr of the Catholic faith for refusing to accept the Act of Supremacy of 1534 making Henry the head of the Church in England, is best known as the author of the satire *Utopia* (1516 in Latin; 1551 in English, safely after the death of Henry).

The work represented More's dedication to reforming English society, its inspiration drawn from both classical models and the Christian life as More had experienced it at Charterhouse under the austere Carthusians during his four years of monastic life prior to being called to the bar in 1501. He could never have envisioned the impact of his literary satire and commentary on the centuries that followed. The second part of the work was written in 1515 in the Netherlands while More was on a diplomatic mission; while there, he discussed the work with his friend and fellow Christian humanist Desiderius Erasmus (Erasmus's *The Praise of Folly* was written in More's home and dedicated to him). The first part of *Utopia* was written back in England in 1516. The form of Utopia probably represents the influence of **Plato**'s *Republic* on the author.

More coined the title of the work, *Utopia,* from two Greek words: *ou topos,* meaning no place, and *eu topos,* meaning an ideal place. *Utopia* represents More's conviction that the only way to change human behavior—specifically that of his native England, which he knew so well and found wanting in many ways—was to improve the environment in which people lived and coordinate the principles of law with public opinion and Christian conscience. All modern utopian works and experiments to one degree or another have been influenced by the literary form and/or the ideas portrayed in More's classical work.

MOREHOUSE UNION. This **Fourierist** colony was established in 1843 at the village of Piseco, five miles north of Lake Pleasant in Hamilton County in northeastern upstate New York. Andrew K. Morehouse offered 10,000 acres of the 60,000 wilderness acres he owned in the counties of Hamilton, Herkimer, and Saratoga to any association willing to organize itself there. Despite this offer of free land on which to build a colony and some improvements actually made on it, the experiment apparently died in less than a year from financial problems and a lack of unanimity of purpose on the part of the wide variety of persons who assembled there.

MOREVILLE COMMUNITORIUM. *See* BARMBY, GOODWYN.

MORGAN, ARTHUR E. (1878–1976). Born in Cincinnati, Ohio, Morgan achieved distinction both as an engineer and as president of Antioch College, where he introduced the Antioch Plan of work-study. Although seen as somewhat of a utopian dreamer heavily influenced by **Edward Bellamy**'s *Looking Backward*, Morgan was tapped by President Franklin D. Roosevelt to be the first chairman of the Tennessee Valley Authority during the New Deal. In 1940 Morgan founded Community Service, Inc. (CSI) to promote family life and small towns in order to assure mutual respect and neighborly cooperation. Always interested in communal settlements, he held regular conferences at Antioch to promote intentional communities. Under his guidance the Inter-Community Exchange was founded, which evolved into the **Fellowship of Intentional Communities**, which worked closely with Community Service, Inc. CSI continues to promote communal values via its headquarters in Yellow Springs, Ohio.

MORGAN, JOSEPH (1671–post 1745). At one time a Congregational and later a Presbyterian minister and always controversial in his day,

Joseph Morgan was the author of the persistently complex *The History of the Kingdom of Basaruah*, an allegory that presents the Calvinist view of human fall and redemption. Basaruah (from Hebrew roots meaning "flesh-spirit"), located somewhere in North America, is described as a kingdom where the people live happily under its king, Pantocrator (the Almighty), until the destruction of a levee redirects the River of Turbulent Waters, cutting Basaruah off from the magnificent land of Shamajim and leaving the people unable to pay their taxes, a failure punishable by slavery in the sulfurous country of Gehenna. But the son of Pantocrator the Almighty becomes a citizen of Basaruah, saves the kingdom by earning the tax money, builds a ford across the river, and offers a home in Shamajim to any citizen willing to follow him. Pantocrator's lord high secretary, Ruah Kadosh (Holy Spirit), is sent to lead them across the river. But not all citizens of Basaruah are willing to follow him to the happy land of Shamajim, preferring less noble alternatives or rejecting the authority of the Publishers of the Proclamation, native Basaruahans appointed to lead them to Shamajim. The obvious allegory to the Christian story of the **Garden of Eden**, the Fall, the Incarnation, and the Redemption concludes with a great judgment of the people of Basaruah and punishment for those who have rejected Pantocrator's offer of salvation.

MORMONS, *or* CHURCH OF JESUS CHRIST OF LATTER-DAY SAINTS. This religion was founded by Joseph Smith (1805–1844), a farm worker near Palmyra, New York, who taught that God had restored his "latter-day" religion in 1823 by sending the angel Moroni to himself to show new divine Scriptures to Smith before returning them to heaven. Smith translated the golden plates on which the Scriptures were printed from their "reformed Egyptian" text by means of accompanying stones, then published them in the *Book of Mormon* (1830), the book being named after Mormon, an ancient prophet in North America. In that same year, Smith organized the church. Mormons accept the *Book of Mormon* as a sacred history of three Middle Eastern groups who had migrated to America prior to 600 B.C. and had been visited by Christ after his Resurrection. It is considered part of the Christian Scriptures.

Converts flocked to Mormonism, and centers of the faith were built in Kirtland, Ohio, and Zion in Missouri. When the Mormons faced violence in Missouri in 1838, they moved to **Nauvoo**, Illinois, and within five years had gained nearly 20,000 members. Because they practiced polygamy, Smith and his brother were jailed in nearby Carthage in 1844. While confined there, a mob of 150 men broke into the jail and shot both men dead. Brigham Young (1801–1877), who had been in England, where he had converted 2,000 to the faith and who had been chosen by Smith in 1835 as one of the Twelve Apostles, returned to lead the church. Then in 1846–1847, amid internal dissention, Young led his followers to the valley of the Great Salt Lake in Utah to establish a utopian society called Desert Free of Harassment and Worldliness. In this location, the church flourished in its "cooperative colonization" on the basis of irrigation-system agriculture and manufacturing, aided by the building of railroads in the area.

Young was appointed to be the Utah Territory's governor in 1850 and served until 1857, when he refused to be replaced by the federal government; this led to the "Mormon War" of 1857–1858. Still, he continued to govern despotically until his death in 1877. The Mormons' practice of polygamy—Young himself had 27 wives and 56 children—was formally repudiated by the Mormon Church in 1890, although it has continued sub rosa in some Mormon families to the present day. Despite a split among the members in the latter part of the 19th century, the Mormons through their missionary work now claim a membership of 5 million in the United States, 2 million in South America, 600,000 in Asia, 750,000-plus in Mexico, and about 400,000 each in Europe and Central America.

MORRIS, WILLIAM (1834–1896). William Morris was educated at Exeter College, Oxford, and subsequently turned to the field of architecture, establishing his own firm in 1861 that changed the art of house decoration and furnishings in Britain. He also published poetry and translated Virgil's *Aeneid* and Homer's *Odyssey*. In 1883 he joined the Social Democratic Federation and became an avid socialist. Under this influence, he published his utopian romance *News from Nowhere* in 1891. He also gained notoriety with his scathing criticism of **Edward Bellamy**'s *Looking Backward*, arguing that it lacked an authentic sense of history, distorted the true nature of socialism, and was naive in believing that society could evolve into an industrial army freed of human greed and failure.

MOUNTAIN COVE COMMUNITY. *See* SPIRITUALIST COMMUNITY AT MOUNTAIN COVE.

MOUNT AIRY COLONY. *See* KELLY, HARRY.

MOUNT LEBANON, *or* **NEW LEBANON COMMUNITY.** Located in New Lebanon Township, Columbia County, New York, this community was the first **Shaker** communitarian settlement based on **Mother Ann Lee**'s **millennialism**. Officially called the United Society of Believers in Christ's Second Coming and also known as the Holy Mount, it grew out of revival meetings of 1779 and was established in 1787, three years after the death of Mother Ann, under the leadership of **James Whittaker** (1751–1787), the major organizer of the sect. As the center of Shakerism, the "Mother-Church," it survived until 1947; during its years of existence, its total membership numbered 3,202 persons. From this base, Shaker missionaries established new communities both in the Northeast and the Midwest during the late 18th and early 19th centuries.

MOVING THE MOUNTAIN. See GILMAN, CHARLOTTE PERKINS.

MUHAMMAD, ELIJAH (1897–1975). *See* NATION OF ISLAM.

MULLER (*or* **MUELLER**), **BERNHARD "COUNT LEON"** (1787–1834). This religious mystic was born in Germany and considered himself a prophet. In 1813 Muller founded a secret order called the *Duchy of Jerusalem* while living in Ireland, then moved on to London and to a number of towns in his native Germany. In 1831 he immigrated to the United States, announcing while en route that he would now be known as "Count Leon." After touring several American cities he arrived at **Economy**, Pennsylvania, announcing to the Harmonists there that he was the Archduke Maximillian and the "Lion of Judah" and that he was divinely sent to usher in the **millennium**.

The following year, after precipitating a dispute with **George Rapp** (1757–1847) over leadership of the colony, he and 176 of his followers left Economy and established the **New Philadelphia Colony** at Phillipsburg (now Monaca) 10 miles northwest of Economy on the Ohio River. Then in September 1833, he led his followers down the Ohio and Mississippi Rivers to establish a New Jerusalem. The next year they settled at **Grand Ecore** in Natchitoches Parish, Louisiana. The colony had failed by 1836. In the meantime, Muller had died and had been buried there at a place his followers named Gethsemane. Those who were left in the colony moved north to **Germantown**, Louisiana, in Webster Parish, where they attempted to carry on the Grand Ecore experiment.

MUNDUS ALTER ET IDEM. *Mundus Alter et Idem Sive Terra Australis ante hac semper incognita* (A World Different and Identical Located in Terra Australis), a precursor to later **dystopias**, was published in 1605 by Joseph Hall (1574–1656), bishop of Exeter and Norwich. It is a satire and a critique of the Land of **Cockaygne** written under the pseudonym "Mercurius Brittanicus." In *Mundus Alter et Idem,* Mercurius tells the story of a voyage to Antarctica where a new society is discovered. It has five divisions: Crapulia where gluttony rules and the state ensures drunkenness and overindulgence in food; Viraginia where women rule men; Moronia where folly is the guide to action; Lavernia where anarchy reigns; and Terra Sancta, which is not described by the pious bishop. Hall's point is that reason alone cannot be a guide for human conduct because of humankind's perversity and self-indulgence; only through living a Christian life, Hall infers, can humankind achieve an ideal existence. The picture Hall paints is of humans acting like primitives or animals. *Mundus,* then, is a parody on **Thomas More**'s *Utopia* and a warning that the civilized world of the early 17th century was in a state of regression and in need of reform.

MUNTZER, THOMAS (1491?–1525). From the Protestant Revolution begun by **Martin Luther** there emerged a number of radical responses to existing authority. Among these was the Peasants' Revolt in Germany that began in 1525 and was directed against landlords and the Church. Monasteries and castles were plundered, and the abolition of serfdom was demanded. In Thuringia, a central German state, the rebels were led by the priest Thomas Muntzer. Thoroughly absorbed in **apocalyptic** speculation, Muntzer was convinced that the people, as God's elect, were the natural leaders of Christianity, that the Last Judgment was at hand, and that a heaven on earth could be created by giving the people the power of the sword and by their living sinlessly. He also taught that theologians, intellectuals, and the wealthy were antiguides to perfection because the common human understood the Bible better than they and that he was an instrument of God given the task of destroying the ungodly and creating God's heaven on earth. Luther, however, was convinced that Muntzer's utopian mixture of religion and politics was "the Devil's work" and encouraged the princes to restore order in the Germanys. In Thuringia as well as throughout the empire, the civil and religious authorities, Catholic as well as reformist, turned against the rebelling peasants and put down their revolt, some 100,000 peasants and religious rebels being killed in a campaign of repression. Muntzer was beheaded on May 15, 1525, and by the next year the movement had been crushed.

MUTUAL AID COMMUNITY. Established by **Alcander Longley** (1832–1918) in 1883 near Glen Allen in Bollinger County in southeastern Missouri, this 120-acre colony had 20 to 30 members. It was disbanded in 1887 because of a lack of members and financial difficulties. This was Longley's final attempt to form a viable commune, the two that followed containing only Longley and his family.

MUTUAL HOME ASSOCIATION. *See* HOME COLONY.

– N –

NABOKOV, VLADIMIR (1899–1977). *See BEND SINISTER.*

NARCOOSSEE. This **Shaker community** was established in 1894 by a small delegation from **Watervliet** called the "Olive Branch" on 7,046 acres in Osceola County in central Florida. Consisting of about two dozen members, these Shakers depended on citrus fruits, fishing, and cattle raising for their subsistence. Many members of the **Koreshan**

Unity at Estero visited the community, and one Koreshan joined Narcoossee in 1906. The community was dissolved in 1924 when the membership of the celibate community reached old age.

NASHOBA. Located on the Wolf River in western Shelby County near Memphis, Tennessee ("Nashoba" means "wolf" in the Chickasaw language), Nashoba, an interracial community on a 640-acre site, was founded by **Frances Wright** (1795–1852) in 1826. She planned to establish an asylum and school of industry for manumitted slaves, who, properly socialized with one another, would repay their masters and then be transported and colonized outside the United States. Additionally, following Wright's belief in full religious and sexual freedom, she allowed the members full social and sexual equality. There were never more than 15 slaves and even fewer whites in the colony. While Wright was absent from the colony in 1827, she left it in the care of James Richardson and two other trustees, and during this time it became public not only that Richardson had sexual relations with a black woman but also that miscegenation was occurring at Nashoba. Richardson had also prepared an article for publication that gave explicit details about free love in the interracial colony. When Wright returned from Europe in 1828, she found the society in a shambles and Richardson gone. Unable to get her experiment back on track, Wright, too, soon left the colony. For all practical purposes, it ceased to exist in 1829. In 1830 she placed 31 blacks in Haiti, the final end for Nashoba.

NATION OF ISLAM. The Nation of Islam first appeared in Detroit in 1930 under the leadership of Wallace D. Ford, later interpreted by members of his movement as Allah. He and **Elijah Muhammad** (1897–1975), his successor and Last Messenger, envisioned a future in which the world would be changed completely after a final battle, a holy war between blacks and whites, initiated by the Mother Ship, or Mother of Planes, carrying 1,500 bombers to crush white America into submission. Thereafter the blacks would rise to their rightful, superior place in the world. In this new age, unrighteousness having been destroyed, there would be perfect peace and happiness. Elijah also demanded a separate state on the North American continent. This **millennial** idea reached its full power in the 1960s during the time of the involvement of Malcolm X (1925–1965) in the movement before his defection to traditional, orthodox Islam in 1964 and his assassination the next year. When the **Apocalypse** failed to occur in 1965 and 1966 as Elijah had prophesied and the nation's economic growth and the government's social programs ameliorated many of the pressing needs of the black community, the Nation of Islam became more moderate.

This was upset, however, with the emergence to prominence of Louis Farrakhan in the 1970s after Elijah Muhammad's death. Minister Farrakhan revitalized the Nation of Islam and preached the millennial doctrine of Elijah and the fall of the United States in an apocalyptic struggle between the races before moving the Nation to a more traditional form of Islam beginning in 1986. Still, the Nation of Islam remains a powerful separatist movement, its millennialist doctrines, including its belief in a coming racial Armageddon, unchanged by the events of the late 20th century.

NATIONAL PRODUCTION COMPANY. *See* SOUTHERN CO-OPERATIVE ASSOCIATION OF APALACHICOLA.

NATIVE TONGUE. See ELGIN, SUZETTE.

NATURE'S CODE. Authored by one Morelly, whose identity has never been ascertained but whose works have been ascribed to **Denis Diderot** and other 18th-century philosophers, *Nature's Code* was published in 1755. It describes an ideal society and reflects Morelly's views that moral evil is not inherent in humans but, rather, is caused by evil-producing institutions. In this beautiful and bountiful land of mountains, forests, fields, and rivers, there is no holding of private property by the inhabitants because they believe that God created humans only to help one another. Work is cooperative and commingled with merrymaking and feasting. As strict vegetarians, the people partake of grains, fruits, vegetables, and milk and honey; live to extreme old age without wrinkles; and die as though gently falling asleep. All persons are supported and employed at public expense and contribute to the public good according to their means. The nation is divided into families, tribes of families, and cities of tribes, all in equal numbers; each share equally in all things, money and bartering being forbidden. Every fifth day is set aside for rest, the year being divided into 73 equal parts; workers may retire at the age of 40; the elderly are meticulously cared for; after age 30 persons can dress as they please (in other words, not uniformly as they have been since age 10);

the head of each family at age 50 becomes a member of the lawmaking Senate; all laws are according to the principle "willed by Reason, prescribed by Law"; all persons must marry at a public ceremony that is held at the beginning of each year; celibacy is forbidden for all persons under 40; and divorce is allowed only once. Whoever Morelly was, his thoughts as presented in *Nature's Code* and other works had a distinct impact on utopian thinkers such as **Francois Noel Babeuf** (1760–1797), **Charles Fourier** (1772–1837), and the founders of **Brook Farm**.

NAUVOO. This town near the Mississippi River in western Illinois was the home to two utopian groups between 1838 and 1859. In 1838 the **Mormons** fled from Zion near Kansas City to Nauvoo and by 1843 had brought 2,000 members to the community. When Joseph Smith (1805–1844) was murdered in nearby Carthage in 1844, Brigham Young (1801–1877) in the beginning of 1846 led the Mormons to the valley of the Great Salt Lake in Utah. Four years later, in 1850, **Etienne Cabet** (1788–1856) led a band of some 280 **Icarian** refugees from Texas and New Orleans to the nearly deserted town. Buying up houses and renting the farms to sustain the people, they soon numbered upward of 1,500 people at Icaria-Nauvoo and enjoyed considerable economic success. But dissension arose over Cabet's leadership and he was voted out of the presidency of the colony, so he left for St. Louis with 180 followers, where he established the colony of Icaria-**Cheltenham**. He died there in 1856, and the Cheltenham project was abandoned in 1864. Meanwhile some of the remaining Nauvoo members moved to Iowa to start a new colony at Icaria-**Corning**, and those who remained in Nauvoo soon dispersed in 1859, ending the town as the site of two major ventures in American utopianism.

NEBRASKA COMMUNITIES. *See* APPENDIX.

NEVADA COLONY. This socialist colony was founded by C. V. Eggleston who, for unclear reasons, left the **Llano del Rio Colony** in California in 1915 and moved to Nevada to establish a colony there, legally separating from Llano the next year. Located in Churchill County, which had the highest concentration of socialists in the state, the colony seemed to have bright prospects for the future. The first settlers moved to the main colony site at Nevada City in May 1916, and by 1918 the colony numbered about 200 persons on 1,540 acres of land. But the Nevada Colony was beset by dissension from the beginning over land rights, and Eggleston resigned from the governing board in 1917. Thereafter more dissension arose over the colony's various industries, and in May 1919 it went into receivership and the few remaining members departed. Today the Nevada Colony exists only as one of Nevada's ghost towns.

NEVADA COMMUNITIES. *See* APPENDIX.

NEW ATLANTIS. This incomplete allegorical romance was authored by **Sir Francis Bacon, Viscount St. Albans** (1561–1626), English scientist and utopian. It was written between 1614 and 1618 and published in Latin in 1626, the year of his death. It describes an imaginary commonwealth, Bensalem, on an island in the South Seas, in which its inhabitants seek to develop a civilization based on knowledge attained through natural science. Visitors, blown off their course on their way to the Far East, arrive and are placed in the House of Strangers. Here they learn that the people of Bensalem live a life of pure Christianity. The core of the island's culture is the Society of Solomon's House where scientific knowledge is cherished and expanded by its scientist-members. They have invented machinery of all types, such as telephones, airplanes, and submarines, and they practice vivisection and the crossbreeding of plants. Ambassadors from Bensalem, called "Merchants of Light," are sent out to inform others of their developments on their isolated commonwealth. Although *New Atlantis* is important for inspiring other writers of utopian literature to work for a better society through scientific knowledge, Bacon's other works, such as his *The Advancement of Learning* (1605) and *Novum Organum* (1620), had an equal or greater impact on Western thought through his advocacy of knowledge gained by collection, comparison, and analysis as a means of attaining a more perfect society.

NEW AUSTRALIA COLONY. This colony was established in Paraguay, South America, in 1893 by 220 Australians under the leadership of William Lane (1861–1917), founder of the New Australian Cooperative Settlement Association. The Association advocated communal ownership of property, savings of capital, communal maintenance of children, and women ranking equally with men. No one was allowed to join who did not speak English, had a bad reputation, was opposed to socialism, drank alcohol, was involved in a de facto marriage, or was Chinese. Members were to be allowed freedom of speech, religious freedom, and leisure. Lane's authoritarianism upset many members on the trip to South America, and the harsh conditions they met only made things worse. Accordingly, in 1894 some of the members broke away and settled at **Cosme** some 45 miles away. Five years later, in 1899, Lane severed all connection with New Australia and left the settlement to some of the original residents. New Australia continued to exist, and the descendants of those who stayed and those who migrated to Cosme still live in the area.

NEW BERGEN. *See* OLE BULL'S COLONY.

NEW DISCOVERY OF TERRA INCOGNITA AUSTRALIS, A. See AUSTRALIANS.

NEW ECONOMY. See GRONLUND, LAURENCE.

NEW ELMSPRING COLONY. This **Hutterite** colony, which had branched off from the **Elmspring Colony**, was founded in 1900 near Ethan, South Dakota, on the Hutchinson-Hanson County line just west of Sioux Falls. Like many other Hutterite colonies that faced hostility during World War I, the colony migrated to Canada in 1918, reestablishing itself at Magrath in Alberta, a short distance north of the Alberta–Montana border.

"NEW ENLIGHTENMENT." By the middle and late decades of the 19th century in European circles—and increasingly in American circles—a broad-based belief had come into existence in what might be termed scientific or positivist realism. This represented a "New Enlightenment" that rejected the Old Enlightenment as too tied to the supernatural and metaphysics and too dogmatic. In its place, the intellectuals espoused scientific and positivist reality and a new emphasis on social problems and their amelioration. Like their forebears, the leaders of the New Enlightenment were optimistic about human nature, believing that history demonstrated an evolutionary linear path of humankind. Whether they took the form of **Auguste Comte**'s "social physics," **Karl Marx**'s "scientific socialism," or other formulae, all their creeds assumed that all of humankind's questions and society's problems could be and should be addressed and solved by science. The older "moral sciences," such as theology, politics, and history, were accepted by these New Enlightenment intellectuals only insofar as their processes and conclusions were demonstrable by science. Only laws discoverable in concrete nature by science (not causes and essences, i.e., theology and metaphysics) were to be accepted as sources of knowledge and power and as guides to action. Philosophy itself was to be a "philosophy of activity" not a "philosophy of spirit," and true philosophers, the doyens of the New Enlightenment insisted, have an obligation to act in the interest of humankind.

Surely, if perhaps imperceptibly, a major shift in Western thought was coming to fruition in the 19th century. God, the supernatural, theology, and metaphysics were being steadily replaced by rationalism and its handmaidens, **scientism** and **positivism**. The "New Enlightenment," accordingly, played a major role not only in advancing the idea of humankind's ability to progress but also in secularizing the accepted means of achieving that progress to perfection.

NEW ERA. Written by **Charles W. Caryl** and published in 1897, this work described in great detail Caryl's imaginary model city designed to assure perfected working and living conditions for the people living there. The worker-owned and -operated New Era model city would be the creation of the cooperative New Era Union and would be populated by generals, majors, captains, lieutenants, sergeants, privates, and recruits ranked "according to their ability and usefulness." Built on a level tract of land 10 miles square, the spiderweb-designed city would feature 239 circular avenues in concentric circles radiating out from the center, glass-covered promenades with electric railways for the convenience of the residents, 100-foot-wide arcades, broad streets, and 150-foot-wide boulevards. A grand "Administration Capital for the New Era Model City and the New Era Union" at the very center of the radiating circles would be surrounded by a circular park and ringed by a "Grand Exposition and Emporium Building." The workers would live in 10-story apartment buildings connected by the arcades and featuring underground pipes and wiring plus an electric railway to convey all supplies and other goods to the residents. Each apartment would have an outside view. The apartment roofs would contain promenades, bicycle paths, and gardens. These apartment buildings would also include public parlors, libraries, lecture rooms and classrooms, amusement halls, and dining rooms.

New Era would also feature a steam railroad to connect all parts of the city, an amusement park, an artists' park, a national park, an exposition park, a university park, a fraternal park, a temple park for all religions, an arcade park for socializing and listening to music during the afternoons and evenings, and a complex of hotels and office buildings. Manufacturing and stock and dairy farming would be carried out in the circles farthest from the center and beyond the residents' apartments.

The apartments themselves would be arranged in order of importance, the first generals' circle estates closest to the center, each to cost $500,000 or more; then the second generals' circle, the third generals' circle, and the generals' apartment building; the first majors' circle, park, and apartment building; the first captain's circle, park, and apartment building; and on down the list to the recruits' apartment buildings. Caryl noted that in the first stage of development of his model city, some 1 million persons would be accommodated in New Era (1,000 generals, 10,000 majors, 100,000 captains, 150,000 lieutenants, 200,000 sergeants, 250,000 privates, and 289,000 recruits), but eventually some 5 million would live in his fully developed city.

Caryl's description of New Era is without a doubt the most fantastic and detailed imaginary city envisioned in the Western world since **Tommaso Campanella**'s *City of the Sun* in the early 17th century. However, there is no evidence that it had any impact either when it was published or since.

NEW GLOUCESTER SOCIETY. *See* SABBATHDAY LAKE.

NEW HAMPSHIRE COMMUNITIES. *See* APPENDIX.

NEW HARMONY. This well-known colony was established in 1825 by the self-made Welsh industrialist and reformer **Robert Owen** (1771–1858) on the 20,000-acre site of a colony called *Harmony* founded by **George Rapp** (1757–1847) 10 years before on the Wabash River in southwestern Indiana. The purchase price of $125,000 included 180 structures. These included public buildings, factories, shops, and housing for 700 persons. New Harmony's membership was made up largely from the ranks of working men but included no skilled craftsmen and no farmers; by the fall of 1825 some 900 persons had been drawn to the site, but they shared little or nothing in religion, work habits, or interests. New Harmony was beset by malingering and confusion from the beginning because Owen, who was rarely there, failed to provide adequate leadership and because he was constantly changing the constitutions under which the colony would operate (seven constitutions were inaugurated over the short life of the colony). As a result, in February 1826 a second colony called *Macluria* after **William Maclure** (1763–1840) broke off from New Harmony, and another colony called *Feiba-Peveli* followed suit. By early 1827 Owen was engaged in selling off the properties of New Harmony, and with Owen himself leaving the colony in July of that year, his initial experiment in communalism—a "study in dissonance," according to Arthur Bestor—came to an end.

NEW HOUSE OF ISRAEL COLONY. See ISRAELITES.

NEW ICARIAN COMMUNITY, *or* **NON-PROGRESSIVES OF NEW ICARIA.** With the bitter split of 1878 in the Icarian **Corning** community in Adams County, Iowa, some of the members formed **Jeune Icarie** while the more conservative members formed the New Icarian Community nearby, about a mile southeast of the old community. Many members were elderly, and many were very young; still, they managed to continue as a community until 1895 as the last of the followers of the ideas of **Etienne Cabet** (1788–1856) in the United States.

NEW ITALY. Established in 1882 in New South Wales, Australia, by Italian immigrants, this communal society established a school, church, and winery. The silk industry instituted there garnered some honors but was not profitable and eventually collapsed. As the original members died off, so too did their socialist-communal ideas. New Italy's Australian-born members opted for individual ownership of property. The colony reached its end in 1955.

NEW JERSEY COMMUNITIES. *See* APPENDIX.

NEW JERUSALEM. According to the **Apocalypse**, after the **millennium** and the final defeat of Satan the present world will end with the Parousia and the Last Judgment; then the New Jerusalem will descend from heaven as the final abode of the souls redeemed by Christ, Satan and his followers being cast into hell for all eternity.

NEW JERUSALEM COMMUNITY. This Jewish Christian community (?–1913) was established by James Fisher in Western Australia east of Narrogin near the southwest coast of the continent. Beginning with 4,000 acres, the 70 members of the community later expanded the colony to 20,000 acres, eventually clearing 30 percent for farming. The venture ended when Fisher, who claimed he had received revelations from Christ, died in 1913.

NEW LANARK. A textile mill in New Lanark, Scotland, was taken over by **Robert Owen** (1771–1858) in 1800 and personally directed by him until 1829. He used it as a reform project, creating a model industrial community by improving working conditions, limiting working hours and child labor, and experimenting with educational innovations. It also offered pensions, cheap housing, and medical care for the workers and their families. Education being at the base of Owen's socialist ideas, infants were admitted to school as soon as they could walk and graduated into the mill at age 12. New Lanark, with some 1,300 inhabitants, became a site visited by thousands of people interested in Owen's model mill and town, which were a reflection of his reform ideas, as spelled out in his *A New View of Society* (1813). Convinced that his ideas should be established on a wider communitarian scale and building on his international reputation as an advocate of welfare capitalism, Owen visited the United States in 1824 and soon after established **New Harmony** in Indiana, one of many ventures worldwide that were attempts to put his communal ideas into practice. His direction of New Lanark ended in 1829.

NEW LEBANON. *See* LEE, MOTHER ANN; MEACHEM, JOSEPH; SHAKERS.

NEW LLANO (*or* **NEWLLANO**) **CO-OPERATIVE COLONY.** Located in Vernon Parish in west central Louisiana, this socialist colony was established in 1917 and led by **Job Harriman** (1861–1925). It was composed of some 40 members from the defunct **Llano del Rio Company** in California plus 25 families from Texas. Located on the site of an abandoned mill town on 20,000 acres of cut-over timber land, the land and property were purchased for $120,000, and its membership grew appreciably during the post–World War I depression of 1920–1921, reaching a maximum of about 500 in 1930. In

1923 the colony became the home of a radical educational institution called **Commonwealth College**, which before long moved to Mena, Arkansas. But hobbled by remaining debts from the Llano venture and the foolish purchase of a large tract of land in Gila, New Mexico, for another 1,000 colonists, the colony became more selective in its membership, refusing membership to anyone who could not pay an admission fee of $2,000. New Llano went bankrupt in 1936, and formally dissolved in 1938.

NEW NORWAY. *See* OLE BULL'S COLONY.

NEW ODESSA COMMUNITY. Founded by **William Frey** (1839–1888) in 1883 on a 760-acre site at Glendale, Douglas County, in southwestern Oregon as a refuge for some 50 Jews fleeing persecution in their native Russia, the community was based on common land holding and other socialist beliefs. Frey, a non-Jew, soon caused dissension by preaching a "religion of humanity." This, combined with economic difficulties despite the fact that all resources and earnings were pooled by the members, led to the demise of the colony by 1887.

NEW PHILADELPHIA COLONY. This colony was established at Phillipsburg (now Monaca), Pennsylvania, in 1832 by **Bernhard "Count Leon" Muller** (1787–1834) and his 250 followers who had broken with **George Rapp** (1757–1847) at **Economy** over celibacy and leadership. It was dissolved the next year to relocate their New Jerusalem on the same latitude as the original; accordingly, in 1834 they reestablished themselves at **Grand Ecore**, Louisiana.

NEWS FROM NOWHERE; OR AN EPOCH OF REST: BEING SOME CHAPTERS FROM A UTOPIAN ROMANCE. This utopian romance was published in 1891 by **William Morris** (1834–1896), the noted English socialist. The work had been serialized the previous year in *Commonwealth,* a socialist weekly published by Morris. In the first part of the book, Morris's chief character, William Guest, awakens during the 21st century in a communist society called Nowhere. As he travels through London, he finds many positive changes: the divisions of society have all but vanished, women are freed from traditional sexual mores, education is voluntary but open to all who desire it, slums and factories have disappeared, political decisions are made by majority vote in the communes, and the people's list of "necessities" (created by the capitalist system) have been whittled down. In the second part of the book, Guest is told by an elderly historian that a violent revolution that took place in 1952 had changed English life completely with politics being abandoned and a pagan form of religion replacing the religion from times past. In the final section of the book, Guest travels up the Thames beyond Oxford to celebrate the haymaking season, revealing the author's vision of a more perfect and innocent nontechnological society. Here the reader finds Morris's repudiation of the ideas presented in **Edward Bellamy**'s *Looking Backward,* for in Morris's new and better society people work with few machines and without managers or factories. *News from Nowhere* was reprinted eight times before Morris's death in 1896. Although its short-term impact was far less than that of *Looking Backward,* it is valued today for its criticism of capitalist society.

NEWTON, ISAAC (1642–1727). This English philosopher-mathematician, inventor of calculus, and creator of Newtonian physics argued that the human mind can understand all of God's creation by the use of science. He was one of the leaders of the Scientific Revolution, which reenforced the ascendancy of reason over faith during the 17th century, and thus he played a key role in establishing **scientism** as one of the cardinal rules of human progress.

NEW VIEW OF SOCIETY, A. See OWEN, ROBERT.

NEW VILLAGE MOVEMENT. *See* LIU SHIHP'EI.

NEW WORLD, THE. See ETZLER, JOHN ADOLPHUS.

NEW YORK COMMUNITIES. *See* APPENDIX.

NEW ZEALAND COMMUNITIES. *See* AUSTRALIAN AND NEW ZEALAND COMMUNITIES in APPENDIX.

NICHOLSON, VALENTINE (1809–1904). *See* PRAIRIE HOME COMMUNITY.

NIEBUHR, REINHOLD (1892–1971). *See* SOFT UTOPIANISM.

NIETZSCHE, FRIEDRICH (1844–1900). Aiding in the acceptance of progressive-utopian ideas in modern times were the teachings of a number of philosophers. One of the most prominent of these was the German philosopher Friedrich Nietzsche, who had a major impact on Western thought, thereby setting the stage for what was to follow. Nietzsche, accepting the 19th-century decay of organized religion, announced the "death of God" not only philosophically but also theologically, not even bothering to prove his assertion but simply accepting the currents of his time. God and Christianity were simply passé, they had been annihilated, and they deserved only ridicule, said Nietzsche. Christians had at last tired of their scriptural fables and theological mythology in an age of enlightenment, psychological maturity, and progress; they had opted for evolutionary reason and science. For this atheist son and grandson of Lutheran ministers, the truth was obvious: God was dead ("God" meaning not only the historical Christian God but also all supersensible reality) and man (finally and rightly) killed him off. That this had occurred was good because Christian morals had made humans effete, smug, and unwilling to embark on the perilous journey toward truth. And since God is dead, he is now to be replaced as the touchstone of life by perfected man, by Superman, as the new god on earth.

To be human, therefore, is to revolt against the fraudulent God of conjecture and begin working for the rediscovery and transformation of natural, historical man wherein the Superman will be the meaning of the earth. Man, through his inherent dynamic Will to Power, his mastery over things, his self-overcoming, and his aspiring to a higher state of being, is man the becoming who will by his efforts continue to advance to infinite utilitarian perfection, to Superman, in time. God is dead, concluded Nietzsche, and man is capable of creating greatness out of the nothingness that surrounds him by his Will to Power. Nietzsche, then, helped set the stage for the secular perfectionism that had come to dominate the Western mind by the end of the 20th century.

NINETEEN EIGHTY-FOUR. This **dystopian** novel published in 1949 was the work of **George Orwell** (the adopted pseudonym of Eric Blair, 1903–1950), English novelist, teacher, socialist, militia member of the leftists during the Spanish Civil War, and bitter critic of all tyrannical states, whether fascist, communist, or capitalist, that threaten to destroy family love, tolerance toward others, and personal

autonomy of mind. Orwell was also the author of ***Animal Farm***
(1945) and other works of fiction and nonfiction. *Nineteen Eighty-
Four,* a grim and powerful warning against the growing power of
modern governments, is set in England in the near future. The world
has been divided into three superstates with England a colony of the
United States ("Oceania"), and two of the three states are constantly
at war with one another to avoid peace, any social discontent, and
challenges to their ruler-dictators.

Orwell's main character is Winston Smith, who works in London for the Ministry of Truth and spends his working hours rewrit-
ing and, therefore, obliterating, history. The new history is written
in Newspeak, an innovative language designed to make "unpatri-
otic" and all other thoughts impossible to formulate and express,
thereby denying the people the ability to think rationally and express their thoughts. And Doublethink, its companion, enables its
followers to hold contradictory ideas simultaneously. Thus the
Ministry of Peace wages war, the Ministry of Truth delivers false
propaganda, the Ministry of Plenty controls rationing, and the
Ministry of Love runs the torture chambers. Doublethink is possible because, metaphysics having been abolished, there is no truth.
Hate is the only emotion allowed to the Party members, and absolute loyalty to the totally intrusive Big Brother is demanded.
Marriage is only for procreation, scientists are working on eradi-
cating the orgasm, and there is a Junior Anti-Sex League. These
measures are designed to create sexual frustration that can be converted into more socially desirable channels, such as witnessing
public executions.

Contrary to Party regulations, Winston Smith begins a love affair
with a saucy female Party member, and they escape London's decay
by fleeing to the countryside. Here they stay in the vicinity of the Pro-
les (proletarians), who embody all that seems to be left of human de-
cency but are too poor and passive to appreciate their own inherent
dignity and resist Big Brother. But Winston and his lover are captured
and imprisoned. He is subsequently "reeducated" (brainwashed) by
O'Brien out of his idea that the truth really exists, that two and two
are in fact four, not five. Winston is told that the truth cannot be discovered in fallible individuals but only in the collective mind of the
immortal Party. The truth is what the Party says it is. Thus the Party
controls not only the actions of the people to the *n*th degree but also
their very thoughts and emotions.

To the astonishment and disappointment of most readers, Winston ends up embracing Big Brother, his ideas, and his state. Thus in *Ninety Eighty-Four,* like **Aldous Huxley** in his *Brave New World,* Orwell in 1949 sent a clear warning to the modern world regarding **scientism**, governmentalism, and incipient totalitarianism.

NINEVEH. This was a branch of the **William Keil's** (1812–1877) Bethel Community of Shelby County in northeastern Missouri. It was established in Nineveh Township in nearby Adair County in 1849, four years after the parent colony began its existence. Having some 150 members at its peak and based on the same religious and communal life as Bethel, it functioned until 1878.

NININGER CITY. *See* DONNELLY, IGNATIUS.

NISKEYUNA. *See* WATERVLIET COLONY—NEW YORK.

NISWONGER, CHARLES ELLIOT (1868–1918). *See ISLE OF FEMININE, THE.*

NON-PROGRESSIVES OF NEW ICARIA. *See* NEW ICARIAN COMMUNITY.

NÖOSPHERE. *See* TEILHARD de CHARDIN, PIERRE.

NORTH AMERICAN PHALANX. This **Fourierist phalanx** was established in 1843 on a 673-acre farm near Red Bank in Monmouth County, New Jersey, some 40 miles south of New York City. Although the phalanx in theory as the basic unit of the Fourierist utopian community was to have 1,620 persons living in common houses called phalansteries on 5,000 acres with all work being done according to individual abilities, the leaders at Red Bank failed to understand fully and teach their members the basic principles of Fourierist phalanxes. Accordingly, disputes arose over questions of organization and governance, work assignments, profits generated by the phalanx, and religion. The phalanx also suffered a disastrous fire in 1854. As a result, the North American Phalanx ended in 1856 despite the eager support of **Albert Brisbane** (1809–1890) and **Horace Greeley** (1811–1872) at its inception, dissidents from Red Bank having already formed the **Raritan Bay Union** in Perth Amboy, New

Jersey, two years before. Still, it was the longest-lived of all of the Fourierist communities.

NORTHAMPTON ASSOCIATION OF EDUCATION AND IN-DUSTRY. Located in Broughton's Meadows in the Town of Northampton, Hampshire County, Massachusetts, this association, which existed from 1842 to 1846, originated in the Northampton Silk Company and was transformed into a communal society with all workers receiving equal pay. In 1835 it consisted of 500 acres, the four-story silk factory, a sawmill, and six houses valued at $31,000.

But problems liquidating the association's debts and the withdrawal of members led to the abandonment of the project in only four years.

NORTH CAROLINA COMMUNITIES. *See* APPENDIX.

NORTH DAKOTA COMMUNITY. *See* APPENDIX.

NORTH UNION SOCIETY. This **Shaker** community was established in 1822 in Warrensville Township (now the Shaker Heights suburb of Cleveland), Cuyahoga County, Ohio. Known as the "Valley of God's Pleasure" by the Shakers, it was organized by the visiting elders from **Union Village** of Warren County. In 1840 its membership totaled 200 persons, but by the mid-1870s this figure had declined to 120. They owned 1,355 acres of land that they farmed and thereby supported themselves by supplying milk and vegetables to Cleveland. The members also operated a sawmill, a broom-making works, and a yarn manufactory and supplied firewood and lumber to their neighbors. It was reported that the community was debt free. It lasted until 1889 and was said to have had an influence on **Joseph Smith** (1805–1844) while the **Mormons** lived in Kirkland, about 30 miles to the northeast.

NOUVEAU CHRISTIANISME. See SAINT-SIMON, CLAUDE HENRI de ROUVROY, COMTE de.

NOVUM ORGANUM. See BACON, FRANCIS.

NOYES, JOHN HUMPHREY (1811–1886). John Humphrey Noyes, the founder of the **Oneida Community**, was born in Brattleboro, Vermont, and attended Dartmouth College from 1826 to 1830. He took up legal studies before turning to theology at Andover Theological Seminary and then at Yale. He was licensed to preach in 1833, believing he was capable of direct contact with God and, after depression and bouts of fanaticizing, he concluded that he was sinless; his license was revoked the following year. Back in Putney, Vermont, his religious doctrines were met with skepticism and outrage, and, after marrying Harriet Holton, a follower, he founded the Putney Society on the basis of **postmillennial** Perfectionism, that is, the idea that the **Apocalypse** had already occurred and that he and his followers were now free to live under postmillennial principles. This included "**complex marriage**," that is, the notion that in the Kingdom of Heaven all believers, being dead to the world by the death of Christ, were now married to one another, exclusive marriage between a man and a woman having been superseded.

When he and Harriet entered into such an arrangement with George and Mary Cragin, Noyes was charged with adultery in Putney, so he and his followers moved to upstate New York in 1847. Here he established the Oneida Community in Madison County the following year. In the Oneida Community, his unique ideas regarding marriage were put into practice. The community prospered until 1880, largely on the basis of the manufacture of animal traps and its agricultural products. Under threat of arrest on a morals charge, he fled to Niagara Falls, Canada, in 1879, where he died in 1886, his son Theodore Noyes having taken over direction of the Community.

– O –

OBERLIN COLONY. Founded in 1833 in Lorain County, Ohio, by eight recent immigrant families from New England and New York, the Oberlin colonists hoped to establish a community based on communal ownership of property. Their leader was John Shipherd. They also wanted to establish a school where children would receive a Christian education. Absorbed by Oberlin College in 1841, the colony faded away within two years.

OCEANA, THE COMMONWEALTH OF. See HARRINGTON, JAMES.

OHIO COMMUNITIES. *See* APPENDIX.

OHIO PHALANX. This **Fourierist phalanx**, originally called the American Phalanx before its actual establishment in 1844, was located in Bell Air (now Bellaire) in Belmont County in eastern Ohio. Organized by Elijah Grant (1808–1874), a disciple of **Albert Brisbane** (1809–1890) and the leading Fourierist in the West, it was located on 30,000 acres on the western bank of the Ohio River downriver from Wheeling, West Virginia. Plagued with internal problems and inadequate financing, it lasted only 16 months. Some members moved on to the **Trumbull Phalanx** west of Warren, Ohio, in Trumbull County.

OLCOTT, HENRY S. (1832–1907). This prominent **Theosophist** was one of the founders of the Theosophical Society, along with Helena Petrovna Blavatsky (1820–1891) and **William Q. Judge** (1851–1896), in 1875. Olcott, a lawyer and journalist, was elected president of the society, and, along with Blavatsky, traveled to India in 1878 to establish a branch of the society at Adyar near Madras (now Chennai). Olcott administered the day-to-day affairs of the society while Blavatsky concentrated on writing and Judge developed the society in the United States. Olcott viewed the society as an open philosophical discussion group and opposed limiting Theosophy to Blavatsky's teachings. In the mid-1880s Blavatsky moved to Europe, and Olcott reorganized the society. In 1888 Olcott formed the Esoteric Section of the Theosophical Society as a separatist organization, which quickly gained major influence in the Theosophist movement, a preview of the split that would rend the movement in 1895. Within a few years, **Annie Besant** (1847–1933) and **Katherine A. Tingley** (1847–1929) would emerge as the leaders of the Theosophists in the United States.

OLE BULL'S COLONY, *or* **NEW NORWAY,** *or* **OLEONA.** Financed and organized by Ole Bull, a Norwegian violinist who had come to the United States on a concert tour in the 1840s, this colony of four villages on 11,444 acres (Oleona, New Norway, New Bergen, and Walhalla) was established in 1852 in Potter County in north central Pennsylvania. But it came to an end in 1853 because of defective land titles. Today it is the site of Ole Bull State Park.

OLEONA. *See* OLE BULL'S COLONY.

OLERICH, HENRY (1852–1926). *See A CITYLESS AND COUNTRYLESS WORLD* . . .

OLIPHANT, LAURENCE (1829–1888). Laurence Oliphant was born to a distinguished English family in Capetown, South Africa, where his father was attorney general of the Cape of Good Hope. His mother, Lady Maria Campbell Oliphant, returned to England with her son in 1837. After extensive travel around Europe with his mother, Oliphant became a lawyer and published a number of travel accounts before covering foreign wars for several British newspapers. In 1860 the mother and son met **Thomas Lake Harris** (1823–1906) in London, but Laurence continued in journalism and was elected to Parliament. In 1867 he resigned his seat in Parliament and joined Harris's community at **Brocton** in upstate New York. His mother had joined the community two years before and donated $100,000 to support Harris's colony. At the colony Laurence was forced to live in degradation by Harris to atone for his past life, and in 1870 he returned to England on Harris's orders to cover the Franco-Prussian War. He returned to Brocton in 1872 with his new wife and his mother. In 1876 Harris separated the couple for possessing too much earthly love in their celibate marriage. In 1879 Laurence led an expedition to Palestine to colonize the land with Jews and eventually established a colony at Haifa. After the death of his first wife, he married Rosamond Owen, the daughter of **Robert Dale Owen** (1801–1877), in 1888. He died shortly thereafter in London.

OLIVE BRANCH. This conservative Protestant communal society was founded in Chicago by Rachel Bradley (?–1893) in 1876 as an evangelical outreach program. In 1883 it began to offer social services to the poor in the city. It has continued since that year, and in 1984 some 17 adults and children were living communally in the society's inner-city facility. Eating and worshiping are done communally, although each family has its own quarters. Olive Branch also provides temporary housing for the homeless, food and clothing for the needy, a summer day camp for the children, and Bible study for all.

ONE. See KARP, DAVID (1922–1999).

ONEIDA COMMUNITY. The Oneida Community was established in 1848 by **John Humphrey Noyes** (1811–1886) at Oneida Creek in Madison County in upstate New York after he fled Putney, Vermont, to avoid charges of adultery. It was based on Noyes's Bible Communism, a return to the practices of the early Church as Noyes saw them, and on **postmillennialist** Perfectionism. This Perfectionist community had as its social-sexual base a belief in what Noyes dubbed "**complex marriage**." Under this doctrine and practice, individuals (with Noyes's approval, not impulsively or spontaneously) could choose sexual partners other than on the basis of a marriage contract, the exclusivity of traditional marriage having been replaced in the Kingdom of God since the beginning of the **millennium** in favor of sexual unions based on love and attraction. Within complex marriage at Oneida was a practice introduced by Noyes known as *male continence*, or *coitus reservatus,* by which the male enjoyed the early stages of sexual intercourse (the amative stage) but never went on to orgasm (the propagative stage), thus providing sexual pleasure without fear of childbearing. In 1868, at Noyes's urging, the community also began to practice **stirpiculture**, a eugenics system based on the sexual union of scientifically selected males and females thereby to produce superior offspring. Fifty-one "stirps" were born that year.

The Oneidans lived in The Mansion House on the property, sharing work on a cooperative basis with mutual criticism being used on a regular basis to ensure proper conduct and adherence to the principles of the colony. Children were removed from their mothers after weaning and raised by other members of the community to prevent the development of undue attachment by the child to his or her parents rather than to the community. A branch of Oneida was established at **Wallingford**, Connecticut, in 1851 that lasted until 1881. Other branches were begun in Brooklyn and Manlius, New York; Newark, New Jersey; and Cambridge, Vermont; but these were closed during 1854–1855 to concentrate the Perfectionists' energies on Oneida and Wallingford. Although Oneida enjoyed prosperity—and popularity, with trainloads of excursionists coming to Oneida each summer—during the 1860s and 1870s, it came to an end in 1880. John Humphrey Noyes had fled the country to Canada in 1876, and the community's silverware manufacturing was absorbing much of its energy and leadership. Oneida as a communal society was transformed into a joint-stock company, Oneida

Community, Ltd., in 1881. Under the name Oneida Limited, it still enjoys a prominent place in the silverplate industry.

ONE MENTION COMMUNITY. This **Owenite** colony about which little is known existed on 800 acres of marginal land in Monroe County in eastern Pennsylvania in 1844–1845. It had 30–40 members and a number of branches. It is sometimes included among the **Fourierist phalanxes**.

ONTARIO PHALANX (*or* ONTARIO UNION). Also known as the Manchester Union, this **Fourierist phalanx** in Ontario County in upstate New York some five miles from Canandaigua was established in 1844 and existed until the following year. Originally called the Rochester Industrial Association and numbering some 150 members, it was led by, among others, Theron C. Leland, who was on the board of directors of the **Sodus Bay Phalanx**.

ON THE REPUBLIC (DE REPUBLICA). This dramatic six-book work by Cicero (106–43 B.C.), the Roman statesman, orator, and author—written in 54 B.C. and perhaps the first discussion of political theory in Latin—takes the form of a dialogue with Scipio the Younger and others of his circle back in the second century B.C. Book 1 outlines the three forms of government (democracy, aristocracy, and monarchy) and judges the Roman Republic as the finest constitutional form as a composite of the three. Book 2 recounts how Rome's constitution was developed. Book 3 speaks of justice relative to expediency. Book 4 deals with education and culture within a community. Books 5 and 6 present a portrait of the ideal statesman and his rewards, culminating in the Dream of Scipio in which he relates how the great Scipio Africanus appeared to him in a dream and revealed to him the promise of an eternal reward amid the harmony of the spheres for those who have served the community and their fellows well. Although not specifically utopian in nature, *On the Republic* had a major impact on Western thought and the ability of humans to build a more perfect state and society.

ORA LABORA COMMUNITY, *or* CHRISTIAN GERMAN AGRICULTURAL AND BENEVOLENT SOCIETY OF ORA LABORA. Located between Caseville and Wildfowl (now Bay Port) in

Huron County, Michigan, on Saginaw Bay, this community consisting of about 30 German Methodist families from Ohio and Pennsylvania was the product of 10 years of planning before it came into existence in 1862. It was modeled after the **Harmony Society** but fell victim to Civil War conscription and the wartime economy and ceased to exist in 1868.

ORBISTON. This **Owenite** colony was established by Abram Combe and A. J. Hamilton on 291 acres east of Glasgow, Scotland, in 1825. In keeping with its communal ideas, its membership, which eventually grew to 290, was to live in a four-story building with common rooms for cooking, eating, leisure, and schooling; the adults' bedroom-sitting rooms were private. They agreed to live by the principles of the Sermon on the Mount, but problems arose over proper compensation for the various levels of skill involved in the members' work. Still, it prospered on the basis of its garden and dairy products, its foundry, and its cobbler shop. Nevertheless, problems persisted over individual ownership, the distribution of food, and members who were reluctant to contribute their "fair share" of the work. With Combe's death in 1827 the community's creditors pressed for payment, so the land was sold and the community ceased to exist.

ORDER OF THEOCRACY. With the death of Cyrus Teed (1839–1908), **Koreshan Unity** split, one group moving from Estero to Fort Myers in Lee County, Florida, to form their own commune in 1910 after its members failed to gain the leadership of the mother colony. This colony, the Order of Theocracy, enjoyed only limited success and ended in 1931.

ORDERVILLE UNITED ORDER. This second experiment of the **Mormon** United Order of Enoch was established in 1875 at Orderville in Kane County in southern Utah. The 100 Mormons who emigrated from Muddy Mission in Long Valley to Orderville had been instructed by Brigham Young (1801–1877) to organize a colony on a communal basis with no private property being held by anyone. The Orderville United Order at one time included more than 600 persons, but it was disbanded in 1884 when its leaders went into hiding after the federal government launched an attack on polygamy, the land being sold off to the highest bidder.

OREGON COMMUNITIES. *See* APPENDIX.

ORIGEN (185?–254?). Origen was a prominent—if not always ortho-dox—theologian in early Christianity who challenged the literal in-terpretation of the Book of Revelation and its description of the **Apocalypse**. He argued that the Scriptures can be interpreted liter-ally, morally, or allegorically and that the Coming of the Kingdom would not take place in time but step by step in the souls of the faith-ful. That is, instead of a collective **eschatology** (the final events in the history of the world), an individual eschatology of the soul was what was intended in St. John's Book of Revelation.

ORIGIN OF THE SPECIES, THE. *See* DARWIN, CHARLES.

ORWELL, GEORGE (1903–1950). *George Orwell* is the pseudonym of Eric Arthur Blair, who was born in Bengal, India, and educated in England and who served in the Indian Imperial Police force in Burma from 1922 to 1927. Moved by a profound distaste for imperialism, he resigned and turned to writing. His early novels reveal his conviction that democratic socialism was the path to be trod, but he became dis-illusioned with communism because of its totalitarianism and fought for the loyalists in the Spanish Civil War in the mid-1930s. Inspired by Yevgeny Zamyatin's *We,* in 1945 he published ***Animal Farm,*** a satire on Stalinism, and followed this up with ***Nineteen Eighty-Four*** in 1949, a frightening view of a totalitarian future under Big Brother. Along with **Aldous Huxley**, he became one of the best-known **dystopians** of the 20th century.

OSCHWALD, AMBROSE (1801–1873). *See* ST. NAZIANZ COM-MUNITY.

OWEN, ALBERT K. (1847–1916). *See* TOPOLOBAMPO BAY COLONY.

OWEN, ROBERT (1771–1858). Born in northern Wales, Robert Owen at an early age became involved in the textile industry and by 1800 had taken control of the mills at **New Lanark**, Scotland. Within 10 years he had amassed a considerable fortune and employed 2,000 workers. It was during these years that he became involved in reform regarding the workers' working and living conditions, leading him to make substantial changes at New Lanark. These changes reflected his conviction that people are made better through universal education and through their improved environment, and that society needed a uniform set of rural-urban communities where cooperation replaced competition. His New Lanark, he believed, would be the exemplary model illustrating that human nature could be reformed. Although many objected to his attacks on organized religion and his radical political views, thousands of visitors came each year to see his model industrial mill and town.

In 1824 Owen went to the United States where he attracted considerable public notice. He then traveled west and purchased 2,000 acres on the Wabash River in Indiana from **George Rapp** (1757–1847), who was in the process of moving his colony, **Harmony**, back to Pennsylvania. On this site Owen established another model community, which he named **New Harmony**. Although some 900 persons joined him at New Harmony, the community was fraught with dissension, Owen instituting no fewer than seven constitutions in the two years the colony was in existence. After the failure of New Harmony, Owen became involved in cooperative and labor movements of many types on both sides of the Atlantic, and his followers in the United States and England founded many colonies based on his reform principles. He died in his hometown of Newton, Wales, in 1858. Although the **Owenite communities** established by him and his followers did not enjoy notable long-term success, Owen is important to the story of utopianism in that he, along with a number of other utopians in the early 19th century, awakened many people to the possibility of improving the human condition by effecting social-economic change.

OWEN, ROBERT DALE (1801–1877). Robert Dale Owen, **Robert Owen**'s eldest son, accompanied his father and his brother William to the United States in 1825. They attempted to put **New Harmony** on a workable basis during their father's frequent absences from the community. Robert Dale also taught school there and edited the *New Harmony Gazette*. After the colony's failure, he became involved with **Frances Wright**'s colony at **Nashoba** and in utilitarian educational reforms, especially the **Pestalozzian** teaching techniques. In 1832 he joined his father in England and coedited *The Crisis* with him for six months before returning to New Harmony. While there, he served in the Indiana legislature from 1836 to 1838, becoming a leading advocate of public school funding. Owen then served in the U.S. House of Representatives from 1843 to 1847 and subsequently entered diplomatic service in 1853. Returning to the United States in 1858, he became an important figure in the abolitionist movement. During the Civil War he wrote an influential pamphlet, *The Policy of Emancipation,* in which he discussed the problems involved in freeing the slaves. During his years in public service, he also played a major role in the establishment of the Smithsonian Institution in Washington, D.C.

OWENITE COMMUNITIES.

Name	Location	Years
New Lanark	Scotland	1800–1829
New Harmony	Indiana	1825–1827
Orbiston	Scotland	1825–1827
Yellow Springs	Ohio	1825–1826
Haverstraw	New York	1826
Feiba Peveli	Indiana	1826
Forestville	New York	1826–1827
Kendal	Ohio	1826–1829
Valley Forge	Pennsylvania	1826
Blue Springs	Indiana	1826–1827
Ralahine	Ireland	1831–
Queenwood	England	1839–1845
Goose Pond	Pennsylvania	1843–1844
Hunt's Colony, *or* **Equality, Society of**	Wisconsin	1843–1847
One Mention Community	Pennsylvania	1844–1845
Utilitarian Association of United Interests	Wisconsin	1845–1848
Fruit Hills	Ohio	1845–1852
Yorkshire	England	1847–
Bournville	England	1893–?

– P –

PACIFIC CITY. *See* TOPOLOBAMPO BAY COLONY.

PAINTED WOODS. This community was organized by a St. Paul, Minnesota, rabbi for Jewish refugees from Russia and was located near Bismarck, North Dakota, in Burleigh County. Begun in 1882, the colony rapidly increased its membership from 20 families to 54, but a combination of crop failures, a prairie fire that destroyed most of the buildings in the community, and a destructive drought in 1886 brought it to an end in 1887.

PARADISE WITHIN REACH OF ALL MEN, THE. *See* ETZLER, JOHN ADOLPHUS.

PARAMANANDA, SWAMI (1833–1940). *See* VEDANTA SOCIETY.

PAROUSIA. *See* APOCALYPSE.

PARTRIDGE, EDWARD (1862–1931). *See* COALSAMAO.

PASCAL, BLAISE (1623–1662). This French mathematician and philosopher opened the door of doubt in the 17th century toward accepting knowledge from the ancients and the medieval theologians by questioning the very basis of human existence in time and the universe. Pascal argued that humans are in Nothingness and always contingent because they occupy a middle position between the infinitesimal and the infinite. By his teachings, Pascal introduced the idea of contingent Nothingness and the search for Somethingness into Western philosophy, a concept picked up by **Helvetius** and carried over into the Enlightenment belief in progress.

PATRIOT COLONY. *See* DOMAIN.

PATTERSON, JOHN S. *See* RISING STAR ASSOCIATION.

PELAGIANISM. Although Christian **millennial** and perfectionist thought had been dealt a stunning blow by **Augustine** (354–430) and was condemned at the Council of Ephesus in 431, it remained alive in the West. Pelagius (ca. 354–post 418), an English lay monk, challenged Augustine's allegorical interpretation of Scripture and argued that people are not burdened by original sin and have the innate ability to perfect themselves on earth, God having commanded man "be ye perfect." It followed that humans were not to wait for perfection in the next world and that the Church is rightly a community of saints on earth striving to perfect themselves. Pelagianism was condemned by the Council of Orange in 529, but the ideas of progress and perfectionism, including **Apocalyptic** visions of the last days, remained alive in the West, at least sub rosa for the next thousand years, to emerge full blown in altered form during the Protestant Revolution and remained a strand of Western thought thereafter.

PENNSYLVANIA COMMUNITIES. *See* APPENDIX.

PEOPLE'S CORPORATION, THE. *See* GILLETTE, KING CAMP.

PEOPLE'S TEMPLE. *See* JONES, JAMES WARREN.

PERFECTIONISTS. *See* NOYES, JOHN HUMPHREY; ONEIDA COMMUNITY.

PESTALOZZI, JOHANN HEINRICH (1746–1827). Johann Heinrich Pestalozzi was a leading educational reformer of the 18th century whose ideas found fertile ground in the thinking of **Robert Owen** (1771–1858) both at **New Lanark** and in **New Harmony**. This native Swiss educational reformer contended that teaching must be by means of things, not words, and that proper educational methods would lead the poor and unfortunate to marked improvement in their lives. He, therefore, recommended that farming and manufacturing be combined for the benefit of the people. These ideas were most clearly illustrated with the publication of his novel *Leinhard und Gertrud: Ein Buch fur das Volk* (Leinhard and Gertrud: A Book for the People; 1781), in which he chronicled the transformation of the village of Bonnal into a model community largely through the establishment of a new school using advanced teaching methods. One of the most avid converts to Pestalozzianism was **William Maclure**

(1763–1840), who attempted to establish education on this basis at New Harmony and in his other reform projects as the key to social-economic-political progress.

PHALANX/PHALANSTERY. *Phalanx* refers to a cooperative community structured according to the ideas of **Charles Fourier** (1772–1837) and altered and simplified for American consumption by **Albert Brisbane** (1809–1890). *Phalanstery* refers to a self-contained structure housing such a community, although the terms are frequently used interchangeably. According to Fourier, each phalanx would consist of 1,620 residents living in common buildings called *phalansteries* in an agrarian setting of 5,000 acres. The type of work each member would contribute to the community would be by the member's choice. All members were to share equally in the work and, with the exception of persons having special skills, receive equal recompense for their labor. The individual phalanxes would eventually link up and form one federation. A number of phalanxes were established in the United States; few lasted an appreciable length of time, and none of them met Fourier's initial specifications of money, members, and acreage.

PHENOMENON OF MAN, THE. *See* TEILHARD de CHARDIN, PIERRE.

PHILADELPHIA INDUSTRIAL ASSOCIATION. This **Fourierist phalanx** was founded in 1845 at the village of Portage (since absorbed by the city of South Bend) in St. Joseph County, Indiana. Despite its name, it apparently had no connection with the city of Philadelphia. It was established on the farm of one William McCartney, who was apparently more interested in getting his land cleared for nothing than in any communitarian ideal. When the members' dispute with McCartney came to a head in 1847, some of them moved to a new site nearby, but this second attempt at communalism also failed.

PHILBRICK, EDWARD (1827–1889). *See* PORT ROYAL EXPERIMENT.

PIERCY, MARGE (1936–). Along with **Charlotte Perkins Gilman** (1860–1935) and **Ursula Le Guin** (1929–), Marge Piercy is considered one of the three major feminist utopian writers of the 20th century. Born in Detroit and educated at the University of Michigan and Northwestern University, she held a number of jobs before gaining success as a writer. As a progressive and feminist, she is known for her poetry and her feminist novels, especially her utopian *Woman on the Edge of Time* (1976).

PIGEON RIVER COLONY. Ten families attempted to establish a **Fourierist phalanx** in Wisconsin in 1846, but they fell into a dispute over where it should be located. Consequently, one group of colonists established their colony at **Spring Farm**; the other chose a site north of Sheboygan on the shores of Lake Michigan in Sheboygan County, Wisconsin, where they set up the Pigeon River Colony. Little is known about this colony except that it ended in 1847.

PILGRIMS. A group calling themselves "the Pilgrims," who originated in lower Canada, settled at South Woodstock, Windsor County, Vermont, in 1817. They were looking for a location where they could return to a biblical way of life. They stayed only until 1818, moving as far west as Missouri in search for a place where they could practice their communal way of Christian life.

PLATO (ca. 427–347 B.C.). The Greek philosopher Plato was a pupil and later a friend of Socrates (ca. 470–399 B.C.). He founded The Academy, where he taught philosophy and mathematics. His work appears in the form of dialogues with Socrates. These examine basic philosophical questions regarding knowing and living. In the dialogue of *The Republic* (360 B.C.) he argues that justice in the state and in the individual must be related to the idea of the Good, the principle that guides both truth and order. *The Republic* contains Plato's argument that the Guardians, the philosopher-kings selected from among the best of the philosophers, are the best rulers because only they are able to understand the harmonious relations between the elements of the universe. In such a perfect state, the philosophers, warriors, and laborers freely and cooperatively enjoy the results of their efforts.

In his utopian work *The Laws* (360 B.C.), Plato discusses a less idealistic and more practical view of the nature of the state. It takes the form of a dialogue regarding a proposed colony in Crete. In it, Plato argues that there is no single best plan for governance, but three models are considered. The best constitution is one where there is equality for all. This may not be achievable by humans but only by the gods or in the mythological **Golden Age**. The second best constitution is intended for the colony of Magnesia in Crete. It establishes a broad-based oligarchy in which only landowners can be citizens. It has a public educational system, women being included here as well as in public life; common meals; and no commerce or currency. The third-best constitution, not fully described because Plato died before finishing it, presents the transitional stage between the ideal society and the real political world and is intended for existing cities. It includes the idea of consultation by the philosopher-kings with the citizens, this being possible even in oligarchies and democracies. Plato's works represent his attempt to blend the constitutional structures of society with ideal models of the good life, that is, to change the institutional infrastructure of politics. They have had a lasting impact on utopian thought.

PLAYER PIANO. The author of this **dystopian** novel, **Kurt Vonnegut**, is probably best known for his novel *Slaughterhouse Five* (1969), but his first novel, *Player Piano: America in the Coming Age of Electronics* (1952), marks him as a prominent dystopian of the 20th century. An extended commentary on the imperfectability of human nature, *Player Piano* describes the land of Illium, which evolved from the urbanized United States in the late 20th century out of a third world war, the technology spawned by the war, and the uncritical hunger after the good life of the American people. The theme of the novel is man versus machine as the Second Industrial Revolution, the electronic revolution, has come to dominate the nation, not out of conscious planning but from a lack of intelligent guidance by its rational and moral agencies. In Illium democracy and freedom are allowed, there is no poverty thanks to technology and higher economic productivity, and war is no more.

But this utopia is only for persons with IQs of 140 and above, the new elite of the new United States. They are given superior educations to become technological experts and managers who each summer indulge in mass games and rituals in The Meadows. The unemployed, who have been replaced by electronic devices and machines, have all the necessities of life and even some luxuries. But they have only two vocational choices: enlisting in the army (for which there is no use) or joining the "Reeks and Wrecks" (Reconstruction and Reclamation Corps) to do essentially nothing. In this state the unemployed and useless have nothing to do but dream about the good old days on the assembly line when they had a useful function. This results in a half-hearted rebellion that leads to some destruction of machines but soon fails. Afterward, the remaining rebels search through the rubble to find the electronic equipment and attempt to rebuild the very instruments of their dehumanization, the very machines that enslaved them.

In Illium technology has guaranteed the good life for everyone, but people cannot now live without the very technology that has dehumanized them. Ironically, the Second Industrial Revolution has led the masses of Illium, the low in intelligence, the untrained and uneducated, those whose sensibilities have been dulled and their self-respect destroyed, those who are willing to listen to the mechanical player piano (not to a human piano player) and to watch television without sound, to a life of spontaneous, habitual nothingness. They are fated to live only as wards of a compassionate society.

The moral of Vonnegut's *Player Piano,* then, is that humans are fallen creatures and that whatever they conceive or create in the name of progress must necessarily contain within itself the seeds of its own destruction. There can be no utopia.

PLEASANT HILL. This **Shaker** community was located on a 5,000-acre site at Shakertown south of Lexington in Mercer County, Kentucky. Founded in 1805 after 1817 novitiates lived on outlying farms while maintaining their normal family life, a very unusual Shaker practice. The community enjoyed economic prosperity on the basis of beef and dairy cattle, grain crops, flax, tobacco, hemp, vegetable gardening, hog and sheep raising, furniture making, and the sale of garden seeds. During the Civil War the community was in the path of the Confederates, and it served 8,000 to 9,000 meals to them free of charge. Pleasant Hill declined economically after the Civil War, ending in 1910. Although no Shakers live there, it is open to the public as a nonprofit public site.

PLOCKHOY, PIETER CORNELIUS (ca. 1620–ca. 1700). The founder of the first American colonial religious communal society was

Pieter Cornelius Plockhoy van Zierikzee. Of Dutch Mennonite parentage, he associated with members of different religious sects in reacting against the religious rigidity found in Holland in the early 17th century. In 1628 he approached Oliver Cromwell, the lord protector, in London with his plans for reforming common British economic and social problems, including the establishment of commonwealths that would relieve those problems. A number of attempts at bringing Plockhoy's plans to fruition were attempted in England, Bristol, and Ireland, but the restoration of the Stuarts ended these projects.

Back in Holland in 1662, Plockhoy made an agreement with the Amsterdam burghers to settle 25 Mennonite emigrants along the Delaware River in New Amsterdam. His projected emigration was delayed for a year, but in May 1663 some 41 colonists sailed from Holland and in July were dropped off on the Delaware shores. The landing site and settlement were known as the Valley of the Swans (*Zwaanendael*), or Horekill, and were near present-day Lewes. Very little is known about the colony, but in September 1664, the next year, when the English took over the Dutch colonies in colonial America, the Valley of the Swans was crushed by the British navy. What became of the colonists is not known; it is speculated that some of them may have been sold into slavery in Virginia. It is known that Plockhoy in 1682–1683 took possession of some property in Lewes and declared his allegiance to England. In 1695 he and his wife were placed on public assistance in Germantown, Pennsylvania, and his will was dated 1700. The Valley of the Swans, or Horekill, stands as the first American utopian settlement.

POINT COUNTER POINT. This 1928 work by **Aldous Huxley** (1894–1963) reveals contemporary disillusionment with the inadequacy of current ideals: religion, false mysticism, sex, art, science, and politics. Its theme is that persons who live solely by exclusionary ideas and absolutes will be both fragmented and unfilled as human beings because the appreciation and acceptance of the reality of the world as it really exists is necessary for all-around living and societal health. These ideas bore fruit four years later in Huxley's famous dystopian novel *Brave New World*.

POINT HOPE COMMUNITY. *See* BERLIN HEIGHTS COMMUNITY.

POINT LOMA, *or* **UNIVERSAL BROTHERHOOD AND THEO-SOPHICAL SOCIETY.** Point Loma was founded on 330 acres on a peninsula just north of San Diego in 1898 by **Katherine Tingley** (1847–1929) as a Theosophical community. Tingley was the leader of one of the **Theosophist** factions that formed after the death of **Helena Petrovna Blavatsky** in 1891. The community was marked by exotic architecture, and a Greek theater overlooking the Pacific was the scene of Shakespearean and classical dramas. Its key feature was the Raja Yoga school where meditation, Theosophy, and the fine arts were taught. The members of Point Loma, nearly 500 by 1917, could live either in individual bungalows or in a large communal house called "the Homestead." The community grew vegetables for market, operated a tailor shop, and published many magazines and books. Point Loma also gained income from tuition charged at the school and contributions given by wealthy patrons. It prospered under the strong guidance of Tingley, but after her death in an automobile accident in 1929 it ran into major financial difficulties. The property (now occupied by Point Loma College) was sold off in 1942 and the remaining members moved to Covina, California, in the Los Angeles area, where they lived noncommunally. The Brotherhood continues to maintain a library and a publishing house.

POLISH BROOK FARM. *See* MODJESKA'S COLONY.

POLITICS. See ARISTOTLE (384–322 B.C.).

PORT ROYAL EXPERIMENT. On November 7, 1861, Union forces landed on the Sea Islands of South Carolina and within the day the territory surrounding Port Royal, between Charleston to the north and Savannah to the south, was in federal hands. Left behind by the local inhabitants were more than 10,000 slaves from the islands plus others who had escaped from the mainland. The Sea Island slaves were Gullahs, among the least civilized of the Southern blacks, confused and without income or prospects. Under directions from Washington, General Thomas W. Sherman put the blacks, considered contraband, to work harvesting the cotton crop, placing them under the supervision of the U.S. Treasury Department's cotton agents. By early 1862, some 3,000 blacks were working on the various plantations in the region and philanthropists from the North were moving into the area to aid the ex-slaves. The government's interest in Port Royal and rehabilitating its black inhabitants waned thereafter, and the decision was made to sell off the plantation lands. This was carried out in 1863 and 1864 with most of the land being reserved for the military and relatively little being bought by the blacks. But this experiment in helping the ex-slaves did not come to an end as the war dragged on and the federal government looked to other matters. During the land sales, a Northern philanthropist named Edward Philbrick (1827–1889) had purchased 11 plantations and leased two others to try his hand at rehabilitating the black victims of slavery.

Having been appointed superintendent of the largest plantation in the region in March 1862, Philbrick was well aware of the situation regarding the Port Royal blacks. Believing that the welfare of the ex-slaves required that they be incorporated into the free labor system and that this could best be done by paying part or all of their wages in food and clothing, Philbrick did away with the gang labor system on his plantations and organized the work on a family basis, each adult family member being assigned one and a half acres for his own use. Each member also worked an assigned plot of cotton for wages. Philbrick proceeded to demonstrate that free black labor could produce a profitable cotton crop. But complications arose regarding Philbrick's centralized direction of economic matters at Port Royal plus the decisions of the government over whether or not the lands actually belonged to the ex-slaves because of the right of preemption. As a result, Philbrick in early 1866 sold his lands to those blacks who wanted them at $5 per acre and the rest to whites in large blocks. Despite the failure of this second phase of the Port Royal experiment, Philbrick had provided an example of how free black labor could be used to make a profit within the boundaries of the American economic system. *See also* BLACK UTOPIAS.

POSITIVISM. *See* COMTE, AUGUSTUS.

POST, C. W. (1854–1914). *See* BEILHART, JACOB.

POSTMILLENNIALIST. A person who believes that the **millennium** has already begun in time. *See also* MILLENNIUM.

PRAGMATISM. *See* DEWEY, JOHN; JAMES, WILLIAM.

PRAIRIE HOME COMMUNITY. This 500-acre community was located near West Liberty, Logan County, Ohio. Its founders were the socialists **John O. Wattles** (1809–1859) and Valentine Nicholson (1809–1904). Most of the 130 original members who came to the site in 1844 were Quaker farmers from the Midwest. This association was very disorganized and loosely structured, having no constitution and no government; its only rule was "Do as you would be done by." It lasted less than a year; in the meantime, a small branch called Highland Home had been established at Zanesfield, some nine miles away. It, too, lasted less than a year.

PRAYING TOWNS. One of the most ambitious utopian schemes carried out in the American colonies was the work of the **Puritan** John Eliot (1604–1690). The "Praying Towns" were established for the remnants of the Algonquian Indians in Massachusetts. Drawing on the Book of Exodus, Eliot, preacher, translator of the Bible into Algonquian, and sometimes referred to as "the Apostle to the Indians," created 19 Praying Towns beginning in 1651. These towns integrated religious and political life into a theocracy in order to Christianize and civilize the Indians, the first town being Natick 18 miles from Boston. According to Eliot, the process would take the Algonquians through four steps: from the state of the unfallen saint to degenerate human to civil human to regenerate saint, that is, from perfection back to perfection, these steps necessary not simply for the Indians but also for all of humanity. The Praying Indians were subjected to cruel laws imposed by the Bay Colony in 1675 and 1676, the first forbidding them to leave the towns under pain of execution, the second offering amnesty if they would report to Boston. Thereafter they were placed in a concentration camp on Deer Island. Here many of them starved to death or died of disease. Soon thereafter, Eliot's project came to an end.

PREMILLENNIALIST. A person who believes that the millennium will occur sometime in the future, either in a religious sense or in a nonreligious sense. See also MILLENNIUM.

PREPARATION. This splinter group of some 50–60 families of **Mormons** led by Charles Blanchard Thompson (1814–1890s) established their own community in 1853 at Preparation, Monona County, on the western border of Iowa, as their "School of Preparation for the Life

Beyond." Obeying a message he said he received from a spirit called "Beneemy," Thompson kept all the rich farming property for himself and imposed tithing on the members. When "Father Empraim" Thompson refused to divide the property and settle with the members, they decided to hang him. He managed to escape from the mob and flee the state. Preparation thus came to an end in 1858, many Mormons leaving the colony and heading for Utah. A 344-acre park now encompasses what was once the town of Preparation.

PRESTER JOHN. *See* BRAGMANS.

PRIMAVERA. *See* BRUDERHOF.

PRINCIPIA. *See* LONGLEY, ALCANDER.

PRODUCT SHARING VILLAGE, THE. *See* HIAWATHA VILLAGE.

PROGRESS AND POVERTY. *See* GEORGE, HENRY.

PROGRESSIVE COMMUNITY, *or* **CEDAR VALE.** The Progressive Community was established in 1871 on 320 acres by **William Frey** (1839–1888) and two Russian associates near Cedar Vale in Howard (now Chautauqua) County in eastern Kansas just north of the border with Oklahoma after the dissolution of the **Reunion Colony** in Missouri the previous year. The communistic community was built on substantial funding from Russia and was initially restricted to Russians, although a number of American spiritualists joined the community. All members lived in a "unitary" home. The community broke up in 1878.

PROUDHON, PIERRE-JOSEPH (1809–1865). The French printer Pierre-Joseph Proudhon was one of the most notable anarchist utopians of the 19th century, known chiefly through his pamphlet *What Is Property?* (1840). Convinced that human labor should be seen in terms of its moral values, Proudhon was opposed to both capitalism and socialism. The solution, as he saw it, was the formation of independent mutual associations of affiliated freed individuals that would follow the overthrow of the capitalist system. Not only would capitalism be abolished when this occurred, but also all state and private property. Out of this would emerge a just, free, egalitarian, and peaceful society of individuals marked by an equal distribution of property plus the elimination of any temptation to accumulate property. Dedicated to the traditional patriarchal family, he envisioned his anarchist society as dominated by males. He tried to initiate a "people's bank" while serving as a deputy to the National Assembly during the Revolution of 1848, but was subsequently imprisoned for advocating radical reforms in France. He later fled to Belgium to escape the police of Napoleon III, but returned to France before his death.

PSEUDO-METHODIUS. This seventh-century tract was part of the **Sibylline prophecies**, dating back to the fourth century, which told of the return of the warrior-Christ leading to the Emperor of the Last Days and which promised a golden age of ease. The *Pseudo-Methodius* emerged from the Eastern Empire, or Byzantium, centered on Constantinople. By the eighth century, it was circulating in the court of the Frankish king Charlemagne in Latin translation. It told of a great emperor who would defeat the Ishmaelites and usher in a period of peace—a peace marked by sensuality and merriment, not by Christian living. This interval of peace, this Golden Age, however, would be shattered by an invasion of people from the north, compelling the emperor to go to Jerusalem. There he would fight a losing battle against the Antichrist, who would reign until Christ descended to defeat him and sit in Last Judgment of all at the end of time. Although the period of peace, the **millennium**, in this case was far from the Christian version of Christ reigning with the saints, the *Pseudo-Methodius* nevertheless helped to keep alive the ideas of a last emperor, earthly salvation, an age of peace, and salvation by God at the end of time.

PUBLIC UNIVERSAL FRIEND. *See* JERUSALEM COLONY.

PUGET SOUND COOPERATIVE COLONY. Founded by **George Venable Smith** (1843– 1919) in 1887 as part of an anti-Chinese labor movement, this colony was located at Port Angeles in Clallam County, Washington. It was to be a model city based on cooperation, and it drew some 400 members from Washington and the Midwest. Most of them were laborers, including some members of the Knights of Labor. Beset by internal management disputes and a turnover of its leadership

(Smith left the colony in 1888), the Puget Sound Colony's members began to drift away. By 1890, the cooperative experiment was defunct.

PURITANS AS UTOPIANS. In New England during the 17th century the Puritans, the Separatists from the Church of England, were able to carry out their ideas for a new beginning for society. Here Calvinist Protestantism would be free from any attack by or influence of the Roman Catholic Church and the quasi-Catholic Church of England. Here the Puritans could engage in constructive Protestantism in humble obedience to Christ thanks to physical distance from the mother country. In the New World, the Protestant Revolution could be completed, manifesting God-the-unfolding, God-the-advancing, God whose religious truths were progressive and successive.

As in the Old Testament after the Fall, when the Jews had to work their way out of darkness as their testing ground, so too the wilderness experience of God's people on the far side of the Atlantic would test their faith and trust in God's ways. Their "errand into the wilderness" would be not unlike the Exodus wherein the children of God were led out of Egypt through the desert by Moses to salvation. They had inherited the mantle and mission of Israel, lost by England under the Stuart kings. They were the new chosen people, a band of saints in a sacred covenant with God. This fit in well with the contemporary Protestant view that the English Colonies represented both the restoration of the **Garden of Eden** and the culmination of history in the **millennium**. The Puritans' belief in their "errand into the wilderness" and their creating a "city upon a hill" (Jerusalem, or the City of God) remained alive until well into the 18th century.

Yet despite their deep belief in the providence of God, the Puritans also saw themselves as active instruments in creating His utopia on earth. This was especially true in their espousal of education as a means of progress, a reflection of their European Renaissance-Enlightenment background. The writings of **Joachim of Fiore** (1135–1202), the 12th-century utopianist, regarding the millennium had a powerful influence upon them; so, too, did the findings of Newtonian physical science. God was still the God of providence, but gradually His role was transferred from a miraculous overriding of natural causes to His operating within natural laws discoverable by humans. These would aid humans to advance by stages to a final, perfect, millennial, **Apocalyptic** end. Thus for the Puritans, education in the arts and sciences was a sign of God's indwelling within them. God-the-advancing as a process of moving to perfection, God the Divine Engineer, and God the watchmaker gradually gained a strong foothold in Puritan thinking, as can be seen in the words of the millennialist Reverend Increase Mather (1639–1723) and especially in the works of his son Cotton Mather (1663–1728), who shared the pulpit of the Old North Church with his father for decades. Cotton Mather, the author of 444 works during his lifetime and an elected member of the Royal Society of London, best illustrates the utopianism-educationism inherent within Puritanism by the 18th century in his works *Magnalia Christi Americana: Or, the Ecclesiastical History of New-England . . .* and in his *Theopolis Americana: An Essay on the Golden Street of the Holy City . . . ,* both works arguing that God's special providences were working through nature in guiding humankind to perfection.

PURNELL, BENJAMIN (1861–1927) **and MARY** (1862?–1953). *See* HOUSE OF DAVID.

PUTNEY SOCIETY. *See* NOYES, JOHN HUMPHREY.

PYTHAGORAS (ca. 580–ca. 500 B.C.)/**PYTHAGOREANS.** The Pythagoreans were the followers of Pythagoras, the Greek philosopher, mathematician, and idealist. Pythagoras taught that mathematics, morals, music, and matter are linked in a single harmonious structure, with mathematical proportion at the root of the universe and human behavior. He formed a religious fraternity in which the members lived together communistically as friends to attain religious holiness, intellectual improvement, and human fellowship. Because of political opposition, Pythagoras sailed to Croton in Italy with 300 of his followers. Here he fashioned a constitution for the Greeks living there based on his principles, a constitution that established a ruling aristocracy, evidence of Pythagoras's belief that there is no greater source of evil than anarchy and that humans to be safe must be governed by others greater than himself. The Pythagoreans, then, represent peaceful communal living for humankind in a fraternal society of subservience to a superior governing class.

– Q –

QUEENWOOD. Queenwood in East Tytherley parish in England was the only **Owenite community** to receive the official sponsorship of the movement. Situated on 534 acres and seen as part of a larger movement toward the establishment of a number of colonies, according to its constitution its members were to have an equal right to settle in all future communities. Within Queenwood (named for Queen Philippa, who had originally been granted the land in the 14th century by Edward III), there was uniformity of dress and furniture and all properties both personal and landed were to be held in common.

When the trustees took possession in October 1839, **Robert Owen** (1771–1858) had already resigned as governor of the association. As a result, management of Queenwood fell to one John Finch. Despite Owen's resignation from the governorship and the fact that the project was marked by financial difficulties from the beginning, on August 31, 1841, Owen himself laid the foundation stone for Queenwood's great building, Harmony Hall. The building featured piped water, private apartments and bedrooms, classrooms, a library, lecture rooms, offices, and a dining room. On this occasion Owen named the community "Economy in the Parish of Harmony," but it became generally known as "Harmony Hall." True to its stated mission, branches with halls of science or social institutions were established in 21 locations, but they failed to flourish. Financial difficulties continued to plague Queenwood, and in 1845 its remaining residents dispersed. Thus this Owenite community, dedicated to illustrating that all laborers at all levels could be united so as to share equally and thereby end excessive wealth in the midst of poverty, came to an end after only six years.

QUIROGA, VASCO de (1470–1565). Vasco de Quiroga first arrived in New Spain (i.e., Mexico) in 1531 as a judge in the High Court of Justice. Inspired by **Thomas More** (1478– 1535), Quiroga was opposed to 16th-century materialism and impressed by the absence of greed, ambition, and luxury among the natives living in the New World. He viewed the Native Americans as "soft wax" that could be molded into members of a reformed Catholic Church in the New

World. Accordingly, he requested and received from the Spanish monarchy permission to establish a utopian community in his territory. Quiroga envisioned communities of 6,000 persons, each governed familially. In pyramid fashion, Quiroga planned that fathers and mothers would govern families, magistrates would govern 30 families, governors would have authority over four magistrates, and a *corregidor* appointed by the *audiencia* would be the chief ruler. He assumed that the Native Americans would agree to work in harmony in agricultural villages, sharing equally the fruits of their labor on their communally owned land. And priests would instruct them in Christian morals and virtues.

His proposal to implement his plans across all of New Spain being rejected by the royal council, Quiroga set up two communal villages (*hospitales-pueblos*) near what is now Mexico City; he called them each Sante Fe. In them, most of his plans were brought to fruition, including women working and a six-hour workday. Quiroga hoped that his *hospitales-pueblos* would serve as a model for a reformed European society. Although this never occurred, the two villages continued to operate under his close supervision until his death 28 years later and perhaps into the early part of the next century.

– R –

RABELAIS, FRANÇOIS (ca. 1483–1553). *See ABBEY OF THELEME, THE.*

RAJNEESH, BHAGWAN SHREE (1931–). *See* RANCHO RAJNEESH.

RALAHINE. This **Owenite** association, officially titled The Ralahine Agricultural and Manufacturing Cooperative Association, was founded in 1831 at Ralahine, County Clare, Ireland, on the 618-acre estate of John Scott Vandeleur. After angry peasants on the estate murdered a steward, Vandeleur decided to experiment following the principles of **Robert Owen** (1771–1858). The proposed draft of the association included the members jointly owning Ralahine's capital; education for all children; an improved standard of living for all members; and care of the aged, the impoverished, and the sickly. Vandeleur hoped that this scheme would satisfy the angry peasants and improve his profits. The commune initially was made up of 52 men, women, and children. Governance of the commune was placed in the hands of a nine-member committee elected twice a year, the peasants' duties were in the hands of an elected committee, weekly meetings of the workers were held to discuss the constitution, a daily infant school was established, vouchers were used as a substitute for money, and the commune and its property were to remain in Vandeleur's hands at 700 pounds rent per year until the cooperative could purchase the land from him. But Ralahine lasted only two years. Vandeleur ran up gambling debts in Dublin and fled the country, leaving great liabilities behind. His creditors demanded payment and seized the estate. With that, the experiment collapsed.

RANCHO ATASCADERO. *See* AMERICAN WOMAN'S REPUBLIC.

RANCHO RAJNEESH. This utopian experiment was established by Bhagwan Shree Rajneesh (1931–) in 1981 near Antelope, Oregon. Comprising 64,229 acres, within one year the land had been modernized with all the necessities of life, such as roads, buildings, electricity, water supplies, and a dairy. In 1982 Rajneesh and his followers were in the process of constructing the largest solar greenhouse in the nation (covering two acres) as they prepared for an inaugural celebration by erecting 2,000 tents for some 7,000 visitors. But three years later, in 1985, Bhagwan was arrested and charged with violation of U.S. immigration laws. He received a 10-year suspended sentence and was fined $400,000. The property, which covered 100 square miles, was offered up for sale, as was an airplane, mobile homes, gambling tables, and place settings for 20,000 persons. Accordingly, Rajneesh's 4,000 followers scattered to their home countries, their four-year effort to create an ecologically sound paradise having come to an end.

RAND, AYN (1905–1982). Born Alissa Zinovievna Rosenbaum in St. Petersburg, Ayn Rand fled the repressive Soviet Union in the 1930s and came to the United States. Employed as a screenwriter in Hollywood for several years, she then turned to serious writing. In *The Fountainhead* (1943), she fictionalized the life of the architectural utopian Frank Lloyd Wright. In *Atlas Shrugged* (1957), she published her most notable contention on behalf of individualism. Her philosophy of objectivism combines emotional antitotalitarianism, capitalism, and atheism. Her **dystopian** polemic *Anthem* reflects that philosophy, picturing the future in dystopian terms as in a primitive state because, she is convinced, the pursuit of any collective and totalitarian ideal must inevitably lead to the decline of industrialism and of humanitarianism.

RAPP, GEORGE (1757–1847). George Rapp, the founder and leader of the **Harmony Society**, was born in Württemberg, Germany. In his youth, he read the Bible and compared conditions in his native Germany with those in the New Testament. Convinced that society should be reformed to conform to the tenets of the New Testament interpreted literally, he found himself in trouble with the local Lutheran clergy, who labeled him and his followers as "Separatists." Seeking to avoid persecution, in 1803 Rapp and 300 followers sailed for the United States. Here Rapp bought 5,000 acres north of Pittsburgh, Pennsylvania, in Butler County for their new home. They were followed by 600 more emigrants in 1804 and formed the Harmony Society. Harmony was marked by common possession of property and celibacy as they awaited the **millennium**, and here they thrived economically through agriculture and some industry. In 1814 the Rappites moved to a new site they named Harmony on the Wabash River in Indiana. Again they prospered. In 1824 they sold the property to **Robert Owen** (1771–1858) and moved back to Pennsylvania to Beaver County and built the village of **Economy**. Once again they prospered despite controversy over Rapp's leadership and a breakaway movement led by **Bernhard "Count Leon" Muller** (1787–1834). Although George Rapp died in 1847, Economy and the Rappites continued in existence until 1905.

RARITAN BAY UNION. This **Fourierist phalanx** was established in 1853 as a joint-stock company on 268 acres at Englewood (now part of Perth Amboy), New Jersey, by 30 dissident members who had withdrawn from the **North American Phalanx**. These breakaway colonists wished to place less emphasis on the principles of **Charles Fourier** (1772–1837) as well as make their colony more religious. Its most notable feature was a coeducational and interracial school based on progressive principles of classical and practical studies and run by Theodore and Angelina Grimke Weld, also prominent members of the current abolitionist crusade. The school attracted a great number of distinguished reformers as lecturers, including Henry David Thoreau, **Horace Greeley** (1811–1872), and **Amos Bronson Alcott** (1799–1888). In 1856, one of the leaders, **Marcus Spring** (1810–1874), a Quaker and New York merchant, purchased all of the shares of the stock in this semicapitalist colony and operated it as a private venture with most communal features coming to an end in 1858. With the outbreak of the Civil War, the school was closed by the Welds. Spring continued to live on the site until his death in 1874.

READERS. *See* BISHOP HILL COLONY.

REFUGEE HOME SOCIETY. The Refugee Home Society was originally established in 1846 as the Sandwich Mission on a 10,000-acre tract of land some 10 miles north of Amherstburg, Ontario, in the Detroit, Michigan-Windsor, Ontario area as a refuge for blacks already crowding into the region who were running into strident local opposition. The land was divided into 10-acre lots and resold (from its original purchase price of $1.50 to $2.00 per acre) for $3.00 down and $6.00 per year for two years. Twenty-five acres were reserved for a church and a schoolhouse.

Despite its efforts to provide a refuge for these expatriate slaves from the United States, by 1850 with the passage of the Fugitive Slave Act and an influx of more runaways from the United States, further steps were needed to take care of these Canadian refugees. Accordingly, in November 1850 the Sandwich Mission was reorganized as the Benevolent Association to purchase an additional 30,000 acres for resale to the blacks so that they might become landowners on the road to economic self-reliance. One of the chief supporters of the move was Josiah Henson of the **Dawn** settlement, another of the **black utopias** of the period. By 1852 the Sandwich-Benevolent Association group and a new group of antislavery enthusiasts from the Detroit-Windsor area had merged into the Refugee Home Society.

Despite buying 2,000 acres of land and settling 150 blacks on it, the Society ran into serious financial difficulties during the 1850s. Added to these was dissension among both the leaders and the settlers themselves. As a result, at the end of the Civil War and the passage of the Thirteenth Amendment, the struggling Refugee Home Society ceased to exist.

REICH, CHARLES (1928–). *See GREENING OF AMERICA, THE.*

RELIGION OF HUMANITY. *See* COMTE, AUGUSTE.

RENEWED CHURCH OF THE UNITED BRETHREN. *See* MORAVIANS.

REPUBLIC. See STOICISM.

REPUBLIC, THE. See ARISTOTLE.

REPUBLIC, THE. See PLATO.

REPUBLICA CHRISTIANA. See LEIBNIZ, GOTTFRIED WILHELM von.

REPUBLIC OF THE FUTURE: OR SOCIALISM A REALITY, THE. This **dystopian** attack on utopian socialism, feminism, and technology was written by Anna Bowman Dodd (1855–1929) in 1887. It is one of approximately 20 popular dystopias that appeared in the United States in the last two decades of the 19th century. The story takes place in New York City in 2050 and takes the form of letters from Wolfgang, a visitor from Sweden, to Hannewig, a friend at home. In the United States, Wolfgang relates, the state has eliminated the capitalist system and has made everyone equal. The result is a deadening uniformity. Every house is the same, and men and women dress and even look the same, which has produced an eradication of erotic sentiment. In the name of utilitarianism, the New Yorkers have built skyscrapers on the Hudson, done away with flowers and lawns, replaced food with bottled pellets, and abolished long meals, as well as servants and even flirtation. People work only two hours a day, machinery having removed the drudgery of work (even cooking and all housework), but they are so bored they simply walk the streets with nothing to do, having "come to the end of things and . . . failed to find it amusing." Wars have been declared illegal, and foreign difficulties are adjusted by arbitration. Religion has been voted out of existence as "immoral" because it brings about discussion; it has been replaced by a system of ethics featuring ethical temples of worship. In Dodd's portrayal of the future, the socialist-egalitarian-technological system into which the United States has evolved has made its citizens neither happy nor contented. This is perhaps, as the novel's narrator says, because "a [man] can't have his dream and dream it too."

RESTIF de la BRETONNE, NICHOLAS-EDME (1734–1806). This 18th-century French writer was the son of a Burgundian peasant who became a master printer in Paris and, with the press at his disposal, published almost 300 books over the next 35 years. Restif was a thoroughgoing rake who squandered his money and ended up in near poverty. He is best known for his erotic novels that earned him the title "Rousseau of the gutters," but he also published utopian novels such as *The French Daedalus* (1781) and *The Andrograph* (1782).

In the first he wrote of an imaginary voyage to peaceful and egalitarian Megapatagonia. Here the people believe in a form of reincarnation in which the dead, burned after death to speed the process of decomposition, return in another form to their beautiful land. They have, therefore, no fear of death, and they practice moderation in their pleasures. In Megapatagonia community feeling is so strong that there is no immoral behavior, laziness, gluttony, or luxury. To assure this happy stage, rules have been established within the state for all to follow faithfully. For example, if a husband abuses his wife he is sent into exile until the age of 35, and if a wife fails her husband she is punished as a felon by the Committee of Ancient Dames. If a woman becomes pregnant, the husband can see her every day for one or two hours. If a wife commits an infidelity and a single eyewitness confirms it, the marriage will be annulled and she will be deported and lowered to the rank of the deformed where she might be given in marriage to a deformed young man. If there are two or more witnesses, she will be deported and given to the most deformed blind men to serve them. If a man seduces an unmarried woman and he is found guilty, he will be required throughout the rest of his life to fall on his knees and beg pardon of her or her parents no matter how many times a day this occurs. If he seduces a married woman, his marriage will be broken if he has no children and his wife demands it, and the wife will be free to marry again. These are just a few of the multitudinous and specific rules in Megapatagonia, happiness in the perfect life, according to Restif, being accomplished not only through community equality and mutual concern but also through minute control of human lives. *Andrograph,* in which Restif also describes a perfected society, also calls for detailed regulation of every aspect of human lives.

REUNION COLONY—MISSOURI, *or* **THE TRUE FAMILY.** Established on a 40-acre site by **Alcander Longley** (1832–1918) in 1868 near Minersville (now Oronogo) in Jasper County in the far southwestern corner of Missouri, this **Fourierist** colony existed only until 1870. Longley, who had spent some time at the Icarian community at **Corning**, Iowa, was joined by only 27 adults in his endeavor. When a faction withdrew from Reunion and mortgage payments could not be met, the colony collapsed in 1870. Longley, the faithful follower of **Etienne Cabet** (1788– 1856), went on to attempt to establish five other colonies after his failure at Reunion.

REUNION COLONY—TEXAS. This **Fourierist** colony was founded in 1855 just outside of Dallas, Texas, across the Trinity River by **Victor Considérant** (1808–1893). Some 150 French followers of **Charles Fourier** (1772–1837) sailed to America that year under the auspices of the European Society for the Colonization of Texas, a group organized by Considérant, to establish a **phalanx** in Texas. By 1856 their colony featured a two-storied main building, a community kitchen, and a dining hall; and they had planted a crop. They soon abandoned communal dining in favor of a nuclear family structure. Five hundred people were part of Reunion during its existence, no more than 350 at any one time, but by 1857 economic problems had arisen and the members could not even pay the interest on the colony's indebtedness. Because of its lack of sufficient capital investment, its weak leadership, the hostility of its neighbors, and two hard Texas winters, the colony came to an end in 1859 even though some members stayed on the site until final liquidation in 1875.

REVELATION, BOOK OF. *See* APOCALYPSE.

REVOLUTIONARY OF THE UPPER RHINE. During the Peasant's Revolt in the wake of the religious revolution set off by **Martin Luther** (1483–1546) in Germany, a person known as the Revolutionary of the Upper Rhine authored the *Book of a Hundred Chapters*. This anonymous author was convinced that God had ordered the massacre of the clergy and rich lords and burghers in a holocaust as a necessary purification of the world on the eve of the **millennium**. He asserted that all church property had to be taken away and used for the benefit of the people, especially the poor. This would lead to the common ownership of property. Furthermore, the Revolutionary stated in the *Book of a Hundred Chapters* that the Germans were the real Chosen People from the time of Adam, not the Jews, and that Adam's kin and descendants came to Europe and settled in Alsace, establishing the capital of the empire they founded at the city of Trier. This German empire, this Paradise, covered all of Europe and was marked by peace, equality, and common ownership but had been destroyed by the Romans and the Church.

Now a great leader from the Black Forest, the resurrected Emperor **Frederick II**, the Emperor of the Last Days, would cleanse German life from Latin corruption, bring back the Golden Age, and restore Germany to the position God had intended for it, reinstating the true religion headquartered not in Rome but in Mainz under a patriarch. In this perfected German state, the emperor would be the supreme priest and an earthly God. Germany, as the center of true religion and civilization, would be a quasi-religious community under a God-ordained savior, the emperor, as both political leader and new Christ. This German national phantasm did not survive the crushing of the Peasant's Revolt and the Catholic Reformation but is an illustration that the idea of a perfected state, a millennium, remained alive in 16th-century Europe.

RICHARDS COLONY. The fifth of the **Hutterite** colonies to emerge from the **Wolf Creek Colony**, it was established in 1906 in Sanborn

ROCKPORT COLONY • 261

County in southeastern South Dakota. In 1918, in the face of local re-
sistance arising from World War I, it was moved to Lethbridge in
southern Alberta, Canada.

RIGNON, SIDNEY (1793–1876). *See* KIRKLAND COMMUNITY.

RIPLEY, GEORGE (1802–1880). This reformer and principal force
behind the establishment of **Brook Farm** had graduated from both
Harvard University and Harvard Divinity School before assuming
the ministry of the Unitarian Purchase Street Church in Boston. He
was also a leading figure in early **Transcendentalism**, the first meeting of the Transcendental Club being held in his home in 1836. He
was also the first president of the Brook Farm Institute of Agriculture
and Education. Not a strong leader, he allowed Brook Farm to drift
into **Fourierism**, and when the Brook Farm property was turned over
to a board of trustees, Ripley moved to Brooklyn but continued to
edit *The Harbinger* before moving on to write for **Horace Greeley**'s
Tribune, where he built a solid reputation as a critic.

RISING STAR ASSOCIATION. Through correspondence with noted
communitarians, including **Albert Brisbane** (1809–1890), John S.
Patterson organized a colony in 1853 on a large farm he had inherited
at Stelvideo in Darke County in western Ohio. The female dress campaign launched by Amelia Bloomer was so popular among the
women of the colony that Rising Star also became known as
"Bloomertown." Patterson and his followers moved to **Berlin
Heights** near Cleveland in 1857.

ROADTOWN. See CHAMBLESS, EDGAR.

ROBERTSON, WARREN. *See* TEMPLE OF THE GOSPEL OF THE
KINGDOM.

ROCHESTER INDUSTRIAL ASSOCIATION. *See* ONTARIO
PHALANX.

ROCKPORT COLONY. This **Hutterite** colony was established in
1891 near Alexandria in Hanson County in southeastern South

Dakota as a spin-off from the parent colony of **Elmspring** in neighboring Hutchinson County. Some of the members moved to Magrath, just across the international border in Alberta, Canada, in 1918. When the remaining members left for Alberta in 1934, the colonists of **Bon Homme** purchased its land and properties for a daughter colony.

ROMANTICISM, 19TH-CENTURY. Although rationalism, **scientism**, and **positivism** made great strides both in Europe and in the United States during the 19th century, they were complemented by a contradictory intellectual movement that also pointed the way toward progress and perfection for humankind. This was romanticism. It promised progress to perfection through the spiritual, nonmaterial dimension of a person's life. Romanticism, whose prophet was **Jean-Jacques Rousseau** (1712–1788), embodied a belief in the natural goodness of humans and a deep concern for his inner life. It valued emotion and simplicity as well as a sense of communication with all of nature. This led the romantic person to a fascination with the strange and nonrational, that is, with the remote that can only be sensed or felt, not intellectually perceived. In turn, it led that person not to earth-bound perception but to seeking out the infinite, the mysterious, the irrational, the spiritual and ultimately unattainable dimensions of life, the what-ifs of human existence that cannot be answered but remain part of a person's very being. Seeking answers to these questions and acting upon them is to be free, argued the romantics. Living authentically and intensely with one's inner creative impulses whatever the cost is more important than the validity of one's vision.

"To thine own self be true" whatever the consequences was taken as the principle of true freedom and humanity by the romantics. This, they said, is true freedom: aspiring toward a higher level of becoming because all life is a process of becoming; living by one's own vision, not by the vision or rules of another; and living according to creative self-expression in accord with nature. In their view, it is by such deep and spontaneous personal exertions that a golden age of humankind will emerge, not by the constructs of reason but by persons being willing to follow the impulses of their souls and by being open to the spiritual unity in all of creation while in communion with other souls doing the same. Romanticism, then, is seeking the greater reality beyond the rules of reason and convention in the deeper conscious and unconscious promptings of the soul.

Of critical importance, it led in most cases to seeing one's history as characterized by change leading to perfectibility because humankind has the ability to bring new and better worlds to life by its creative and inventive powers. Different as it was from optimistic positivist-scientist thought during the 19th century, romanticism, which occupied the same stage during this critical century, also assumed human progress to ever higher levels. In tandem with the positivist-scientists, the romantics infused into the 19th century a continuing and growing conviction that humankind was progressing toward perfection in time, toward a perfected, utopian existence.

ROSEDALE COLONY. This **Hutterite** colony was established in 1901 in Hanson County in southeastern South Dakota as the first granddaughter colony from the **Milltown Colony** in Beadle County to the north. It was moved to Elie, Manitoba, Canada, near Winnipeg in 1918 because of the hostility of its neighbors during World War I.

ROSENHAYN. Established at Rosenhayn in Cumberland County, New Jersey, in 1882 and aided by the Hebrew Emigrant Aid Society, the colony began with six families but gradually increased in membership to 67 families and 250 individuals by 1889. Many came because of the success of the neighboring **Alliance Colony**. The members of Rosenhayn built a clothing factory and although some communal practices were maintained, the community ceased to be a cooperative enterprise after 1889.

ROUSSEAU, JEAN-JACQUES (1712–1778). Jean-Jacques Rousseau, the son of a Swiss watchmaker and author of the classic political tract *The Social Contract* (1762), believed that a tension existed between the individual and society. This is clearly illustrated in his famed novel *The New Heloise* (1761). As a faithful child of the Enlightenment and friend of the *philosophe* **Denis Diderot** (1713–1784), Rousseau also argued for the importance of proper rational education, as brought out in his *Emile* (1762). But his greatest impact on French and Western intellectual development came from his *The Social Contract* and his earlier *Discourse on Political Economy* (1755?) in which he proposed a model for government that would assure individual moral freedom—for men only—by all persons submitting their individual interests to a social contract that represented the common good, the General Will of the community, the collective consciousness of all male citizens, even to the point that they must "be forced to be free."

In his works, Rousseau makes clear that he wanted humans to return to the state of nature in which no greed or selfishness will be found. Here humans simply delight in existence, needing only food, sleep, and copulation. All humans are not totally equal in this idyllic state, but their natural differences, their natural advantages and disadvantages, are not enhanced by the accumulation of goods furnished by the arts and sciences. In this utopian state, humans are independent; their only goal in life is liberty in self-actualization. But paradoxically, Rousseau, while emphasizing the importance of the autonomous "I" in his writings, also argued for the dominance of the General Will of the moral community. Attaining the General Will involved taking away a human's private being and absolute existence and creating a collective moral body in which his relative existence predominates. Rousseau, a consummate egalitarian, was in effect denouncing the political, social, and religious void of civilization with its inequality and privilege in favor of an egalitarian utopian community that would bring happiness and peace to all through the dominance of the all-powerful General Will.

This to Rousseau was progress; this was utopia. People, once in an idyllic state of nature but diverted from progress by inequality and property, will regain their proper destiny and superior civilization by a forced equality in subservience to the General Will. The resulting absolute state will even be the object of worship (as occurred during the French Revolution) with the creation of a civil religion possessing the power to impose its dogmas on everyone under the penalty of death. Whatever this Enlightenment icon's intentions, his concept of the utopian totalitarian state as the answer to people's problematic life on earth had a powerful effect on Western ideas and institutions, justifying absolutism of the Left as well as the Right both in his lifetime and in the centuries to come. His concept of the individual being subject to the General Will was also found in most utopian societies that flourished in the 19th and 20th centuries. *See also* ROMANTICISM, 19TH-CENTURY.

ROYAL SALT WORKS. *See* LEDOUX, CLAUDE-NICOLAS.

ROYCROFT. This unique profit-sharing, semicommunal corporation was founded by Elbert Hubbard in 1900 at East Aurora in Erie County, New York. Its economic activities included a farm, a bank, a printing plant, a bookbindery, a furniture factory, and a blacksmith shop. These were manned by 300 to 500 persons, some of whom lived in quarters called the Roycroft Phalanstery (so named to evoke the memory of **Charles Fourier**), all of whom worked in pleasant conditions and shared in the corporation's multimillion dollar sales. Roycrofters enjoyed common meals, meetings, sports, studies, and a library. Hubbard became a considerable economic and social force in the country through the Roycrofters' publishing efforts, but with his death (and that of his wife) aboard the *Lusitania* in 1915 the cooperative features of Roycroft were ended and the community became a typical commercial enterprise under the leadership of his son, lasting until 1938.

RUGBY COLONY. Central to the establishment of this Anglo-American cooperative was Thomas Hughes, who hoped to establish a settlement on the American frontier for the second and third sons of English gentry to give them a chance to develop skills and become productive citizens. Opened in 1880 on the Cumberland Plateau in Morgan County in eastern Tennessee on 7,000 acres (plus 33,000 more for farming), Rugby by 1884 had over 400 residents (only about 40 percent were English) and 42 buildings, including a church, a school, a 7,000-volume library (Hughes hoped to start an Anglo-American university on the site), and a hotel. It also featured social clubs and literary and dramatic groups. Its commissary, its only cooperative feature, supplied the members with everything they needed. Most of the cooperative aspects of the colony were phased out after 1887, and its governing body was reorganized into a landholding company in 1892.

RUINES, OU MEDITATION SUR LES REVOLUTIONS DES EMPIRES, LES (THE RUINS, OR A MEDITATION ON THE REVOLUTIONS OF EMPIRES). *See* VOLNEY, CONSTANTIN FRANCOIS CHASSEBOUF, COMTE de.

RUSKIN COLONY. Named in honor of the influential English art critic and reformer **John Ruskin** (1819–1900), the first Ruskin colony, the Ruskin Cooperative Association, was founded by **Julius A. Wayland** (1854–1912), the prominent editor of the socialist newspaper *The Coming Nation.* It was established in 1894 on two 500-acre tracts some 50 miles west of Nashville, Tennessee, in Dickinson County. The membership of the colony eventually reached 250, with persons coming from over 32 states. But Wayland left the colony the next year over his editorial control of *The Coming Nation,* and the colony was weakened by turnover in membership plus quarrels over religion, schools, and monogamy. Still, by 1897 the colony had 1,800 acres, a number of business enterprises, and several dozen buildings. However, plagued with general dissatisfaction over life at the colony, it was dissolved in 1899. In the meantime, some families had left Ruskin and reformed themselves into a separate colony at Dixie on the Tennessee River. But this breakaway colony, made up of middle-class urbanites and intellectual socialists, lasted only until the end of 1898. Most of the faithful believers at Ruskin voted to abolish the Ruskin Cooperative Association and create a new colony called the Ruskin Commonwealth. Then, having lost their land in Tennessee, most of the remaining members of the Ruskin Cooperative Association joined the Duke Colony, also known as the ***American Settlers Association,*** on the edge of the Okefenokee Swamp near Waycross, Georgia, the Duke colonists thereafter dissolving their organization and becoming members of the Ruskin Commonwealth; this colony lasted only until 1901. Others quit and joined the **single-tax** colony at **Fairhope** in Alabama; still others joined the **Cooperative Brotherhood** at Burley in Washington.

RUSKIN, JOHN (1819–1900). This foremost English art critic during the mid-19th century was also a noted reformer and critic of industrialization and its effects. He advocated, among other things, old age pensions, the nationalization of education, and the organization of labor. His positive program for social reform appeared in *Sesame and Lilies* (1865), *The Crown of Wild Olive* (1866), *Time and Tide* (1867), and *Fors Clavigera* (8 vols., 1871–1884).

RUSS, JOANNA (1937–). Joanna Russ, a graduate of Cornell and Yale Universities and a professor of English at the University of Washington, is prominent as a feminist science fiction writer. She is also the author of *The Female Man* (1975), which centers around four female characters. In this utopian futurist novel, Russ paints a picture of an all-female world called Whileaway. Whileaway was created when a plague 600 years before killed off all the males. Motherhood is portrayed as a necessity and is achieved mechanically. The community is based on the extended female family, usually numbering 30 females, who use technology to remove the drudgery of work and live in peace and contentment.

RUSSELL, CHARLES TAZE (1852–1916). *See* JEHOVAH'S WITNESSES.

– S –

SABBATHDAY LAKE. Located at New Gloucester, Maine, just southwest of Lewiston, the Sabbathday Lake **Shaker** Village was founded in 1793 on what was then called Thompson's Pond Plantation by a group of Shaker missionaries. Within a year almost 200 people had gathered on the site, living in existing homes and outbuildings. In 1794 these Shakers built a Meeting House for public worship, and during the next decade their first communal Dwelling House, mills, barns, and other buildings were constructed.

Referred to as "the least of Mother's children in the east," Sabbathday Lake was one of the smallest and poorest of the eastern Shaker communities, its members struggling to pay off debts incurred by dishonest business agents. Still, the community overcame its problems and continued to function. Today it is the only active Shaker community, encompassing 18 buildings on 1,800 acres of land dedicated to agricultural production. Sabbathday Lake members also manufacture fancy goods, baskets, and small woodenware. Its membership consists of two women ("sisters") and two men ("brothers"), but new members are still accepted.

SACRED ORDER OF UNIONISTS. *See* SPEAR, JOHN MURRAY.

SADE, DONATIEN ALPHONSE FRANCOIS, COMTE de (1740–1814). The Marquis de Sade is best known in history as a notorious and unapologetic libertine who died incurably insane after being placed in an institution in 1803. Yet he was also a utopian of a sort, picturing and urging the adoption of a lascivious utopia of total human and sexual permissiveness, as best revealed in his *Philosophy in the Bedroom*. Rejecting Christian values and moral teachings completely, as well as confining civil laws based upon them, he argued against modesty other than as a means of coquetry, any restrictions on sexual acts, and any restrictions on prostitution, adultery, or fornication, seeing all three as being positively beneficial to society. On the other hand, he argued in favor of incest and sodomy and urged that brothels for both men and women be established by the government. Despite the hue and cry that greeted de Sade's writings, his arguments in favor of total human happiness based on sensual openness and practice have continued to affect the Western world down to the present time.

SAINT-SIMON, CLAUDE HENRI de ROUVROY, COMTE de (1760–1825). Saint-Simon was born in Paris to a distinguished and noble, but impoverished family. He served as a volunteer in the American Revolution and, after making his fortune in confiscated lands from the French Revolution (during which he was imprisoned for a time), he turned to the study of philosophy. His major ideas were contained in his *Nouveau Christianisme* (1825). These were basically utopian and socialist in nature, calling for a state system of socialist government and a new Christianity. The cardinal belief of Saint-Simon was that humankind must work for an organic society for the benefit of the greatest number of citizens. This organic, utopian society would be based on the state possessing all property with no inheritance allowed, that the rewards for labor would not be equal but would be given according to their service to the common good, that society would be based on a new spiritual power or new religion proper for the forthcoming industrial age, and that the old feudal and military state systems would be replaced by a new order headed by scientists, engineers, and artists, not by politicians.

The new state would be made up of **phalanxes**, part garden cities and part agricultural communes. The new religion to give spiritual direction to the people, his "new Christianity," would be based on true and reliable knowledge founded on science rather than on the traditional authority of the church, thereby ensuring that all its members accept the principle of love for one another. In this new religion, the scientists and intellectuals would be its priests, presiding over the Council of Newton (God's *logos,* or word) representing God on earth. Temples of Newton would serve as worship and research centers. When all of this is accomplished—including the oceans of the world being transformed into lemonade and having 37 million each of poets, mathematicians, and dramatists!—it will be the culmination of the ascending **postmillennial** history of the world in stages, urged Saint-Simon, with the first stage that of the ancient world, the second that of the Christian Middle Ages, and the final and culminating stage that of the Age of Reason and the Enlightenment. Saint-Simon's ideas, largely stripped of their religious content, became the basis of French socialism in the 19th century, thanks to a group of brilliant young disciples.

SALTAIRE. This industrial utopia was opened next to Shipley and just north of Bradford in West Yorkshire, England, in 1853. It was the creation of the wealthy manufacturer Sir Titus Salt (1803–1876) for his woolen workers as an alternative to the dark mill towns of Bradford and Leeds. Conceived as the model town for his employees to integrate their home, work, and leisure, its buildings were arranged like the letter *T* with an elongated room on the sixth floor with great glass windows, giving the workers fresh air and good light. Around the *T* and situated on 26 acres were 800 houses with all the modern conveniences for the workers. Saltaire also featured shops, schools, and other social amenities—except alcohol, which Salt believed, combined with lust, created social problems. Today Salt's mill has been converted into a art gallery featuring the works of David Hockney, and other buildings in the village have been transformed into shops, restaurants, and pubs. In December 2001 Saltaire was designated a World Heritage Site by the United Nations Educational, Scientific and Cultural Organization (UNESCO).

SALVATION ARMY FARM COLONIES. These colonies represented the working out of the idea of William Booth in his *In Darkest England and the Way Out* (1890) that the way to alleviate a nation's poverty was by establishing self-sufficient cities and farm colonies for the poor. In 1896 Frederick Booth-Tucker (1853–1929), the commander of the Salvation Army in the United States, proposed that wasted labor (the urban unemployed) be placed on wasted land by means of wasted capital. Such notables as Grover Cleveland, Theodore Roosevelt, Henry C. Lodge, and Mark Hanna came out in support of the idea. Accordingly, during 1897 Salvation Army representatives chose sites in Colorado, California, and Ohio for the project. The resulting colonies were **Fort Amity** in Colorado, **Fort Romie** in California, and **Fort Herrick** in Ohio. The colonies stressed the family as the basic social unit and practiced only minimal economic cooperation. Still, all were utopian in outlook and character. Despite some successes, the Salvation Army closed the program in 1910.

SANCTIFICATIONISTS. *See* MCWHIRTER, MARTHA (1827–1904).

SANDWICH MISSION. *See* REFUGEE HOME SOCIETY.

SANGAMON PHALANX. *See* INTEGRAL PHALANX.

SARTRE, JEAN-PAUL (1905–1980). Jean-Paul Sartre, philosopher, novelist, playwright, chief exponent of French existentialism, and author of *Being and Nothingness* (1943), argued that each person is the sole master of his destiny in a world of absurdity, spiritual decay, social injustice, and war. Yet humans are impelled to exercise their freedom to create somethingness out of nothingness to create some meaning out of meaningless reality. Their self-essence, then, consists in what they make of themselves through their freedom until death, even though they know that they are moving in a nothingness of perpetual instability and contingency of all things including themselves. In doing so, they create their own laws and values, these being the true exercise of their freedom and being. Self-realization through freedom, the individual struggle to escape from nothingness to somethingness, from absurdity to meaning, represents the summit of human aspiration and must be exercised. Sartre's philosophy has become part and parcel of the widespread struggle for perfection in the 20th century.

SAVOY COMMUNITY. This **Shaker** community was established in Berkshire County in western Massachusetts in 1817. Owing to a severe drought, the community was abandoned in 1821, its members moving to **Mount Lebanon** and **Watervliet** in New York.

SCHOOL OF LIVING COLONY. *See* BORSODI, RALPH.

SCIENTISM. Scientism is an assumption that knowledge can be gained only by the methods of inductive reasoning. It represents a singular trust in the efficacy of the methods of natural science applied to all areas of investigation including philosophy, the social sciences, and the humanities. Scientism was one of the chief assumptions accepted by many reformers and utopians during the Enlightenment and continues to enjoy wide approval to the present day.

SCOTT, SARAH (1723–1795). This 18th-century British writer was the author of one of the earliest examples of feminist utopias with the publication of her *A Description of Millennium Hall* (1762). The work was based on a female commune that Scott and a female companion had established in 1754 after the failure of her marriage and apparently in reaction against Scott's earlier ultra-patriarchal home environment. In the work a male stumbles upon a female commune, Millennium Hall, populated by single and socially ostracized women who have created a perfect state. It is run according to the rational principles of the Enlightenment, the labor undertaken by the women being according to their abilities and interests rather than being based on gender as in the "outside world." The women of Millennium Hall view God as their "Supreme Legislator," thereby building their society on divine ordinances of kindness and compassion for others and loving one another like sisters.

SEGARELLI, GERARD (?–1300). *See* APOSTOLIC BRETHREN.

SEPARATISTS OF ZOAR. Established as a haven for southern German Separatists from the Lutheran Church and suffering religious persecution in their native land, the colony of the Society of Separatists of Zoar was founded in 1817 on 5,500 acres in Tuscarawas County in eastern Ohio. The emigration was aided by financial help from English Quakers. Zoar was the biblical city where Lot found refuge after the destruction of the cities on the plain. Zoar's 150 pioneers, poverty-stricken in the beginning, established communal ownership of property two years later after their leader, Joseph Bimeler (1778–1853), became convinced that this was the proper economic remedy. After 10 years, the Separatists dropped their belief in celibacy when Bimeler fell in love with one of his maidservants. Additionally, the colonists became concerned over the future growth of the community. By 1875 it was estimated that the colony was worth $1 million. This model Christian society continued in existence until 1898, drawing income from its brewery and its woolen and linen mills, although it had been in slow economic decline since the Civil War.

SEVARAMBIANS. In the utopian tale *Histoire des Sevarambes* (1677–1679), written by Denis Vairasse d'Allais (ca. 1630–ca. 1700), a Frenchman about whom little is known but who had spent considerable time in England, the mythical land of the Sevarambians is described in detail. The land is ruled by a benevolent monarch, the Viceroy of the Sun, who is accepted as their god and who governs absolutely in justice and equity with the unquestioning obedience of his subjects who acknowledge him as the source of all their goodness. The people live in *osmasies* (communal dwellings) with no private property, but all their needs for a comfortable life are gathered into public warehouses and then distributed to the *osmasies,* where they are in turn distributed to the people. Any surplus, especially from the agricultural communes, is sent to a central warehouse where it is distributed to other *osmasies,* again according to need alone. Each *osmasie* has its own officials and teachers. It also has slaves to do the lowest tasks. In the Sevarambians' educational program, some are taught the arts and trades, and others are directed to more intellectual tasks in the community and the art of governing. Equity being the rule of the land—except for the slaves—no one is poor and without the necessities for useful and pleasurable existence. Furthermore, there are no taxes, private property, or dowries, so advancement is by merit, not by wealth. Vairasse happily concludes that this land is as perfect as can be in the world, all other nations being most unlucky by comparison.

SEVENTH-DAY BAPTIST CHURCH. *See* SNOW HILL NUN-NERY.

SHAKER COMMUNITIES.

Name	Location	Years
Mount Lebanon (New Lebanon)	New York	1787–1947
Watervliet (Niskeyuna)	New York	1788–1938
Hancock (West Pittsfield)	Massachusetts	1790–1960
Enfield	Connecticut	1790–1917
Harvard	Massachusetts	1791–1918
Tyringham	Massachusetts	1792–1875
Canterbury	New Hampshire	1792–1992
Shirley	Massachusetts	1793–1908
Enfield	New Hampshire	1793–1923
Alfred	Maine	1793–1931
Sabbathday Lake	Maine	1793–
Gorham	Maine	1794–1819
Union Village	Ohio	1805–1912
Pleasant Hill (Shakertown)	Kentucky	1805–1910
Watervliet	Ohio	1806–1900
South Union (Gasper Springs)	Kentucky	1807–1922
West Union	Indiana	1807–1827
Savoy	Massachusetts	1817–1821
North Union	Ohio	1822–1889
Whitewater	Ohio	1822–1916
Sodus Bay	New York	1826–1836
Groveland	New York	1836–1895
Narcoossee	Florida	1894–1924
White Oak	Georgia	1898–1902

SHAKERS, *or* **UNITED BELIEVERS IN CHRIST'S SECOND COMING.** This society was founded in 1747 in Manchester, England. Its members soon earned the disparaging epithet "Shaking Quakers" because of their bodily agitation in worship. To this group came **Ann Lee** (1736–1784). While imprisoned for her religious views, she experienced a series of visions. From that time on, she was acknowledged as the leader of the Shakers and was known as "Mother Ann."

In 1774 Mother Ann and eight of her followers boarded *The Mariah* in Liverpool and sailed to New York City. Several of them then went up the Hudson River to a site outside Albany called Niskeyuna, or *Watervliet*. Again the Shakers suffered persecution and derision. Mother Ann died in 1784, and **James Whittaker** (1751–1787), one of the eight Shakers who sailed to the United States with her, assumed the leadership of the group. After his death in 1787, the society was headed by American converts to the faith, **Joseph Meachem** (1741–1796) and **Lucy Wright** (1760–1821), and began to be gathered together into "Gospel Order." The first gathered community was at **Mount Lebanon**, or New Lebanon; thereafter 22 communities were established in Maine, New Hampshire, Massachusetts, Connecticut, New York, Kentucky, Ohio, Indiana, Georgia, and Florida. By the 1850s the Shakers numbered some 6,000 adherents, but the years after the Civil War witnessed falling numbers and a decrease in religious practice. From 1847 to 1947, Shakerism declined as fewer people were attracted to the life and the celibate population aged. The colonies' property was sold off, and a necessary consolidation of members from the various sites took place. Today **Sabbathday Lake** in Maine is the only remaining Shaker colony.

The basic tenets of the Shaker faith include a belief that all men and women are called to that holiness without which no one can see the Lord; that God is the omniscient, omnipotent, omnipresent Great First Cause and of pure spirit embodying both maleness and femaleness; that Christ became the anointed of God with his baptism; that Mother Ann was not Christ but rather the first of many Believers totally imbued by His spirit; that the Second Coming is in Christ's Church, so Christ will not return in the flesh; that the community of goods and living a life of simple poverty is God's way; and that celibacy is mandatory because sexual intercourse is a covenant with the devil and the cause of human suffering. Additionally, the Shakers are pacifists.

SHAKERTOWN. *See* UNION VILLAGE.

SHAKING QUAKERS. *See* SHAKERS.

SHAPE OF THINGS TO COME, THE. *See* WELLS, H. G.

SHAW, GEORGE BERNARD (1856–1950). *See BACK TO METH-USALAH*.

SHELLEY, MARY WOLLSTONECRAFT (1797–1851). *See LAST MAN, THE*.

SHEPHERD'S ROD. *See* BRANCH DAVIDIANS; DAVIDIAN SEVENTH-DAY ADVENTISTS; HOUTEFF, VICTOR.

SHIRLEY COMMUNITY. Eleven years after four prosperous farmers were converted to Shakerism in Middlesex County, Massachusetts, some 70 **Shakers** gathered and formed a community on a 2,000-acre site at Shirley northwest of Boston in 1893. The main economic activity at Shirley was the processing of applesauce; the members sold five to six tons of the product each year. By the 1820s the community had a membership of 150, but the numbers gradually declined thereafter, standing at only 48 in 1875. The project ended in 1908.

SIBYLLINE PROPHECIES. Although the idea of an earthly **millennium** was condemned by the Church in the fifth and sixth centuries, the concept continued to exist in the popular mind during the Middle Ages. In some instances, it took the form of full-blown movements that forced the Church as the guardian of orthodoxy to counter them and condemn their adherents. This can partially be explained by the continued circulation of the Sibylline prophecies, dating back to the fourth century, which told of the return of the warrior-Christ leading to the Emperor of the Last Days and which promised a golden age of ease. Prominent among these prophecies was the seventh-century tract known as the ***Pseudo-Methodius***, which emerged from Byzantium.

SICILY ISLAND COLONY. Founded in 1881 by Herman Rosenthal on Sicily Island in Catahoula Parish, Louisiana, some 90 miles from New Orleans, this colony was set up to aid 60 Jewish families fleeing the pogroms in Russia. Each family was offered 160 acres of land, but it was hoped that the migrants would also establish factories and industries and reinvest their earnings in cooperative enterprises. Arriving in the winter of 1882, they soon found with the coming of spring that the heat and outbreaks of malaria warred against their success, culminating with the Mississippi River flooding their land and structures. Some of the colonists moved to the **Cremieux Colony** in South Dakota; others simply dispersed to other parts of Louisiana. By 1883 the experiment had collapsed.

SILKVILLE COLONY. *See* BOISSIERE, ERNEST VALETON de.

SINAPIA. This Spanish utopian novel by an anonymous author (but attributed to the Count of Campomanes) was written in 1682 but discovered only in 1975. Its contents indicate that the author borrowed heavily from **Thomas More**'s *Utopia*; it is also reflective of the ideas of the humanist Desiderius Erasmus. It is fundamentally a critique of 17th-century Spain, the story being set on a peninsula similar to Iberia. It recounts the adventures of a Dutch navigator, Abel Tasman, who landed on Sinapia (originally called Bireia, it was renamed for Prince Sinap of Persia who conquered and ruled the country). Prince Sinap and his patriarch, Bishop Codabend, were driven from their native Persia to China and then to Bireia (Iberia) in search of religious freedom. The population of Sinapia (Hispania) is cosmopolitan and includes people from many lands. It has its own language and elects its leaders, who must be well trained and experienced whether serving in a religious or governmental capacity. Christian education, therefore, is very important in Sinapia. Because it is a communal society, there is no private property. Sinapian society and government are organized around the patriarchal family, and, therefore, women cannot vote or hold office. The moral code is rigidly enforced in the land because it is a Christian commonwealth; social injustices and economic inefficiencies do not exist; and there is no war or violence, the people being pacifists.

Sinapia is both a singular example of utopian literature censoring 17th-century Spain itself—Spanish writers in all other instances locating utopia in the New World, not at home—and a condemnation of 17th-century secularism and the decadence that had arisen in Europe because its rulers had abandoned Christian principles.

SINCLAIR, UPTON BEALL (1878–1968). Known primarily as a novelist, Upton Sinclair was also the leader of Helicon Hall located at Englewood on the Palisades in New Jersey. Using the royalties from his popular muckraking work *The Jungle* (1904), Sinclair started the cooperative colony in 1906. It was more of a Bohemian experiment than a communal colony as the members, including Sinclair Lewis, lived a gracious and expensive lifestyle. After a fire destroyed the main house in 1907, Sinclair found that interest in the Helicon Hall scheme was feeble. He thereafter became an apostle of pure foods. Sinclair ran for governor of California in 1934 on the End Poverty in California ticket. He also worked as an advocate for temperance, the American Civil Liberties Union, and cooperative societies until his death.

SINGLE TAX. *See* GEORGE, HENRY.

SKANEATELES COMMUNITY. Founded by John A. Collins (1810–1890), a salaried abolition agent from Boston, in 1844 in Onondaga County in the Finger Lakes region of upstate New York, this **Fourierist** colony grew out of a number of reform meetings held in the Syracuse area the previous year. Formed as a joint-stock company, the community was located on a 300-acre site and, under Collins's leadership, stressed anarchist political principles, community of ownership, and abstaining from meat, narcotics, and alcohol. It accepted a free love philosophy and forbade organized religion. Although the colony enjoyed some economic success, a dispute between Collins and an important member, who disapproved of Collins's radical social and religious beliefs, led to a weakening of the community. Collins subsequently withdrew from the **phalanx**, which came to an end in 1846. Several members thereafter joined the **Oneida Community**.

SKINNER, B. F. (1904–1990). The author most responsible for the resurgence of American utopianism in the post–World War II era was the **behaviorist** psychologist B(urrhus) F(rederic) Skinner. Skinner, longtime professor of psychology at Harvard University, argued during his career that people are controlled by external factors. Good behavior is encouraged and bad behavior is discouraged by external reactions to them; therefore, positive and negative reinforcement from the outside is the key to understanding a person's behavior. People are not capable of independent, self-willed actions. He also advocated that "behavioral technology" as used with laboratory animals be applied to society in order to eliminate crime, poverty, and war. These behaviorist ideas formed the basis of his utopian novel *Walden Two* (1948) and his *Beyond Freedom and Dignity* (1971).

In *Walden Two,* a utopian alternative to 20th-century society in which people are exhausted and demoralized, Skinner portrayed a society, a "pilot experiment," a "model for imitation," in which positive and negative behaviorist reinforcements would be built into its very structure, thereby eliminating conspicuous consumption, pursuit of power, crime, and even the need for legislation. Children would be raised in communal nurseries and taught to think and learn, not to memorize facts. Sexual relations would take place freely between adolescents, and girls would begin having children as early as 16, but monogamy would be the general rule. There would be no theology, religion, or history in Skinner's ideal society; rather, all of its members would seek harmony and happiness by utilizing positive and negative reinforcement to ensure socially approved behavior, free will gradually receding as a factor in human action.

In Skinner's idealized society, Walden Two, the six Planners govern the community (utilizing society as a laboratory because human actions can be studied empirically) and select their replacements when their 10-year terms are up; the Managers, chosen by the Planners, are in charge of the functioning of the community; the Scientists specialize in the physical and natural sciences; and the Workers, a category that includes all members of the community, labor at least four hours per day and accumulate labor credits based on the psychological pleasure or displeasure associated with each given task.

In his highly controversial *Beyond Freedom and Dignity,* Skinner again advocated utilitarian behaviorism, a technology of behavior wherein humans' destructive behavior would be altered through systematic positive and negative reinforcement. This, he argued, would cure all of society's problems involving human decision making, the outmoded belief in autonomous, free will judgments and the related, old-fashioned concepts of freedom and dignity having been discarded. In Skinner's projected society, the person would not be held responsible for his or her conduct; rather, the responsibility would properly lie in the environment.

Skinner's teachings have sparked heated debate over their validity and implications, but they have found wide acceptance in the fields of psychology, sociology, criminology, penology, and education. They thus have furthered the belief that persons, given the correct insights and direction, can improve society by the adoption of the behaviorist techniques of positive and negative reinforcement. And less obviously but crucially, the belief that a more perfect society, a utopia, can be achieved on earth received support from his preaching. Inspired by what they had read in *Walden Two,* a small group in 1967 formed a utopian community at **Twin Oaks**, near Louisa, Virginia, and enjoyed some success in the years thereafter. It continues to this day.

SLUYTER, PETER (1645–1722). *See* LABADISTS.

SMITH, GEORGE VENABLE (1843–1919). Born in Kentucky, Smith came to California with his father as a young child and was schooled in Sacramento. Admitted to the bar in 1864, he practiced law in Portland, Oregon, then served as a delegate to the California State Constitutional Convention in 1879. He subsequently became district attorney for Kern County, California, and in 1883 moved to Seattle, Washington. In 1885 he became involved with an anti-Chinese labor group interested in founding a cooperative colony. The next year, the **Puget Sound Cooperative Colony** was formed near Port Angeles with Smith as its president. The colony enjoyed some early success but was weakened by leadership disputes. Smith left the colony in 1888 and opened a law practice in Port Angeles. Five years later he published a pamphlet called *A Co-operative Plan for Securing Home and Occupations at Port Angeles, Washington,* calling for another collective experiment, the Puget Sound Colony having been defunct for three years. Smith went on to become a probate judge, a prosecuting attorney, and the city attorney for Port Angeles before his death in 1919.

SMITH, JOSEPH (1805–1844). *See* MORMONS.

SMOLNIKAR, ANDREAS BERNARDUS (1795–?). Born in Austria and ordained a priest, Smolnikar then became a Benedictine monk in 1825. He served as a professor of biblical literature and in 1826 took a new middle name, Bernardus, after St. Bernard. Then in 1837 he recorded that he had a vision in which Christ appointed him as a messenger to prepare people for the **millennium** and to form a new universal republic. In November of that year, he arrived in the United States to carry out this divine charge and thereafter published his views in five volumes between 1838 and 1842. He was familiar with and apparently influenced by the writings of **John Adolphus Etzler** (ca. 1796–?), who had argued that four stages existed in the transformation of human society into a utopian setting. In 1844 Smolnikar was one of six vice presidents, along with **Albert Brisbane** (1809–1890) and **Horace Greeley** (1811–1872), of the National Convention of Associationists when it met in New York City. The following year he attempted to form a colony of Germans in Warren County, Pennsylvania; it was called the Peace Union Settlement. It apparently failed. Then in 1846 he became involved with the **Grand Prairie Community** in Indiana. During the decade of the 1850s, he was in attendance at many reform conventions trying to receive the endorsement of those present for his millennialist schemes. In 1859 he purchased land in Pennsylvania for another colony, published a tract attacking the Catholic Church and President James Buchanan, and talked about the coming of a New Era. No record of his activities after that year exist, including the year of his death.

SNOW HILL NUNNERY, *or* **SEVENTH-DAY BAPTIST CHURCH AT SNOW HILL.** This colony was founded in 1798 at Snow Hill in Franklin County in south-central Pennsylvania, by a group of German Seventh-Day Baptists as an offshoot of the Ephrata Colony founded by **Johann Conrad Beissel** (1690?–1768) in Lancaster County. It began operation about 1800. The breakaway members at Snow Hill sought to perpetuate the mysticism of Ephrata, as well as that colony's writing and musical styles. Members were required to be baptized and single and to belong to the church. Celibacy was not required, but married members had to reside outside the cloister, as did any secularist members. There were separate orders for men and women, and the community followed monastic practices, the members rising at dawn for hymns and prayers. Although it remained a small community with never more than 40 members, during the 1830s several buildings were erected, including a convent for the brothers. In 1843, a convent for the sisters was built. The school at Snow Hill empha-sized history, music, and theology and welcomed children from the area. But by the end of the 19th century, only one brother and one sis-ter remained in the community, and the monastic order was dissolved in 1900, the Snow Hill Nunnery becoming a church society.

SOCIAL CONTRACT, THE. See ROUSSEAU, JEAN-JACQUES.

SOCIAL DARWINISM. *See* SPENCER, HERBERT.

SOCIAL DEMOCRACY OF AMERICA. *See* DEBS, EUGENE VICTOR.

SOCIAL DESTINY OF MAN. *See* BRISBANE, ALBERT.

SOCIAL GOSPELISM. Social Gospelism emerged in the late 19th century within American Protestantism. A form of liberal and mod-ernist religious outlook arising out of a desire to make Christianity more relevant to American worshipers, it was marked by a desire to retain religious belief yet blend it with rational and scientific valida-tion. It attempted to achieve this fusion by arguing that God was im-manent in the development of society and that society was necessar-ily progressing linearly through time toward the kingdom of God, toward perfection here on earth.

From this belief, it followed that today's religious ideas and non-literal interpretations of the Bible were by definition superior to those of the past, God's truths being in a state of evolution. This included reinterpreting or ignoring traditional doctrinal matters in favor of working toward the amelioration of human problems in the present.

Marked in particular by the writings of Walter Rauschenbusch (1861–1918) and Washington Gladden (1836–1918), this new version of Protestantism emphasized that Christianity means Christian in-volvement for the good of others. Because of its tendency to blend tra-ditional revealed religious truth with modern ideas of reason, science, evolution, experimentation, ceaseless change, and necessary progress toward the realization of a heaven on earth, Social Gospelism played an important role in the acceptance of necessary societal progress—if not to declared utopianism—during the 20th century.

SOCIALISM. *See* UTOPIAN SOCIALISM.

SOCIALIZING THE STATE. See GRONLUND, LAURENCE.

SOCIAL REFORM UNITY. This first **Fourierist** community was formed in 1842 on 2,000 acres of timbered and bouldered land in the Pocono Mountains in Pike (now Monroe) County, Pennsylvania, outside of Skytop, by some laborers, many unemployed, from Brooklyn. Although it began with the support of **Albert Brisbane** (1809–1890) and **Horace Greeley** (1811–1872), it lasted only 10 months and never operated on Fourierist principles despite its elaborate constitution. After its failure, the **Owenite community** of **Goose Pond** was formed in 1843 on the site.

SOCIETY OF BELIEVERS OF CHRIST'S SECOND APPEARING. *See* SHAKERS.

SOCIETY OF BROTHERS. *See* BRUDERHOF.

SOCIETY OF INDUSTRY. *See* MCKEAN COUNTY ASSOCIATION.

SOCIETY OF TRUE INSPIRATION. *See* AMANA SOCIETY.

SOCIETY OF UNITED GERMANS. *See* TEUTONIA—PENNSYLVANIA.

SOCIETY OF UNIVERSAL FRIENDS. *See* JERUSALEM COLONY.

SOCIOCRACY. *See* WARD, FRANK LESTER.

SODUS BAY PHALANX. This **Fourierist phalanx** was in existence from 1844 to 1846 on a 1,400-acre tract of land abandoned in 1836 by the **Shakers** on Sodus Bay on Lake Ontario in Wayne County, New York. It was formed in Rochester and led by one of the city's wealthiest citizens, Benjamin Fish. The members, ill equipped for the tasks they faced, fell into disagreement between the "religious group" and the "liberal group," resulting in the religious group withdrawing.

The remainder, some 12–15 men (down from about 300 men, women, and children the year before), maintained the colony as the Sodus Phalanx until 1846.

"SOFT UTOPIANISM." Reinhold Niebuhr (1892–1971), the American theologian, has described the United States' 20th-century intellectuals (professors, writers, journalists, and so on) as wedded to "soft utopianism." By this he means that modern intellectuals no longer seek to understand how things are and have ever been, that is, how, as a study of history reveals, human affairs are imperfect given the nature of people and their societies. Rather, dismissing such evidence, they draw up blueprints of how society could and should be and then seek ways in which to implement their idyllic blueprints. These intellectuals, who would deny being utopianists at all, are not devotees of "hard utopianism," such as in fascism or communism. However, as "children of light" (Niebuhr's term) they are quite willing to tinker with the status quo to "improve" it.

But their tinkering always involves **behaviorist** coercion in one way or another. This coercion they regard as necessary and proper because they are speaking from an "elevated" position in society and thus have an obligation to make things right for the "non-elevated" on whose behalf they act. As Niebuhr makes clear, intellectuals as existentialist ideologues of progress judge national and world affairs against theoretical ideas of how they believe things *should* be. This, in turn, impels them to demand changes to create an ideal nation and world in which benevolent social and political structures will cure all problems. As inheritors of Enlightenment rationalism and **scientism** plus 19th- and 20th-century behaviorism and pragmatism, these "soft utopianists" believe that a flawless or near flawless nation and world is attainable, making them utopianists in fact if not in name.

SOLITARY BRETHREN OF THE COMMUNITY OF THE SEVENTH-DAY BAPTISTS. *See* BEISSEL, JOHANN CONRAD.

SOME THOUGHTS CONCERNING EDUCATION. *See* LOCKE, JOHN.

SONS OF FREEDOM. *See* BETHLEHEM YEHUDAH.

SOUTH CAROLINA COMMUNITY. *See* APPENDIX.

SOUTH DAKOTA COMMUNITIES. *See* APPENDIX.

SOUTHERN CO-OPERATIVE ASSOCIATION OF APALA-CHICOLA, *or* **CO-OPERATIVE ASSOCIATION OF AMERICA.** Earlier known as the Brotherhood of the New Age, a Swedenborgian group, the founders of this 1,700-acre experiment in cooperative living began their project in 1900 at Apalachicola on the southern shore of the Florida panhandle under the auspices of the National Production Company. Its purpose was to change the very basis of society. Led by Harry C. Vrooman, the 17 members of the Southern Co-operative Association were mainly refugees from the **Christian Commonwealth Colony** in Georgia that had become defunct earlier that year. The experiment apparently ended in 1904 when Vrooman left for Indianapolis.

SOUTH UNION SOCIETY. The **Shaker** community at South Union, or Gasper Springs, in Logan County, Kentucky, was founded in 1807 on the site of the Kentucky revival of that year by the converts from the New Light Presbyterians. Former slaves lived in the 6,000-acre South Union community on the same terms as the whites. The society subsisted on grain and stock farming, a hotel, broom making, preserving fruits, tanning, and the maintenance of various other shops designed to serve their own members plus persons from the outside. The population of South Union reached a high point in 1827 with 349 members. The society continued in existence until 1922.

SPAIN AND THE NEW WORLD AS UTOPIA. *See* MENDIETA, JERONIMO de; QUIROGA, VASCO de.

SPEAR, JOHN MURRAY (1804–1877). Spear was a Universalist minister who founded Harmonia, the Association of Beneficents, or the **Domain**, in western New York in 1853. Little is known about his life prior to that time except that he was active in the antislavery crusade and in prison reform. He reported that in 1852 he received a series of spirit messages from John Murray, the founder of Universalism, and others, including Benjamin Franklin and Thomas Jefferson, instructing him to make radical changes in society via a model community. The next year he received more spirit messages from a "heavenly directorate," which gave him specific directions as to what this colony was to embody. These included house designs, areas of reform, and the like. In 1855 the National Spiritualist Convention was held at the site, but Harmonia was the target of local agitation against it because it was viewed as a free love colony (which may have been true). In 1859 Spear received a spirit message to organize a group called the Sacred Order of Unionists to promote world government. Accordingly, a group boarded a steamer to spread the word all the way to New Orleans. By 1861 the scheme had failed, and two years later the Order was dissolved. Spear then moved to London, returning to the United States shortly before his death.

SPENCER, HERBERT (1820–1903). The English philosopher Herbert Spencer was the embodiment of 19th-century belief in progress and a conduit of European ideas to the United States. He argued in his voluminous writings that the world and everything in it is in the process of organic evolution. His vigorous commitment to the **Darwinian** principle of adaptive evolution and progress of humans, which came to be called Social Darwinism, brought him worldwide renown and made his name familiar even today. A devotee of what he termed "the development hypothesis" even before the publication of Darwin's *Origin of the Species* in 1859, Spencer had earlier written of the law of organic growth as the law of progress inherent not only in lower order natural species but also in human affairs. All things, contended Spencer, have been and are moving *necessarily* upward by means of warfare from the homogeneous to the heterogeneous, wherein all unfitness or imperfection will disappear.

Spencer's writings brought evolutionary Darwinism to the United States and popularized it in his 10-volume *First Principles* in 1862. In these volumes he argued that everything from the solar system to the tiniest of natural creatures was evolving upward by natural selection toward a more perfect stage by the "law of evolution." The acceptance of Darwinism via Spencerian naturalism in all things including morals and ethics gained ascendancy in American intellectual life with more and more emphasis being placed on human aggressiveness and kinship with the animal world. It is not an exaggeration to say that this Englishman as the popularizer of Darwinian evolutionism was perhaps the most important figure in American intellectual life in the latter half of the 19th century, a century already open to the acceptance of utopian theories regarding the end of humanity's and the nation's history.

SPERANZA, *or* **ICARIA-SPERANZA.** This **Icarian** commune was organized in 1881 by seceders from **Jeune Icarie** in Iowa, together with some French socialists from the San Francisco area. Three years later, they were joined by some 55 more from Jeune Icarie. Located 75 miles north of San Francisco near Cloverdale in Sonoma County, California, on 900 acres, this last group of disciples of **Etienne Cabet** (1788–1856) permitted some private ownership of property. In 1885, realizing that neither additional Icarians nor money would be forthcoming from Jeune Icarie, the commune was dissolved with the property being divided among the remaining members.

SPINK COLONY. This **Hutterite** colony was located in Spink County in eastern South Dakota. It was established in 1905 as a spin-off of the **Wolf Creek Colony** in Hutchinson County to the southeast. Because of hostility to the Hutterites in Spink County during World War I, the members moved to Fort MacLeod in southern Alberta, Canada, in 1918.

SPIRIT FRUIT SOCIETY. Organized by **Jacob Beilhart** (1867–1908) with 13 followers on a five-acre site at Lisbon in Columbiana County in eastern Ohio in 1899, this spiritualist colony was often the target of denunciation because of its disavowal of conventional marriage. Some members were in the state of conventional wedlock, some changed mates occasionally, and some were celibate. In 1905 the society moved to a 90-acre farm at Wooster Lake near Ingleside, Illinois, outside of Chicago. There they built a great communal dwelling, "The Spirit Temple House," with at least 18 bedrooms and ample social spaces. After Beilhart's death in 1908, the colony continued under the leadership of Charlena "Ma" Young (1848–ca. 1935), who received spiritual communications from Beilhart. These she announced daily after lunch. In 1914 the group moved to a hilltop ranch near Santa Cruz, California; they remained there for the next 14 years, supporting themselves by dairy farming and growing crops. The Spirit Fruit Society ended in 1929.

SPIRITUAL COMMUNITY AT MOUNTAIN COVE. The 1840s witnessed an outbreak of spiritualism, that is, communication with spirits, particularly with the dead, through "rappings." So widespread was the phenomenon in upstate New York that the area became known as "The Burned Over District." Influenced by the doctrines of **Charles Fourier** (1772–1837) and Emanuel Swedenborg, some spiritualists opted for communal living according to their precepts. One of these was the Mountain Cove Community, about which little has been ascertained except for its brief existence. What is known is that it originated with a large circle of Spiritualists at Auburn, New York, sometime between 1851 and 1853, drawing additional followers from Oneida and Madison Counties, the locale of **John Humphrey Noyes**'s **Oneida Community.** Some of the Oneidans joined the movement to Fayette County, Virginia (now West Virginia), southeast of Charleston, to establish the community at a place they claimed was the **Garden of Eden**, undisturbed since The Fall.

The spiritualists claimed that Mountain Cove was to be the center of human redemption and where adjacent lands would be restored to their primeval state. This claim was based on revelatory "rappings" from St. Paul and from a vision given to a James L. Scott, the leader of the group, of an approaching time in which the "sun will be darkened, and [the] moon turned into blood, and [the] stars shall fall from . . . heaven." Thereafter all sin and suffering will pass away and the people at Mountain Cove, "the Holy Mountain," will find perfect happiness before their Maker's throne. The members were subjected to the infallible rules of Scott and **Thomas Lake Harris** (1823–1906), a Universalist-Swedenborgian minister, who claimed that God communicated with the two of them directly. These rules included giving all their property to the control of Scott and Harris as God's vice regents. The community came to an end in 1853 over disputes regarding property, although Harris went on to form three other colonies.

SPIRITUAL FRANCISCANS. *See* FREE SPIRITISTS.

SPIRITUALIST COMMUNITY. Also known as The Brotherhood, the Spiritualist Community was begun by **John O. Wattles** (1809–1859) and other prominent citizens of Cincinnati, Ohio, in 1846 on part of the site of the old **Clermont Phalanx** in Clermont

County. Some 100 members rebuilt the building, which is still standing on the Ohio River bank. They also erected a large store in Cincinnati to sell their agricultural goods. But a flood in December 1847 destroyed all their work and ended the community.

SPIRITUAL MAGNETIC ASSOCIATION. *See* ST. NAZIANZ COMMUNITY.

SPIRITUALS. *See* AMAURIANS.

SPRING CREEK COLONY. This **Hutterite** colony, an offspring of the **Wolf Creek Colony**, was established near Lewiston, Fergus County, in central Montana, in 1912. This was the first Hutterite colony outside of South Dakota. But like the other pacifist Hutterite colonies, its members suffered local opposition during World War I. Part of the colony moved to Alberta, Canada, in 1919, and others returned to Beadle County, South Dakota, in 1920.

SPRING FARM COLONY. This **Fourierist** colony existed from 1846 to 1848 and was located in Sheboygan County, Wisconsin. It grew out of a group of 10 families in the town of Sheboygan Falls who agreed to establish a **phalanx**. When disagreements arose over the location of the projected phalanx, the group split into two, and each group of families decided to start their own colony. The group of six families who established Spring Farm as a joint-stock venture 20 miles inland and cultivated 30 acres of prairie land requested incorporation after a year but were turned down by the territorial legislature. Consequently, the group disbanded by mutual agreement. The other group founded the **Pigeon River Colony** on Lake Michigan, but it, too, enjoyed only a brief existence.

SPRING, MARCUS (1810–1874). This successful cotton merchant, Quaker abolitionist, philanthropist, and reformer, along with his wife, Rebecca Buffum Spring, was very active in a number of **Fourierist** utopian projects. They were stockholders in **Brook Farm** and served as directors of the **North American Phalanx**. In 1853 they bought 270 acres of land at Perth Amboy, New Jersey, for the **Raritan Bay Union**, founded for dissidents from the North American Phalanx.

They bought back the land of the Raritan Bay colony from the stockholders in 1856 and continued to live on the site until Marcus's death.

STIRPICULTURE. This experiment in eugenics was instituted by **John Humphrey Noyes** (1811–1886) at the **Oneida Community** in 1869. Under the direction of Noyes, 24 males were selected to have sexual relations with 20 females in the community, all participants chosen for their "spiritual, intellectual, and moral qualities," to produce superior offspring to be the nucleus of a new society. Fifty-eight children were born under the plan, Noyes himself having fathered nine of the "stirps." The stirpiculture experiment lasted until 1880, ironically failing in part because it led to the very exclusivity between men and women that had been condemned by Noyes in establishing **"complex marriage,"** practiced at Oneida until 1868.

ST. LOUIS-WESTERN COLONY. *See* WESTERN COLONY.

ST. NAZIANZ COMMUNITY. This community was established in 1854 at St. Nazianz in Manitowoc County, Wisconsin, and lasted until 1874. It was founded by a group of German immigrants under Father Ambrose Oschwald (1801–1873). Oschwald had been released from his priestly duties in 1849 for outrageous predictions, including that a New Jerusalem would be established by the year 1900 and other errors. He had organized his followers into the Spiritual Magnetic Association with St. Gregory Nazianzen as its patron and had urged his followers to emulate St. Gregory and flee the wickedness of this world. Accordingly, in 1854 some 100-plus of his followers immigrated to the United States and established the St. Nazianz Community. The colony encompassed 3,840 acres of land held in common, and all labor was performed without compensation except for food and clothing. Some 450 persons made up the community. After Oschwald's death in 1873 the married members were given their share of the property, and the remaining land was taken over by the Society of Our Divine Savior. As far as can be determined, this was the only Roman Catholic communal society established in the United States.

STOICISM. This philosophy was founded by Zeno of Citium about 300 B.C. It taught that the wise person, having achieved a total harmony between individual will and total reason, should be, on the basis of that harmony, free from passion, unmoved by joy or grief, and submissive to natural law if he would be happy and find tranquility in life. In his *Republic,* Zeno envisioned a whole world of "cities" in which no money is needed, warfare has been eliminated, a more egalitarian society has been achieved, the temples of the gods have been destroyed because Reason alone is to be worshipped, women have attained equality, and only the wise are fit for leadership in the state, in the economy, and in the household. When such a perfected society and world has been achieved, a form of utopia will exist. The task of humans in the meantime is to strive for those qualities that would be the hallmarks of that perfected society, being free of passion, unmoved by joy or grief, and submissive to reason and the law of nature.

STRANG, JAMES JESSE (1813–1856). *See* BEAVER ISLAND COLONY.

STRIKE OF MILLIONAIRES AGAINST MINERS, A. See LLOYD, HENRY DEMAREST.

SUNRISE COMMUNITY—MICHIGAN. Founded by Jewish anarchists from New York City led by Joseph Cohen (1878–1953) in 1932 at Alicia in Saginaw County, Michigan, as a solution to the economic hardships of the Great Depression, the Sunrise Community was envisioned as having its members live communally and engage in cooperative enterprises. Cohen in 1933 bought a 10,000-acre working farm as the site of the community. Interested families were expected to pay a membership fee of $1,000, and individuals over 45 years of age, those with large families, and communists were discouraged from joining. The initial membership consisted of 100 families, but lack of experience and skill in running a large commercial farm, disagreements between the Yiddishists and the anarchists, and problems with Cohen's leadership led to the withdrawal of some of the families. Despite federal aid, the colony never made a profit and the land was sold off to the Resettlement Administration in 1936.

SUNRISE COMMUNITY—NEW JERSEY. This predominantly Jewish community, also known as the Sunrise Co-operative Farms, was established in 1933 near Hightstown in Mercer County east of Trenton, New Jersey, on a 1,000-acre site purchased by a group of Jewish philanthropists for the purpose of settling poor urban Jews in a country setting. It eventually was composed of about 100 families, each of which had a private home and a one-acre allotment for gardening. All other work was undertaken communally, be it gardening, dairy farming, or light industry. But most of the members drifted away, and in 1936 the colony was closed, its property being taken over by the Resettlement Administration.

SWAMI KRIYANANDA (DONALD WATERS) (1926–). *See* ANANDA COOPERATIVE COMMUNITY.

SWEVEN, GODFREY (1846–1935). *See LIMANORA*.

SYLVANIA ASSOCIATION. This **Fourierist phalanx**, the first phalanx in the United States, was located at Darlingville (now Greeley), Pike County, Pennsylvania. It was started in New York City and Albany by economically distressed working people in 1843 with **Horace Greeley** (1811–1872) as its treasurer. It contained 2,300 acres. It lasted only until 1845, falling victim to poor land, inadequate farming techniques, and a lack of sufficient capital. The original owner of the land accepted the improvements made by the members and released them from any financial obligations.

SYNANON COMMUNITY. Synanon was founded in California in 1958 by Charles E. "Chuck" Diederich, a charismatic alcoholic, as a resident treatment center for drug addicts. At its peak more than 2,000 men, women, and children resided in its various communities. Using confrontational psychological methods within highly structured, self-contained communities, Synanon gained the reputation for being a utopian, diverse, nonviolent, caring organization. However, it was also marked by tensions, crime, violence, and arbitrary expulsions. Governance in the Synanon communities was authoritarian and solely in the hands of Diederich, his family, and an inner circle of privileged members. In time, Diederich decreed that members must change marital partners and defend themselves with lawsuits and violence. Since no more children were to be admitted, the men were ordered to get vasectomies.

By the late 1980s, Synanon's reputation had fallen drastically. The organization lost its tax-exempt status, and federal tax charges forced it into bankruptcy in 1991. Diederich died in 1997 at age 83. Ultimately, the Synanon Community failed because Diederich transformed it from a drug rehabilitation center into a "utopia" of his own imagining and ruled it dictatorially despite the behavioral, financial, and emotional damage inflicted on its members.

– T –

TABORITES. Religious dissent combined with **millennialism** was present in Europe prior to the Protestant Revolution of the 16th century. John Wycliffe (ca. 1330–1384) and his followers, the Lollards, had challenged the Church in England in the 14th century before the movement was suppressed by the bishops early in the next century. However, in Bohemia religious dissent turned into open revolt by the followers of Jan Hus (ca. 1372–1415) and Jerome of Prague (ca. 1365–1416), this movement having adopted **Free Spiritism** and the ideas of **Joachim of Fiore** (1135–1202). When Hus and Jerome were burned at the stake for criticizing papal and clerical privilege, this set off open revolution against the Church and the state, the more radical of the Hussites becoming Taborites.

The Taborites, faced with repression by Sigismund, the Holy Roman Emperor, withdrew to a mountain in southern Bohemia they called "Mt. Tabor," where, according to the New Testament, the transfiguration of Christ had taken place. Here they established their own communal society in five cities free from papal authority with their own bishop, and here they would await the Second Coming and the end of the world. One of their most important leaders was a Free Spiritist priest named Martin Huska, who preached the imminent coming of Christ after a period of strife but followed by a millennium, the New Age of peace and plenty. They also changed both the meaning and form of the Mass and denied the Real Presence in the Eucharist. In addition, the Taborite leaders took it upon themselves as "men of the Law of God" to rob the possessions of all non-Taborites to fill the communal coffers. The more radical of the Taborites, the **Adamites**, were exterminated by armed Taborites in 1421. In turn, the main body of the Taborites held off five attacks by troops representing Sigismund and the pope until they were overcome in 1436.

TA T'ING SHU. See GREAT EQUALITY, THE.

TEED, CYRUS REED (1839–1908). *See* KORESHAN UNITY.

TEILHARD de CHARDIN, PIERRE (1881–1955). One of the major philosophic influences in the mid-20th century in both Europe and the United States was Pierre Teilhard de Chardin, a French priest, paleontologist, geologist, and spiritual evolutionist who gained international attention with the publication of his *Phenomenon of Man* (1938–1940 in French; 1959 in English after his death). Essentially, Teilhard argued that spirituality (i.e., God) and science (i.e., the universe in the process of evolution) are one and the same moving toward unity and perfection in time.

This evolution to perfection occurs through a buildup of psychic energy until it reaches a point when a transition occurs toward a higher level of complexity and consciousness. At this point in time, with the evolution of human thought, an envelope or period of emerging, freely accepted common consciousness, the *nöosphere* (from the Greek *noos,* meaning mind) has been superimposed upon the earlier simply organic biosphere (and before that, the lithosphere of inorganic matter), placing it on the path to a final and necessary evolutionary advance to accelerating the "hominization" (the process of increased consciousness) of the world to perfection in which humans come to dominate the entire evolutionary process. From this process, the spiritual (God) and the physical (the world) will become one and the biosphere (including planet earth) will die off as a material entity.

Thus the world, humans, and God are all in the process of becoming in discernable stages—the lithosphere, the biosphere, and finally the *nöosphere*—as part of an irresistible evolution to perfection or completion in which super-humanity as a super-organism meets Super-Christ in the Second Coming, the Parousia—which may not come for several million years. Until then, God is not; He, too, is becoming. And Christ has not yet completed His own forming and has not attained His full growth. The only spiritual or physical absolute to Teilhard de Chardin is evolutionary change. And this evolutionary change, no matter how radical, is to be welcomed and accepted—even **Marxism** and fascism because of their "thirst for fuller being"—because it is truly a holy process bringing humans closer to God, a process that is moving humans in the final stage of history to the superior and final cosmic and spiritual level of understanding and the brotherhood of all.

Teilhard, then, is the super-evolutionist of the 20th century, combining natural evolution with divine evolution to portray perfected Man-God in time as the end of human existence.

TEMPLE HOME ASSOCIATION, *or* HALCYON THEOSOPHISTS. This colony of **Theosophists** originated in 1903 when, under the leadership of William H. Dower, a group who rejected **Katherine Tingley** (1847–1929) as successor to the Theosophical Society left Syracuse and formed the Temple Home Association at Halcyon south of Pismo Beach in San Luis Obispo County, California. By 1906 these Theosophists could boast of 140 residents on their 300-acre site plus a sanatorium and hotel. Each member received half an acre on which to farm to take care of his or her own needs, but all land and other economic enterprises, including farming and a construction business, belonged to the community. The system of co-operative enterprise ended in 1912 because of financial problems; however, the members of the community developed independent businesses and the movement prospered. In the 1920s, the Halcyon Theosophists built a classical-revival "Temple of the People" there. A few dozen members (some of whom claim to still receive spiritual messages) remain at Halcyon, and the temple remains on the site.

TEMPLE OF THE GOSPEL OF THE KINGDOM. This community of black Jews was founded about 1900 by Warren Robertson in Virginia. It embodied a version of Jewish orthodoxy that emulated Jewish cultural patterns, including learning Yiddish. Communal living and celibacy were parts of the beliefs of this group, as was the assurance that its members would enjoy eternal life on earth. Many of the practices found here would later be emulated by **Father Divine**'s **Peace Mission Movement**. By 1917 the Temple had moved to Harlem, where it enjoyed considerable success, establishing some 150 additional communal households ("kingdoms"). But the movement came to an abrupt end in the 1920s when it was charged that at one kingdom near Atlantic City various women had borne the children of the leader. Robertson was also charged with transporting women across state lines for immoral purposes in 1926 and was sentenced to prison, ending the community.

TENNESSEE COMMUNITIES. *See* APPENDIX.

TEUTONIA—PENNSYLVANIA. *See* MCKEAN COUNTY ASSOCIATION.

TEXAS COMMUNITIES. *See* APPENDIX.

THELEME, ABBEY OF. *See* ABBEY OF THELEME.

THEOPOLIS AMERICANA. See PURITANS AS UTOPIANS.

THEOSOPHISTS. The Theosophists were the persons ascribing to Theosophy (meaning "divine wisdom," derived from the Greek *theos,* meaning God, and *sophia,* meaning wisdom), a combination of Oriental religions and philosophical thought, including the belief in a universal oversoul and reincarnation, as found in Hinduism and Buddhism. Elements were also derived from the Jewish Kabala and Islamic Sufism. The Theosophy movement began in the United States in 1875, although its cardinal ideas can be traced back to the 17th and 18th centuries. The conversion of the movement from esoteric Christianity to "modern spiritualism" came about in 1848 at the hands of the sisters Leah, Kate, and Margaretta Fox, who allegedly communicated with the dead at Hydesville, New York. It was furthered by the publication of Emma Britten's *Modern American Spiritualism* in 1870.

The founders of the Theosophy movement in the United States were Helena Petrovna Blavatsky (1820–1891), a devotee of **Edward Bellamy** and his Nationalist clubs; **William Q. Judge** (1851–1896); **Henry S. Olcott** (1832–1907); and **Annie Wood Besant** (1847–1933). All, as Theosophists of one stripe or another, sought to unite humanity spiritually into a universal brotherhood through the practice of toleration and charity. These would lead to perfect justice and thereby alleviate the injustices in the world. The three basic tenets of Theosophy were (and are) to create a universal brotherhood of persons without distinction of race, creed, sex, caste, or color; to study the great thoughts and religious literature of the ancient and modern world; and to investigate the laws of nature and psychic powers latent in humans.

By the end of the 1870s, branches of the Theosophical Society, which had been formed in New York in 1875 by Blavatsky, Judge, Olcott, and others, had been established in India and the major European cities. After Blavatsky's death in 1891, the movement continued to grow under the guidance of her successor, **Katherine A. Tingley** (1847–1929). Tingley founded a Theosophic experiment at **Point Loma**, California, in 1898, devoting special attention to a school to create spiritually sensitive humans, specifically to see life as a school in which the soul through successive reincarnations becomes godlike. When Tingley died in 1929, leadership fell to Gottfried de Prucker, but the hard times of the Great Depression forced the Pont Loma settlement to move to Covina, California, in 1942, where many of its communal features gradually disappeared. Another Theosophical colony called the **Cooperative Brotherhood** was established at Burley, Washington, in 1898. When it broke up in 1908, many of its members moved to Point Loma.

The Theosophical Society, headquartered in Pasadena, California, continues to function in the United States with a membership of about 5,000. Here it persists in its efforts to popularize Eastern philosophy and religion in the United States. The Theosophists' early communal practices have long ago been abandoned, but many of their ideas continue to play a major role in the ideas and values of the age.

THOMAS, CHAUNCEY (1822–1898). This literary utopianist of the late 19th century was the author of *The Crystal Button: or, Adventures of Paul Prognosis in the Forty-Ninth Century* (1891), in which Chauncey advocated that the government take control of all industries of public interest, including communication, transportation, and insurance.

His utopian City of Tone (Boston) of 4872, now a gigantic metropolis of beauty, prosperity, and justice, is presided over by the

Government of Settled Forms (accepted by all nations in the Congress of Nations). Tone is marked by universal free education, resulting in public opinion that by definition can never be in error or unjust. It is also marked by full employment and no poverty. The world now features electrically powered airships; electric or compressed-air automobiles; underground monorail railways capable of speeds of up to 200 miles per hour; solar power; ownership of all land by the government; and no wasteful military spending because warfare has ceased to exist, the world having enjoyed peace for over a millennium. People are now free and happy with no cares or fears in Chauncey's imaginative utopian world depicted in *The Crystal Button,* which appeared just one year after **Ignatius Donnelly**'s epic *Caesar's Column.*

THOMPSON, CHARLES BLANCHARD (1814–1890s). *See* PREPARATION.

THOMPSON COLONY. Established in 1880 near Salina, Kansas, this communal agricultural settlement was organized in New York City. The members had their separate homes and fields, but the large fields were worked jointly and a certain amount of time was devoted to working for the colony. When it ended is not known.

THOMPSON, WILLIAM (1775–1833). This Irish socialist from County Cork was a contemporary of **Robert Owen** (1771–1858) and a leading figure in the formation of the London Co-operative Society in 1826. This society espoused community of property, self-government by majority vote, an eight-hour workday, the end to all unhealthy occupations, guardians appointed to assure public health, and freedom from domestic drudgery for women.

It can be argued that Thompson was of greater importance in the history of socialism because he went beyond the concept of community and the labor theory of value by also espousing the acquisition of political power for the laboring classes to gain their just needs. He had advanced this principle in his 1824 treatise *An Inquiry into the Principles of the Distribution of Wealth Most Conducive to Human Happiness.* Thompson asserted that with the adoption of cooperative communities based on a free division of labor among the members and mutual assistance, government as then existing would be nearly superfluous because the communities would be crime free and low taxation (levied as a graduated rent on the wealth of each community) and only limited governmental apparatus would be needed to protect persons and property.

Little remembered today, Thompson, it can be argued, was a major figure in pre-Marxist socialist theory. His assumptions regarding the necessity of political involvement to assure equality for the working classes foreshadowed the socialist agitation of the late 19th century.

THROUGH THE EYE OF THE NEEDLE. *See* HOWELLS, WILLIAM DEAN.

TIDIOUTE COLONY. This **Hutterite** colony was formed in 1884 when 19 families from the **Tripp Colony** in South Dakota accepted an invitation from the followers of **George Rapp** (1757–1847), who were facing problems because of their aging and celibacy, to move onto some of their land in Warren County in western Pennsylvania, near the Titusville oil fields. However, faced with working a hilly and wooded area with which they, as plains farmers, were unfamiliar, and perhaps feeling isolated from the other Hutterite colonies, the Tidioute Hutterites two years later returned to southeastern South Dakota and founded the **Milltown Colony** in Hutchinson County.

TIME MACHINE, THE. *See* WELLS, H. G.

TINGLEY, KATHERINE (1847–1929). This leading **Theosophist**, successor to Helena Blavatsky, leader of one of the Theosophist factions that emerged after Blavatsky's death in 1891, and founder of the **Point Loma** Community, came to Theosophy after three marriages and extensive reform experience. She was converted to Theosophy by **William Q. Judge** and soon emerged as one of the leaders of the movement. In 1896 she began to formulate plans for a Theosophical "School for the Revival of the Lost Mysteries of Antiquity" and community in California. Point Loma was started by her two years later to embody her idea of a worldwide cultural and ethical renovation through education. It also served as the national headquarters for the

Universal Brotherhood and Theosophical Society. The communal aspects of life were not emphasized or even insisted upon at Point Loma. During the Spanish-American War, Tingley organized relief activities. As a committed reformer, she also campaigned against vivisection and capital punishment and strongly opposed American entry into World War I. She died as the result of an automobile accident in Europe.

TOMORROW: A PEACEFUL PATH TO REAL REFORM. See GARDEN CITY.

TOPOLOBAMPO BAY COLONY. This utopian community was established in the state of Sinaloa on the Pacific coast of Mexico by Albert Kimsey Owen (1847–1916) in the early 1870s with an eye toward the integration of capital investment, labor, and urban planning to end the more sordid aspects of urban living. With a background in railroad and town development, Owen believed that a railroad should be built from Virginia to the port of Topolobampo on the Gulf of California, thus cutting 400–600 miles off the route from the east coast to the west coast and providing more convenient shipping to the Orient. With this in mind, he visited Topolobampo Bay in 1872 and thereafter proposed that a colony be developed there along with the railroad to that site. His "Pacific City" of 29 square miles with streets laid out in a grid pattern, public amenities, and buried utility lines would be home to those who sought to organize cooperative industries and thereby pursue good lives without the evils of advertising, saloons, lawyers, and prostitutes but with cooperative credit available for entrepreneurial investment, traditional family structures intact, and dress codes.

Work on the Texas, Topolobampo, & Pacific Railroad actually began in the 1880s, and by 1886 the colony had been established with over 1,400 colonists on site and with 2,500 investors having advanced capital for the project. However, the harbor was unsuitable for shipping, malaria was rampant, and conflicts within the colony over land and water rights resulted in Owen leaving the project in 1893, having by then given up on restructuring Pacific City along the lines of **Theodor Hertzka**'s *Freeland*. The railroad was never finished despite surveys having been made across northern Mexico to Texas, and litigation between factions led to evictions from Pacific City. Almost all of the colonizers had returned to the United States by the mid-1890s.

TRABUCO COLLEGE. *See* HEARD, HENRY FITZGERALD; VEDANTA SOCIETY.

TRANSCENDENTALISM. This intellectual movement of the first half of the 19th century was largely the creation of the poet **Ralph Waldo Emerson** (1803–1882). Especially popular among New England intellectuals, it taught that a higher metaphysical truth exists that transcends the human physical senses, that the earth is first and foremost spiritual, and that all things are united in an "oversoul." Because the oversoul is God's essence existing in humans and nature, human beings are capable of perfection and charged with perfecting all things in their power. This led the Transcendentalists to undertake many reforms such as abolitionism and the equality of women plus communal experiments in the decades prior to the Civil War.

Prominent among the Transcendentalists, besides Emerson, were **George Ripley** (1802–1880), the founder of **Brook Farm**; Henry David Thoreau; **Bronson Alcott** (1799–1888); and Nathaniel Hawthorne. Borrowing the ideas of **Charles Fourier** (1772–1837) and **Robert Owen** (1771–1858), the Transcendentalists accepted socialist utopian theories. Brook Farm was the best known, but equally prominent at the time were two other Massachusetts communities, the Universalist colony **Hopedale** in Milford, founded in 1841, and Fruitlands in Harvard, established in 1843 by the Transcendentalist Bronson Alcott.

TRAVELER FROM ALTRURIA, A. *See* HOWELLS, WILLIAM DEAN.

TRIALVILLE. *See* UTOPIA COMMUNITY.

TRIPP COLONY. Organized as a daughter colony of the **Hutterites'** **Bon Homme Colony**, Tripp Colony, 36 miles to the northwest, was begun in 1879 in Hutchinson County, South Dakota. Facing financial problems, the Tripp colonists borrowed money from the **Amana So-**

ciety, then moved to land offered to them by the followers of **George Rapp** (1757–1847) in western Pennsylvania. Here they established the **Tidioute Colony** in 1884. This arrangement, however, did not work, and the families from Tripp moved back to South Dakota and established the **Milltown Colony** in 1886.

TROPICAL EMIGRATION SOCIETY. *See* ETZLER, JOHN ADOLPHUS.

TRUE FAMILY. *See* REUNION COLONY—MISSOURI.

TRUE LEVELLERS. *See* DIGGERS.

TRUMBULL PHALANX. This **Fourierist phalanx** was established in 1844 on a 280-acre site with a house and five mills of various purposes eight miles west of Warren in Trumbull County, Ohio, by a group of Pittsburgh Associationists. Thirty-five families consisting of 140 persons made up its original membership. The socialist phalanx living in "the spirit of Christianity" increased its membership to 250 members and its land holdings to 1,500 acres, but the colony suffered from defection by members unwilling to endure the Spartan life demanded by the phalanx's circumstances and from indebtedness, internal discord, and fevers and ague brought on by the low-lying land on which the phalanx was situated. It was first dissolved in the winter of 1847–1848 but struggled on with the aid of supporters from Pittsburgh for a few more months.

TRUTH, SOJOURNER (1797–1883). *See* MATTHEWS, ROBERT.

TUCKER, FREDERICK BOOTH (1853–1929). *See* SALVATION ARMY FARM COLONIES.

TURGOT, ANNE ROBERT JACQUES (1727–1781). Turgot, Baron de l'Aulne, was controller general of France at the court of King Louis XVI. He urged the Crown to take a leading role in reform for France, including utilizing elite scientists to undertake coordinated research for the perfection of humankind, and to carry out a series of economic reforms including the removal of all restraints on trade, labor, and market pricing. He also urged a reform of the tax system, granting subsidies to certain industries, and abolishing the corvée (forced labor service by the citizens). These were reflections of his view of the history of humankind and the place of government within it. However, his plans died when he was dismissed by the king in 1776 for his lack of tact in pushing for his reforms, among other reasons. Of equal or greater importance, Turgot envisioned history as a series of cultural stages as part of a grand scheme of progress.

In his *Plan de deux discours sur l'histoire universelle* (The Scheme of Two Discourses on Universal History), he described the human condition in successive stages: the hunting stage, the pastoral life stage, the agricultural stage, and the introduction of government. His seminal idea of progressive development inherent in history only gained widespread acceptance, however, in 1793 with the publication of the **Marquis de Condorcet**'s *Esquisse d'un tableau historique de progrès de l'esprit humain* (Sketch of a Historical View of the Human Mind), Condorcet having picked up the idea from Turgot. Thereafter, the concept of human progress through successive stages became a prominent strain in the intellectual concepts of the West.

TUSCARAWAS. Located on 400 acres in Tuscarawas County, Ohio, Tuscarawas was founded by **Josiah Warren** (1798–1874) in 1831 as the first anarchist community in the United States. Members voluntarily invested their money in a steam sawmill. Their capital drew no interest, but they could withdraw it at any time. But between 1833 and 1835 the community was destroyed by disease, especially malaria and influenza. Warren and most of the inhabitants simply left in 1835; those who remained stayed until 1837. They lost everything they had invested in the project.

TWIN OAKS COMMUNITY. This community was founded in 1967 at Twin Oaks in Louisa County, Virginia, east of Charlottesville, by eight persons under the leadership of Kathleen Kinkade (1931–). These originators wished to put the behavior modification theories of **B. F. Skinner** (1904–1990) into practice, although they never intended that his *Walden Two* would be the working model for their experiment. They hoped to phase out the biological family in favor of a communal family with "child managers" entrusted with the care of children and rewards being given to children for proper behavior and self-discipline. To aid in the demise of the biological family, first names only are allowed, never family names. Although the 465-acre commune initially utilized agriculture as its economic base, it now relies also on hammock- and casual furniture–making, indexing books, making tofu, visitors' fees, and some members' outside employment. Within Twin Oaks, the workers were initially paid according to a labor credit system with less desirable jobs paying more, but this was eventually abandoned because of a lack of proper measuring devices for the various tasks. Presently each income-sharing member works 42 hours per week in the community's business and domestic areas, and each person has a room of his or her own, a certain amount of privacy being accepted as necessary even within communal life. Having no central leader, the members hold weekly meetings to discuss utopian history and community projects and problems. About 100 adults and children reside at Twin Oaks, which continues to be nonsectarian but heavily involved in issues of peace, ecology, antiracism, and feminism.

2001: A SPACE ODYSSEY. This 1968 science fiction **dystopia** written by Arthur C. Clarke (1917–) deals with an adventurous voyage into space and the human utopian quest for perfection. It revolves around a contest between man and machine, between the astronaut Dave and the supercomputer HAL, which has developed a mind and intent of its own. The novel illustrates Clarke's fear of the negative consequences of technology. Man, in his desire for a perfected life, has created technologies whose outcome can be less than positive, Clarke argues by this popular novel.

TYRINGHAM COMMUNITY. Formed in 1792 under the influence of **Joseph Meachem** (1741–1796) in Berkshire County, Massachusetts, this **Shaker** community was dissolved in 1875, its members moving to the **Hancock** Community nearby and the **Enfield Community** in Connecticut.

– U –

UNION, THE. The Union was established in 1804 at Clark's Crossing between Potsdam and Norwood in St. Lawrence County in upstate New York. It was founded by a shoemaker named William Bullard, who led a group of Vermonters across the border into New York State. It was located on a 2,427-acre site. Three years after its establishment, in 1807, a constitution was adopted, but by 1810 the communitarian experiment had become irreparably ruptured. The land was divided among its members with a dozen or so families continuing to live on the site.

UNION COLONY. This colony was founded by **Nathaniel C. Meeker** (1817–1879) in 1869 in Weld County, Colorado. Meeker had previously been a member of the **Trumbull Phalanx**, a **Fourierist** colony in Ohio, and had visited the **Shakers**, **Mormons**, and the **Oneida Community** before establishing this colony. The original 442 members came from New York, Ohio, and Pennsylvania and paid a $150 fee to join. They were allowed to own their homes, businesses, and farmland, but there was collective housekeeping, irrigation, and fencing. Some 300 single-family residences were constructed in the first year. The Union Colony was Christian nonsectarian, but forbade any liquor on the site. Beset by problems of insufficient funds and a lack of knowledge of farming and cattle-raising techniques, in 1872 the members transformed the communal colony into private property, and the colony became the city of Greeley. Some of the members later joined the **Puget Sound Cooperative Colony** in Washington.

UNION GROVE. Located in Meeker County, Minnesota, and established in 1856, Union Grove was an offshoot of the **Hopedale Community** in Massachusetts and a part of the Practical Christians' western movement. Made up of transplants from Hopedale and some Minnesota enthusiasts, it consisted of 800 acres of land secured under the U.S. Preemption Act. But by 1858 the project had been abandoned because of troubles with the Native Americans in the region and a lack of support from its Hopedale backers. Its members had returned to Massachusetts.

UNION HOME COMMUNITY. This Spiritualist community was established in 1842 or 1844 at Cabin Creek near Huntsville in Randolph

County, Indiana, close to the Ohio border. Its founder was **John O. Wattles** (1809–1859), and it was located on 700 acres donated by Hiram Mendenhall (1801–1852), an extensive landowner from nearby Unionsport. This socialist experiment soon encountered serious economic problems. It was dissolved in 1846, Mendenhall moving to California.

UNION MILL COMPANY. Little is known about this community located in Tillamook County, Oregon, east of Portland, except that it was founded in 1891 by Daniel and Catherine Cornen. Apparently all property was held in common and lumbering was carried on cooperatively with all the workers receiving equal pay. It ended in 1897 when its property was seized by the county sheriff.

UNION VILLAGE. Union Village (commonly referred to as Shakertown) was established in 1805 as the first **Shaker** community west of the Appalachians. It was located in Warren County in southeastern Ohio four miles west of Lebanon. Coming into existence as the result of missionaries sent out from **Mount Lebanon**, it was made up largely of Presbyterian schismatics from the revivals that swept Kentucky and its neighboring states after 1800. It served as the center of western Shakerism, and its membership of 3,873 was the largest of all the Shaker communities. It continued to exist until 1912. The site is now occupied by the Lebanon State Prison Farm.

UNITAS FRATRUM. *See* MORAVIANS.

UNITED BELIEVERS IN CHRIST'S SECOND COMING. *See* SHAKERS.

UNITED ORDER OF ENOCH. *See* ORDERVILLE UNITED ORDER.

UNITED STATES COMMUNITIES. *See* APPENDIX.

UNIVERSAL BROTHERHOOD AND THEOSOPHICAL SOCIETY. *See* POINT LOMA.

UNIVERSAL COMMUNITARIAN ASSOCIATION. *See* BARMBY, GOODWYN.

UNVEILING A PARALLEL. This utopian fantasy novel was published in 1893, the work of two middle-class women from Cedar Rapids, Iowa, Alice Ilgenfritz Jones (1846–1906) and Ella Merchant (1857–1916), who labeled themselves two "Women of the West." The novel, which satirizes 19th-century gender roles and discrimination against women, tells of a rather stuffy gentleman who travels to Mars and is shocked by the emancipated women he finds there. On this planet, women are not only equal to men but also smoke, drink, use drugs, and gain sexual gratification in gardens of prostitution with young males. In contrast, a more perfect state of development has been reached in a second country on Mars where unselfishness, nurturing, and mutual support offer a viable alternative to passive femininity and greedy, lustful masculinity. *Unveiling* stands as a precursor to 20th-century feminist utopian novels such as **Charlotte Perkins Gilman**'s *Herland* and **Marge Piercy**'s ***Woman on the Edge of Time***.

UTAH COMMUNITIES. *See* APPENDIX.

UTILITARIAN ASSOCIATION OF UNITED INTERESTS. This **Owenite** colony was begun in 1845 in Waukesha County, Wisconsin, just west of Milwaukee by a group of 16 London mechanics and their families on 200 acres of land some 13 miles from Hunt's Experiment of **Equality**. Their cooperative venture failed after only three years and, facing starvation, they moved to Milwaukee in 1848.

UTOPIA. This famous literary satire written by **Thomas More** (1478–1535) was first published in Latin in Louvain, Belgium, in 1516 for international consumption by the educated, then was translated into English in 1551. More, a Renaissance man and social reformer, began the work in the Netherlands in 1515 while on a diplomatic mission as lord chancellor of England under Henry VIII. Here he conceived the idea of the need for a description of a perfect state as a model for Christian political reform and discussed the project with his friend Desiderius Erasmus. After completing the second part of the work in the Netherlands, More wrote the first part while back in England the next year and had it published. A second translation into English came only in 1684, and a third not until 1923.

The form of *Utopia* was undoubtedly derived from the classics, in particular **Plato**'s *Republic,* where the ideal imaginary societies were isolated from the real world. The title *Utopia* was More's imaginative invention; it was taken from two Greek terms: *ou topos,* meaning nowhere, and *eu topos,* meaning an ideal place.

In Book I, the reader is introduced to Raphael Hythloday (from the Greek, meaning "a storyteller," "a talker of nonsense," or "one knowing in trifles"), a Portuguese traveler who tells More of his accidental discovery of the island of Utopia. Here the evils of the world are discussed in detail, setting up a contrast between the peaceful and productive island society of Utopia and the real world of More's day. Book II contains Hythloday's account of Utopia, an isolated island some 200 miles by 500 miles, formerly called Abraxis before being conquered by King Utopos, who created the perfect society Hythloday happened upon. Utopia contains 54 cities all alike in design and divided into four sectors. In each city there are 6,000 households, and every 30 households holds an annual election for a phylarch. A protophylarch is elected for every 10 phylarchs, and the 200 phylarchs elect a city governor who holds power for life unless he becomes tyrannical. Each city is governed by a senate composed of the governor, the protophylarchs, and two phylarchs. Self-government is the norm in Utopia despite the fact that there is a central council over the 54 cities.

The basic social unit in Utopia is the extended family, and the economy is based upon agriculture, manufacturing, and trade with all citizens taught the necessary skills to allow the inhabitants to function in their six-hour, and therefore pleasurable, workday, the city dwellers and the farmers alternating work functions. And since the Utopians practice communism with everything held in common, there is no striving for material goods. Gold, for example, is used for bracelets for criminals and for toilets. But Utopian society is regimented with severe punishment for vices such as adultery, although crimes of violence do not exist since all property is communal, not personal. Socially, men may not marry until the age of 22 and women until 18, and prospective grooms and brides inspect one another in the nude before marriage to reveal any "foul deformities." Euthanasia is normal and suicide is practiced, and slavery is the punishment for serious crimes. The Utopians (who are in a pre-Christian state) are to believe in a god-creator and some sort of afterlife, but all are guaranteed freedom of religion, and the small priestly class is limited in its function. Good Christian that he was, More's vision of Christianity in Utopia is that of imitation of the earthly ministry of Christ, that is, expressions of love and concern for one's fellow humans, not the organized Christianity of his day.

More's great work in many ways became the pattern of modern utopias in the centuries that followed, especially in that it emphasized regimentation and discipline in order to change society. As More saw it, the only way to improve society was to improve human behavior by refashioning people's environment. This is achieved by coordinating and enforcing the laws, mores, and consciences that mold and sustain a society. Following these precepts, in More's static imaginary land of Utopia there is no tyranny, no private property, and no luxury.

Whatever More's intention in writing *Utopia*—Robert Nisbet has called it "a kind of hair shirt for the nobility of England"—he created a whole new literary genre. And his assumptions regarding human nature's need for external regimentation and personal equality to achieve the more perfect functioning of societies have become the hallmarks of all modern utopias.

UTOPIA COMMUNITY. Also known as Trialville, the **Fourierist** colony of Utopia was located in Clermont County, Ohio, on the site of the **Clermont Phalanx** after that experiment failed. **Josiah Warren** (1798–1874) visited those who were left at Clermont, about two dozen in number, in 1847. The members accepted Warren's "equitable commerce" through 1848, although Warren left the community that year. The community continued to exist into the late 1850s, but its cooperative arrangements gradually faded from practice.

UTOPIANISM. Utopianism is the concept and belief that a perfect or more perfect society or subset of a society can be achieved in time through human efforts to change the circumstances within which that society or subset finds itself. Although it achieved its name only in recent centuries because of the impact of Sir **Thomas More**'s literary satire *Utopia* of 1516, the idea of creating a perfect society has been in existence since ancient times. It has sometimes been religious in nature and at other times secular. It has sometimes been presented in the form of description only, and sometimes in the form of actual attempts to create a perfect society. It has become more prominent in

UTOPIAN NOVELS (MAJOR) • 309

the Western world and beyond since the Renaissance, especially in the 19th and 20th centuries. Utopianism, ancient or modern, has almost always been marked by the following: group-based isolation from contemporary worldly corruption, often the utopia being placed on an isolated island away from civilization; equality of goods and a rejection of luxury; regimentation of the lives of the participants (humans being malleable) to assure the perceived common good; and direction of the new model society being placed in the hands of leaders (whether in an oligarchy, a theocracy, a republic, or a democracy) endowed with a vision (whether based on religion, reason, or science) that will bring peace and justice to all adherents within time.

Utopianism is neither mere reformism to improve or perfect a single or a limited number of aspects of a society nor mere escapism. True utopianism envisions fundamental transformation in a society or one of its subsets based on concrete ideas on how this essential transition to indefectibility can and must be achieved.

UTOPIAN NOVELS (MAJOR).

Title	Author	Year
Utopia	**Thomas More**	1516
Abbey of Theleme in *Gargantua and Pantagruel*	François Rabelais	1567
City of the Sun	**Tommaso Campanella**	1623
Macaria	Samuel Hartlib *or* Gabriel Plattes	1641
Histoire des Savarambes (*see* **Sevarambians**)	Denis Vairasse d'Allais	1666–1679
New Discovery of Terra Incognita Australis	**Gabriel de Foigni**	1676
Sinapia	Anonymous	1682
History of the Kingdom of Basaruah	**Joseph Morgan**	18th c.
L'An 2440	**Louis Mercier**	1771
The French Daedalus	**Restif de la Bretonne**	1781
Leinhard und Gertrud	**Johann Pestalozzi**	1781
The Andrograph	**Restif de la Bretonne**	1782

Ching-bua yuan (Flowers in the Mirror)	**Li Ju-chen**	1828
Voyage en Icarie	**Etienne Cabet**	1839
Margaret, a Tale of the Real, Blight and Bloom	**Sylvester Judd**	1845
What Is to Be Done?	**N. G. Chernyshevsky**	1863
Man's Rights	**Annie Denton Cridge**	1870
The Coming Race	Edward Bulwer-Lytton	1871
Germinal	Emile Zola	1885
Looking Backward	**Edward Bellamy**	1888
Caesar's Column	**Ignatius Donnelly**	1890
Crystal Button	**Chauncey Thomas**	1891
News from Nowhere	**William Morris**	1891
Golden Bottle	**Ignatius Donnelly**	1892
Building of the City Beautiful	**Joachim Miller**	1893
A Cityless and Countryless World	Henry Olerich	1893
Unveiling a Parallel	Alice I. Jones and Ella Merchant	1893
A Traveler from Altruria	William Dean Howells	1894
The Garden of Eden, U.S.A.	William H. Bishop	1895
Equity	**Edward Bellamy**	1897
Utopia, The Great Awakening	**Albert A. Merrill**	1899
A Modern Utopia	**H. G. Wells**	1905
Lost Horizon	**James Hilton**	1933
The Shape of Things to Come	**H. G. Wells**	1933
Islandia	**Austin Wright**	1942
Walden Two	**B. F. Skinner**	1948
The Island	**Aldous Huxley**	1962
Ecotopia	Ernest Callenbach	1975
Ecotopia Emerging (see **Ecotopia**)	Ernest Callenbach	1981
A Door into Ocean	Joan Slonczewski	1986

See also DYSTOPIAN NOVELS (MAJOR); FEMINIST UTOPIAN NOVELS (MAJOR); UTOPIAN WORKS (MAJOR MULTIFORM).

UTOPIAN SOCIALISM. Socialism by definition is a political-economic theory that advocates collective and/or governmental ownership and administration of the most important means of production and distribution of goods. As it has been put into practice throughout the world in the 20th and 21st centuries, it is normally reflected in national policies and practices. The more extreme form of socialism is communism in which total, as opposed to partial, state ownership and administration of the economy is put in place. In a milder form of common ownership of goods and centralized control of the economy of a societal unit, socialism was prominent in utopian ideas and communities in the 19th century and has remained so to the present.

As the 19th century witnessed the effects of both the Agricultural and Industrial Revolutions and the dislocations they caused, a search for a more just and humane economic system evolved, drawing heavily on **Thomas More**'s *Utopia,* on the scientific approach to progress advocated by **Francis Bacon** (1561–1626), and on the Enlightenment's dependence on human reason to ameliorate the economic problems weighing heavily on the shoulders of the victims of the vast economic changes then underway. Accordingly, socialistic solutions were an integral part of the utopian ideals and plans spelled out by utopians such the **Comte de Saint-Simon** (1760–1825), **Charles Fourier** (1772–1837), **Etienne Cabet** (1788–1856), **Robert Owen** (1771–1888), and many others in Europe and in the United States by **Albert Brisbane** (1809–1890), **Horace Greeley** (1811–1872), and myriad other founders or leaders of the utopian communities established in the United States in the first half of the 19th century. Thereafter, socialist ideas of common ownership of property and centralized control of the economy continued to be advocated by utopian novelists and social philosophers such as **Marge Piercy** (1936–) and **B. F. Skinner** (1904–1990) thereafter and then put into practice by the new utopian movements of the late 20th century—although sharply criticized and satirized by **dystopian** dissenters such as **George Orwell** (1903–1950) and **Aldous Huxley** (1894–1963).

Thus because virtually all utopian communities have advocated communal property and control, it is true that socialism historically has been an integral part of utopianism. However, it is also true that socialist national states and the social-economic policies practiced by them have not been utopian either in theory or in reality because they have not seen these policies and practices as means of achieving a perfect or near perfect society. Virtually all utopias have been socialist, but virtually no socialist state has been utopian.

UTOPIAN WORKS (MAJOR MULTIFORM).

Title	Author	Year
Works and Days	**Hesiod**	9th c. B.C.
Prometheus Bound	**Aeschylus**	4th c. B.C.
Ecclesiazusae, or *Women in Parliament*	**Aristophanes**	ca. 393 B.C.
Republic	Zeno (*See* **Stoicism**)	ca. 300 B.C.
Metamorphosis (*see* **Golden Age, Myth of the**)	Ovid	1st c. A.D.?
Concordance of the Old and New Testaments	**Joachim of Fiore**	1196?
Mandeville's Travels (*see* **Bragmans**)	Sir John Mandeville	1322?
Wolfaria	Johan von Gunsburg	1521
Book of a Hundred Chapters	**Revolutionary of the Upper Rhine**	16th c.
I Mondi	Anton Francesco Doni	1552
Reipublicae Christianopolitanae Descriptio	**Johann Valentin Andreae**	1619
Anatomy of Melancholy	**Robert Burton**	1621
New Atlantis	**Francis Bacon**	1629
The Law of Freedom in a Platform (*see* **Diggers**)	Gerrard Winstanley	1652
The Commonwealth of Oceana	**James Harrington**	1656
History of the States of the Moon	**Cyrano de Bergerac**	1657
History of the States of the Sun	**Cyrano de Bergerac**	1662
Glorious Kingdom of Christ	**Richard Baxter**	1691
Some Thoughts Concerning Education	**John Locke**	1693
Republica Christiana	**Gottfried von Leibniz**	18th c.
Nature's Code	Morelly	1755
Discourse on Political Economy	**Jean-Jacques Rousseau**	1755

The Social Contract	**Jean-Jacques Rousseau**	1762
Philosophy in the Bedroom	**Marquis de Sade**	1772
Supplement to Bougainville's Voyage	**Denis Diderot**	1772
Manifesto of the Equals	**François Noel Babeuf**	1790
Les Ruines	**Comte de Volney**	1791
Enquiry Concerning Political Justice	William Godwin	1793
Esquisse d'un tableau historique de progrèss de l'esprit humain	**Marquis de Condorcet**	1794
Plan de deux discours sur l'historie universelle	**Robert Turgot**	17??
New View of Society	**Robert Owen**	1813
Millennial Laws	**Joseph Meachem**	1821
A Few Days in Athens	**Frances Wright**	1822
An Inquiry into the Principles of the Distribution of Wealth	**William Thompson**	1824
Nouveau Christianisme	**Claude Saint-Simon**	1825
The Paradise within Reach of All Men	**John Adolphus Etzler**	1833
Voyage en Icarie	**Etienne Cabet**	1839
The Social Destiny of Man	**Albert Brisbane**	1840
What Is Property?	**Pierre-Joseph Proudhon**	1840
The New World	**John Adolphus Etzler**	1841
The Phalanx	**Albert Brisbane**	1843–1845
Emigration to the Tropical World	**John Adolphus Etzler**	1844
Two Visions of John Adolphus Etzler	**John Adolphus Etzler**	1844
The Harbinger	**Brook Farm Phalanx**	1845–1847
The Communist Manifesto	**Karl Marx**	1848
First Principles	**Herbert Spencer**	1862
History of American Socialisms	**John Humphrey Noyes**	1870
Progress and Poverty	**Henry George**	1879
The Coming Revolution	**Laurence Gronlund**	1879

The Watchtower	Jehovah's Witnesses	1879–
The Cooperative Commonwealth	Laurence Gronlund	1884
The Path	William Q. Judge	1886–
Freiland	Theodor Hertzka	1890
In Darkest England and the Way Out (see **Salvation Army Farm Colonies**)	William Booth	1890
Wealth against Commonwealth	Henry Demarest Lloyd	1894
The Human Drift	King Camp Gillette	1894
New Era	Charles W. Caryl	1897
Tomorrow: A Peaceful Path to Real Reform (see **Garden City**)	Ebenezer Howard	1898
The New Economy	Laurence Gronlund	1898
Socializing the State	Laurence Gronlund	1898
Altneuland	Theodor Herzl	1902
Gillette's Social Redemption	King Camp Gillette	1907
Gillette's Industrial Solution	King Camp Gillette	1908
World Corporation	King Camp Gillette	1910
Roadtown	Edgar Chambless	1910
The People's Corporation	King Camp Gillette	1924
Flight from the City	Ralph Borsodi	1933
The Great Equality	K'ang Yu-wei	1935
The Phenomenon of Man	Teilhard de Chardin	1938
Eros and Civilization	Herbert Marcuse	1955
The Greening of America	Charles Reich	1970
The Late Great Planet Earth	Hal Lindsey	1970
Beyond Freedom and Dignity	B. F. Skinner	1971
The Dispossessed: An Ambiguous Utopia	Ursula Le Guin	1974
Always Coming Home	Ursula Le Guin	1987

See also DYSTOPIAN NOVELS (MAJOR); FEMINIST UTOPIAN NOVELS (MAJOR); UTOPIAN NOVELS (MAJOR).

– V –

VALLEY OF GOD'S PLEASURE. *See* NORTH UNION SOCIETY.

VALLEY OF THE SWANS. *See* PLOCKHOY, PIETER COR-NELIUS.

VEDANTA SOCIETY. Following the path laid out by predecessors in the Vedanta movement since the 1890s, such as Swami Vivekananda; Swami Turiyananda; Swami Trigunatita; and Vedanta communities in the Thousand Islands in the St. Lawrence River; at San Jose and Concord, California; and at West Cornwall, Connecticut, the 135-acre Ananda Ashram at La Crescenta, near Pasadena, was founded by Swami Paramananda (1833–1940) in 1923. The name of this society and movement comes from two Sanskrit words indicating final wisdom: *veda,* meaning wisdom, and *anta,* meaning the end. The members of the Vedanta movement lived a communal life in ashrams (religious retreat locations) to purify themselves through work and meditation, thereby losing their "self" through self-realization and meditation.

The membership of the Ananda Ashram at La Crescenta, consisting of a community house, homes for lay brothers and nuns, and a Temple of the Universal Spirit, was never more than 20, most being American middle- and upper-class women. As a highly disciplined community, the members submitted themselves to Paramananda's direction, and their lives were marked by meditation, prayer, and striving to attain the community's goals. Branches of the Ananda Ashram were established at Cohasset, 20 miles from Boston, and in India. Swami Paramananda died at Cohasset in 1940. Since the 1920s, a number of Vedanta communities have been created, including Trabuco College, making them among the longest living Indian religious communities in the United States.

VERMONT COMMUNITIES. *See* APPENDIX.

VICTORY CITY. Hailed as "The City of the Future" by its imaginative creator, Orville Simpson II of Cincinnati, a real estate investor and manager, Victory City promises no crime, no pollution, and no overcrowding. Conceived as a series of cities, each situated under one roof, located in the scenic countryside, and built and operated by private enterprise, it is presented as "a veritable utopia" designed to "keep the human race going" and the solution to today's urban problems. Each city will be able to accommodate 332,000 persons. Promised benefits for Victory City residents will be free city services and no city taxes, stress-free and pollution-free commuting since all persons will walk or take elevators to their destinations, health care for all through health insurance as part of their rent, large cafeterias to feed all residents, and the bulk of the city's food being produced on its own farms and greenhouses. Investors are being sought by Mr. Simpson for the project.

VINELAND COLONY. *See* ALLIANCE COLONY.

VINTON, ARTHUR DUDLEY (1852–1906). A native of Brooklyn, Vinton received a law degree from Columbia Law School in 1873 and went on to practice law in New York City. He was the inventor of the automatic railway signal and served as managing editor of the *North American Review.* He is important to utopianism as the author of the **dystopian** novel *Looking Further Backward* (1890), a parody and satire on **Edward Bellamy**'s popular utopian novel *Looking Backward,* published two years before. In his novel, Vinton uses the characters, setting, and design of *Looking Backward* to warn of the consequences of socialism and the ongoing Chinese and European immigration into the country. In *Looking Further Backward,* Vinton tells the story of Julian West 23 years after the close of Bellamy's story. By this time, Bellamy's Nationalist policies have created a decadent Boston that has surrendered to China with thousands of Bostonians being shipped off to Chinese slave camps. New York, however, has rebelled against Chinese rule, resulting in the bombing of Manhattan and killing 4 million people. Chinese have been imported into the United States to repopulate the country. As a result, by 2023 the socialist United States has become a colony of China.

Julian West has been replaced as narrator by General Wong Lung Li, the history professor-dictator, who reveals through West's diary how the American people lost their self-reliance and willingness to resist oppression through their passive acceptance of an oversized government ruled by "gossiping women," the socialists in power thereafter having mistakenly welcomed people of all races, encouraged woman's equality, and abolished the army. Julian West, having escaped on an abandoned railroad handcar, is the only American left to resist the new state. He is an atavistic hero who now leads the attack on the "progress" that has been made. But West dies in an **apocalyptic** contest against the nation's oppressors, knowing that the Chinese have gained control of all but a small part of the Midwest and will soon conquer all. Thus Vinton has reversed Bellamy's picture of a happy, socialist utopian future for the United States, replacing it with a warning to the nation that socialism, governmentalism, and unrestricted immigration will inevitably lead to weakness and to a cataclysmic end to the nation in the 21st century.

VIRGINIA COMMUNITIES. *See* APPENDIX.

VISIT TO FREELAND. See HERTZKA, THEODOR.

VOLNEY, CONSTANTIN FRANCOIS CHASSEBOUF, COMTE de (1757–1820). This French aristocrat and man of letters was a student of law, medicine, and the Middle East and associated with the *Idéologues,* who believed in the perfectibility of the human race. He represented Anjou in the Estates-General in 1789. The following year he became secretary of the Constituent Assembly, but he was imprisoned for 10 months during the Terror as a Girondist—even though he was a Royalist. Escaping the guillotine, he eventually reentered public life and traveled to the United States in 1795. Here he visited Thomas Jefferson at Monticello and George Washington at Mount Vernon, but prudently left the country during a rising tide of anti-French sentiment. He spent his last years engaged in scholarship and literature.

His major contribution to libertarian ideas and utopianism took the form of his *Les Ruines, ou Méditation sur les Révolutions des Empires* (The Ruins, or a Meditation on the Revolutions of Empires), published in 1791, a grandiose survey of human progress and decay that advocated a future based on liberty, justice, and the general will of the people. Although Volney is rarely read today, 26 editions of his *The Ruins* had been published in English by 1890.

VONNEGUT, KURT (1922–). Born in Indianapolis, Vonnegut studied at Cornell, Carnegie Tech, and the University of Chicago. He served in the Army from 1942 to 1945, and his experiences as a prisoner of war influenced his future work, specifically his novel *Slaughterhouse Five* (1945). Since that time he has produced a steady stream of novels, short stories, nonfiction, and plays. His first novel was the **dystopian** *Player Piano.*

VON ZINZENDORF, NICHOLAS LUDWIG (1700–1760). *See* MORAVIANS.

VOREE. *See* BEAVER ISLAND COLONY.

VOYAGE EN ICARIE. See CABET, ETIENNE.

– W –

WAIPU. *See* MCLEOD, NORMAN.

WALDEN TWO. See SKINNER, B. F.

WALK TO THE END OF THE WORLD. See CHARNAS, SUZY MCKEE.

WALLINGFORD COMMUNITY. This offshoot of the **Oneida Community** instituted by **John Humphrey Noyes** (1811–1886) in upstate New York in 1848 was established in Wallingford in New Haven County, Connecticut, in 1851. Other branches of Oneida were established at Brooklyn and Manlius, New York; Newark, New Jersey; and Putney and Cambridge, Vermont. These were eliminated between 1854 and 1855 to concentrate the Perfectionists' interests here and at Oneida. Wallingford kept in close contact with Oneida and remained in existence until the demise of the mother community in 1881, its membership varying between 25 and 85 during the 30 years it remained a Perfectionist enclave.

WARD, FRANK LESTER (1841–1913). Frank Lester Ward, government geologist, social philosopher, psychologist, and cultural evolutionist, asserted in his *Dynamic Sociology* (1883) and other works that acquired characteristics in humans included social ethics as part of the inherent synergy that took place in the entire universe. Ward argued that human beings had acquired reason as part of their adaptations to life by the development of the nervous system and brain, enabling them to substitute conscious judgment for the blind forces of evolution and suppress the animal ego domination. This allowed them to come to a state of mutuality and cooperation instead of a **Darwinian** tooth-and-nail struggle for survival. Thus Ward in his "cosmic monism" (the belief that all reality is one material, organic whole) modified, but did not deny, evolution, and in doing so brought the "science" of human actions and attitudes into the evolutionary scheme of nature and history. Man, he insisted, could therefore by his judgments and actions, especially by acquiring knowledge and by social engineering, ameliorate society's problems and enhance life in the areas of equality, security, and justice.

Because of government's role in carrying out these beneficent policies, this was a positive good in that it replaced ego-driven individualism with a higher form of decision making. Ward urged the formation of a new type of political organization he labeled "sociocracy" to replace not only autocracy and aristocracy but also democracy. Under sociocracy all decisions would be made on a strictly scientific basis, thereby abolishing from governance fear, favor, bias, and, in time, the historic social evils of ignorance, crime, and war. Ward's influence made progress to perfection, to utopianism, more acceptable to the American people both academic and nonacademic. *See also* SCIENTISM.

WAR OF THE WORLDS, THE. *See* WELLS, H. G.

WAR ON POVERTY. *See* COALSAMAO.

WARREN, JOSIAH (1798–1874). Josiah Warren, writer, community planner, anarchist, libertarian, and musician, settled in Cincinnati, Ohio, in his early years. Here he became an orchestra leader and music teacher. After hearing a lecture by **Robert Owen** (1771–1858) in 1825, he sold his lamp manufactory and moved to **New Harmony**, where he displayed a notable independence of thought. He returned to Cincinnati in 1827 and opened a "time store," where persons exchanged hours of labor for goods available in the store. This lasted until 1830. In 1831 he helped to establish Equity (**Tuscarawas**), a communitarian colony in Ohio, but then abandoned it in 1835. Warren then dedicated himself to improving the printing trade, publishing the *Herald of Equity* in 1841 and *Equitable Commerce* in 1847. Two years later he moved to the **Utopia Community** and thereafter helped to establish the **Modern Times** colony in Suffolk County on Long Island, where anarchists preached and practiced free love, which met with Warren's disapproval. By 1861 he had returned to his native Massachusetts, and for the last decade of his life dedicated himself to his continuing love of music.

WARREN RANGE COLONY. This **Hutterite** colony was established in 1913 in Fergus County in north-central Montana as an offshoot of the **Wolf Creek** and **Richards** colonies in South Dakota. In 1918 during World War I, it was moved just across the border to Cardston, Alberta, Canada.

WASHINGTON COLONY. This colony was organized in Kansas for the purpose of bringing people to Puget Sound, Washington. Located in Whatcom County, Washington, the settlement was established in 1881 with 25 families as original members. They agreed with the local promoters that they would build a sawmill, a wharf, and 50 homes. Plans went well and the lumber business brought prosperity to Bellingham Bay, but the colony ended in 1884 with disputes over land titles.

WASHINGTON COMMUNITIES. *See* APPENDIX.

WATERS, DONALD, *or* **SWAMI KRIYANANDA** (1926–). *See* ANANDA COOPERATIVE VILLAGE.

WATERVLIET COLONY—NEW YORK. Also known as Niskeyuna, this colony was located eight miles north of Albany, New York, and is where the eight original **Shakers** settled after arriving in the United States in 1774. Organized as a colony in 1788, it comprised 2,580 acres on its home site and owned another 32,000 acres in the area. Its chief industry was farming and the raising of sheep and cattle, as well as shops for the making of shoes, carpets, furniture, and clothing. Watervliet included a library and a school. It also had a branch of black female Shakers in Philadelphia, the sisters working as day servants in the city during the day. When it was dissolved in 1938, the remaining members moved to **Mount Lebanon**, the center of Shakerism.

WATERVLIET COLONY—OHIO. This **Shaker** community was located some six miles southeast of Dayton in Montgomery County, Ohio. Established in 1806 and named after the **Watervliet Colony** in New York, it existed under the supervision of the **Union Village** leaders in Warren County. Much of its 1,350 acreage was leased out to tenants. Its only manufactory produced woolens. In 1825 there were 100 members in the colony; this had declined to 55 by 1875. It was dissolved in 1900.

WATSON, JOHN BROADUS (1878–1958). A major influence in the 20th century on the growing conviction in academic circles and indirectly among the general public in the United States that society could be improved even to perfection or near perfection, especially through rational knowledge and governmental intervention, was the psychologist John B. Watson, the founder of **behaviorism**. Watson taught that there was very little, if anything, inherent in human nature, that is, that persons are blank slates at birth; are formed in their early years in response to outside stimuli, this process forming their personalities and character; and are capable of being re-formed at will for the general good. Watson's theory became the basic article of faith upon which many, if not most, modern institutions were built, especially government and education and not excluding mainstream religion, thereby adding academic and "scientific" corroboration to the peoples' existing belief that increased perfection is inherent in American history.

WATTLES, JOHN OTIS (1809–1859). Born in Connecticut, this reformer and communitarian moved to Cincinnati in 1836. Heavily involved in abolitionism and having taught black students in a school organized by the abolitionists, Wattles came to believe that all forms of coercive force, especially those of governments, were un-Christian. They should, he argued, be replaced by the establishment of the

Government of God on earth, this to be brought about by founding communities based on the principles of nonresistance. In 1842 he and other reformers formed the Society for Universal Inquiry and Reform, an organization committed to "organizing the social system in accordance with the principles of God's government." Accordingly, in 1843 Wattles and Valentine Nicholson established the **Prairie Home Community** near West Liberty in Logan County, Ohio. The community was mainly composed of Quaker farmers and had no constitution or ruling government. Its only principle was "Do as you would be done by." It failed in less than a year, partially by Wattles's insistence on visiting jails and poorhouses and inviting the persons there to take up residence at Prairie Home.

Sometime during 1844 he visited a number of Spiritualists in Randolph County, Indiana, and convinced them to form the **Union Home** community on 700 acres donated by an extensive landowner in the area. This second of Wattles's socialist communities lasted only until 1846. That same year, Wattles and a number of prominent citizens of Cincinnati organized a Spiritualist community called *The Brotherhood,* or the Spiritualist Community, on part of the site formerly occupied by the failed **Clermont Phalanx** upriver from Cincinnati on the Ohio River. They also built a store in the city to sell their farm produce, but a flood in December 1847 destroyed their buildings, claimed the lives of 16 residents, and ended the community.

In these same years Wattles was also listed as one of the trustees of the **Kristeen Community** of Marshall County, Indiana, which began in 1845 and ended in 1846. Wattles's fifth and final attempt at community building took the form of the **Grand Prairie Harmonial Institute** of Warren County, Indiana, in 1853; this school-community was to be an "association of educational and social reform." The Grand Prairie Harmonial Institute, as with Wattles's previous attempts at community building, lasted only a year, the students withdrawing amid rumors of its being a "free love" community. It ended in 1854. Despite these communal failures, Wattles did enjoy some prominence as a reformer and writer during the 1840s, serving as editor of the *Herald of Progression,* a monthly periodical "devoted to the cause of God and Humanity," during 1845–1846 and authoring *A Few Thoughts on Marriage* in 1844 and the *Annual Report of the Educational Conditions of the Colored People of Cincinnati* in 1849.

WAUGH, EVELYN (1903–1966). *See* "LOVE AMONG THE RUINS: A ROMANCE OF THE NEAR FUTURE."

WAYLAND, JULIUS (1854–1912). Wayland was a newspaper publisher in Indiana and Ohio and a successful real estate developer in Colorado before turning to socialism. He was the founder of **Ruskin Colony** in Tennessee, where he hoped to blend John Ruskin's aesthetics with pragmatic socialism. He used his widely circulated radical newspaper *The Coming Nation* (published in Greensburg, Indiana, since 1893 and with a circulation of over 50,000 in 1894) to promote the colony and support it financially. But Wayland had left the colony by the end of 1895 and had returned to his newspaper. In that same year, he started *The Appeal to Reason* in Kansas City, Missouri.

WE. This **dystopian** novel was published in 1921, the work of Yevgeny Zamyatin (1884–1937). Displaying an indebtedness to **H. G. Wells**'s *When the Sleeper Wakes,* it had a marked influence on later dystopian novels such as **Aldous Huxley**'s *Brave New World* and **George Orwell**'s *Nineteen Eighty-Four.* As is clearly reflected in this post–World War I novel, Zamyatin believed that humans cannot cope with too much individual freedom and end up relishing and embracing their lack of liberties. In *We,* the author portrays humans as being of two types: the pragmatic majority seeking their own self-fulfilling ends, represented by D-503, and a small minority of rebels willing to challenge the status quo at the price of their own security, represented by I-330. In the "United State," or "One State," which came into being after a 200-year war that destroyed human civilization, people exist like robots, living under the benevolent despotism of the Benefactor and his Guardians, a character based on Fyodor Dostoyevsky's Grand Inquisitor and later presented in the person of Orwell's Big Brother. Reason, science, and mathematics are at the base of all United State institutions; citizens are ciphers without names and live in glass rooms with only two hours of privacy each day; sex is separated from love and reproduction; childbirth is controlled by eugenics; and tragedy does not exist because the people have no deep feelings about anything.

As long as the citizens have security, they continue to live in their state of inert uniformity. D-503, an engineer, is willing to accept this lack of freedom until he meets and falls in love with I-330, a zealous female

324 • WEALTH AGAINST COMMONWEALTH

member of the Mephi, a group dedicated to attempting to restore a more simple society that values and promotes human freedom. They seek to breach the glass Green Wall that separates the United State from the natural world of freedom beyond. Zamyatin makes it clear that the Mephi cannot and will not succeed in their plans, but they continue to struggle anyway rather than accept the collectivism that enslaves the individual. As the story proceeds, D-503 is captured and forced to undergo a surgical procedure known as "fantasierectomy" that eliminates his desire for change, and he betrays the members of the Mephi, including his lover I-330, and all are executed by being placed in a vacuum.

Despite his portrayal of the failure of I-330 and the Mephi to break through to freedom, Zamyatin suggests that people must resist totalitarianism and avoid allowing themselves to become "dead-alive" creatures if they are to be truly human; therein lies the enduring value of this portentous dystopian novel.

WEALTH AGAINST COMMONWEALTH. *See* LLOYD, HENRY DEMAREST.

WEITLING, WILHELM (1808–1871). *See* COMMUNIA.

WELD, THEODORE (1803–1895) *and* **ANGELINA GRIMKE WELD** (1805–1879). *See* RARITAN BAY UNION.

WELLS, H. G. (1866–1946). Herbert George Wells, English novelist, science fictionist, short story writer, literary critic, Fabian socialist, historian, and philosopher, is best known for his early science fiction novels *The Time Machine* (1895), *The Island of Doctor Moreau* (1896), *The Invisible Man* (1897), and *The War of the Worlds* (1898). Although Wells's early *The Time Machine* was a story of human degeneration and his *When the Sleeper Wakes* (1899) a warning against dictatorships, his *A Modern Utopia* (1905) was created during an optimistic period of his career and presents a hopeful picture for humans if only they can escape the deadening hand of outmoded religious beliefs and social conventions.

Wells's utopia is situated on an earth-like planet, but it is dynamic ("kinetic") and creative as one stage of man's unending ascent up the ladder of progress. This is true even of the lower classes on Utopia, the

Dull and the Base. As a part of Utopia's "social surgery," the Dull are accorded a comfortable life and are allowed to marry providing they do not reproduce; the Base are exiled to the Island of Incurable Cheats, the Island of Drink, and so on, along with criminals of their own sex. Both the Dull and the Base are expected to eliminate themselves over time, Wells arguing that they would have failed anyway in the struggle for life because of competitive selection by which humankind will improve. To ensure that neither Malthusian overpopulation nor genetic deterioration adversely affect the state, two persons desiring to marry must be solvent, physically adequate, and free of communicable disease.

The entire planet-wide World State owns all the land and resources and consists of interlocking local and central governments to coordinate resources and labor and to provide for the inhabitants' material needs. Planning and coordination are the keys, as is scientific research, toward which the universities are geared almost completely. Order and design being the goal of the state, the World Index of Population is maintained. It records every individual's physical and social characteristics, family history, occupational history, criminal record, residence, and all of his or her movements across the planet.

The entire system is administered by *samurai,* a power elite of scientists and technicians who have brought their passions and lower selves under control and have realized their intellectual and emotional potential. The *samurai* basically maintain the status quo and discuss changes that have been suggested because of accidents beyond the control of humans with a legislative assembly, but politicians as such have been eliminated by the vast increase in intelligence in the state. Wells's utopia pictures the future to which man is moving; indeed, it is immanent in existing reality and will come to fruition when scientific creativity is released from the bonds of egotism and artificial distinctions between persons.

Wells's second utopian novel, *Men like Gods* (1932), displays his continued faith in the progress of humankind through pure and social science, as does his third, *The Shape of Things to Come* (1933). He remains in the forefront of utopian novelists of the 20th century.

WESTERN COLONY. This colony, later renamed the St. Louis-Western Colony, was organized in Illinois by the Reverend Andrew C. Todd, a Reformed Presbyterian minister, and his parishioners in 1870. The headquarters were later moved to St. Louis. It was decided to move to Weld County, Colorado, at a site only four miles from Greeley. Some 500 members were part of the colony that year, but it never flourished, perhaps because of its proximity to Greeley and **Union Colony**.

WESTERN NEW YORK INDUSTRIAL ASSOCIATION. *See* CLARKSON INDUSTRIAL ASSOCIATION.

WEST UNION. This **Shaker** community was located at Busro on Busseron Creek on the Knox-Sullivan County border in western Indiana 16 miles above Vincennes. Four years after West Union was established in 1807, the members were joined by a number of other Shakers from Ohio. During the War of 1812, with violence on the frontier, the West Union Shakers moved to **Union Village** in Ohio for two years. When hit by a series of epidemics, the members left Busro in 1827. Some moved to **South Union** in Kentucky, and others moved to **Pleasant Hill** in that same state.

WEST VIRGINIA COMMUNITY. *See* APPENDIX.

WHAT IS PROPERTY? *See* PROUDHON, PIERRE-JOSEPH.

WHAT IS TO BE DONE? *See* CHERNYSHEVSKY, NICKOLAI G.

WHEN THE SLEEPER WAKES. *See* WELLS, H. G. (1866–1946).

WHITE OAK COMMUNITY. After attempting to settle in 1897 near Brunswick in Glynn County, Georgia, a small number of **Shakers** established a 4,000-acre community the following year at White Oak in Camden County in southeastern Georgia. Most were from the **Union Village** Community in Ohio. This was probably the last Shaker colony established. In 1902 the members of White Oak sold out and returned to Ohio.

WHITEWATER COMMUNITY. This **Shaker** community was established in 1822 at Dry Forks Creek on the Hamilton County–Butler County line in southeastern Ohio. The original founders were joined by others from the defunct community at **West Union**, or Busro, in Indiana two years later. In 1856 some 33 Shakers from Whitewater joined **Union Village** in nearby Warren County to strengthen it. In 1916, on orders from **Mount Lebanon**, the community was dissolved.

WHITTAKER, JAMES (1751–1787). Long associated with **Mother Ann Lee** (1736–1784) in England, Whittaker was among the eight **Shakers** who sailed with her to the United States in 1774. As the successor to Mother Ann upon her death in 1784, he organized the Shaker communities of the East into a network, traveling through New England to encourage the scattered Shakers to gather into covenanted Orders. He also ordered the construction of the first meeting house at **Mount Lebanon**. Upon his death in 1787, he was succeeded as leader of the Shakers by **Joseph Meachem** (1741–1796).

WILBERFORCE. Named in honor of William Wilberforce (1759–1833), the prominent English abolitionist, this first of the **black utopias** arose from the efforts of Cincinnati abolitionists who, angered at the enforcement of a series of laws known collectively as the Ohio Black Code and antiblack rioting in the city, in 1829 sent agents to Canada to find a place of refuge for the city's blacks. The result was an agreement to purchase land in the so-called Huron Tract from the Canada Company near Leucine, northwest of London in western Ontario, Canada, for this purpose. The plan was to purchase 4,000 acres of land for $6,000 to be resold to the new black settlers, the profits to be used to buy the entire 1-million-acre Huron Tract for the refugees. But the projected settlers had little or no money, and probably less than 200 blacks settled there. Quaker organizations in Ohio and Indiana managed to purchase 800 acres for the project from the Canada Company, but the Company thereafter refused to sell any land directly to the blacks. Despite an attempt to save the project by reorganization in 1831, problems based on the Cincinnati urban-dwelling blacks' inability to subdue the wilderness and undertake successful farming, dishonesty in fundraising by its agents, and disputes and downright incompetence among its leaders spelled an end to the noble experiment in the 1850s.

WILLARD CO-OPERATIVE COLONY. This colony was organized in Andrews, Cherokee County, North Carolina, in 1895 by some 50 prohibitionists who sought a better environment in which to educate their children. It was named after Frances Willard, the founder of the Women's Christian Temperance Union. Its leaders, William C. Damon (1838?–?), a classics professor from California, and **Ralph Albertson** (1866–ca. 1926), a Congregational minister, made plans for a "People's University" there. The prospectus for the university asserted that the political economy of Jesus was practical and that "the love and brotherhood of the Kingdom of Heaven may be realized on earth." But the 1,000-acre colony came to an end in 1896 with Albertson and others affiliating with the **Christian Commonwealth Colony** in Georgia.

WILLARD, CYRUS FIELD (1858–1935). A native of Massachusetts, Willard was a reporter with the *Boston Globe* in 1888 and, in this capacity, played a major role in forming the first Nationalist Clubs in the wake of **Edward Bellamy**'s *Looking Backward.* He was a lifelong **Theosophist** and confidant of **Annie Besant** (1847–1933), **William Q. Judge** (1851–1896), and **Katherine Tingley** (1847–1929). In 1897 Willard became involved with **Eugene V. Debs**'s Social Democracy Party, which sought land in the West to establish a socialist colony there. He also played a major role in the 1898 Social Democracy convention in Chicago, arguing unsuccessfully for the establishment of that colony. He later joined Richard Hinton in purchasing land for what became the Burley Colony, or **Cooperative Brotherhood**, in Kitsap County, Washington. Leaving the colony after two years, he joined the Theosophists at **Point Loma** in southern California and continued to work for the Theosophical Society until his death.

WILSON, EDWARD ARTHUR (BROTHER XII) (1878–1934). *See* AQUARIAN FOUNDATION.

WINSTANLEY, GERRARD (1609–1676). *See* DIGGERS.

WISCONSIN COMMUNITIES. *See* APPENDIX.

WISCONSIN PHALANX. This **Fourierist phalanx** was begun in 1844 by New Englanders on 1,800 acres at Ceresco (now part of Ripon) in Fond du Lac County in eastern Wisconsin. Most of its 100-

plus members were liberal Christians and Whigs in politics. Although this phalanx ranks second in longevity among the Fourierist associations, it ended in 1850 for a number of reasons, including the lure of riches to be made on the frontier, a lack of working capital, a gradual erosion of communal practices, and the development of towns nearby that attracted the colonists away from the phalanx.

WOLFARIA. A reflection of the teachings of **Martin Luther** (1483–1546), Johan Eberlin von Gunzburg's (ca. 1470–1533) brief, 20-page Protestant utopian work written in 1521 portrayed an ideal Christian community, in contrast to Middle Ages German society shaped by the Catholic Church. Written in the vernacular, it was a call to ordinary Germans to cast off the traditional institutions of church and state. As an ex-Franciscan friar and devoted follower of Luther, Gunsburg's description of the state of Wolfaria, which resembled Reformation Germany, was marked in its religious doctrines, which were in sharp contrast to those of the Catholic Church. These included the abolition of the begging friars, liberal laws regarding divorce, the abolition of tithing, advocating that monks and nuns should leave their orders, the election of the clergy by their parishioners, and the clergy being married and subject to secular laws.

In the secular realm, he advocated the election of magistrates; the abolition of serfdom; government supported hospitals, schools, poor houses, and orphanages; city planning; the military being led by elected officials; capitalist-tinged professionals such as bankers, lawyers, and merchants being allowed to function only under government license; no importation of goods into the country; state control of commodity pricing; and mandatory charity toward the poor by the rich. Gunzburg's proposals as spelled out in *Wolfaria* were a reflection of his peasant background and anticipated the Peasants' Revolt that occurred in Germany in 1524–1525.

WOLF CREEK COLONY. This **Hutterite** colony was established in 1875 near Freeman in the James River Valley in Hutchinson County in southeastern South Dakota. The **Jamesville Colony** of Yankton County branched off from it in 1886. By 1889 Wolf Creek had a population of 160 members in 27 families. In 1890 the **Kutter Colony** of Hanson County was established as a branch of Wolf Creek, and the **Spink Colony** was founded as a third offspring of Wolf Creek in

1905. Thereafter the **Spring Creek Colony** of central Montana was established as a daughter colony in 1912, and the **Warren Range Colony** was established as the same in 1913. The colony moved to Stirling, Alberta, Canada, in 1930.

WOMAN IN THE WILDERNESS COMMUNITY. *See* KELPIUS, JOHANN.

WOMAN ON THE EDGE OF TIME. In this feminist **utopian** novel published in 1976, the author, **Marge Piercy** (1936–), recounts the story of Connie Ramos, a Chicana women in a New York mental hospital. Ramos discovers and comes to accept the utopian pastoral state of Mattapoisset of 2137. Here there has been established a complete androgynous and anarchist society depending entirely on cooperation between its members and the communities. Women's values are respected equally with men's because men have been "maternalized" and all persons, men and women alike, have become "mothers," with children being machine bred by genetic selection and raised by three male and female mothers (during their first years, the men even breastfeeding the babies). And to ensure the permanent separation of the mother/female-child bonding, the children in this egalitarian and androgynous society are reared in communal day care centers where they are taught to be sensitive and artistic humans and to identify themselves as future mothers. Still, Mattapoisset is not perfect, but it is evolving and hopeful—Piercy's major point—as she makes her reading audience aware of the imperfections of the present state of society and points the way to a possible future. This process can be termed "defamiliarization" by which Piercy's readers can be coaxed out of blind acceptance of the familiar present to examine it anew by considering how it might be different and better.

WOMEN IN PARLIAMENT. See ARISTOPHANES.

WOMEN'S COMMONWEALTH. *See* MCWHIRTER, MARTHA.

WOODCREST. *See* BRUDERHOF.

WORLD CORPORATION, THE. See GILLETTE, KING CAMP.

WORLD DIFFERENT AND IDENTICAL LOCATED IN TERRA AUSTRALIS. See MUNDUS ALTER ET IDEM.

WORLDS, THE. See I MONDI.

WRIGHT, AUSTIN (1883–1931). *See ISLANDIA.*

WRIGHT, FRANCES (1795–1852). This self-educated Scottish-born radical reformer came to the United States in 1818, and in 1822 published a utopian tract entitled *A Few Days in Athens.* Two years later she accompanied her friend the Marquis de Lafayette on his farewell tour of the United States and thereafter decided to stay to work for the emancipation of the slaves. After publishing a pamphlet urging Congress to set aside tracts of land for slaves where they could earn money and purchase their freedom, she began to plan for a communal society based on racial emancipation and equality. In 1826 she founded **Nashoba** in Shelby County, Tennessee. Meanwhile, she also kept in contact with **Robert Owen**'s colony at **New Harmony**.

When New Harmony failed, she returned to England to attempt to gain support for Nashoba, but came back to her colony when it began to fail under the weight of scandal under James Richardson. She defended Nashoba vociferously and also launched attacks on religion, segregation, and marriage, these views pronounced without apology and making her persona non grata for virtually all of American society. In the aftermath of the failure of Nashoba, Wright abandoned all cooperative utopian schemes and turned her reforming zeal toward the causes of women's rights and public education. She joined **Robert Dale Owen** (1801–1877) in New York City in 1829 where they published the *Free Enquirer,* a vehicle by which she promulgated her various reform views. After sailing for Paris in 1830 and marrying a French doctor and reformer, she returned to the United States in 1835 with her husband and child and settled in Cincinnati. Here she continued to lecture on various reform issues until her death.

WRIGHT, LUCY (1760–1821). Born of a prominent Massachusetts family and married at 18, Lucy Wright and her husband joined the **Shakers** in the 1780s and soon became prominent in the movement. After **Mother Ann Lee**'s death in 1784, **Joseph Meachem**

(1741–1796) appointed Wright to lead the Shaker sisters and assume equal symbolic leadership with himself. Thereafter she played an important role in Shaker affairs, encouraging the spread of Shakerism into the West and introducing singing and dancing into Shaker worship. After Meachem died in 1796, she advanced to the leadership role in the **Mount Lebanon** community, bearing that responsibility until her death in 1821.

WU CHIH-HUI (1864–1954). As an anarchist socialist who rejected **Karl Marx**'s eventual dictatorship of the proletariat in favor of the immediate destruction of capitalism and private property and a spontaneous creation of a moral society without government or laws, Wu Chih-hui led the movement to attain this utopian society in China. Wu and his fellow anarchists attempted to combine modern social Darwinism, libertarianism, and Taoist teachings. They desired a progressive anarchist state for their native country. And, rejecting the traditional beliefs of **Confucianism** and Taoism that a perfect society could be created by returning to the past and to the natural order, Wu and his fellow Chinese anarchists looked to a future built on evolution, technology, and individual growth as the remedy for the disappointments their country had endured over the centuries. Despite the efforts of Wu and the anarchists, their proffered solution to China's problems was overwhelmed first by the nationalist movement and then by communism under **Mao Zedong** in the 20th century.

– Y –

YAMAGISHI-KAI. This is a Japanese association of **kibbutzim**-like communes, the name being derived from Miyoco Yamagishi (1901–1961), a chicken farmer who developed a movement in 1953 dedicated to personal development and improved social relations. In short order, it enrolled 1,500 members living in communes and had an estimated 30,000 supporters in Japan. Yamagishi's philosophy, "Kensan," was a combination of Chinese philosophy, Zen Buddhism, Marxism, anarchism, and nonviolence that emphasized the connection between the body and the spirit, anger management, the unity of society, and property sharing. The largest of the Yamagishi-Kai communes is Toyosato ("rich village"), begun in 1970, where members are grouped into heterogeneous, self-governing "families" and live in a communal house. As of 1994, more than 4,800 members were living in 35 communes in Japan, and seven Yamagishi-Kai communities existed outside of that country, in Australia, Brazil, Germany, Thailand, South Korea, Switzerland, and the United States.

YELLOW SPRINGS COMMUNITY. This first **Owenite community** in the United States was founded in Yellow Springs, Greene County, Ohio, by Daniel Roe, the Swedenborgian minister of the New Jerusalem Church in Cincinnati. After meeting with **Robert Owen** (1771–1858), Roe formed the community of 500 mostly wealthy enthusiasts in 1825. Located some 75 miles north of Cincinnati, it was modeled after the plans for Owen's **New Harmony**. The community failed to flourish because of disputes over social and labor equality. By 1826 only nine members were left on the property. Others had established a hotel at Yellow Springs and refused to share the profits. The community ended in 1826 after only six months and was formally disestablished in 1827. The Yellow Springs site is now occupied by Antioch College.

YORKSHIRE COMMUNITIES. Forty-two "utopian" communities located in Yorkshire, England, between 1325 and 1945 have been identified. The great majority were very limited in their goals and designed only to ameliorate problems among certain occupations and classes. Among the most important were Smith House (1739–1744), Fulneck (1744–), Copley (1847–1853), the Wincobank Land Colony (1848), **Saltaire** (1851–), the Christian Israelite Institute (1857–1863), and the Brotherhood Church/Stapleton Colony (1921–present).

YOUNG, BRIGHAM (1801–1877). *See* MORMONS.

YOUNG, CHARLENA (1848–ca. 1935). *See* SPIRIT FRUIT SOCIETY.

– Z –

ZAMYATIN, YEVGENY IVANOVICH (1884–1937). *See WE.*

ZENO (ca. 335–ca. 263 B.C.). *See* STOICISM.

ZION CITY. Also known as the Christian Catholic Apostolic Church in Zion, this community was founded in 1901 at Zion, in Lake County, Illinois, 42 miles north of Chicago on Lake Michigan. Its leader and prophet was a Scotsman, John Alexander Dowie (1847–1907), who wanted to isolate his followers from the outside world and to reform American politics through his Theocratic party, formed in 1902. Dowie was very autocratic, but the community prospered with a bank, general stores, a planing mill, brickyards, a laundry, and lace manufactories, all under Dowie's absolute ownership and control. The colony did not practice communal housing and dining. When Dowie's enterprises began to fail, including an attempt to start a new Zion in Mexico, his followers revolted against him and deposed him in 1906, ending Zion City as a reformist community, although it has continued to exist to date.

ZION HILL COMMUNITY. *See* MATTHEWS, ROBERT.

ZIONISM. *See* KIBBUTZ MOVEMENT.

ZOARITES. *See* SEPARATISTS OF ZOAR.

ZODIAC. Founded by Lyman Wight (1796–1858) in 1847 and located near Fredericksburg in Gillespie County, Texas, this colony represented a break from the leadership of the **Mormons** by Brigham Young on the part of Wight. The members engaged in simple agriculture, but abandoned the colony in 1853 after their mill on the Pedernales River was destroyed by a flood.

ZOLA, EMILE (1840–1902). *See GERMINAL.*

Bibliography

The materials available to the student of utopianism as a long-term component of Western thought that has existed since ancient times and is now spreading across the globe are scattered but readily available to those who would pursue this subject of historical inquiry with diligence. Although depositories for primary materials on the various utopian communities are limited, a surprising amount of valuable utopian history can be obtained in many collegiate libraries either as part of their collections or through the interlibrary loan network. We have included in this *Historical Dictionary of Utopianism* and this bibliography primary and secondary descriptions and accounts of the hundreds of utopian projects that have been attempted through the centuries. We have also included philosophical, economic, and even religious reformist treatises that, most strikingly since the time of the Enlightenment and not usually thought of as "utopian," nevertheless represent consequential ideas on how to improve the condition of persons and families within their societies by altering the conditions within they live—the very essence of utopian thought.

Some utopian works argue for changes of whole societies or nations through governmental, economic, or social changes. Others call out to a more limited audience of those with shared beliefs and aspirations who are undergoing distressful living conditions to remove themselves from their society and collectively create new communal societies free of the debilities that surround them, these new communities not only bringing relief from their troubles but also serving as models for others to follow. Still other utopianists hope to spread their message through literature wherein they are able to picture a more perfect society based on peace, economic and sexual equality, and justice. On the other hand, some works are dystopian, or antiutopian, in nature, seeking through literature to warn against attempting to alter society to perfect it because such attempts inevitably result in a state of affairs basically worse than the one in which their readers find themselves. This is because utopian thought, the dystopian authors argue, is based on the fallacious belief that human nature can be changed for the better because it is malleable.

These movements, political, social, economic, and ethical—some successful, some unsuccessful—must be understood to appreciate this creedal phenomenon we call *utopianism.* It is interesting within itself as an area of intellectual inquiry, but, of greater importance, it is crucial to appreciating this strand of thought that has influenced the Western world and is now spreading to nations and cultures that, until now, have not been notably affected by it. It is to this better understanding of utopias and utopianism that we have assembled this dictionary and extensive bibliography, hoping to lead others to a deeper understanding of their world and times by means of historical inquiry.

We have divided this bibliography into five sections: general works, reference works, European utopianism, North American utopianism, and utopianism in other areas of the world, the three geographical area sections being divided into primary and secondary source materials.

The **general works** section consists of monographs and special studies that attempt to examine utopianism or utopias as they have existed over the centuries. These works cast a descriptive and critical eye on utopian thought and action, seeking to reveal both the strengths and weaknesses of each. Some view utopianism against the background of Western thought, such as Isaiah Berlin's *The Crooked Timber of Humanity* (1991) or Rene Dubos' *The Dreams of Reason: Science and Utopia* (1961). Some, such as Ernest Tuveson in his *Millennium and Utopia: A Study in the Background of the Idea of Progress* (1949), Elisabeth Hansot in her *Perfection and Progress* (1974), and Arthur Morgan in his *Nowhere Was Somewhere: How History Makes Utopias and How Utopias Make History* (1946, 1976), seek to explain it as a rather unique phenomenon created by time-based conditions. Persons interested in the impact of modern feminism and its emergence in utopianism should consult two outstanding anthologies on the subject: Marleen Barr and Nicholas D. Smith's *Women and Utopia: Critical Interpretations* (1983) and Libby Falk Jones and Sarah Webster Goodwin's *Feminism, Utopia, and Narrative* (1990).

The general work that cannot be overlooked is Frank and Fritzie Manuel's *Utopian Thought in the Western World* (1979), the supreme example of effective scholarly utopian studies. The Manuels approach the subject with well-reasoned depth and breadth, a reflection of their lifelong dedication to the subject and their ability to blend it into the entire intellectual development of the West. This is a book to be examined with care not as an introduction to the subject but as a vehicle for thereafter availing oneself of fine minds carefully delineating utopian thought from the ancients to the near present.

The **reference works** section herein included contains works that are absolutely valuable for researching the subject of utopianism. All should be examined. But of particular importance because of their clarity, completeness, and format are Robert Fogarty's *Dictionary of American Communal and Utopian History* (1980), which includes Otohiko Okugawa's annotated list of communal societies, and Timothy Miller's *American Communes, 1860–1960: A Bibliography* (1990) for the American communal experience. Students of the subject will also find Daniel Hollis's *ABC-CLIO World History Companion to Utopian*

Movements (1997) a valuable tool in helping them to unearth information and resources to better understand utopianism in its many dimensions.

The **European utopianism** section of this bibliography is extensive. Particularly to be recommended as primary sources are, first of all, Thomas More's classic *Utopia* (1515), which should be familiar to all students of utopianism not only because of its prominence as a literary classic but also because of its impact on utopianism as a separate genre of literature. Students of the subject should also examine other primary sources such as Augustine's fifth-century *City of God*; Tommaso Campanella's *City of the Sun* (1623 or 1624); James Harrington's *The Commonwealth of Oceana* (1656); Robert Owen's *A New View of Society* (1813); Etienne Cabet's *Voyage en Icarie* (1848), available in translation; and Charles Fourier's *The Passions of the Human Soul and Their Influence on Society and Civilization* (1851). At the same time, they should become familiar with notable dystopian novels such as Yevgany Zamyatin's *We* (1924), George Orwell's *Animal Farm* (1946) and *Nineteen Eighty-Four* (1949), and William Golding's *Lord of the Flies* (1954), all having become literary classics in their own right.

Among the secondary sources, we highly recommend Owen Chadwick's *The Secularization of the European Mind in the Nineteenth Century* (1975); Gregory Cleays's *Modern British Utopias, 1700–1850*, 8 volumes (1997); Doyne Dawson's *Cities of the Gods: Communist Utopias in Greek Thought* (1992); Arthur Lovejoy's *The Great Chain of Being* (1936); Frank Podmore's *Robert Owen: A Biography*, 2 volumes (1936); Marjorie Reeves's *Joachim of Fiore and the Prophetic Future* (1976); and Andrew Wernick's *Auguste Comte and the Religion of Humanity* (1975).

North American utopianism contains a plethora of first-class sources, the United States and Canada having been the major world testing ground for attempts to establish utopian communities in the 19th and 20th centuries. Although it borders on the impossible to recommend all the first-rate work done on this topic, among the primary sources we recommend are Edward Bellamy's *Looking Backward* (1888), Ignatius Donnelly's *Caesar's Column* (1890), Henry George's *Progress and Poverty* (1879), William Dean Howells's *A Traveler from Altruria* (1894), Henry Demarest Lloyd's *Wealth against Commonwealth* (1894), and Charles Nordhoff's *The Communist Societies of the United States* (1875). Outstanding American dystopian works include Aldous Huxley's *Brave New World* (1932), Arthur Koestler's *Darkness at Noon* (1941), Vladimir Nabokov's *Bend Sinister* (1973), Charles Elliot's *The Isle of Feminine* (1893), Ayn Rand's *Anthem* (1938), Ray Bradbury's *Fahrenheit 451* (1953), and Kurt Vonnegut's *Player Piano* (1952). The United States has also witnessed the publication of a number of feminist utopian novels; among these are Margaret Atwood's *The Handmaid's Tale* (1985), Suzy McKee Charnas's *Walk to the End of the World* (1989), Suzette Elgin's *Native Tongue* (1984) and *The Judas Rose*

(1987), Charlotte Perkins Gilman's *Herland* (1915), Marge Piercy's *Woman on the Edge of Time* (1976), and Joanna Russ's *The Female Man* (1986).

The list of secondary sources for North American utopianism appears to be virtually limitless. Indeed, a whole volume could be published on the primary and secondary bibliographic materials available on this subject. Nevertheless, among those that should be consulted are Edward Andrews's *The People Called Shakers* (1953), Karl Arndt's *George Rapp's Harmony Society* (1965), Leonard Arrington and Davis Bitton's *The Mormon Experience: A History of the Latter-Day Saints* (1979), Diane Barthel's *Amana: From Pietist Sect to American Community* (1984), Arthur Bestor's *Backwoods Utopias* (1950), Kenneth Burnham's *God Comes to America: Father Divine and the Peace Mission Movement* (1979), Maren Lockwood Carden's *Oneida: Utopian Community to Modern Corporation* (1969), Hugh Gardner's *The Children of Prosperity: Thirteen Modern American Communes* (1978), Carl Guarneri's *The Utopian Alternative: Fourierism in Nineteenth-Century America* (1991), Uri D. Herscher's *Jewish Agricultural Utopias in America* (1981), John Hostetler's *Hutterite Life* (1983), Martha Lee's *The Nation of Islam: An American Millenarian Movement* (1988), Timothy Miller's *The Quest for Utopia in Twentieth-Century America* (1998) and *The 60s Communes* (1999), Robert Allerton Parker's *A Yankee Saint: John Humphrey Noyes and the Oneida Community* (1935), William and Jane Pease's *Black Utopias: Negro Communal Experiments in America* (1963), Donald Pitzer's *America's Communal Utopias* (1997), Stephen Stein's *The Shaker Experience in America* (1992), and Ernest Tuveson's *Redeemer Nation: The Idea of America's Millennial Role* (1968). On the experience of the Hutterites in Canada, the reader should consult Morris Davis and Joseph K. Krauter's *Other Canadians: Profiles of Six Minorities* (1971) and Wallace Turner's "Hutterites During World War I," in *Mennonite Life* (1969).

The number of publications covering **other areas** of utopianism is limited as Western utopianism has not at this time had a major impact to date on the rest of the world. However, one primary source that students of utopianism should be familiar with is Charles Krause's *Guyana Massacre: The Eyewitness Account* (1978). Complementing it is George Klineman, Sherman Butler, and David Conn's *The Cult That Died: The Tragedy of Jim Jones and the People's Temple* (1980). For utopianism "Down Under," see Bill Hornadge's *The Search for an Australian Paradise* (1999). And for utopianism in neighboring New Zealand, see Maureen Molloy's *Those Who Speak to the Heart—The Nova Scotian Scots at Waipu, 1854–1920* (1991). Both primary and secondary sources for other areas where utopianism has had a minimal impact, such as the Middle East, Far East, and Latin America, are clearly lacking, but Daniel Gavron's *The Kibbutz: Awakening from Utopia* (2000) covers the 20th-century kibbutz movement in Israel very well.

Archival collections for scholarly research on utopianism are, as one would expect, available but require extensive travel to utilize their holdings. However, among those that contain important primary materials are the American Jewish Archives at Hebrew Union College/Jewish Institute of Religion in Cincinnati, Ohio; Community Service, Inc., at Yellow Springs, Ohio; the Institute for the Study of American Religion at the University of California, Santa Barbara; the State Historical Society of Wisconsin Library in Madison; the Center for Communal Studies at the University of Southern Indiana at Evansville; the East Wind Collection at Tecumseh, Missouri; the Alternative Library at Cornell University in Ithaca, New York; the Social Protest Project collection at the Bancroft Library at the University of California, Berkeley; and the American Communities Collection, part of the Oneida Community Collection, in the Syracuse University library in New York.

A tremendous amount of information on utopianism is also available via the Internet. The best way to access it is to go to www.google.com, then to the web page "Utopianism on the Internet." This site contains information on utopian organizations, classical and modern utopian works, and modern utopian communities, plus lists of resources, literature sites, utopian conferences, and many other useful resources for further study.

CONTENTS

I. GENERAL WORKS

Albinski, N. B. *Women's Utopias in British and American Fiction.* New York: Routledge, 1988.
Alexander, Peter, and Roger Gill, eds. *Utopias.* LaSalle, Ill.: Open Court Publishing, 1984.

Anderson, Kristine J. "The Great Divorce: Fictions of Feminist Desire." In *Feminism, Utopia, and Narrative,* eds. Libby Falk Jones and Sarah Webster Goodwin, 88–95. Tennessee Studies in Literature. Knoxville: University of Tennessee Press, 1990.

Baczko, Bronislaw. *Utopian Lights: The Evolution of the Idea of Social Progress.* Translated by Judith L. Greenberg. New York: Paragon House, 1989.

Baker, Robert S. *Brave New World: History, Science, and Dystopia.* Boston: Twayne Publishers, 1990.

Barr, Marleen, and Nicholas D. Smith, eds. *Women and Utopia: Critical Interpretations.* Lanham, Md.: University Press of America, 1983.

Bartkowski, Frances. *Feminist Utopias.* Lincoln: University of Nebraska Press, 1989.

Barzun, Jacques. *From Dawn to Decadence: 500 Years of Western Cultural Life: 1500 to the Present.* New York: HarperCollins, 2000.

Baumer, Franklin L. *Modern European Thought: Continuity and Change in Ideas, 1600–1950.* New York: Macmillan, 1977.

Berlin, Isaiah. *The Crooked Timber of Humanity.* Edited by Henry Hardy. New York: Alfred A. Knopf, 1991.

Bloomfield, Paul. *Imaginary Worlds: or, The Evolution of Utopia.* London: H. Hamilton, 1932.

Chianese, Robert L., ed. *Peaceable Kingdom: An Anthology of Utopian Writings.* New York: Harcourt Brace Jovanovich, 1971.

Cioran, E. M. *History and Utopia.* Translated by Richard Howard. New York: Seaver Books/Henry Holt, 1987.

Dawson, Christopher. *Progress and Religion: An Historical Enquiry.* London: Sheed & Ward, 1929, 1938.

Dubos, Rene J. *The Dreams of Reason: Science and Utopia.* New York: Columbia University Press, 1961.

Eliade, Mircea. *Myth and Reality.* Translated by Willard R. Trask. New York: Harper & Row, 1963.

Erasmus, Charles J. *In Search of the Common Good: Utopian Experiments Past and Present.* New York: Free Press, 1977.

Friedlander, Saul. *Visions of Apocalypse, End or Rebirth?* New York: Holmes & Meier, 1985.

Frost, William P. *What Is the New Age? Defining Third Millennium Consciousness.* Lewiston, N.Y.: Edwin Mellen Press, 1992.

Geertz, Clifford, ed. *Myth, Symbol, and Culture.* New York: W. W. Norton, 1971.

Hansot, Elisabeth. *Perfection and Progress: Two Modes of Utopian Thought.* Cambridge, Mass.: MIT Press, 1974.

Hertzler, Joyce Oramel. *The History of Utopian Thought.* New York: Macmillan, 1923. Reprint, edited by Frank Manuel. New York: Cooper Square, 1965.

Jelenski, K. A., ed. *History and Hope: Progress in Freedom.* London: Routledge & Kegan Paul, 1962.

Jones, Libby Falk, and Sarah Webster Goodwin, eds. *Feminism, Utopia, and Narrative.* Tennessee Studies in Literature. Knoxville: University of Tennessee Press, 1990.

Kanter, Rosabeth. *Commitment and Community: Communes and Utopias in Sociological Perspective.* Cambridge, Mass.: Harvard University Press, 1972.

———. *Communes: Creating and Managing the Collective Life.* New York: Harper & Row, 1973.

Kateb, George. *Utopia and Its Enemies.* New York: Free Press of Glencoe, 1963.

Kitch, Sally. *Chaste Liberation: Celibacy and Female Cultural Status.* Urbana: University of Illinois Press, 1989.

Kumar, Krishan. *Utopia and Anti-Utopia in Modern Times.* New York: Basic Blackwell, 1987.

———. *Utopianism: Concepts in Social Thought.* Minneapolis: University of Minnesota Press, 1991.

Lash, Christopher. *The True and Only Heaven: Progress and Its Critics.* New York: W. W. Norton, 1991.

Lasky, Melvin J. *Utopia and Revolution: On the Origins of a Metaphor . . .* Chicago: University of Chicago Press, 1976.

Levitas, Ruth. *The Concept of Utopia.* Syracuse, N.Y.: Syracuse University Press, 1991.

Mannheim, Karl. *Ideology and Utopia: An Introduction to the Sociology of Knowledge.* New York: Harcourt Brace, 1936.

Manuel, Frank E., ed. *Utopias and Utopian Thought.* Boston: Beacon Press, 1965.

Manuel, Frank E., and Fritzie P. Manuel. *Utopian Thought in the Western World.* Cambridge, Mass.: Belknap Press of Harvard University Press, 1979.

McCord, William. *Voyages to Utopia: From Monastery to Commune: The Search for the Perfect Society in Modern Times.* New York: W. W. Norton, 1989.

Molnar, Thomas. *Utopia: The Perennial Heresy.* New York: Sheed and Ward, 1967.

Morgan, Arthur E. *Nowhere Was Somewhere: How History Makes Utopias and How Utopias Make History.* Chapel Hill: University of North Carolina Press, 1946. Reprint, Westport, Conn.: Greenwood Press, 1976.

Negley, Glenn, and J. Max Patrick, eds. *The Quest for Utopia: An Anthology of Imaginary Societies.* New York: Henry Schuman, 1952.

Nisbet, Robert. *History of the Idea of Progress.* New York: Basic Books, 1980.

North, Robert C. *The World That Could Be.* New York: W. W. Norton, 1976.

Noziak, Robert. *Anarchy, State, and Utopia.* New York: Basic Books, 1974.

Passmore, John. *The Perfectibility of Man.* New York: Charles Scribner's Sons, 1970.

Phillips, Derek L. *Looking Backward: A Critical Appraisal of Communitarian Thought.* Princeton, N.J.: Princeton University Press, 1993.

Richter, Peyton E., comp. *Utopias: Social Ideals and Communal Experiments.* Boston: Holbrook Press, 1971.

Rothstein, Edward, Herbert Muschamp, and Martin Marty. *Visions of Utopia.* Oxford: Oxford University Press, 2003.

Sanford, Charles L. *The Quest for Paradise: European and the American Moral Imagination.* Urbana: Illinois University Press, 1961.

Schaer, Roland, and Gregory Claeys, eds., and Lyman Tower Sargent. *Utopia: The Search for the Ideal Society in the Western World.* Oxford: Oxford University Press, 2000.

Shklar, Judith N. *After Utopia: The Decline of Political Faith.* Princeton, N.J.: Princeton University Press, 1957.

Siebers, Tobin, ed. *Heterotopia: Postmodern Utopia and the Body Politic.* Ann Arbor: University of Michigan Press, 1994.

Sterns, Peter N. *Millennium III, Century XXI.* Boulder, Colo.: Westview Press, 1998.

Thrupp, Sylvia, ed. *Millennial Dreams in Action: Studies in Revolutionary Religious Movements.* New York: Schocken, 1970.

Tuveson, Ernest. *Millennium and Utopia: A Study in the Background of the Idea of Progress.* Berkeley: University of California Press, 1949.

Vahanian, Gabriel. *God and Utopia: The Church in a Technological Civilization.* New York: Seabury Press, 1977.

Walsh, Chad. *From Utopia to Nightmare.* London: Geoffrey Bleo, 1962.

Weber, Eugen. *Apocalypses: Prophesies, Cults, and Millennial Beliefs through the Ages.* Cambridge, Mass.: Harvard University Press, 1999.

Wilson, A. N. *God's Funeral.* New York: W. W. Norton, 1999.

II. REFERENCE WORKS

Albertson, Ralph. "Survey of Mutualistic Communities in America," *Iowa Journal of History and Politics* 34 (October 1936): 375–444. Reprint as *Survey of Mutualistic Communities in America.* New York: AMS Press, 1973.

Alexander, Peter, and Roger Gill. *Utopias.* LaSalle, Ill.: Open Court Publishing, 1984.

Bassett, T. D., bibliographer; Donald Drew Egbert, and Stow Persons, eds. *Socialism and American Life.* 2 vols. Princeton, N.J.: Princeton University Press, 1952.

Bitton, Davis. *Historical Dictionary of Mormonism.* Lanham, Md.: Scarecrow Press, 2000.

Booker, M. Keith. *Dystopian Literature: A Theory and Research Guide.* Westport, Conn.: Greenwood Press, 1994.

Burbridge, John W. *Historical Dictionary of Hegelian Philosophy.* Lanham, Md.: Scarecrow Press, 2000.

Chryssides, George D. *Historical Dictionary of New Religious Movements.* Lanham, Md.: Scarecrow Press, 2001.

Dare, Philip, ed. *American Communes to 1860: A Bibliography.* New York: Garland, 1990.

Diethe, Carol. *Historical Dictionary of Nietzscheanism.* Lanham, Md.: Scarecrow Press, 1999.

Duffield, Holley Gene. *Historical Dictionary of the Shakers.* Lanham, Md.: Scarecrow Press, 2000.

Fellowship for Intentional Community. *Communities Directory.* Langley, Wash.: Fellowship for Intentional Community, 1995.

Fellowship for Intentional Community and Communities Publications Cooperative. *The 1990/91 Directory of Intentional Communities: A Guide to Cooperative Living.* Evansville, Ind.: Author, 1990.

Fogarty, Robert S. *Dictionary of American Communal and Utopian History.* Westport, Conn.: Greenwood Press, 1980.

Hollis, Daniel W., III. *ABC-CLIO World History Companion to Utopian Movements.* Santa Barbara, Calif.: ABC-CLIO, 1997.

Kent, Alexander. "Cooperative Communities in the United States." *Bulletin of the Department of Labor* 35 (July 1901): 563–646.

Medoff, Rafael, and Chaim I. Waxman. *Historical Dictionary of Zionism.* Lanham, Md.: Scarecrow Press, 2000.

Melton, J. Gordon. *Biographical Dictionary of American Cult and Sect Leaders.* Garland Reference Library of Social Science, vol. 212. New York: Garland, 1986.

Miller, Timothy. *American Communes, 1860–1960: A Bibliography.* Sects and Cults in America Bibliographical Guides, vol. 13. New York: Garland, 1990.

Moussalli, Ahmad S. *Historical Dictionary of Islamic Fundamentalist Movements in the Arab World, Iran and Turkey.* Lanham, Md.: Scarecrow Press, 1999.

Negley, Glenn R. *Utopian Literature: A Bibliography with a Supplemental Listing of Works Influential in Utopian Thought.* Lawrence: Regents Press of Kansas, 1977.

Okugawa, Otohiko. "Annotated List of Communal and Utopian Societies, 1787–1919." Appendix to Robert S. Fogarty, *Dictionary of American Communal and Utopian History.* Westport, Conn.: Greenwood Press, 1980.

Oved, Yaacov. *Two Hundred Years of American Communes.* New Brunswick, N.J.: Transaction Press, 1988.

Richmond, Mary L. *Shaker Literature: A Bibliography.* 2 vols. Hanover, N.H.: University Press of New England, 1977.

Riley, Marvin P. *Hutterite Brethren: An Annotated Bibliography with Special Reference to South Dakota Hutterite Colonies.* Brookings: South Dakota State University Experiment Station, 1965.

Sargent, Lyman Tower. *British and American Literature, 1516–1985: An Annotated Chronological Bibliography.* New York: Garland, 1988.

Snodgrass, Mary Ellen. *Encyclopedia of Utopian Literature.* Santa Barbara, Calif.: ABC-CLIO, 1995.

Trahair, Richard C. S. *Utopias and Utopians: An Historical Dictionary.* Westport, Conn.: Greenwood Press, 1999.

III. EUROPEAN UTOPIANISM

1. Primary Sources

Aeschylus. *Prometheus Bound.* New York: Heritage Press, 1966.

Andreae, Johann Valentin. *Reipublicae Christianopolianae Descripto* (Description of a Christian Republic). Strasbourg, France: Zetzner, 1619.

Aristophanes. *Ecclesiazusae* (Women in Parliament). Oxford: J. H. Parker, 1833. Reprint, London: Franfrolico Press, 1929.

Aristotle. *Politics.* Chapel Hill: University of North Carolina Press, 1997.

Augustine. *City of God.* Garden City, N.Y.: Image Books, 1958.

Babeuf, Francois Noel. *L'eclaireur du peuple: ou Le défenseur de 24 millions d'opprimés* (The Manifesto of the People: or the Defense of 24 Million Oppressed). Paris: n.p., 1796. Reprint, Barcelona: Peninsula, 1970.

Bacon, Francis. *New Atlantis.* London: Printed by J. H. for William Lee, 1627. Reprint, W. J. Black, 1942.

Baxter, Richard. *A Holy Commonwealth.* London: Printed for Thomas Underhill and Francis Tyton, 1659. Reprint, New York: Cambridge University Press, 1994.

Bergerac, Cyrano de. *The Comical History of the States and Empires of the Worlds of the Moon and Sun.* London: H. Rhodes, 1687. Reprint, London: New English Library, 1976.

Bohme, Jakob. *Der Weg zu Christo* (The Way to Christ). 1623. London: Printed by M. S. for H. Blunden, 1648. Reprint, New York: Paulist Press, 1978, translated by Peter C. Erb and W. Zeller.

Booth, William. *In Darkest England and the Way Out.* Chicago: Charles H. Sergel, 1890.

Bulwer-Lytton, Edward. *The Coming Race.* Edinburgh: W. Blackwood & Sons, 1871. Reprint, Stroud, UK: Alan Sutton, 1995.

Burton, Robert. *The Anatomy of Melancholy.* Oxford: Printed by John Lichfield and James Short for Henry Cripps, 1621. Reprint, East Lansing: Michigan State University Press, 1965.

Cabet, Etienne. *Voyage en Icarie.* Paris: Au Bureau du Populaire, 1848. Reprint, Clifton, N.J.: Augustus M. Kelley, 1973.

Campanella, Tommaso. *Civitas Solis* (City of the Sun). 1623 or 1627. Berkeley: University of California Press, 1981.

Chernyshevsky, Nikolai. *What Is to Be Done?* 1863. Boston: B. R. Tucker, 1886. Reprint, Ithaca, N.Y.: Cornell University Press, 1989.

Clarke, Arthur Charles. *2001: A Space Odyssey.* New York: World Publishing, 1968. Reprint, New York: ROC, 1993.

Columbus, Christopher. *Christopher Columbus's Book of Prophecies.* Translated by Kay Brigham. Barcelona: CLIE, 1991.

Comte, Auguste. *A General View of Positivism.* New York: R. Speller, 1957.

Condorcet, Marquis de. *Esquisse d'un tableau historique de progrès de l'esprit humain* (Sketch of an Historical Account of the Progress of the Human Spirit). Paris: Agasse, 1795. Reprint, Paris: J. Vrin, 1970.

Diderot, Denis. *Supplément au voyage de Bougainville* (Supplement to Bougainville's Voyage). 1772. New York: Zone Books, 1997.

Doni, Anton. *I Mondi* (The Worlds). Vinegia, Italy: F. Marcolini, 1552. Reprint, Turin, Italy: G. Einaudi, 1994.

Etzler, John Adolphus. *Emigration to the Tropical World for the Melioration of All Classes of People of All Nations.* Ham Common, Surrey, UK: Stollmeyer, 1844.

Fleming, Robert. *Apocalyptical Key.* London: Printed for G. Terry, 1701. Reprint: New York: American Protestant Society, 1850.

Foigny, Gabriel de. *A New Discovery of Terra Incognita Australis, or the Southern World.* London: Printed for John Dunton, 1693.

Fourier, Charles. *The Passions of the Human Soul and Their Influence on Society and Civilization.* London: H. Bailliere, 1851. Reprint, New York: Augustus M. Kelley, 1968.

———. *The Utopian Vision of Charles Fourier: Selected Texts on Work, Love, and Passionate Attraction.* Translated and edited by Jonathan Beecher and Richard Bienvenu. Columbia: University of Missouri Press, 1983.

Godwin, William. *An Enquiry Concerning Political Justice.* 2 vols. London: G. G. & J. Robinson, 1793. Reprint, Toronto: University of Toronto Press, 1946.

Golding, William. *Lord of the Flies.* London: Faber & Faber, 1954. Reprint, New York: Aeonian Press, 1975.

Gunsberg, Johan Eberlin von. *Wolfaria.* Basel, Switzerland: Pamphilus Gegenbach, 1521.

Hall, Joseph. *Mundus Alter et Idem.* London: H. Lownes, 1605.

Harrington, James. *The Commonwealth of Oceana.* London: Printed for D. Pakeman, 1656. Reprint, Westport, Conn.: Hyperion Press, 1979.

Harting, Pieter. *Anno 2065; Een blik in de teokomst* (The Year 2065: A Glance into the Future). Utrecht, the Netherlands: J. Greven, 1865.

———. *Anno 2070* (The Year 2070). Utrecht, the Netherlands: J. Greven, 1870.

———. *Anno Domini 2071* (The Year of Our Lord 2071). Translated by Alexander V. W. Bikkers. London: William Tegg, 1871.

Hartlib, Samuel. *Macaria.* London: Printed for Francis Constable, 1641. Reprint facsimile, Corte Madera, Calif.: Wallace Kibbee, 1961.

Hertzka, Theodor. *Frieland* (Freeland). New York: Appleton, 1891. Reprint, New York: Gordon Press, 1972.

Herzl, Theodor. *Altneuland* (Old New-Land). Leipzig, Germany: H. Seemann, 1902. Princeton, N.J.: M. Weiner, 1997.

———. *The Jewish State.* London: D. Nutt, 1896. New York: American Zionist Emergency Council, 1946.

Hesiod. *Works and Days.* Oxford: Clarendon Press, 1978.

Howard, Ebenezer. *Tomorrow: A Peaceful Path to Real Reform.* London: S. Sonnenschein, 1898. Reprint, London: Routledge, 2003.

Ideal Commonwealths: Comprising More's Utopia, *Bacon's* New Atlantis, *Campanella's* City of the Sun *and Harrington's* Oceana. Introductions by Henry Morley. London: G. Routledge, 1885. Rev. ed., New York: Colonial Press, 1901.

Kant, Immanuel. *Critik der reinen Vernunft* (The Critique of Pure Reason). Riga, Latvia: Johann Friedrich Hartknoch, 1781. Reprint, New York: St. Martin's Press, 1965.

Lucretius. *On the Nature of Things.* Baltimore, Md.: Johns Hopkins University Press, 1995.

Mandeville, John, Sir. *The Travels of Sir John Mandeville* [of 1322–1356]. Exeter, UK: University of Exeter, 1496, 1980. In Italian as *Tractato de le Piu Maravigliose Cosse e Piu Notabili.* Milan, Italy: Ductu & auspicijs Magistri Petri de Corneno, 1480. In Latin as *Itinerarium.* Gouda, the Netherlands: Gerard Leeu, 1484.

McGinn, Bernard, trans. and intro. *Apocalyptic Spirituality: Treatises and Letters of Lactantius, Adso of Montier-en-Der, Joachim of Fiore, the Franciscan Spirituals, Savonarola.* Classics of Western Spirituality. Preface by Marjorie Reeves. New York: Paulist Press, 1979.

Mercier, Louis. *L'An 2440* (The Year 2440). Paris: n.p., 1787. Reprint, Paris: La Découverte, 1999.

More, Thomas. *Utopia.* Lovanii (Leuven), Belgium: n.p., 1516. Reprint, New Haven, Conn.: Yale University Press, 2001.

Morelly, M. *Code de la nature* (Nature's Code). n.p.: Sage, 1755. Reprint, Paris: Editions Sociales, 1970.

Morris, William. *News from Nowhere.* London: Kellmscott, 1892. Reprint, New York: Cambridge University Press, 1995.

Orwell, George. *Animal Farm.* New York: New American Library, 1946, 1961.

———. *1984.* New York: New American Library, 1949.

Owen, Robert. *The Book of the New Moral World.* London: Home Colonization Society, 1842–1844. Reprint, New York: Augustus M. Kelley, 1970.

———. *The Life of Robert Owen. Written by Himself. With Selections from His Writings and Correspondence.* 2 vols. London: Effingham Wilson, 1857–1858. Reprint, New York: Augustus M. Kelley, 1967.

———. *A New View of Society: or, Essays on the Principle of the Formation of the Human Character, and the Application of the Principle to Practice.* London: J. M. Dent & Sons, 1813. Reprint, New York: Augustus M. Kelley, 1972.

Pestalozzi, Johann Heinrich. *Leinhard und Gertrud: Ein buch fur das Volk* (Leonard and Gertrude: A Book for the People). Leipzig: Philipp Reclam, 1781. Reprint, Zurich: Rascher, 1927.

Plato. *The Laws.* Chicago: University of Chicago Press, 1988.

———. *The Republic.* New York: Cambridge University Press, 2000.

Proudhon, Pierre-Joseph. *What Is Property?* 1840. Princeton, Mass.: B. R. Tucker, 1876. Reprint, Cambridge: Cambridge University Press, 1994.

Rabelais, François. *Les oeuvres . . . contenant cinq livres, de la vie, faicts, and dits heroiques de Gargantua and de son fils Pantagruel* (The Works . . . Containing Five Books of the Life, Deeds, and Heroic Days of Gargantua and his son Pantagruel). Lyon, France: Jean Martin, 1558. Reprinted as *Gargantua and Pantagruel,* New York: W. W. Norton, 1990.

Restif de Bretonne, Nicholas-Edme. *La découverte australe par un homme volant* (The Southern Discovery by a Flier; usually translated as The French Daedalus). Leipzig, Germany: n.p., 1781. Reprint, Paris: France Adel, 1977.

Sade, Marquis de. *The Complete Justine, Philosophy of the Bedroom and Other Writings.* New York: Grove Press, 1965, 1990.

Saint-Simon, Claude-Henri, Comte de. *Nouveau Christianisme* (New Christianity). Paris: Bossange Pere, A. Sautelet, 1825. Reprint, London: B. D. Cousins and P. Wilson, 1834.

Shaw, George Bernard. *Back to Methuselah.* New York: Brentano's, 1921. Reprint, London: Oxford University Press, 1947.

Shelley, Mary Wollstonecraft. *The Last Man.* London: H. Colburn, 1826. Reprint, Oxford: Oxford University Press, 1998.

Stapledon, Olaf. *Last and First Men.* London: Methuen, 1930. Reprint, New York: J. P. Tarcher, 1988.

Teilhard de Chardin, Pierre. *The Future of Man.* Translation by Norman Denny. New York: Harper & Row, 1964.

———. *The Phenomenon of Man.* New York: Harper, 1959.

Thompson, William. *An Inquiry into the Principles of the Distribution of Wealth.* London: Longsman, Hurst, Ross, etc., 1824.

Turgot, Anne-Robert-Jacques. *Turgot on Progress, Sociology and Economics: A Philosophical Review of the Successive Advances of the Human Mind, on Universal History [and] Reflections on the Formation and Distribution of Wealth.* N.p., 1788. Reprint, Cambridge Studies in the History and Theory of Politics. Edited by Ronald L. Meek. Cambridge: Cambridge University Press, 1973.

Volney, Constantin, Comte de. *Les Ruines, ou méditation sur les révolutions des empires* (The Ruins, a Meditation on the Revolutions of the Empires). Paris: Desenne, Vollard, Plassan, libraireo, 1791. Reprint, Baltimore, Md.: Black Classics Press, 1991.

Waugh, Evelyn. *Love among the Ruins: A Romance of the Near Future.* London: Chapman & Hall, 1953, 1962.

Wells, H. G. *The First Men in the Moon.* Serially, *Strand Magazine,* 1900–1901. Reprint, Oxford: Oxford University Press.

———. *Men like Gods.* New York: Macmillan, 1923. New York: Penguin, 1987.

———. *A Modern Utopia.* London: Chapman & Hall, 1905. Reprint, Lincoln: University of Nebraska Press, 1967.

Winstanley, Gerrard. *The Law of Freedom in a Platform or True Magistracy Restored.* London: Author, 1652. Reprint, Cambridge: Cambridge University Press, 1983.

Zamyatin, Yevgany. *We.* Translation by Gregory Zilboorg. New York: Dutton, 1924. Reprint, translation and introduction by Clarence Brown. New York: Penguin, 1993.

Zola, Emile. *Germinal.* Paris: G. Charpentier, 1885. Reprint, Gloucester, Mass.: Peter Smith, 1968.

2. Secondary Sources

Armytage. W. H. G. *Heavens Below: Utopian Experiments in England, 1560–1960.* Studies in Social History, ed. Harold Perkin. Toronto: University of Toronto Press, 1961.

Baumer, Franklin L. *Modern European Thought: Continuity and Change in Ideas, 1600–1950.* New York: Macmillan, 1977.

Bax, Ernest Belfort. *The Last Episode of the French Revolution; Being a History of Gracchus Babeuf and the Conspiracy of the Equals.* London: Grant Richards, 1911.

Beecher, Jonathan. *Charles Fourier: The Visionary and His World.* Berkeley: University of California Press, 1986.

Bonansea, Barnadino M. *Tommaso Campanella.* Washington, D.C.: Catholic University of America Press, 1969.

Brabant, Frank Herbert. *Time and Eternity in Christian Thought.* New York: Longmans, Green, 1937.

Caird, Edward. *The Social Philosophy and Religion of Comte.* New York: Macmillan, 1893.

Chadwick, Owen. *The Secularization of the European Mind in the Nineteenth Century.* New York: Cambridge University Press, 1975.

Cioranescu, Alexandre. "Utopia: Land of Cocaigne and Golden Age." *Diogenes* 75 (1971): 85–121.

Cleays, Gregory, ed. *Modern British Utopias, 1700–1850.* 8 vols. London: Pickering and Chatto, 1997.

Coates, Chris. *Utopia Britannica.* Vol. 1. *British Utopian Experiments: 1325 to 1945.* London: Diggers & Dreamers Publications, 2001.

Cohn, Norman. *Cosmos, Chaos, and the World to Come: The Ancient Roots of Apocalyptic Faith.* New Haven, Conn.: Yale University Press, 1993.

——— . *The Pursuit of the Millennium: Revolutionary Millenarians and Mystical Anarchism of the Middle Ages.* Revised and expanded. New York: Oxford University Press, 1971.

Cole, Margaret. *Robert Owen of New Lanark.* New York: Oxford University Press, 1953.

Dawson, Doyne. *Cities of the Gods: Communist Utopias in Greek Thought.* New York: Oxford University Press, 1992.

Emmerson, Richard K. *The Apocalypse in the Middle Ages.* Ithaca, N.Y.: Cornell University Press, 1992.

Estep, William Roscoe. *The Anabaptist Story.* Grand Rapids, Mich.: Eerdmans, 1975.

Ferguson, John. *Utopias of the Classical World.* Ithaca, N.Y.: Cornell University Press, 1975.

Garnett, R. G. *Co-operation and the Owenite Socialist Communities in Britain, 1824–1845.* Manchester, UK: Manchester University Press, 1972.

Garrett, Clarke. *Respectable Folly: Millenarians and the French Revolution in France and England.* Baltimore, Md.: Johns Hopkins University Press, 1975.

Gerber, Richard. *Utopian Fantasy: A Study of English Utopian Fiction since the End of the Nineteenth Century.* London: Routledge & Paul, 1955.

Goertz, Hans-Jurgen. *Thomas Muntzer: Apocalyptic, Mystic, and Revolutionary.* Edinburgh: T & T Clark, 1993.

Hardy, Dennis. *Alternative Communities in Nineteenth-Century England.* London: Longman, 1979.

Holstun, James. *A Rational Millennium: Puritan Utopias of Seventeenth-Century England and America.* Oxford: Oxford University Press, 1987.

Holyoake, George Jacob. *The History of Co-operation in England: Its Literature and Its Advocates.* 2 vols. London: Trubner, 1876–1885. Reprint, New York: AMS Press, 1971.

Johnson, Christopher. *Utopian Communities in France: Cabet and the Icarians, 1839–1851.* Ithaca, N.Y.: Cornell University Press, 1974.

Jones, Judith P. *Thomas More.* Boston: Twayne, 1979.

Kaminsky, Howard. *A History of the Hussite Revolution.* Berkeley: University of California Press, 1967.

Kenny, Anthony. *Thomas More.* Oxford: Oxford University Press, 1983.

Kenyon, Timothy. *Utopian Communism and Political Thought in Early Modern England.* London: Pinter, 1989.

Laurent, Benoit. *Les Béguins.* Saint-Etienne, France: Le Henaff, 1944, 1980.

Lee, Martha F. *Earth First: Environmental Apocalypse.* Syracuse, N.Y.: Syracuse University Press, 1995.

Levin, Harry. *The Myth of the Golden Age in the Renaissance.* Bloomington: Indiana University Press, 1969.

Lovejoy, Arthur O. *The Great Chain of Being.* Cambridge, Mass.: Harvard University Press, 1936.

Lowith, Karl. *From Hegel to Nietzsche: The Revolution in Nineteenth-Century Thought.* New York: Holt, Rinehart and Winston, 1964.

Lubac, Henri de. *La Posterité Spirituelle de Joachim de Flore* (The Spiritual Posterity of Joachim of Fiore). Paris: Culture et Verite, 1979.

———. *Teilhard de Chardin: The Man and His Meaning.* New York: Hawthorn Books, 1965.

Manuel, Frank. *The New World of Henri Saint-Simon.* Cambridge, Mass.: Harvard University Press, 1956.

———. *Prophets of Paris.* Cambridge, Mass.: Harvard University Press, 1962.

———. and Fritzie P. Manuel, eds. and trans. *French Utopias: An Anthology of Ideal Societies.* New York: Free Press, 1966.

Marius, Richard. *Thomas More: A Biography.* New York: Alfred A. Knopf, 1984.

McGinn, Bernard. *Visions of the End: Apocalyptic Traditions in the Middle Ages.* New York: Columbia University Press, 1979.

Morton, A. L. *The English Utopia.* London: Lawrence & Wishart, 1969.

Oliver, W. H. *Prophets and Millennialists: The Uses of Biblical Prophecy in England from the 1790s to the 1840s.* Oxford: Oxford University Press, 1978.

Pankhurst, R. K. P. *William Thompson, 1775–1833: Britain's Premier Socialist, Feminist, and Co-operator.* London: Watts, 1954.

Podmore, Frank. *Robert Owen: A Biography.* 2 vols. London: Hutchinson, 1906. Reprint, New York: Augustus M. Kelley, 1968.

Reeves, Marjorie. *The Influence of Prophecy in the Later Middle Ages: A Study in Joachism.* Oxford: Clarendon Press, 1969.

———. *Joachim of Fiore and the Prophetic Future.* London: SPCK, 1976.

Riasanovsky, Nicholas M. *The Teaching of Charles Fourier.* Berkeley: University of California Press, 1969.

Ronzeaud, Pierre. *L'utopie Hermaphrodite: la terre Australe connue de Gabriel de Foigny* (The Diverse Utopia: The Land of Australia as Known by Gabriel of Foigny). 1676. Marseilles, France: C.M.R., 1982.

Rose, R. B. *Gracchus Babeuf: The First Revolutionary Communist.* Stanford, Calif.: Stanford University Press, 1978.

Surtz, Edward. *The Praise of Pleasure* [re: Thomas More]. Cambridge, Mass.: Harvard University Press, 1957.

———. *The Praise of Wisdom* [re: Thomas More]. Chicago: Loyola University Press, 1957.

Talmon, J. L. *The Rise of Totalitarian Democracy.* Boston: Beacon Press, 1952.

Thompson, E. P. *William Morris: Romantic to Revolutionary.* London: Merlin, 1977.

Verbeke, Werner. *The Use and Abuse of Eschatology in the Middle Ages.* Leuven, Belgium: Leuven University Press, 1988.

Voegelin, Eric. *From Enlightenment to Revolution.* Edited by John H. Hallowell. Durham: Duke University Press, 1975.

Wernick, Andrew. *Auguste Comte and the Religion of Humanity: The Post-Theistic Program of French Social Theory.* Cambridge: Cambridge University Press, 2001.

Williams, George Hunston. *The Radical Reformation.* Philadelphia: Westminster Press, 1962.

IV. NORTH AMERICAN UTOPIANISM

1. Primary Sources

Atwood, Margaret. *The Handmaid's Tale.* Boston: Houghton Mifflin, 1985.

Bellamy, Edward. *Looking Backward: 2000–1887.* Boston: Houghton, Mifflin, 1888. Reprint, Cambridge, Mass.: Belknap Press of Harvard University Press, 1967.

Bishop, William Henry. *The Garden of Eden, U.S.A.: A Very Possible Story.* Chicago: C. H. Kerr, 1895.

Blavatsky, H. P. *The Key to Theosophy.* London: Theosophical Publishing, 1889.

Borsodi, Ralph. *Flight from the City: An Experiment in Creative Living on the Land.* New York: Harper Brothers, 1933. Reprint, New York: Harper & Row, 1972.

——. *This Ugly Civilization.* New York: Simon & Schuster, 1929.

Bradbury, Ray. *Fahrenheit 451.* New York: Ballantine Books, 1953, 1996.

Brisbane, Albert. *The Social Destiny of Man; or, Association and Reorganization of Industry.* Philadelphia: C. F. Stollmeyer, 1840. Reprint, New York: Burt Franklin, 1968.

Brown, Paul. *Twelve Months in New Harmony.* Cincinnati, Ohio: Wm. Hill Woodward, 1827. Reprint, Philadelphia: Porcupine Press, 1973.

Brown, Thomas. *An Account of the People Called Shakers.* Troy, N.Y.: Parker & Bliss, 1812. Reprint, New York: AMS, 1972.

Callenbach, Ernest. *Ecotopia.* Berkeley, Calif.: Banyan Tree Books, 1975.

Caryl, Charles W. *New Era: Presenting the Plans for the New Era Union to Help Develop and Utilize the Best Resources of This Country.* Denver, Colo.: the author, 1897. Reprint, New York: Arno Press, 1971.

Chambless, Edgar. *Roadtown.* New York: Roadtown Press, 1910.

Charnas, Suzy McKee. *The Furies.* New York: TOR, 1994.

——. *Walk to the End of the World; and Motherlines.* London: The Women's Press, 1989.

Cridge, Annie Denton. *Man's Rights: or, How Would You Like It? Comprising Dreams.* Boston: W. Denton, 1870.

Dodd, Anna Bowman. *The Republic of the Future.* New York: Cassell, 1887. Reprint, Upper Saddle River, N.J.: Literature House/Gregg Press, 1970.

Donnelly, Ignatius. *Caesar's Column: A Story of the Twentieth Century.* Chicago: F. J. Schulte, 1890. Reprint, Cambridge, Mass.: Belknap Press of Harvard University Press, 1960.

Elgin, Suzette. *The Judas Rose.* New York: DAW Books, 1987.

——. *Native Tongue.* New York: DAW Books, 1984.

Etzler, John Adolphus. *The New World, or Mechanical System to Perform the Labours of Man and Beast by Inanimate Powers.* Philadelphia: Stollmeyer, 1841.

——. *The Paradise within the Reach of All Men without Labour by Powers of Nature and Machinery.* Pittsburgh, Pa.: Etzler and Reinhold, 1833. Reprint, London: John Brooks, 1972.

Evans, Frederick W. *Autobiography of a Shaker and Revelation of the Apocalypse.* New York: American News Company, 1869. Reprint, Philadelphia: Porcupine Press, 1973.

——. *Shakers; Compendium of the Origin, History, Principles, Rules and Regulations, Government and Doctrine of the United Society of Believers in Christ's Second Appearing.* New York: D. Appleton, 1859. Reprint, New York: Burt Franklin, 1972.

Fairbairns, Zoe. *Benefits.* New York: Avon Books, 1979.

Fairfield, Richard, and Consuelo Sandoval. *Communes U.S.A.: A Personal Tour.* New York: Penguin, 1972.

Fogarty, Robert S., ed. *American Utopianism.* Itasca, Ill.: Peacock Publishers, 1972.

———. *Special Love/Special Sex: An Oneida Community Diary.* Syracuse, N.Y.: Syracuse University Press, 1994.

George, Henry. *Progress and Poverty.* New York: H. George, 1879. Reprint, New York: Robert Schalkenbach Foundation, 1954.

Gillette, King Camp. *The Human Drift.* Boston: New Era Publishing, 1894. Reprint, New York: Scholars' Facsimilies & Reprints, 1976.

Gilman, Charlotte Perkins. "Herland." *Foreunnner* 6 (1915). Reprint as *Herland,* Mineola, N.Y.: Dover Publications, 1998.

Gronlund, Laurence. *The Coming Revolution: Its Principles.* St. Louis, Mo.: Slawson & Pierrot, 1878.

———. *The Co-operative Commonwealth.* London: S. Sonnenschein, 1896. Reprint, Cambridge, Mass.: Belknap Press of Harvard University Press, 1965.

Gross, Paul S. *Hutterite Way: The Inside Story of the Life, Customs, Religion and Tradition of the Hutterites.* Saskatoon, Saskatchewan, Canada: Freeman Publishing Co., 1965.

Harbinger, The. Vols. 1–8, 1845–1849. Reprint, New York: AMS Press, 1971.

Heard, Henry Fitzgerald. *The Ascent of Humanity.* New York: Harcourt, Brace, 1929.

Hilton, James. *Lost Horizon.* New York: W. Morrow, 1933. Reprint, Pleasantville, N.Y.: Reader's Digest Association, 1990.

Howells, William Dean. *Through the Eye of the Needle.* New York: Harper & Brothers, 1907. Reprint, New York: AMS Press, 1977.

———. *A Traveler from Altruria.* New York: Harper & Brothers, 1894. Reprint, Boston: Bedford Books of St. Martin's Press, 1996.

Howland, Marie. *Papa's Own Girl.* New York: J. P. Jewett, 1873. Reprint as *The Familistere,* Philadelphia: Porcupine Press, 1975.

Hughes, Thomas. *Rugby, Tennessee.* London: Macmillan, 1881.

Huxley, Aldous. *Brave New World.* Garden City, N.Y.: Doubleday, Doran, 1932. Reprint, New York: Harper & Brothers, 1946.

———. *Island.* New York: Harper, 1962. Reprint, New York: Perennial, 2002.

Jones, Alice Ilgenfritz, and Ella Merchant. *Unveiling a Parallel: A Romance.* Introduction by Carol A. Kolmerten. Boston: Arena Publishing, 1893. Reprint, Syracuse, N.Y.: Syracuse University Press, 1991.

Jordan, Clarence. *Substance of Faith and Other Cotton Patch Sermons by Clarence Jordan.* Edited by Dallas Lee. New York: Association Press, 1972.

Judd, Sylvester. *Margaret, a Tale of the Real, Blight and Bloom.* Boston: Jordan & Wiley, 1845. Reprint, Upper Saddle River, N.J.: Gregg Press, 1968.

Karp, David. *One.* New York: Vanguard Press, 1953. New York: Grosset & Dunlap, 1962.

Koestler, Arthur. *Darkness at Noon.* New York: Macmillan, 1941.

Koresh [Cyrus R. Teed], and U. G. Morrow. *The Cellular Cosmogony . . . Or . . . The Earth a Concave Sphere.* Chicago: Guiding Star, 1899. Reprint, Philadelphia: Porcupine Press, 1975.

Lamson, David R. *Two Years' Experience among the Shakers.* West Boylston, Mass.: Author, 1848. Reprint, New York: AMS, 1971.

Lane, Mary E. Bradley. *Mizora: A Prophecy.* New York: G. W. Dillingham, 1890. Reprint, Syracuse, N.Y.: Syracuse University Press, 2000.

Le Guin, Ursula. *Always Coming Home.* New York: Harper & Row, 1985.

——— . *The Dispossessed: An Ambiguous Utopia.* New York: Harper & Row, 1974.

Lewis, Sinclair. *It Can't Happen Here.* Garden City, N.Y.: Doubleday, Doran, 1935. Reprint, New York: New American Library, 1970.

Lindsey, Hal. *The Late Great Planet Earth.* Grand Rapids, Mich.: Zondervan, 1970.

Lloyd, Henry Demarest. *Wealth against Commonwealth.* New York: Harper & Brothers, 1894. Reprint, Westport, Conn.: Greenwood Press, 1976.

London, Jack. *The Iron Heel.* New York: Macmillan, 1907. Westport, Conn.: L. Hill, 1980.

Longley, Alcander. *Communism, the Right Way, and the Best Way for All to Live.* St. Louis: n.p., 1880.

——— . *What Is Communism?* St. Louis, Mo.: Altruist Community, 1890.

Marcuse, Herbert. *Eros and Civilization, Philosophical Inquiry into Freud.* New York: Vintage Books, 1955, 1962.

Mather, Cotton. *Magnalia Christi Americana; or, The Ecclesiastical History of New England.* London: T. Parkhurst, 1702. Reprint, New York: Arno Press, 1972.

[Meachem, Joseph]. *A Concise Statement of the Principles of the Only True Church . . .* Bennington, Vt.: Haswell & Russell, 1790.

Merrill, Albert Adams. *The Great Awakening: The Story of the Twenty-Second Century.* Boston: George Book Publishing, 1899.

Miller, Joaquim. *The Building of the City Beautiful.* Chicago: Stone & Kimball, 1893. Reprint, Trenton, N.J.: A Brandt, 1905.

Modjeska, Helena. *Memories and Impressions of Helena Modjeska.* New York: Macmillan, 1910.

Morgan, Joseph. *The History of the Kingdom of Basaruah.* Boston: n.p., 1715. Reprint, Cambridge, Mass.: Harvard University Press, 1995.

Nabokov, Vladimir. *Bend Sinister.* New York: Time Incorporated, 1947. Reprint, New York: McGraw-Hill, 1973.

Niswonger, Charles Elliot. *The Isle of Feminine.* Little Rock, Ark.: Brown Printing, 1893.

Nordhoff, Charles. *The Communistic Societies of the United States from Personal Visit and Observation.* New York: Harper and Bros., 1875. Reprint, New York: Hillary House Publishers, 1960.

Noyes, John Humphrey. *Bible Argument Defining the Relation of the Sexes in the Kingdom of Heaven.* Oneida Reserve, N.Y.: Leonard, 1849.

——. *Bible Communism.* Oneida, N.Y.: Office of Oneida Circular, 1872. Reprint, Philadelphia: Porcupine Press, 1973.

Noyes, Pierrepont B. *My Father's House: An Oneida Boyhood.* New York: Holt, Rinehart and Winston, 1937.

Nydahl, Joel, ed. *The Collected Works of John Adolphus Etzler, 1833–1844.* Delmar, N.Y.: Scholars' Facsmilies & Reprints, 1977.

Olerich, Henry. *Cityless and Countryless World.* Holstein, Iowa: Gilmore & Olerich, 1893. Reprint, New York: Arno Press, 1971.

Owen, Robert. *The Book of the New Moral World.* London: Home Colonization Society, 1842–1844. Reprint, New York: Augustus M. Kelley, 1970.

——. *Life of Robert Owen. Written by Himself. With Selections From His Writings and Correspondence.* 2 vols. London: Effingham Wilson, 1857–1858. Reprint, New York: Augustus M. Kelley, 1967.

Phalanx, The. Nos. 1–23, 1843–1845. Reprint, New York: AMS Press, 1971.

Piercy, Marge. *Woman on the Edge of Time.* New York: Knopf, 1976.

Rand, Ayn. *Anthem.* London: Cassell, 1938. Reprint, New York: Dutton, 1995.

Rapp, George. *Thoughts on the Destiny of Man, Particularly with Reference to the Present Times.* New Harmony, Ind.: Harmonie Society Press, 1824.

Reich, Charles. *The Greening of America.* New York: Random House, 1970.

Robertson, Constance Noyes, ed. *Oneida Community: An Autobiography, 1851–1876.* Syracuse, N.Y.: Syracuse University Press, 1970.

Russ, Joanna. *The Female Man.* New York: Bantam, 1975. Reprint, Boston: Beacon Press, 1986.

Russell, Charles Taze. *The Object and Manner of Our Lord's Return.* Rochester, N.Y.: Office of the Herald of the Morning, 1877.

Simpson, Orville, II. "Victory City." Available at www.victorycities.com.

Sinclair, Upton. *Autobiography.* New York: Harcourt, Brace & World, 1962.

Skinner, B. F. *Walden Two.* New York: Macmillan, 1948, 1962.

Slonczewski, Joan. *A Door into Ocean.* New York: Arbor House, 1986.

Smith, Joseph. *The Book of Mormon.* 1830. Reprint, Salt Lake City, Utah: Church of Jesus Christ of Latter-Day Saints, 1986.

Strang, James J. *Prophetic Controversy.* St. James, Mich.: Cooper and Chidester, 1856.

Teed, Cyrus. *The Cellular Cosmogony; or Earth a Concave Sphere.* 1905. Reprint, Philadelphia: Porcupine Press, 1974.

Thomas, Chauncey. *The Crystal Button: or, Adventures of Paul Prognosis in the Forty-Ninth Century.* Boston: Houghton, Mifflin, 1891. Reprint, Boston: Gregg Press, 1975.

Twin Oaks Community. *Journal of a Walden Two Commune.* Yellow Springs, Ohio: Distributed by Community Pub. Cooperative, 1972.

Vinton, Arthur Dudley. *Looking Further Backward.* Albany, N.Y.: Albany Book, 1890. Reprint, New York: Arno Press, 1971.

Vonnegut, Kurt. *Player Piano: America in the Coming Age of Electronics.* New York: Charles Scribner's Sons, 1952. Reprint, New York: Holt, Rinehart and Winston, 1966.

Ward, Frank Lester. *Dynamic Sociology.* New York: D. Appleton, 1883. Reprint, New York: Greenwood Press, 1968.

Wattles, John O. *Annual Report of the Educational Condition of the Colored People of Cincinnati.* Cincinnati, Ohio: John Write, 1849.

——. *A Few Thoughts on Marriage.* Salem, Ohio: H. Painter, 1844.

Wright, Austin. *Islandia.* New York: Farrar & Rinehart, 1942. Reprint, New York: Overlook Press, 2001.

2. Secondary Sources

Adkin, Clare. *Brother Benjamin: A History of the Israelite House of David.* Berrien Springs, Mich.: Andrews University Press, 1990.

Albertson, Ralph. "A Survey of Mutualistic Communities in America." *The Iowa Journal of History and Politics* 3 (October 1936): 375–444. Reprint as *Survey of Mutualistic Communities in America*, New York: AMS Press, 1973.

Alderfer, E. G. *The Ephrata Commune: An Early American Counterculture.* Pittsburgh, Pa.: University of Pittsburgh Press, 1985.

Alexander, Peter, and Roger Gill. *Utopias.* LaSalle, Ill.: Open Court Publishing, 1984.

Alyea, Paul E., and Blanche Alyea. *Fairhope, 1894–1954.* Tuscaloosa: University of Alabama Press, 1956.

Andelson, Jonathan G. "The Gift to Be Single: Celibacy and Religious Enthusiasm in the Community of True Inspiration." *Communal Societies* 5 (1985): 1–32.

Anderson, Olive. *Utopia in Upper Michigan: The Story of a Cooperative Village* [Hiawatha Village]. Marquette: Northern Michigan University Press, 1982.

Andrews, Edward Deming. *The People Called Shakers: A Search for the Perfect Society.* New York: Oxford University Press, 1953. Reprint, Mineola, N.Y.: Dover, 1963.

Armytage, W. H. G. "J. A. Etzler, an American Utopist." *American Journal of Economics and Sociology* 16 (October 1956): 83–88.

Arndt, Karl J. R. *George Rapp's Harmony Society, 1785–1847.* Philadelphia: University of Pennsylvania Press, 1965.

———. *George Rapp's Successors and Material Heirs, 1847–1916.* Madison, N.J.: Fairleigh Dickinson University Press, 1972.

Arnold, Eberhard, and Emmy Arnold. *Seeking for the Kingdom of God: Origins of the Bruderhof Communities.* Rifton, N.Y.: Plough, 1974.

Arrington, Leonard J. *The Great Basin Kingdom: An Economic History of the Latter-Day Saints.* Cambridge, Mass.: Harvard University Press, 1958.

Arrington, Leonard J., and Davis Bitton. *The Mormon Experience: A History of the Latter-Day Saints.* New York: Alfred A. Knopf, 1979.

Arrington, Leonard J., Feramorz Y. Fox, and Dean L. May. *Building the City of God: Community and Cooperation among the Mormons.* 2nd ed. Urbana: University of Illinois Press, 1992.

Baer, Hans A. *Recreating Utopia in the Desert: A Sectarian Challenge to Modern Mormonism.* Albany: State University of New York Press, 1988.

Bailie, William. *Josiah Warren: The First American Anarchist.* Boston, Mass.: Smal, Maynard, 1906.

Ballou, Adin. *History of the Hopedale Community from its Inception to its Virtual Submergency in the Hopedale Parish.* Lowell, Mass.: Thompson & Hill, 1847. Reprint, Philadelphia: Porcupine Press, 1972.

Barkun, David. *Disaster and the Millennium.* New Haven, Conn.: Yale University Press, 1974.

Barkun, Michael. *Crucible of the Millennium: The Burned-Over District of New York in the 1840s.* Syracuse, N.Y.: Syracuse University Press, 1986.

Barthel, Diane L. *Amana: From Pietist Sect to American Community.* Lincoln: University of Nebraska Press, 1984.

Bell, Daniel. *The End of Ideology: On the Exhaustion of Political Ideas in the Fifties.* Glencoe, Ill.: Free Press of Glencoe, 1960.

Bercovitch, Sacvan. *The American Jeremiad.* Madison: University of Wisconsin Press, 1978.

Bernini, Marie Louise. *Journey through Utopia.* Foreword by George Woodcock. New York: Schocken Books, 1971.

Berry, Brian J. L. *America's Utopian Experiments: Communal Havens from Long-Wave Crises.* Hanover, N.H.: Dartmouth College/University Press of New England, 1992.

Bestor, Arthur E. *Backwoods Utopias: The Sectarian and Owenite Phases of Communitarian Socialism in America: 1663–1829.* Philadelphia: University of Pennsylvania Press, 1950.

Block, Marguerite Beck. *The New Church in the New World: A Study of Swedenborgianism in America.* London: Octagon Press, 1969.

Bowman, Sylvia. *The Year 2000: A Critical Biography of Edward Bellamy.* New York: Bookman Associates, 1958.

Boyer, Paul. *When Time Shall Be No More: Prophecy Belief in Modern American Culture.* Cambridge, Mass.: Belknap Press of Harvard University Press, 1992.

Braden, Charles S. *Those Who Believe: A Study of Modern American Cults and Minority Religious Movements.* New York: Macmillan, 1949.

Brandes, Joseph. *Immigrants to Freedom: Jewish Communities in Rural New Jersey since 1882.* Philadelphia: University of Pennsylvania Press, 1971.

Brewer, Priscilla J. *Shaker Communities, Shaker Lives.* Hanover, N.H.: University Press of New England, 1986.

Brommel, Bernard J. "Deb's Cooperative Commonwealth Plan for Workers." *Labor History* 12 (fall 1971): 560–69.

Brostowin, Patrick R. "John Adolpus Etzler: Scientific-Utopian during the 1830's and 1840's." Ph.D. diss., New York University, 1969.

Brown, Margaret Ann. "Not Your Usual Boardinghouse Types: Upton Sinclair's Helicon Home Colony, 1906–1907." Ph.D. diss., George Washington University, 1993.

Brundage, W. Fitzhugh. *A Socialist Utopia in the New South: The Ruskin Colonies in Tennessee and Georgia, 1894–1901.* Urbana: University of Illinois Press, 1996.

Buder, Stanley. *Visionaries and Planners: The Garden City Movement and the Modern Community.* New York: Oxford University Press, 1980.

Burnham, Kenneth. *God Comes to America: Father Divine and the Peace Mission Movement.* Boston: Lambeth Press, 1979.

Burns, Edward McNall. *The American Idea of Mission: Concepts of National Purpose and Destiny.* New Brunswick, N.J.: Rutgers University Press, 1957.

Bushee, F. A. "Communistic Societies in the United States." *Political Science Quarterly* 20 (December 1905): 625–64.

Carden, Maren Lockwood. *Oneida: Utopian Community to Modern Corporation.* Baltimore, Md.: Johns Hopkins University Press, 1969.

Carpenter, Garrett R. *Silkville.* Emporia: Kansas State Teachers College, 1954.

Clark, Bertha W. "Huterian [sic] Communities." *Journal of Political Economy* 32 (1924): 357–74, 468–86.

Clark, Elmer Talmadge. *The Small Sects in America.* New York: Abingdon, 1944.

Clark, Thomas D., and F. Gerald Ham. *Pleasant Hill and Its Shakers.* 2nd ed. Pleasant Hill, Ky.: Pleasant Hill Press, 1983.

Clebsch, William A. *From Sacred to Profane America: The Role of Religion in American History.* New York: Harper & Row, 1968.

Codman, John Thomas. *The Brook Farm Association.* Boston: Coming Age Company, 1899. Reprint, New York: AMS Press, 1971.

Cobb, William H. "From Utopian Isolation to Radical Activism: Commonwealth College." *Arkansas Historical Quarterly* 23 (summer 1964): 132–47.

Cohen, Joseph J. *In Quest of Heaven: The Story of the Sunrise Co-operative Community.* New York: Sunrise History Publishing Committee, 1957. Reprint, Philadelphia: Porcupine Press, 1975.

Coleman, Marion Moore. *Fair Rosalind: The American Career of Helena Modjeska.* Cheshire, Conn.: Cherry Hill Books, 1969.

Conkin, Paul K. *Two Paths to Utopia: The Hutterites and the Llano Colony.* Lincoln: University of Nebraska Press, 1964.

Cook, Philip L. *Zion City, Illinois: Twentieth Century Utopia.* Syracuse, N.Y.: Syracuse University Press, 1996.

Cotkin, George. *Reluctant Modernism: American Thought and Culture, 1880–1900.* New York: Twayne, 1992.

Cross, Whitney. *The Burned-Over District: The Social and Intellectual History of Enthusiastic Religion in Western New York, 1800–1850.* Ithaca, N.Y.: Cornell University Press, 1950. Reprint, New York: Harper & Row, 1965.

Curti, Merle. *Human Nature in American Thought: A History.* Madison: University of Wisconsin Press, 1980.

Curtis, Edith Roelker, *A Season in Utopia: The Story of Brook Farm.* New York: Nelson, 1961.

Curtis, Susan. *A Consuming Faith: The Social Gospel and Modern American Culture.* Baltimore, Md.: Johns Hopkins University Press, 1991.

Davidson, Gabriel. *Our Jewish Farmers and the Story of the Jewish Agricultural Society.* New York: L. B. Fischer, 1943.

Davidson, James West. *The Logic of Millenial Thought.* New Haven, Conn.: Yale University Press, 1977.

Davis, Morris, and Joseph F. Krauter. *Other Canadians: Profiles of Six Minorities* [incl. Hutterites]. Toronto: Methuen, 1971.

Deets, Lee Emerson. *The Hutterites: A Study in Social Cohesion.* Gettysburg, Pa.: n.p., 1939. Reprint, Philadelphia: Porcupine Press, 1973.

Delano, Sterling F. *The Harbinger and New England Transcendentalism: A Portrait of Associationism in America.* Rutherford, N.J.: Fairleigh Dickinson University Press, 1983.

Desroche, Henri. *The American Shakers.* Amherst: University of Massachusetts Press, 1971.

Doig, Ivan. *Utopian America: Dreams and Realities.* Rochelle Park, N.J.: Hayden Book Company, 1976.

Dubrovsky, Gertrude Wishnick. *This Land Was Theirs: Jewish Farmers in the Garden State.* Tuscaloosa: University of Alabama Press, 1992.

Eckhardt, Celia Morris. *Fanny Wright: Rebel in America.* Cambridge, Mass.: Harvard University Press, 1984.

Egbert, Donald, and Stow Persons, eds. *Socialism and American Life.* 2 vols. Princeton, N.J.: Princeton University Press, 1952.

Egerton, John. *Visions of Utopia: Nashoba, Rugby, Ruskin, and the "New Communities" in Tennessee's Past.* Knoxville: University of Tennessee Press, 1977.

Eisenberg, Ellen. *Jewish Agricultural Colonies in New Jersey, 1882–1920.* Syracuse, N.Y.: Syracuse University Press, 1995.

Ekirch, Arthur Alphonse, Jr. *The Idea of Progress in America, 1815–1860.* Studies in History, Economics and Public Law, no. 511. New York: Columbia University Press, 1944. Reprint, New York: Peter Smith, 1951.

Etzioni, Amatai. *The Spirit of Community: Rights, Responsibilities, and the Communitarian Agenda.* New York: Crown Publishers, 1993.

Fellman, Michael. *The Unbounded Frame.* Westport, Conn.: Greenwood Press, 1973.

Firchow, Peter Edgerly. *The End of Utopia: A Study of Aldous Huxley's* Brave New World. London: Associated University Presses, 1984.

Firkins, Oscar W. *William Dean Howells: A Study.* Cambridge, Mass.: Harvard University Press, 1924.

Flanders, Robert B. *Nauvoo: Kingdom on the Mississippi.* Urbana: University of Illinois Press, 1965.

Flint, David. *Hutterites: A Study in Prejudice.* Toronto: Oxford University Press, 1975.

Fogarty, Robert S. *All Things New: American Communes and Utopian Movements, 1860–1914.* Chicago: University of Chicago Press, 1990.

———. *American Utopianism.* 2nd ed. Itasca, Ill.: F. E. Peacock, 1977.

———. *The Righteous Remnant: The House of David.* Kent, Ohio: Kent State University Press, 1981.

Foster, Lawrence. *Religion and Sexuality: Three American Communal Experiments of the Nineteenth Century.* New York: Oxford University Press, 1981. Reprinted as *Religion and Sexuality: The Shakers, the Mormons, and the Oneida Community.* Urbana: University of Illinois Press, 1984.

———. *Women, Family, and Utopia: Communal Experiments of the Shakers, the Oneida Community, and the Mormons.* Syracuse, N.Y.: Syracuse University Press, 1991.

Frost, William P. *What Is the New Age? Defining Third Millennium Consciousness.* Lewiston, N.Y.: Edwin Mellen Press, 1992.

Gardell, Mattias. *Countdown to Armageddon: Louis Farrakhan and the Nation of Islam.* London: Hurst, 1996.

———. *In the Name of Elijah Muhammed: Louis Farrakhan and the Nation of Islam.* Durham, N.C.: Duke University Press, 1996.

Gardner, Hugh. *The Children of Prosperity: Thirteen Modern American Communes.* New York: St. Martin's Press, 1978.

Gleick, Elizabeth. "The Marker We've Been . . . Waiting For." [Heaven's Gate cult] *Time* 149 (7 April 1997): 28–29.

Goering, Violet, and Orlando J. Goering. "The Agricultural Communes of the Am Olam." *Communal Societies* 4 (1984): 74–86.
———. "Jewish Farmers in South Dakota—The Am Olam." *South Dakota History* 12 (winter 1982): 232–47.
Gollin, Gilliam Lindt. *Moravians in Two Worlds: A Study of Changing Communities.* New York: Columbia University Press, 1967.
Goodman, Percival. *Communitas: Means of Livelihood and Ways of Life.* Chicago: University of Chicago Press, 1947.
Grant, H. Roger. *Spirit Fruit: A Gentle Utopia.* DeKalb: Northern Illinois University Press, 1988.
Greenwalt, Emmett. *The Point Loma Community in California, 1897–1942: A Theosophical Experiment.* Berkeley: University of California Press, 1955. Rev. ed. published as *California Utopia: Point Loma: 1897–1942.* San Diego, Calif.: Point Loma Publications, 1978.
Gross, Paul S. *The Hutterite Way: The Inside Story of the Life, Customs, Religion, and Traditions of the Hutterites.* Saskatoon, Saskatchewan, Canada: Freemen, 1965.
Guarneri, Carl J. *The Utopian Alternative: Fourierism in Nineteenth-Century America.* Ithaca, N.Y.: Cornell University Press, 1991.
Gutek, Gerald Lee. *Joseph Neef: The Americanization of Pestalozzianism.* Tuscaloosa: University of Alabama Press, 1978.
Harder, Leland, and Marvin Harder. *Plockhoy from Zurik-zee: The Study of a Dutch Reformer in Puritan England and Colonial America.* Newton, Kans.: [Mennonite] Board of Education and Publication, 1952.
Harris, Leon. *Upton Sinclair, American Rebel.* New York: Thomas Y. Crowell, 1975.
Harris, Sara. *The Incredible Father Divine.* London: W. H. Allan, 1954.
Harrison, John F. C. *Quest for the New Moral World: Robert Owen & the Owenites in Britain and America.* New York: Charles Scribner's Sons, 1969.
———. *Robert Owen and the Owenites in Britain and America.* London: Routledge & K. Paul, 1969.
———. *The Second Coming: Popular Millenarianism, 1780–1850.* New Brunswick, N.J.: Rutgers University Press, 1979.
Hatch, Nathan O. *The Sacred Cause of Liberty: Republican Thought and the Millennium in Revolutionary New England.* New Haven, Conn.: Yale University Press, 1977.
Hayden, Dolores. *The Second Coming: Popular Millennarianism, 1780–1850.* New Brunswick, N.J.: Rutgers University Press, 1979.
———. *Seven American Utopias: The Architecture of Communitarian Socialism, 1790–1975.* Cambridge, Mass.: MIT Press, 1976.
Hecht, David. *Russian Radicals Look to America, 1825–1894.* Cambridge, Mass.: Harvard University Press, 1947.

Hendricks, Robert. *Bethel and Aurora: An Experiment in Communism as Practical Christianity: With Some Account of Past and Present Ventures in Collective Living.* New York: Press of the Pioneers, 1933. Reprint, New York: AMS Press, 1971.

Herscher, Uri D. *Jewish Agricultural Utopias in America, 1880–1910.* Detroit, Mich.: Wayne State University Press, 1981.

Hill, Mary A. *Charlotte Perkins Gilman: The Making of a Radical Feminist, 1860–1896.* Philadelphia: Porcupine Press, 1974.

Hinds, William A. *American Communities and Co-Operative Colonies.* Chicago: C. H. Kerr, 1902. Reprint, Philadelphia: Porcupine Press, 1974.

Hine, Robert V. *California's Utopian Colonies.* San Marino, Calif.: Huntington Library, 1953. Reprint, New Haven, Conn.: Yale University Press, 1966.

Holloway, Mark. *Heavens on Earth: Utopian Communities in America, 1680–1880.* 2nd ed. New York: Dover Publications, 1966.

Holstun, James. *A Rational Millennium: Puritan Utopias of Seventeenth-Century England and America.* Oxford: Oxford University Press, 1987.

Horowitz, Irving Louis. *Ideology and Utopia in the United States, 1956–1976.* New York: Oxford University Press, 1977.

Hostetler, John A. *Hutterite Life.* Scottdale, Pa.: Herald, 1983.

———. *Hutterite Society.* Baltimore, Md.: Johns Hopkins University Press, 1974.

Hughes, Thomas. *Rugby, Tennessee: Being Some Account of the Settlement Founded on the Cumberland Plateau by the Board of Aid to Land Ownership, Limited. . . .* New York: Macmillan, 1891. Reprint, Philadelphia: Porcupine Press, 1975.

Isaksson, Olov. *Bishop Hill: A Utopia on the Prairie.* Stockholm: L. T. Solna Seelig, 1969.

Jackson, Carl T. *Vedanta for the West: The Ramakrishna Movement in the United States.* Bloomington: Indiana University Press, 1994.

James, Bartlett. *The Labadist Colony in Maryland.* Baltimore, Md.: Johns Hopkins University Press, 1899.

Janzen, Rod. *The Rise and Fall of Synanon: A California Utopia.* Baltimore, Md.: Johns Hopkins University Press, 2001.

Jewish Agricultural Society. *Jews in American Agriculture.* New York: Jewish Agricultural Society, 1954.

Johnson, K. Paul. *The Masters Revealed: Madam Blavatsky and the Myth of the Great White Lodge.* Albany: State University of New York Press, 1994.

Johnson, Paul E., and Sean Wilentz. *The Kingdom of Matthias: A Story of Sex and Salvation in 19th-Century America.* New York: Oxford University Press, 1994.

Kagan, Paul. *New World Utopias: A Photographic History of the Search for Community.* New York: Penguin, 1975.

Kanter, Rosabeth Moss, ed. *Communes: Creating and Managing the Collective Life.* New York: Harper and Row, 1973.

Katscher, Leopold. "Owen's Topolobampo Colony, Mexico." *American Journal of Sociology* 12 (September 1906): 145–75.

Kent, Alexander. "Cooperative Communities in the United States." *Bulletin of the Department of Labor* 35 (July 1901): 563–646.

Kern, Louis J. *An Ordered Love: Sex Roles and Sexuality in Victorian Utopias—the Shakers, the Mormons, and the Oneida Community.* Chapel Hill: University of North Carolina Press, 1981.

Kinkade, Kathleen *A Walden Two Experiment: The First Five Years of Twin Oaks Community.* New York: William Morrow, 1973.

Klaw, Spencer. *Without Sin: The Life and Death of the Oneida Community.* New York: Penguin, 1993.

Klein, W. C. *Johann Conrad Beissel: Mystic and Martinet, 1690–1768.* Philadelphia: University of Pennsylvania Press, 1942.

Koch, Raymond, and Charlotte Koch. *Educational Commune: The Story of Commonwealth College.* New York: Schocken, 1972.

Kolmerten, Carol A. *Women in Utopia: The Ideology of Gender in the American Owenite Communities.* Bloomington: Indiana University Press, 1990.

Lankes, Frank J. *The Ebenezer Society.* West Seneca, N.Y.: West Seneca Historical Society, 1963.

Lauer, Robert H., and Jeanette C. Lauer. *Spirit and the Flesh: Sex in Utopian Communities.* Metuchen, N.J.: Scarecrow Press, 1983.

Lee, Martha F. *The Nation of Islam: An American Millenarian Movement.* Studies in Religion and Society, vol. 21. Lewiston, N.Y.: Edwin Mellen Press, 1988.

Legler, Henry E. "Moses of the Mormons [James J. Strang]," *Michigan Pioneer and Historical Collections* 32 (1903): 180–224.

LeWarne, Charles P. *Utopias on Puget Sound.* Seattle: University of Washington Press, 1975.

Lockwood, George B. *The New Harmony Movement.* New York: D. Appleton, 1905. Reprint, Mineolta, N.Y.: Dover, 1971.

Loomis, Mildred. *Alternative Americas.* New York: Universe Books, 1982.

Mackle, Elliott. "Koreshan Unity in Florida, 1894–1910." Master's thesis, University of Miami, 1971.

Martin, James Joseph. *Men against the State: The Expositors of Individualist Anarchism in America, 1827–1908.* De Kalb, Ill.: Adrian Allen Associates, 1953. Reprint, Colorado Springs, Colo.: Ralph Myles, 1970.

May, Henry F. *The Divided Heart: Essays on Protestantism and the Enlightenment in America.* New York: Oxford University Press, 1991.

McNiff, W. J. *Heaven on Earth: A Planned Mormon Society.* Oxford, Ohio: Mississippi Valley Press, 1940. Reprint, New York: AMS Press, 1974.

Meade, Marion. *Madame Blavatsky.* New York: G. P. Putnam's Sons, 1980.

Melcher, Marguerite F. *The Shaker Adventure.* Cleveland, Ohio: Press of Case Western Reserve University, 1968.

Menes, Abraham. "The Am Oylom Movement." *YIVO Annual of Jewish Social Science* 4 (1949): 9–33.

Meyering, Sheryl L. *Charlotte Perkins Gilman: The Woman and Her Work.* Ann Arbor, Mich.: UMI Research Press, 1988.

Mikkelsen, Michael. *The Bishop Hill Colony: A Religious Communist Settlement in Henry County, Illinois.* Baltimore, Md.: Johns Hopkins Press, 1892. Reprint, Philadelphia: Porcupine Press, 1973.

Miller, Timothy. *The Quest for Utopia in Twentieth-Century America.* Vol. I, *1900–1960.* Syracuse, N.Y.: Syracuse University Press, 1998.

——. *The 60s Communes: Hippies and Beyond.* Syracuse, N.Y.: Syracuse University Press, 1999.

Moment, Gairdner B., and Otto F. Kraushaar, eds. *Utopias: The American Experience.* Metuchen, N.J.: Scarecrow Press, 1980.

Morgan, Arthur. *Edward Bellamy.* New York: Columbia University Press, 1944.

Murphy, James L. *The Reluctant Radicals: Jacob L. Beilhart and the Spirit Fruit Society.* Lanham, Md.: University Press of America, 1989.

Niebuhr, H. Richard. *The Kingdom of God in America.* Chicago: Willett, Clark, 1937.

Noyes, John Humphrey. *History of American Socialisms.* New York: Hillary House Publishers, 1870, 1961.

Oliphant, John. *Brother Twelve: The Incredible Story of Canada's False Prophet and His Doomed Cult of Gold, Sex, and Black Magic.* Toronto: McClelland and Stewart, 1991.

Ortiz, Victoria. *Sojourner Truth: A Self-Made Woman.* Philadelphia: Lippincott, Williams & Wilkins, 1974.

Oved, Iaacov. *Two Hundred Years of American Communes.* New Brunswick, N.J.: Transaction Press, 1988.

——. *The Witness of the Brothers: A History of the Bruderhof.* New Brunswick, N.J.: Transaction Press, 1996.

Parker, Robert Allerton. *Incredible Messiah: The Deification of Father Divine.* Boston: Little, Brown, 1937.

——. *A Yankee Saint: John Humphrey Noyes and the Oneida Community.* New York: G. P. Putnam's Sons, 1935. Reprint, Philadelphia: Porcupine Press, 1973.

Parrington, Vernon Louis, Jr. *American Dreams: A Study of American Utopias.* 2nd ed. New York: Russell & Russell, 1964.

Pearson, Carol. "Coming Home: Four Feminist Utopias and Patriarchal Experience." In *Future Females: A Critical Anthology,* ed. Marleen S. Barr, 63–70. Bowling Green, Ohio: Bowling Green State University Popular Press, 1981.

Pease, William H., and Jane H. Pease. *Black Utopia: Negro Communal Experiments in America.* Madison: State Historical Society of Wisconsin, 1963.

Peters, Victor. *All Things Common: The Hutterian Way of Life.* Minneapolis: University of Minnesota Press, 1966.

Pfaelzer, Jean. *The Utopian Novel in America, 1886–1896: The Politics of Form.* Pittsburgh, Pa.: University of Pittsburgh Press, 1984.

Pickering, William S. F. *The Hutterites: Christians Who Practice a Communal Way of Life.* London: Ward Lock Educational, 1982.

Pitts, William L. "Davidians and Branch Davidians: 1929–1987." In *Armageddon in Waco: Critical Perspectives on the Branch Davidian Conflict,* ed. Stuart A. Wright, 20–42. Chicago: University of Chicago Press, 1995.

Pitzer, Donald E., ed. *America's Communal Utopias.* Chapel Hill: University of North Carolina Press, 1997.

Pletcher, David. *Rails, Mines, and Progress: Seven American Promoters in Mexico, 1867–1911.* Ithaca, N.Y.: Cornell University Press, 1958.

Quaife, Milo. *The Kingdom of St. James: A Narrative of the Mormons.* New Haven, Conn.: Yale University Press, 1930.

Quint, Howard H. *The Forging of American Socialism: Origins of the Modern Movement.* Columbia: University of South Carolina Press, 1953. Reprint, Indianapolis: Bobbs Merrill, 1964.

Reynolds, Ray. *Cat'spaw Utopia* [Topolobampo]. El Cajon, Calif.: Author, 1972.

Rhodes, Harold V. *Utopia in American Political Thought.* Institute of Government Research, Political Theory Studies, no. I. Tucson: University of Arizona Press, 1967.

Riegel, Oscar H. *Crown of Glory: Life of J. J. Strang, Moses of the Mormons.* New Haven, Conn.: Yale University Press, 1935.

Roberts, Ron. *The New Communes: Coming Together in America.* Englewood Cliffs, N.J.: Prentice-Hall, 1971.

Robertson, Constance Noyes. *The Oneida Community: The Breakup, 1876–1881.* Syracuse, N.Y.: Syracuse University Press, 1972.

Roemer, Kenneth M., ed. *America as Utopia.* American Cultural Heritage Series. New York: Burt Franklin, 1981.

——. *The Obsolete Necessity: America in Utopian Writings, 1888–1890.* Kent, Ohio: Kent State University Press, 1976.

Rooney, Charles J., Jr. *Dreams and Visions: A Study of American Utopias, 1865–1917.* Contributions in American Studies, no. 77. Westport, Conn.: Greenwood Press, 1985.

Rose, Willie Lee. *Rehearsal for Reconstruction: The Port Royal Experiment.* New York: Oxford University Press, 1964.

Royle, Edward. *Robert Owen and the Commencement of the Millennium: A Study of the Harmony Community.* Manchester, UK: Manchester University Press, 1998.

Ryan, Charles J. *H. P. Blavatsky and the Theosophical Movement.* Pasadena, Calif.: Theosophical University Press, 1975.

Sachse, Julius Friedrich. *The German Pietists of Provincial Pennsylvania.* Philadelphia: Author, 1895. Reprint, New York: AMS Press, 1970.

——. *The German Sectarians of Pennsylvania, 1708–1800: A Critical and Legendary History of the Ephrata Cloisters and Dunkers.* 2 vols. Philadelphia: Author, 1899–1900. Reprint, New York: AMS Press, 1971.

Sandall, Robert. *History of the Salvation Army.* London: T. Nelson, 1955.

Saxby, Trevor. *The Quest for the New Jerusalem, Jean de Labadie and the Labadists, 1610–1744.* Boston: Kluwer Publishers, 1987.

Schneider, Herbert W., and George Lawton. *A Prophet and a Pilgrim, Being the Incredible History of Thomas Lake Harris and Laurence Oliphant, Their Sexual Mysticisms and Utopian Communities.* New York: Columbia University Press, 1942. Reprint, New York: AMS Press, 1970.

Shambaugh, Bertha. *Amana, the Community of True Inspiration.* Iowa City: The State Historical Society of Iowa, 1908. Reprint, Des Moines: The State Historical Society of Iowa, 1988.

Shaw, Albert. *Icaria, A Chapter in the History of Communism.* New York: G. P. Putnam's, 1884. Reprint, Philadelphia: Porcupine Press, 1973.

Shields, Steven L. *Divergent Paths of the Restoration: A History of the Latter Day Saint Movement.* 3nd ed. Bountiful, Utah: Author, 1892.

Shpall, Leo. "Jewish Agricultural Colonies in the United States," *Agricultural History* 24 (July 1950): 120–46.

Solis, Miguel J. *American Utopias, 1693–1900.* Bloomington: Indiana University Printing Services, 1984.

Spann, Edward K. *Brotherly Tomorrows: Movements for a Cooperative Society in America, 1820–1920.* New York: Columbia University Press, 1989.

Spence, Clark C. *The Salvation Army Farm Colonies.* Tucson: University of Arizona Press, 1985.

Sperber, Mae T. *Search for Utopia: A Study of Twentieth Century Communes in America.* Middleboro, Mass.: Country Press, 1976.

Spurlock, John C. *Free Love: Marriage and Middle-Class Radicalism in America, 1825–1860.* New York: New York University Press, 1988.

Stagg, Brian L. "Tennessee's Rugby Colony." *Tennessee Historical Quarterly* 27 (fall 1968): 209–24.

Stein, Stephen. *The Shaker Experience in America: A History of the United Society of Believers.* New Haven, Conn.: Yale University Press, 1992.

Stern, Peter. *Millennium III, Century XXI.* Boulder: University of Colorado Press, 1996.

Suksong, Duangrudi. "A World of Their Own: The Separatist Utopian Vision of Mary E. Bradley Lane's *Mizora.*" In *Redefining the Political Novel: American Women Writers, 1797–1901,* ed. Sharon M. Harris, 128–48. Knoxville: University of Tennessee Press, 1995.

Sutton, Robert P. *Les Icariens: The Utopian Dream in Europe and America.* Urbana: University of Illinois Press, 1994.

Swank, George. *Bishop Hill, Swedish-American Showcase: History of the Bishop Hill Colony.* Galva, Ill.: Galvaland Press, 1987.

Swift, Lindsay. *Brook Farm: Its Members, Scholars and Visitors.* New York: Macmillan, 1900. Reprint, Secaucus, N.J.: Citadel Press, 1973.

Tabor, James D., and Eugene V. Gallagher. *Why Waco? Cults and the Battle for Religious Freedom in America.* Berkeley: University of California Press, 1995.

Taylor, R. James. *Mary's City of David.* Benton Harbor, Mich.: Mary's City of David, 1996.

Thomas, John L. *Alternative America: Henry George, Edward Bellamy, Henry Demarest Lloyd and the Adversary Tradition.* Cambridge, Mass.: Belknap Press of Harvard University Press, 1983.

Thomas, Norman. "Hutterite Brethren." *South Dakota Historical Collections* 25 (1950): 265–90.

Thomas, Robert D. *The Man Who Would Be Perfect: John Humphrey Noyes and the Utopian Impulse.* Philadelphia: University of Pennsylvania Press, 1977.

Thrupp, Sylvia Lettice, ed. *Millennial Dreams in Action: Studies in Revolutionary Religious Movements.* New York: Schocken, 1970.

Turner, Wallace. "Hutterites during World War I," *Mennonite Life* 24 (July 1969): 130–37.

Tuveson, Ernest. *Redeemer Nation: The Idea of America's Millennial Role.* Chicago: University of Chicago Press, 1968.

Tyler, Alice Felt. *Freedom's Ferment: Phases of American Social History to 1860.* Minneapolis: University of Minnesota Press, 1944.

Van Dusen, Glyndon G. *Horace Greeley, Nineteenth Century Crusader.* Philadelphia: University of Pennsylvania Press, 1953.

Van Noord, Roger. *King of Beaver Island: The Life and Assassination of James Jesse Strang.* Urbana: University of Illinois Press, 1988.

Veysey, Laurence. *The Communal Experience: Anarchist and Mystical Counter-Cultures in America.* Chicago: University of Chicago Press, 1978.

Waterman, William. *Frances Wright.* New York: n.p., 1924. Reprint, New York: AMS Press, 1972.

Watts, Jill. *God, Harlem, U.S.A.: The Father Divine Story.* Berkeley: University of California Press, 1992.

Webber, Everett. *Escape to Utopia: The Communal Movement in America.* New York: Hastings House, 1959.

Weisbrot, Robert. *Father Divine and the Struggle for Racial Equality.* Urbana: University of Illinois Press, 1983.

Williams, Aaron. *The Harmony Society, at Economy, Penn'a Founded by George Rapp, 1805; with an Appendix.* Pittsburgh, Pa.: W. S. Haven, 1866. Reprint, New York: AMS Press, 1971.

Williams, David R. *Wilderness Lost: The Religious Origins of the American Mind.* Selinsgrove, Pa.: Susquehanna University Press/Associated University Presses, 1987.

Wright, Stuart A., ed. *Armageddon in Waco: Critical Perspectives on the Branch Davidian Conflict.* Chicago: University of Chicago Press, 1995.

Yarmolinsky, Avrahm. *A Russian's American Dream: A Memoir of William Frey.* Lawrence: University of Kansas Press, 1965.

Zablocki, Benjamin. *The Joyful Community: An Account of the Bruderhof, a Communal Movement Now in Its Third Generation.* New York: Penguin, 1971.

V. OTHER AREAS

1. Primary Sources

Kang You-wei. *Ta T'ung Shu* (Book of the Great Unity). Shanghai, China: Chung-hua shu chu, 1935.

Krause, Charles A. *Guyana Massacre: The Eyewitness Account.* New York: Berkeley Publishing Group, 1978.

Li Ju-Chen. *Ching-Bua Yuan* (Flowers in the Mirror). Translated and edited by Tai-y Lin. Berkeley: University of California Press, 1965. Reprint, London: Arena, 1985.

Mendieta, Geronimo de. *Historia Eclesiastica Indiana.* 1870. Lewiston, N.Y.: Edwin Mellen Press, 1997.

2. Secondary Sources

Claeys, Gregory. "John Adolphus Etzler, Technological Utopianism, and British Socialism: The Tropical Emigration Society's Venezuelan Mission and Its Social Context, 1833–1848." *English Historical Review* 101 (April 1986): 351–75.

Gavron, Daniel. *The Kibbutz, Awakening from Utopia.* Lanham, Md.: Rowman & Littlefield, 2000.

Hornadge, Bill. *The Search for an Australian Paradise.* Bondi Junction, Australia: Imprint, 1999.

Klineman, George, Sherman Butler, and David Conn. *The Cult That Died: The Tragedy of Jim Jones and the People's Temple.* New York: Putnam, 1980.

Lowenthal, Bennett. "The Topolobampo Colony in the Context of Porfirian Mexico." *Communal Societies* 7 (1987): 47–66.

Molloy, Maureen. *Those Who Speak to the Heart—The Nova Scotian Scots at Waipu, 1854–1920.* New Zealand: Dunmore Press, 1991.

Phelan, John Leddy. *The Millennial Kingdom of the Franciscans in the New World: A Study of the Writings of Geronimo de Mendieta (1524–1604).* Berkeley: University of California Press, 1956.

Reinhard, Wolfgang. "Missionaries, Humanists and Natives in the Sixteenth-Century Spanish Indies—A Failed Encounter of Two Worlds?" Translated by Ursula Cairns Smith. *Renaissance Studies* 6, Nos. 3–4 (1892): 360–76.

Appendix: Utopian Communities

AUSTRALIA AND NEW ZEALAND

Name	Location	Years
Waipu (*see* MCLEOD, NORMAN)	North Island, New Zealand	1853–?
Herrnhut Commune	Victoria, Australia	1853–1889
New Italy	New South Wales, Australia	1882–1955
New Jerusalem	Western Australia, Australia	?–1913

CANADA

Name	Location	Years
St. Ann (*See* MCLEOD, NORMAN)	Nova Scotia	1822–1840?
Wilberforce	Ontario	1829–1850s
Dawn Colony, *or* British-American Institute	Ontario	1842–1868
Refugee Home Society	Ontario	1846–1866?
Elgin Association	Ontario	1849–1873
Coalsamao	(Western provinces)	Never attempted
Cardston Company	Alberta	1890–1895?
Hutterite Colonies (12)	Alberta and Manitoba	1918–present
Aquarian Foundation	Vancouver Island, B.C.	1927–1934

EUROPE

Name	Location	Years
Yorkshire Communities (42)	England	1325–present
Mt. Tabor (*see* TABORITES)	Bohemia	15th c.
Anabaptists	Germany	1534–1535
Family of Love (*see* FAMILISTS)	Kent, England	1552
	Cambridgeshire, England	1574
Weinwerd (see LABADISTS)	Holland	1675–17??
New Lanark	Scotland	1800–18??
Orbiston	Scotland	1825–1827?
Ralahine	Ireland	1831–1833
Queenwood	England	1840?–1845
Hanwell Communitorium (*see* BARMBY, GOODWIN)	England	1841–?
Saltaire	England	1853–?
Bournville	England	1893–?
Bruderhof	Germany and England	1926–1962
Yamagishi-Kai	Germany and Switzerland	1947–present

LATIN AMERICA

Name	Location	Years
Tropical Emigration Society (see ETZLER, JOHN)	Venezuela	1846–1847?
New Australia Colony	Paraguay	1893–1899
Cosme	Paraguay	1894–1900?
Primavera (*see* BRUDERHOF)	Paraguay	1941–1962
Jonestown	Guyana	1977–1978
Yamagishi-Kai	Brazil	1994?

MEXICO

Name	Location	Years
Sante Fe (see QUIROGA, VASCO DE)	Near Mexico City	1537–1565?
Topolobampo	Sinaloa	1886–1893

UNITED STATES

Alabama

Name	Location	Years
Fairhope	Baldwin County	1894–1937

Arizona

Name	Location	Years
Molokans	Glendale	1911–1921?

Arkansas

Name	Location	Years
Harmonial Vegetarian Society	Benton County	1860–1864
Commonwealth College	Polk County	1925–1940

California

Name	Location	Years
Fountain Grove	Sonoma County	1876–1896
Modjeska's Colony	Anaheim	1877–1878
Speranza	Sonoma County	1881–1885
Esoteric Fraternity	Placer County	1880s–present
Koreshan Unity	San Francisco	1890–1891
Co-operative Brotherhood of Winters Island	Contra Costa County	1893–1898
Altruria	Sonoma County	1894–1896

Fort Romie Colony	Soledad	1898–?
Point Loma	San Diego	1898–1842
Temple Home Association	San Luis Obispo County	1903–present
Molokan Communities	Los Angeles, San Francisco, and Baja California	1904?–present
Krotona Community of Adyar Theosophists	Hollywood and Ojai Valley	1912–present
Rancho Atascadero of **American Woman's Republic**	Atascadero	1913–1920
Llano Del Rio Company	Los Angeles County	1914–1918
Spirit Fruit Society	Santa Cruz	1914–1929
Vedanta Society	Pasadena	1923–present
Trabuco College (*See* HEARD, HENRY F.)	Laguna Beach	1942–1947
Christ's Church of the Golden Rule (*See* MANKIND UNITED)	Willits	1944–present
Synanon Community	Various	1958–1991
People's Temple	Ukiah and San Francisco	1965–1977
Ananda	Nevada City	1967–present
Heaven's Gate	San Diego	1970s–1997

Colorado

Name	Location	Years
Union Colony	Weld County	1869–1872
Western Colony	Weld County	1870–?
Colorado Cooperative Colony	Pinon	1894–1906
Fort Amity Colony	Holly	1898–1910

Connecticut

Name	Location	Years
Enfield Community	Hartford County	1790–1917

Wallingford Community New Haven County 1851–1881

Delaware

Name	Location	Years
Valley of the Swans (see PLOCKHOY, PIETER)	Lewes	1663–1664
Arden	New Castle County	1900–present

District of Columbia

Name	Location	Years
Koreshan Unity	Washington	1908
Women's Commonwealth (*see* MCWHIRTER, MARTHA)	Washington	1899–1906

Florida

Name	Location	Years
Narcoossee	Osceola County	1894–1912
Koreshan Unity	Estero	1894–1961
Southern Co-operative Association of Apalachicola	Apalachicola	1900–1904
Order of Theocracy	Lee County	1910–1931

Georgia

Name	Location	Years
Christian Commonwealth Colony	Muskogee County	1896–1900
White Oak Community	Glynn County	1897
American Settlers Association, *or* Duke Colony	Ware County	1898–1899
White Oak Community	Camden County	1898–1902
Kinder Lou	Lowndes County	1900–1902

| **Macedonia Cooperative Community** | Habersham County | 1937–1958 |
| **Koinonia Farm** | Sumter County | 1942–present |

Illinois

Name	Location	Years
Nauvoo (Mormons)	Hancock County	1838–1846
Bureau County Phalanx	Bureau County	1843–1844
Sangamon Phalanx (*see* INTEGRAL PHALANX)	Sangamon County	1845–1846
Canton Phalanx	Fulton County	1845
Bishop Hill Colony	Henry County	1846–1862
Nauvoo (Icarians)	Hancock County	1849–1859
Olive Branch	Chicago	1876–present
Zion City	Lake County	1901–1906
Spirit Fruit Society	Lake County	1905–1914
Heaven City	McHenry County	1923–1927

Indiana

Name	Location	Years
West Union	Knox-Sullivan Counties	1810–1827
Harmony	Posey County	1814–1825
New Harmony	Posey County	1825–1827
Coal Creek Community and Church of God	Fountain County	1825–1827
Blue Springs Community	Bloomington	1826–1827
Feiba-Peveli	Posey County	1826–?
Macluria	Posey County	1826–?
LaGrange Phalanx	LaGrange County	1843–1846
Union Home Community	Randolph County	1844?–1846
Grand Prairie Community	Warren County	1845–1847
Kristeen	Marshall County	1845–1847
Philadelphia Industrial Association	St. Joseph County	1845–1847

Grand Prairie	Warren County	1853–1854
Harmonial Institute		
Fourier Phalanx	Dearborn County	1858–1858
Patriot (see DOMAIN)	Switzerland County	1860–1863

Iowa

Name	Location	Years
Iowa Pioneer Phalanx	Mahaska County	1844–1845
Communia	Clayton County	1847–1857?
Jasper Colony	Iowa County	1851–1853
Preparation	Monona County	1853–1858
Corning	Adams County	1854–1878
Amana Society	Iowa County	1855–1932
New Icarian Community	Adams County	1878–1895
Jeune Icarie	Adams County	1879–1887

Kansas

Name	Location	Years
Silkville Colony (see BOISSIERE, ERNEST)	Franklin County	1868–1886
Progressive Community	Chautauqua County	1871–1878
Investigating Community	Chautauqua County	1875–1876?
Cedarvale, or Cedar Vale Benevolent and Educational Society	Chautauqua County	1875–1877
Esperanza	Neosho County	1877–1878?
Thompson Colony	Salina	1880–?
Beersheba Colony	Hodgeman County	1882–1885
Freedom Colony	Fulton	1898–1905

Kentucky

Name	Location	Years
Pleasant Hill	Mercer County	1806–1910
South Union Society	Logan County	1809–1922

Louisiana

Name	Location	Years
Grand Ecore	Natchitoches Parish	1834–1836
Germantown	Webster Parish	1836–1871
Sicily Island Colony	Catahoula Parish	1881–1883
New Llano	Vernon Parish	1917–1936

Maine

Name	Location	Years
Sabbathday Lake	New Gloucester	1783–present
Alfred Community	York County	1793–1932
Gorham Community	Cumberland County	1794–1819

Maryland

Name	Location	Years
Bohemia Manor (*see* LABADISTS)	Cecil County	1683–1727
Women's Commonwealth (*see* MCWHIRTER, MARTHA)	Unknown	1899?–1983

Massachusetts

Name	Location	Years
Hancock, *or* West Pittsfield	Berkshire County	1790–1960
Tyringham Community	Berkshire County	1792–1875
Harvard Society	Worcester County	1793–1918
Savoy Community	Berkshire County	1817–1825
Brook Farm	West Roxbury	1841–1847
Northampton Association of Education and Industry	Hampshire County	1842–1846
Hopedale Community	Milford	1842–1868
Adonai-Shomo Corporation	Athol and Petersham	1861–1897

Shirley Community	Middlesex County	1893–1908
Fellowship Farm Association	Westwood	1907–1918
The Farm	West Newburyport	1909–1980s
Gould Farm	Great Barrington	1913–present
Vedanta Society	Cohasset	1920s

Michigan

Name	Location	Years
Washtenaw Phalanx	Ann Arbor	1843?
Alphadelphia Phalanx	Kalamazoo County	1844–1846
Beaver Island Colony, or		
Kingdom of St. James	Beaver Island	1851–1856
Ora Labora Community	Huron County	1862–1868
Hiawatha Village	Schoolcraft County	1893–1895
Drummond Island	Chippewa County	1902–1914
House of David	Benton Harbor	1903–present
Sunrise Community	Saginaw County	1932–1936

Minnesota

Name	Location	Years
Union Grove	Meeker County	1856–1858

Missouri

Name	Location	Years
Bethel (see KEIL, WILLIAM)	Shelby County	1844–1880
Nineveh	Adair County	1849–1878
Cheltenham Colony	St. Louis	1856–1864
Reunion Colony	Jasper County	1868–1870
Friendship Community	Dallas County	1872–1877
Bennett Co-operative Colony	Dallas County	1873–1877
Mutual Aid Community	Bollinger County	1883–1887
Home Employment Co-operative	Dallas County	1894–1904?

Altruist Community	Sulphur Springs	1907–1908
Fruit Crest	Independence	1911–1912
American Woman's Republic	St. Louis	1912–1913

Montana

Name	Location	Years
Spring Creek Colony	Fergus County	1912–1920
Warren Range Colony	Fergus County	1913–1918

Nebraska

Name	Location	Years
Bookwalter	Bookwalter	1891–?
Christian Corporation	Lancaster County	1896–1897

Nevada

Name	Location	Years
Llano Del Rio Company of Nevada	Churchill County	1916–1918
Nevada Colony	Churchill County	1916–1919

New Hampshire

Name	Location	Years
Canterbury Community	Merrimack County	1792–1992
Enfield Community	Grafton County	1793–1923

New Jersey

Name	Location	Year
North American Phalanx	Monmouth County	1843–1856
Oneida branch	Newark	185?–1855
Raritan Bay Colony	Englewood	1853–1858
Rosenhayn	Cumberland County	1882–1889
Alliance Colony	Salem County	1882–1908
The Lord's Farm	Woodcliff	1889–1910

Helicon Hall Colony (*see*
SINCLAIR, UPTON)   Bergen County   1906–1907
Ferrer Colony   Middlesex County   1915–1946
Sunrise Community   Mercer County   1933–1936

New York

Name	Location	Year
Mount Lebanon	Columbia County	1787–1947
Jerusalem Colony	Yates County	1788–1863
Watervliet	Albany County	1788–1938
The Union	St. Lawrence County	1804–1810
Haverstraw Community	Rockland County	1826
Forrestville Community	Green County	1826–1827
Kingdom of Matthias, *or* Zion Hill (*see* MATTHEWS, ROBERT)	Ossining (Sing Sing)	1830s
Groveland Society	Livingston County	1836–1895
Morehouse Union	Hamilton County	1843–1844?
Jefferson County Association	Jefferson County	1843–1844
Ebenezer (*see* AMANA SOCIETY)	Erie County	1843–1855
Bloomfield Association	Honeoye Falls	1844–1845
Clarkson Industrial Association	Monroe County	1844–1845
Mixville Association	Allegheny County	1844–1845
Ontario Phalanx	Ontario County	1844–1845
Skaneateles Community	Onandoga County	1844–1846
Sodus Bay Phalanx	Wayne County	1844–1846
Oneida Community	Madison County	1848–1881
Oneida branches	Brooklyn and Manlius	185?–1855
Modern Times	Suffolk County	1851–1863
Domain	Chautauqua County	1853–1863
Amenia Community, *or* Brotherhood of the True Life	Dutchess County	1861–1867

Brocton Community, *or* Salem-on-Erie	Chautauqua County	1867–1881
Roycroft	Erie County	1900–1938
Ferrer Colony	New York City	1912–1915
Temple of the Gospel of the Kingdom	Harlem	1917–1926
Father Divine's Peace Mission	Sayville and Harlem	1920s–1942
Mohegan Colony (*see* KELLY, HARRY)	Lake Mohegan	1925–?
Mount Airy Colony (*see* KELLY, HARRY)	Harmon	1925–?
School of Living Colony (*see* BORSODI, RALPH)	Suffern	1935–?
Woodcrest (*see* BRUDERHOF)	Rifton	1954–1962

North Carolina

Name	Location	Years
Moravian communities	Wachovia and Bethabara	1740s–?
Warm Springs Colony	Madison County	1871–1872?
Christian Socialist Colony	Andrews	1895?

North Dakota

Name	Location	Years
Painted Woods	Burleigh County	1882–1887

Ohio

Name	Location	Years
Union Village	Warren County	1805–1912
Watervliet	Montgomery County	1806–1910

Separatists of Zoar	Tuscarawas County	1817–1898
North Union Society	Cuyahoga County	1822–1889
Yellow Springs	Greene County	1825–1827
Whitewater Community	Hamilton-Butler Counties	1825–1907
Kendal Community	Stark County	1826–1829
Teutonia	Columbiana County	1827–1831
Kirkland Community	Lake County	1830–1835
Tuscarawas	Tuscarawas County	1831–1837
Oberlin Colony	Lorain County	1833–1841
Marlborough Association	Stark County	1841–1845
Abram Brooke's Experiment	Clinton County	184?–?
Clermont Phalanx	Clermont County	1844–1846
Prairie Home Community	Logan County	1844–1845?
Highland Home (*see* PRAIRIE HOME COMMUNITY)	Logan County	1844?–1845?
Ohio Phalanx	Belmont County	1844–1846
Trumbull Phalanx	Trumbull County	1844–1848
Columbian Phalanx	Franklin County	1845
Integral Phalanx	Butler County	1845–1846
Fruit Hills	Warren County	1845–1852
Spiritualist Community	Clermont County	1846–1847
Utopia Community	Clermont County	1847–1850s
Rising Star Association	Darke County	1853–1857
"Free Lovers at Davis House"	Erie County	1854–1858
Memnonia Institute	Yellow Springs	1856–1857
Berlin Heights Community, *or* Point Hope Community	Erie County	1860–1861
Berlin Community, *or* Christian Republic	Erie County	1865–1866
Fort Herrick Colony	Cuyahoga County	1898–?
Spirit Fruit Society	Columbiana County	1899–1905

Oregon

Name	Location	Years
Aurora Community	Willamette Valley	1856–1881
New Odessa Community	Douglas County	1883–1887
Union Mill Company	Tillamook County	1891–1897
Bride of Christ	Benton County	1903?–1906
Rancho Rajneesh	Antelope	1981–1985

Pennsylvania

Name	Location	Years
Woman in the Wilderness (*see* KELPIUS, JOHANN)	Coxsackie	1694–post-1708
Ephrata Colony (*see* BEISSEL, JOHANN)	Lancaster County	1732–1770
Moravian colonies	Bethlehem, Lititz, Nazareth	1742–1762
Snow Hill Nunnery	Franklin County	1798–1900
Harmony Society	Butler County	1805–1814
Economy	Beaver County	1825–1898
Valley Forge Community	Chester County	1826–1826
New Philadelphia Colony	Beaver County	1832–1833
Social Reform Unity	Monroe County	1842–1843?
McKean County Association	McKean County	1842–1844
Goose Pond Community	Pike County	1843–1844
Sylvania Association	Pike County	1843–1845
One Mention Community	Monroe County	1844–1845
Leraysville Phalanx	Bradford County	1844–1845?
Peace Union Settlement (*see* SMOLNIKAR, ANDREAS)	Warren County	1845–?
Ole Bull's Colony	Potter County	1852–1853
Celesta	Sullivan County	1863–1864
Tidioute Colony	Warren County	1884–1886
Father Divine's Peace Mission	Philadelphia	1942–present

South Carolina

Name	Location	Years
Port Royal Experiment	Sea Islands	1862–1866

South Dakota

Name	Location	Years
Bon Homme Colony	Beadle County	1874–present
Wolf Creek Colony	Hutchinson County	1875–1930
Elmspring Colony	Hutchinson County	1878–1929
Tripp Colony	Hutchinson County	1879–1884
Cremieux Colony	Davison-Aurora Counties	1882–1885
Bethlehem Yehudah	Aurora County	1882–1885
Milltown Colony	Hutchinson County	1886–1907
Jamesville Colony	Yankton County	1886–1918
Kutter Colony	Hanson County	1890–1918
Rockport Colony	Hanson County	1891–1934
Maxwell Colony	Hutchinson County	1900–1918
New Elmspring Colony	Hutchinson-Hanson Counties	1900–1918
Rosedale Colony	Hanson County	1901–1918
Spink Colony	Spink County	1905–1918
Beadle Colony	Beadle County	1905–1922
Huron Colony	Beadle County	1906–1918
Richards Colony	Sanborn County	1906–1918
Buffalo Colony	Beadle County	1907–1913
Milford Colony	Beadle County	1910–1918
James Valley Colony	Beadle County	1913–1918

Tennessee

Name	Location	Years
Nashoba	Shelby County	1826–1829
Rugby Colony	Morgan County	1880–1892
Ruskin Colony	Dickinson County	1894–1899
Willard Co-operative Colony	Roane County	1895–1896

Ruskin breakaway movement (*see* RUSKIN COLONY)	Dixie	1897–1898
Bohemian Co-operative Farming Company	Cumberland County	1913–1916
The Farm Eco-Village	Lawrence County	1971–present

Texas

Name	Location	Years
Bettina, *or* Darmstaedter Kolonie	Llano County	1847–1848
Zodiac	Gillespie County	1847–1853
Icaria (*see* ICARIANS)	Denton County	1848–1849
Reunion Colony	Dallas County	1855–1859
Women's Commonwealth (*see* MCWHIRTER, MARTHA)	Belton	1876–1899
Israelites, *or* New House of Israel	Polk County	1895–1920
Commonwealth Colony of Israel	Mason County	1899–1902?
The Burning Bush, *or* Metropolitan Institute of Texas	Smith County	1913–1919
Shepherd's Rod (*see* HOUTEFF, VICTOR)	McLennan County	1934–1942
Branch Davidians	McLennan County	1934–1993

Utah

Name	Location	Years
Deseret (*see* MORMONS)	Valley of the Great Salt Lake	1846–present
Orderville United Order	Kane County	1875–1884

Vermont

Name	Location	Years
Pilgrims	Windsor County	1817–1818
Oneida branch	Cambridge	185?–1855

Virginia

Name	Location	Years
Mahanaim (*see* ECKERLIN, ISRAEL)	New River	1745?–1750?
Spiritual Community at Mountain Cove	Fayette County (now West Virginia)	1851–1853
Temple of the Gospel of the Kingdom	Unknown	1900–1917
Twin Oaks Community	Louisa County	1967–

Washington

Name	Location	Years
Daviesite Kingdom of Heaven	Walla Walla	1867–1881
Washington Colony	Whatcom County	1881–1884
Puget Sound Cooperative Colony	Clallam County	1887–1890?
Glennis Cooperative Industrial Company	Pierce County	1894–1896
Cooperative Brother-hood, *or* Burley	Kitsap County	1898–1906
Equality, *or* Brotherhood of the Cooperative Commonwealth	Skagit County	1897–1907
Home Colony, *or* Mutual Home Association	Puget Sound	1898–1919
Freeland Association	Whidby Island	1900–1906?
Lopez Island Community	Lopez Island	1911–1920?

West Virginia

Name	Location	Years
Mountain Cove Community	Fayette County	1851–1853?

Wisconsin

Name	Location	Years
Society of Equality, *or* Hunt's Colony	Waukesha County	1843–1847
Wisconsin Phalanx	Fond du Lac County	1844–1850
Voree (*see* BEAVER ISLAND COLONY)	Kenosha County	1845–?
Utilitarian Association of United Interests	Waukesha County	1845–1848
Pigeon River Colony	Sheboygan County	1846–1847
Spring Farm Colony	Sheboygan County	1846–1848
Ephraim-Green Bay	Brown County	1850–1853
Ephraim-Door County	Door County	1853–1864
St. Nazianz Community	Manitowoc County	1854–1874
Germania Company	Marquette County	1856–1879

About the Authors

James M. Morris, a native of Michigan and the holder of three academic degrees, including a Ph.D. in history from the University of Cincinnati, has spent four decades in the classroom at both the high school and collegiate level. Having retired in 2002, he presently holds the title of emeritus professor of history at Christopher Newport University in Newport News, Virginia. The author or editor of six previous books, most on American military and naval history, he is presently completing for publication a book-length manuscript entitled *America as Utopia.*

Andrea L. Kross, a native of Alberta, Canada, and the holder of four academic degrees, including a master of library and information studies degree from Dalhousie University, Nova Scotia, has enjoyed a distinguished career in librarianship. From 1996 until 2001, she served as cataloging and reference librarian at the Captain John Smith Library of Christopher Newport University. She now holds the position of implementation consultant at Innovation Interfaces, Inc., in California providing data profiling and indexing services to libraries across the nation. She is the author of numerous articles on effective librarianship, served as coeditor of *Making the Grade: Academic Libraries and Student Success* (2002), and also works as a freelance editor.